The M68000 Family
Volume 1

Werner Hilf · Anton Nausch

The M68000 Family

Volume 1

Architecture, Addressing Modes and Instruction Set

PRENTICE HALL, Englewood Cliffs, New Jersey 07632

© 1989, 1988 by Markt & Technik Verlag Aktiengesellschaft
8013 Haar bei München (Germany)

Cover design: Tom Turley
Translated by: Jack L. Davies, Munich, West-Germany

UNIX is a registered trademark of AT&T Bell Laboratories.
EXORmacs, VERSAdos, RMS68K are trademarks of Motorola, Inc.

Printed in the United States of America

10 9 8 7 6 5 4 3 2 1

ISBN 0-13-541525-X

Prentice-Hall International (UK) Limited, *London*
Prentice-Hall of Australia Pty. Limited, *Sydney*
Prentice-Hall Canada Inc., *Toronto*
Prentice-Hall Hispanoamericana, S.A., *Mexico*
Prentice-Hall of India Private Limited, *New Delhi*
Prentice-Hall of Japan, Inc., *Tokyo*
Simon & Schuster Asia Pte. Ltd., *Singapore*
Editora Prentice-Hall do Brasil, Ltda., *Rio de Janeiro*

Table of Contents

Preface to the English Edition

The original German edition of this book that first appeared in 1984 has been a major success on the German market, primarily

- as an official training manual in many courses on microcomputers by many professional and public schools,
- as a reference work for designers and developers of both hardware and software for the M68000 family, and
- as an introduction to microprocessors in general and the M68000 family in particular for many enthusiasts.

In particular, it consolidates a large amount of relevant information from a variety of both English and German sources into one book that is convenient for the reader to use. This success led to the decision to publish an English edition of the book.

Several additions and changes have been incorporated into this new English edition. Due to the later release, all information has been updated to include new support devices and microprocessors (such as the 68030 microprocessor). The literature on the M68000 family comes from a variety of sources and points-of-view, with the result that there are many apparent logical inconsistencies in the information. We have therefore made a major effort to resolve these apparent inconsistencies in one single consistent treatment of the subject. Examples include such simple problems as how to count the number of instructions and addressing modes for each microprocessor in the family.

Realizing that many readers of this new edition will be beginners in the field of computers, we have included a more complete history of computers that tries to show why the M68000 family was designed the way it was–in its historical context. The emphasis of Chapter 2 was changed, from a presentation on the architecture of the 68000 microprocessor to a presentation on the architecture of all M68000 microprocessors with emphasis upon the 68000 microprocessor as an example. Therefore, specific differences between the 68000, 68008, 68010, 68012, 68020, and 68030 microprocessors are at least mentioned as the general architecture is described in Chapter 2. These differences are explained in more detail in Chapter 8 where the later processors are presented separately. The description of the additional addressing modes for the 68020 and 68030 microprocessors has been expanded and brought forward from Chapter 8 to the last section of Chapter 3 on addressing modes in general. Likewise, the additional instructions and changed instructions for the 68010 and 68012 microprocessors have been brought forward from Chapter 8 and integrated in alphabetical order in Chapter 4. However, the additional instructions for the 68020 and 68030 microprocessors have only been presented separately in summary form as the last section of Chapter 4. They are presented in more detail in Chapter 8.

Our special thanks to Jack L. Davies for his excellent translation and supportive ideas in issuing this book.

Munich, West Germany   W. Hilf, A. Nausch

Preface to the Second German Edition

This book is intended for use both as an introduction to the M68000 family and as a reference work. The authors have attempted to present complex information explicitly in detail. This is one of the main reasons why this book had to be divided into two volumes shortly before it was first published in 1984. Fortunately, a separation was possible that is convenient for the reader.

In Volume I, the fundamentals are presented and the architecture for both hardware and software is presented more or less theoretically. You will find a brief historical background and second sources in Chapter 1. Fundamentals for a microcoded CPU and the pin layouts for the 68000 microprocessore are given in detail in Chapter 2. Important concepts and definitions that you will encounter in both volumes are also presented in Chapter 2. The addressing modes are presented in detail in Chapter 3 and the individual instructions are presented in detail with numerous small examples in Chapter 4. The last chapter in this volume presents the different versions of the 68000 microprocessor at the mask level.

Volume II is particularly suitable for those readers who have already acquired some experience with the M68000 family. It has the subtitle of "Applications and the M68000 Devices". You will find supplementary information and practical hints for working with the 68000 microprocessor in it. The software aspects are covered in Chapter 6, with many examples of short programs in assembler with M68000 instructions. Chapter 7 covers the most important support devices in both the 8-bit M6800 and 16-bit M68000 families. Chapter 8 covers the new and future microprocessors in the M68000 family. A complete single-board computer system, including software monitor, is described in Chapter 9 and a more complete illustrative example. Since the VME bus should not be overlooked in any discussion of the M68000 family, it is described in Chapter 10.

Both volumes present additional information concerning the 68000 microprocessor, e.g. laying the foundations for new programming techniques, new operating systems, and support devices for the next generation within the M68000 family.

The authors are in the fortunate position to have been intimately involved with the M68000 family, as employees of the prime source, from the day when this family was first introduced to the market. In creating and presenting numerous training courses internationally, the authors were able to develop their own understanding of this information, as well as to experiment with techniques for explaining this information to typical users. This experience played an important role in developing the format for this book.

The reader should realize that the information in this book assumes some prior knowledge about microprocessors. As an example, the basic functions of a microprocessor are not explained in detail in this book. However, the reader will find a variety of other good books available for this type of introduction.

The authors wish to thank Motorola Inc. for the information and illustrations that they have made available to us for this purpose. We also wish to thank the companies Hitachi Europe, Rockwell International GmbH, and Valvo (Hamburg) for the information that they gave to us, particularly for Chapter 7 in Volume II.

In the second edition, a number of typographical errors were corrected and some of the formulations were improved. In particular, an extra subchapter, 2.4.4, was added to Chapter 2 in order to explain the differences between user and supervisor modes in more detail. The treatment of interrupts was expanded to include summaries. The "MC68000 16-bit Microprocessor Programming Reference Card" from Motorola, that is included separately with this book should be a welcome supplement for most readers. We thank Motorola Inc. for having provided the master copy for printing this card. The addition of an index in this edition emphasizes the role of this book as a training and reference work.

Munich, West Germany   W. Hilf, A. Nausch

1
General Background Information

1.1 Introduction

1.1.1 Definition of the "M68000 Family"

When Motorola introduced its 8-bit "M6800 family" in 1974, the 6800 was approximately the 20th 8-bit microprocessor released to the market–but it was the first microprocessor that was released as a family, together with various support devices. Since then, other manufacturers have adopted the same procedure of developing and releasing families rather than individual processors. In this context, it is not surprising that in 1979 Motorola also introduced its first 16-bit microprocessor, the 68000 microprocessor, as a member of a new family, called "the M68000 family".

The "M68000 family" has two dimensions or subfamilies:
– a subfamily of different microprocessors and
– a subfamily of different support devices.

In addition, the microprocessors of the M68000 family can also use the support devices from the related 8-bit M6800 family.

The subfamily of microprocessors is illustrated in Figure 1-1 below:

The subfamily of support devices contains the following categories of devices:
– peripheral-interface devices, including
– serial-interface devices
– parallel-interface devices
– data-communications devices
– floppy-disk controllers
– graphics controllers
– multi-function devices
– DMA devices
– memory-management units
– clocks and timers

As you can see from this listing, the availability of single devices for these complex functions can greatly simplify the task of an engineer in designing a new computer system around a new microprocessor. Otherwise, the engineer would have to design all of these circuits in detail himself, rather than to connect standard building blocks with predefined interfaces to the new microprocessor.

Since different terminolgy is used to describe the microprocessors and support devices of the M68000 family by
– Motorola (all device names begin with the prefix "MC", but the family is called the "M68000 family"),
– the second sources (all device names have the same number but different prefixes and suffixes), and
– the neutral literature (uses no prefixes),

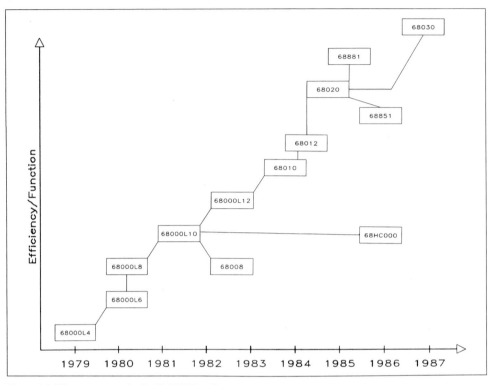

Figure 1-1: Microprocessors in the M68000 Family

we have established the following conventions for this book:
- "the M68000 family" refers to all microprocessors and support devices in the family,
- "an M68000 microprocessor" refers to any one of the several microprocessors in the M68000 family,
- "a 68000 microprocessor" refers to the single microprocessor with the Motorola designation of "MC68000",
- the names of individual support devices also have no prefix, and
- a "C" is sometimes used in a number or as a suffix for a device that is implemented in CMOS technology.

In addition, references to the literature that is listed in the bibliography are enclosed in square brackets, [ ]'s.

1.1.2   Who the Book is Designed for

This book is designed for both
- hardware engineers, who want to design the hardware for a simple or complex computer system that is based upon the M68000 family of microprocessors and support devices, and
- software engineers, who want to develop system software or specialized application software for use on computer systems that are based upon the M68000 family (at the level of an assembler language),
as well as
- owners or users of computer systems that are based upon the M68000 family, who have an interest in understanding more clearly how their computer systems and software work, and

– computer enthusiasts who are curious and want to know more about how microprocessors work and how the microprocessors in the M68000 family work as specific examples.

Therefore, the potential reader can be

– a beginner, with some basic knowledge of the binary number system and access to a computer system that is based upon the M68000 family (with an assembler for some simple experimentation) or
– an experienced professional who wants to study the details of how the M68000 family works or to use the book as a reference work (from one single consistent source).

This book, or subsets thereof, can be used as a part of a neutral course on microcomputers in general, hardware design with microprocessors, or software design with microprocessors. In this case, this book presents the M68000 family as one example and other books can be used to present other families in order to maintain neutrality.

The reader does not have to read this book from A to Z, but rather can select most any order for reading the individual chapters. Cross references are included in each chapter to sections of the same or other chapters that may be relevant for understanding a particular point. This enables a casual reader to read the book in most any order, to browse through the main points, and then to study particular points of interest in more detail. An expert with prior experience with the M68000 family can use the book as a reference work for more detailed information on most aspects from one single source.

Volume I presents a more general background, including:

– a general history of microprocessors, that shows the relationships between the M68000 microprocessors within this historical framework,
– an explanation of the architecture of the M68000 microprocessors, with particular emphasis upon the 68000 microprocessor as the first in this family,
– an explanation of the basic concepts that are necessary to understand how M68000 microprocessors work, such as registers, data formats, exceptions, interrupts, buses and timing for the 68000 microprocessor,
– an explanation of the addressing modes that are available within the M68000 family (extended for the 68020 and 68030 microprocessors), and
– a complete description of each instruction in the instruction sets for the 68000, 68008, 68010, and 68012 microprocessors (some additions for the 68010 and 68012) and a summary description of the instructions added for the 68020 and 68030 microprocessors.

Volume II presents more specific information, including:

– how to program M68000 microprocessors, with practical examples (based upon the instruction set of the 68000 and 68008 microprocessors – that is a subset of the instruction sets of the other microprocessors),
– a detailed description of all major support devices in the M68000 family,
– a detailed description of the differences of the 68008, 68010, 68010, 68020, and 68030 microprocessors to the first 68000 microprocessor (the emphasis is on the differences in this volume, whereas it was on the similarities in the first volume), and
– a detailed description of a single-board computer system, as a practical example, including a monitor program as system software.

1.2   History of the M68000 Family

Where does the history of the M68000 family begin? To be complete, we would have to start with the discovery of the number systems and ancient tools to aid in computations with numbers. Then, we would have to trace the development of mathematics and computers, as well as related technologies. However, we must limit the presentation here to the more recent developments that have a more direct bearing upon explaining why the M68000 family has become what it is today.

1.2.1   General History of Computers

One way of classifying computers into different groups is by the criterion of the technology that they use for performing computational tasks. With this approach, there are four generations, as follows:

Generation 0: Mechanical and Electromechanical

Examples of mechanical computers include:
– the abacus
– the slide rule
– the Jacquard loom
– the analytical engine of Charles Babbage
Examples of electromechanical computers include:
– the Bush differential analyzer
– the Mark I computer (with relays)

Generation 1: Electronic Tubes

The ENIAC was the first of the "first-generation computers". It was developed by the US Army in order to meet the computational requirements for calculating ballistic trajectories during the second world war. It was followed by the EDVAC and EDSAC computers, with improved architectures. The first commercial computers were based upon the EDVAC and EDSAC computers.

Generation 2: Transistors

Seymour Cray pioneered in designing the first computer that used only transistors without any electronic tubes in 1960 at the Control Data Corporation (he later formed his own company). However, the basic architecture and design remained essentially the same. (It was difficult to combine transistors and electronic tubes in the same computers, since both the signal levels and the required power voltages are quite different.)

Generation 3: Integrated Circuits

Since integrated circuits are essentially several transistors on one crystal "chip", the transition from using transistors to integrated circuits was more gradual, whereby many computers were made using both transistors and integrated circuits during this transition.
It is semantically incorrect to speak of 4th and 5th generation computers in this sequence, since the so-called 4th and 5th generation computers are really only third-generation computers that differ from one another in other ways than their basic technology. Therefore, we are still in the middle of the third generation in this sequence defined by basic technology as the criterion. The true 4th and 5th generations, in this sequence, will use other technologies, such as optics, 3-dimensional integrated circuits or biological molecules.
IBM came close to developing the first 4th-generation computer in this sequence, based upon Josephson junctions as the basic technology. However, both IBM and its competitors encountered technical dif-

ficulties in transfering the Josephson junction from the laboratory to real computers, and IBM dropped the project. Gene Amdahl, the architect of the IBM 360 architecture as well as the later Amdahl computers, tried through his new company of Trilogy to develop simultaneously a new technology (wafer-scale integration) and a new computer based upon this technology. Although Trilogy achieved interesting advances in the direction of wafer-scale integration, there are still technical obstacles, and the proposed new computer was dropped. If a change from using silicon to using gallium arsenide as the basis for integrated circuits is sufficient to qualify as a new technology in this sense, then there is a good chance that Seymour Cray may go down in history as the pioneer who not only introduced the first second-generation computer with transistors in 1960 but also the first large fourth-generation computer with gallium arsenide in the near future. (During the more than one quarter of a century between these two events, at any given point in time, the fastest commercially available computer in the world has nearly always been a computer designed by Seymour Cray, at first for Control Data and later for Cray Research.)

In the case of the transitions from each of the preceding computer generations, the transitions were inevitable. "There was no other way. It was only a question of when and by whom." Once pioneers made the transition, their competitors were forced to follow their footsteps. However, the approaching transition from the third generation to the fourth generation appears to be qualitatively different. It appears that the current third generation still has considerable room for continued development and that there will be no single technology that will replace the third generation. New technologies will gradually be introduced, particularly for specialized applications, without superseding the third generation.

With the prospect that we will be dealing with the third generation of computers for some time, it is interesting to examine the advances that are taking place within this generation. Two dimensions are leading to subgenerations:

- changes in the architecture at the logical level and
- changes in the architecture at the physical level.

At the logical level, we have started out with the von-Neumann architecture. There are increasingly stronger impulses to break away from this architecture, particularly in the direction of using more than one processing unit to do either the same or different things parallel in time, as explained in Chapter 2.1.6 below. At the physical level, we started out by applying integrated circuits to combinatorial logic and memory separately. Microprocessors, that include registers with combinatorial logic, may be a first step in a different direction.

The M68000 family of microprocessors was influenced historically in particular by

- the development of the von-Neumann architecture for 1st-generation computers and
- the development of microprocessors as a special type of integrated circuits for use in 3rd-generation computers.

The von-Neumann-Architecture

The von-Neumann-architecture dates back to the time of the ENIAC as the first electronic computer with electronic tubes. An Army officer at the Aberdeen Proving Grounds, Paul N. Gillon, perceived the need for much faster means for calculating ballistic firing tables prior to World War II, identified the potential of electronic tubes versus electronic relays as the basic technology, obtained funding for the ENIAC project during the war, obtained highly qualified personnel to work on this project and directed this project through to its completion. Therefore, Gillon was the "father" of the ENIAC, although not its inventor, designer or constructor. There were many inventors, designers and constructors who worked on this project as well as others who had laid important foundations earlier.

The concept of an "architecture" for a computer had not yet arrived and the ENIAC was designed, starting with a basic concept from John William Mauchly at the University of Pennsylvania, as a translation of an existing class of computational methods into electronic circuitry that was designed by John Presper

Eckert, Jr, also at the Univ. of Pennsylvania. The coordination between the computational methods and requirements of the Army with the electronic design was managed by another Army officer and applied mathematician, Herman H. Goldstine, who played a major role in designing what we would today call the architecture of this machine. During the construction phase of the ENIAC, John von Neumann became closely involved with the project as an external consultant.

The architecture of the ENIAC was a logical translation from the given mathematical problems (solving differential equations) and used several processing units in parallel that could perform one multiplication and several additions at the same time. The adding processor units performed 5000 additions or subtractions per second each, and the multiplication unit took up to 14 addition cycles per multiplication, using decimal look-up tables. The ENIAC operated with decimal numbers internally, using ring counters composed of D-flip-flop circuits to store one of 10 possible states for each digit in the word size of 10-digit numbers (plus signs) – thereby emulating the counter wheels of mechanical calculators. The ENIAC had 20 accumulators for holding such numbers – corresponding roughly to modern registers – and had 3 function look-up tables for 104 words of 12 digits each, where the values were set by switches – corresponding roughly to modern look-up tables in ROM. Control instructions were set mainly by switches. Therefore, it had no main memory in the conventional sense, since devices for implementing such memory at reasonable prices were not yet available.

With approximately 18,000 electronic tubes, it was a gamble to build such a machine at the time – due to the reliability aspects. It was a major feat of engineering, due largely to Eckert, that the ENIAC had an average of less than one tube failure per day and that it took less than 1 hour on an average to identify and replace a defective tube. (The substantial improvements in reliability since then make modern computers the most reliable devices that man has created.)

During the design and construction of the ENIAC, several important architectural concepts were developed but were deliberately not included in the ENIAC. The reason was that the expenditure of effort upon such a risky project during the war could only be justified by at least the hope that the ENIAC could be completed quickly enough to be used and to make a contribution to the war effort – before the war was over. Two accumulators were built and tested successfully in August, 1944 as a preliminary technical-feasibility test and the first useful computations were performed on the complete ENIAC in November, 1945 – indicating how critical this timing was at that time. Therefore, Goldstine proposed a second project for a more general-purpose computer to be constructed after the war that was called the EDVAC. The concept of a stored program is an example of such a concept that was developed early in the ENIAC project but was deliberately delayed until the EDVAC for implementation. Again, Gillon launched and sponsored the EDVAC project. Von Neumann naturally took over the leadership within the ENIAC team for the theoretical design work on the logical structure for the EDVAC, ie. its "architecture", with particularly significant contributions from Goldstine and Arthur Burks. With Looking-back, it is difficult to say who invented or discovered what aspects of this architecture that became known as the "von-Neumann architecture".

One of the major contributions of the new architecture for the EDVAC was the switch to using a binary representation for numbers internally and the use of the octal number system for representing them externally for users of the computer. This greatly simplified the arithmetic and storage circuits of the computer. Going one step further, only one single processing unit was used, instead of parallel processing, and this processing unit was programmable to perform a wider variety of operations than in the ENIAC. Although this new concept was architecturally slower than that of the ENIAC, economic and technical aspects made it superior at that time. In particular, it was important to reduce the number of tubes significantly in order to increase reliability – which it did. Due to its increased simplicity and improved electronic circuits, it was ultimately faster (this is already a prelude to the RISC philosophy discussed in Section 1.2.5 below). It is indeed surprising that drastically changing economic and technological factors across 3 generations of computers continued to lead to the same conclusion that this architecture was optimal for most applications. It is ironic to note that modern attempts to go "beyond" the von-Neumann architecture consist primarily of attempts to return from the single processor of this architecture to the multiple parallel processors of the ENIAC, i.e. simply undoing this major innovation in advancing from the ENIAC to the EDVAC – in a new environment of different economic and technological conditions.

In addition, the concept of a stored control, where both the instructions and the data are stored in the same memory, was implemented. Initially, one bit was proposed to identify each word in memory as either an instruction or an operand of data (this is at least similar to the concept of Function-Code Outputs for the M68000 family of microprocessors, discussed in Chapter 2.7 below). It is also interesting to note that this concept for mixing instructions and data in one central memory was developed and established before the first magneticcore memory devices were invented (by Jay W. Forrester) – that made the first large random-access main memory technologically and economically feasible. Although the general concept of a program with iteration that can influence itself depending upon the results of calculations (with conditional jumps) was first proposed by Charles Babbage and Lady Lovelace 100 years earlier, this concept was developed in more detail within the concept of the "von-Neumann architecture".

Lady Augusta Ada Byron, Countess of Lovelace, is credited with being the first computer programmer – for her work in collaboration with Charles Babbage on his Analytical Engine around 1850 (the US Department of Defense named the computer language ADA after her). It is perhaps less well known that a woman played a similar role for the ENIAC. Adele Katz Goldstine (wife of Herman Goldstine) was a member of the design team for the ENIAC, developed programming techniques for the ENIAC, wrote the first operating manual for the ENIAC, trained others to program the ENIAC and programmed many of the important applications that later were processed on the ENIAC. She, together with her husband and von Neumann, developed the concept for a flow chart as a programming aid. When von Neumann proposed in 1947 that the lack of a physical central control unit could be overcome by a virtual central control unit, Adele Goldstine developed the software (should we call it "switchware") for implementing this proposal. It implemented 51 instructions, that were later expanded to 92 instructions. Although it slowed the ENIAC somewhat, it made the machine so much easier to use, that it was used exclusively thereafter. At least to a certain extent, this makes the ENIAC the first "virtual machine", with a simulated physical unit that was not physically present. (This concept of a "virtual machine" is important for the 68010/12 microprocessors, as discussed in more detail in Chapter 8.)

The M68000 microprocessors are modern implementations of a "von-Neumann architecture", minus the memory that is external to these microprocessors. As modern implementations, they have many obvious refinements over early implementations, such as in the power of their sets of instructions, their use of registers, and their variety of modes for addressing and accessing memory. Internally and largely hidden to the user other than through faster performance, the M68000 microprocessors advance beyond the "von-Neumann architecture" by including parallel processing in both space and time (pipelining) as explained in Chapter 2.1.6 below. Due to their small sizes, small power requirements and low costs, it is possible and feasible to use several M68000 microprocessors together in a larger and more complex multiprocessor architecture than a simple single-processor "von-Neumann architecture."

The Development of Microprocessors

The evolution of microprocessors took a different path than most users realize. Even with electronic tubes, it was technically feasible and advantageous to build electronic tubes with two electronic valves in the same glass tube. Therefore, when transistors began to replace electronic tubes, it was natural to try to create transistor pairs, particularly for use as preamplifiers in analog circuits (so that both transistors would be closely matched in their properties). Jack Kilby (Texas Instruments) developed a way for creating two transistors on the surface of one chip. With his approach, once more than one transistor could be made on the surface of a chip, the field was open for increasing the number of transistors so that we now can create integrated circuits with the equivalent of several million transistors on the surface of one chip. A large number of different technological developments were necessary to development this technology to the state that we have today.

The technology for placing increasing numbers of transistors on the surface of one chip seems to have grown faster than the theory for what we should do with this new technology. The SN 7400 is a typical integrated circuit with "small-scale integration", using TTL technology (Transistor-Transistor Logic). It has four NAND gates (with two inputs and one output per NAND gate). For some applications, such as memory circuits, no new theoretical developments were necessary in order to apply the increasing scales of integration to construct very useful integrated circuits with very large numbers of transistor equivalents per chip. However, for other applications, such as replacing logic circuitry in particular, it was extremely difficult and expensive to design complex logic circuits that took full advantage of the new technology for very large-scale integration. In practise, we still needed large numbers of small-scale integrated circuits, such as the SN 7400, on each printed-circuit board.

Therefore, the practical need was perceived to replace large numbers of small-scale integrated circuits for logic with a small number of inexpensive general-purpose integrated circuits with very large-scale integration. There was no sound theoretical approach available for solving this problem. The idea arose that one might be able to use something like a general-purpose programmable minicomputer to replace logic. From the practical point-of-view, tested architectures were available and flexibility appeared to be only a problem of programming software.

As a first step in this direction, Texas Instruments developed the MSI (medium-scale integration) 74181 arithmetic logic unit in TTL technology. The 74181 performs 16 arithmetic operations (such as addition, subtraction, shift, etc.) and 16 logic operations (such as AND, NAND, OR, and NOR) on 4-bit operands. It can be cascaded for words of arbitrary lengths, with fast look-ahead carry, which is faster than simple ripple carry. However, it is not normally classified as a microprocessor, since it does not have registers or even a program counter. Complete minicomputer systems were built, using this 74181 as the arithmetic logic unit at the center of the central processing unit, and it could also be used, together with several other integrated circuits, for replacing SSI (small-scale integration) circuits.

Intel was the first to develop a true "microprocessor". Their 4004 microprocessor was also a 4-bit device, like the 74181, but it contained registers and had a mini "von-Neumann architecture", like a conventional minicomputer. Intel designed their 4004 microprocessor for the specific purpose of replacing logic circuitry in a sophisticated electronic calculator. (It was a 4-bit device as the natural size to handle BCD numbers in a calculator.)

It is very important to understand that the early microprocessors were designed specifically as universal replacements for large numbers of small-scale integrated circuits in logic circuitry. It was only coincidental that they had architectures much like the central processor of a minicomputer. Most of the designers, developers and manufacturers of these microprocessors were convinced that microprocessors would NEVER be used as central processors in computer systems.

Since Digital Equipment Corporation was the leading supplier of minicomputers for scientific applications, the engineers who developed the first microprocessors were most acquainted with the architectural concepts of their DEC computers. Since there was no clear theory to specify the architectures that would be optimal for the new application of replacing logic circuitry, these engineers often took a subset of the architectural concepts from the DEC computer systems that they already knew. To a large extent, the architectural choices and decisions were arbitrary and based upon the immediate requirement of replacing random logic, rather than to form a sound foundation for building computer systems around microprocessors as central processing units.

1.2.2   The History of 8-bit Microprocessors and Microcomputers

The history of microprocessors began at Intel with their 4-bit 4004 microprocessor. Intel itself was only one-year old when it started the design of the 4004 in 1969. Intel developed the 4004 exclusively for one single customer but released it later onto the general market in November 1971. This history continued at Intel with the development of their 8-bit 8008 microprocessor that had a size of 8-bits because of its first application in replacing logic in a terminal that worked with bytes of data. It was released in April, 1972. Masatoshi Shima, who had been indirectly related with the development of the 4004, directed the design of the 8080 microproccessor that Intel released in April, 1974. It was designed to be an improvement over both the 4004 and 8008 for their application in replacing logic circuitry, and it was designed more generally, without a single specific application in mind. However, even in this evolutionary stage, the concept of maintaining "upward compatibility" was already present, and the instruction set of the 8080 included the instruction set of the 8008, with some corrections.

Since the mid 1950's, there was a small but determined group of computer amateurs in the USA. They bought old scrapped 1st- generation computer systems and tried to build minimal systems from these components. A hobby system with a few hundred bytes of magneticcore memory that could add two numbers in binary form was a great success. This was a very expensive and difficult hobby at that time.

When these amateurs heard about the new microprocessors, it was natural for them to want to use these microprocessors as the central processing units in their hobby computers. As a result, the first "microcomputers" were designed and built by these computer amateurs – outside of the main evolutionary process that was occuring inside of companies such as IBM, DEC, Intel and Texas Instruments. The first of these microcomputers were based upon the 8008 microprocessor. They were sold as kits to hobbyists starting in the Summer of 1974. The first commercially successful microcomputer was the Altair 8800 from MITS. It was based upon the 8080 microprocessor and it was actually developed as a kit for the purpose of having an interesting "do-it-yourself" article to boost the sales of a popular electronics magazine. This article appeared in January 1975, and the kit was priced at $ 439. Neither the designer, Ed Roberts, nor the magazine realized at the time that the computer itself would be far more successful and interesting than the magazine article.

Nearly the same problem existed for software as for hardware regarding microprocessors. The prevalent official opinion was that it was technically impossible to develop an operating system or an interpreter or compiler for a high-level language that would run on a microprocessor, such as the 8080 from Intel. Microprocessors were programmed only with cross assemblers and an occassional cross compiler until Intel released its resident version of PL/M for their Intellec Development System in 1974. Bill Gates, who later founded Microsoft together with Paul Allen, emulated an 8080 microprocessor on a DEC minicomputer and wrote the first BASIC interpreter for a microprocessor. It was first tested on a real 8080 microprocessor with the Altair 8800 microcomputer from MITS. The first versions of their BASIC interpreter were self contained, with their own input/output routines and ran without an operating system (since there were no operating systems for the 8080 microprocessor at that time). The combination of the language BASIC together with the low price for the hardware of the Altair 8800 made this pair a commercial success in the early days of microcomputers. In cooperation with Intel, Gary Kildall of Digital Research developed the CP/M operating system for the 8080 microprocessor of Intel – that later played a major role in the historical development of microprocessors and microcomputers.

The designer of the 8080 microprocessor at Intel, Masatoshi Shima left Intel to design the Z-80 8-bit microprocessor for the new startup company of Zilog (he later returned to Intel). It was released in 1976. The Z-80 used the concept of upward compatibility to provide a super set of 158 instructions, compared to the subset of 75 instructions for the 8080 (and subset of 45 instructions for the 8008). Programs that were written for the 8080, using its limited set of instructions, also ran on the Z-80. It also had other architectural advantages over the older 8080 microprocessor. Intel countered later, with its 8085 8-bit microprocessor that also used a super set of the instructions of the earlier 8080 – but was too late. The Z-80 captured the largest share of the market for 8-bit microprocessors within this family that started with the 4-bit 4004 and included the 8008, 8080, Z-80 and 8085 8-bit microprocessors. It is ironical that the much larger instruction sets of the Z-80 and 8085 were seldom used by software developers. They prefered to develop software using the subset of instructions for the 8080, in order to maintain portability to a larger number of different microcomputers. Therefore, in practise, the increased speed of the Z-80 over the earlier 8080 was its primary practical advantage.

In the meantime, Motorola was in the process of diversifying from its original business of making radios for automobiles (the source of its name) into the area of semiconductors. When Motorola designed the 6800 as its first 8-bit microprocessor, as an improvement over the 8008 from Intel, Motorola was able to make a fresh start, without any obligations that the 6800 be upward compatible from any older 4-bit or 8-bit microprocessors. The result was a new design that more systematically took advantage of the existing experience from minicomputers. Motorola and Intel released their 6800 and 8080 8-bit microprocessors at approximately the same time, in mid 1974. Although Intel was the pioneer with the headstart, programmers who were starting with microprocessors generally prefered working with the 6800.

At the time that Motorola released its 6800 microprocessor in mid 1974, there were about 20 other microprocessors on the market. However, the 6800 quickly became the main competitor to the 8080 from Intel, due to several important innovative features, including the use of a single 5-volt power supply and the simultaneous release of peripheral devices to support it. There was already a shift of emphasis from designing a microprocessor to replace random logic to designing a microprocessor for use as the central processor in a complete computer system.

Similar to the history at Intel, Chuck Peddle left the design team for the 6800 at Motorola to design the very similar 6502 microprocessor at MOS Technology. The major difference between the 6502 and the 6800 was an onboard clock timer that saved a few supporting components in making low-cost systems. By contrast with the Z-80, that added 83 instructions to the instruction set of the 8080, the 6502 only changed two instructions in the instruction set of the 6800 and did not add any new instructions. Even with this minor difference, and lower prices, the 6502 quickly stole the market for microprocessors for the 6800 family, just as the Z-80 stole the market for the 8080 family.

One important consequence of this historical development is that the later M68000 family of 16-bit and 32-bit microprocessors from Motorola is the logical successor to both the M6800 and 6502 families of 8-bit microprocessors. By contrast, the later 16-bit and 32-bit microprocessors from Intel are not logical succesors to the popular Z-80 8-bit microprocessor from Zilog. Programmers who prefered to work with either the 6800 or 6502 families of 8-bit microprocessors usually prefer to work with the M68000 family of 16/32-bit microprocessors.

Both Intel and Motorola, as the pioneers and developers of the two most important families of 8-bit microprocessors, lost the major shares of their respective markets to new upstart companies, Zilog and MOS Technology (later taken over by their largest customer, Commodore).

In the ensuing battle between these two families, the following technical factors evolved as decisive:

- The 8080 family (dominated by the Z-80) had one single standard operating system (CP/M from Digital Research) that made it easier to develop standard applications software for the hardware of different manufacturers.
- The 6800 family (dominated by the 6502) was easier to program and faster in processing.
- The Microsoft BASIC interpreter was available in many versions for both families, with small differences for graphics and sound capabilities of different hardware systems, which created a broad-based standard for the BASIC language.

Overall, the result was a draw, with each family winning in a different area as follows:

- The 8080 family won the market for business applications, due to the need for standard software packages that ran on the hardware of a large number of hardware manufacturers (possibly due to the CP/M operating system). Due to the standard operating system, it was easy for a very large number of hardware manufacturers to enter this market with a base of compatible applications software ready to run on their systems. These companies started with MITS and were followed by IMSAI, Cromemco, North Star and Osborne – to mention only a few in the order that they entered the market).
- The 6800 family won the market for personal computers where the demands were highest for high

speeds in processing graphics and sound (A 6502 at 2 MHz was typically 20% faster than a Z-80 at 4 MHz for such demanding applications). The high demand for performance in this market was also a factor that led each hardware manufacturer to develop its own operating system, that was optimized for its own graphics and sound capabilities. Therefore, there was a smaller number of successful companies in this market, including Ohio Scientific, SW Technical, Apple, Commodore and Atari (roughly in the order of their entry).

Figure 1-2 below summarizes the statistical results of this competition as the total number of microprocessors shipped through the end of 1984.

6800	Motorola	5,283,000	
	2nd Sources	4,616,000	
	Total	9,899,000	3.9%
650X	MOS Tech/Commodore	15,300,000	
	2nd Sources	39,016,000	
	Total	54,316,000	21.3%
6802/8	Motorola	8,620,000	
	2nd Sources	14,841,000	
	Total	23,461,000	9.2%
6809	Motorola	6,771,000	
	2nd Sources	4,899,000	
	Total	11,670,000	4.6%
	Subtotal	99,346,000	38.9%
8080	Intel	5,085,000	
	2nd Sources	11,738,000	
	2Total	16,823,000	6.6%
Z-80	Zilog	27,654,000	
	2nd Sources	50,888,000	
	Total	78,542,000	30.7%
8085	Intel	16,820,000	
	2nd Sources	22,764,000	
	Total	39,584,000	15.4%
	Subtotal	134,949,000	52.8%
	Others	21,286,000	8.3%
		255,581,000	100.0%

Source = Dataquest

Figure 1-2: Total Number of 8-bit Microprocessors Shipped (from 1975 through 1984)

Many other 8-bit microprocessors made their way to the market and some were reasonably successful in small corners of the market. Some had interesting innovative concepts that may be important in the future, such as the first use of CMOS technology by RCA for their 1802 microprocessor in 1974. However, none came close to the 8080 and 6800 families in terms of the number of units sold for use as the central processors of microcomputers. Within the original market of replacing random logic, the TMS 1000 series of 4-bit microprocessors was introduced by Texas Instruments in 1974 and became very important for controller applications, such as in toys.

The 12-bit 6100 microprocessor from Intersil should also be mentioned here, between the larger families of 8-bit and 16-bit microprocessors. It has the unusual size of 12-bits because it implements the architecture and instruction set of the very popular PDP-8 microcomputer from Digital Equipment Corporation. This was the one of the two early attempts to reduce a minicomputer to a microcomputer directly (the other was by Texas Instruments with their 16-bit 9900 microprocessor, also in 1976). Although the PDP-8 was rather old at the time when Intersil introduced the 6100 microprocessor in 1976, a large base of software already existed and the PDP-8 minicomputer was probably the minicomputer most familiar to people who used the first microcomputers. As mentioned earlier, many of the other designs for microprocessors borrowed heavily from practical experience with DEC computer architectures – however without trying to duplicate them, as in this case.

1.2.3   The History of 16/32-bit Microprocessors

The distinction between 16-bit and 32-bit processors is somewhat blurred. The reason is that you can use several different parameters, measured as a number of bits, to define the "size" of a microprocessor. They include:
- the size of the operands processed internally by the processor,
- the size of the registers used internally by the processor,
- the size of the data path used internally by the processor,
- the size of the data path used externally by the processor and
- the size of the address bus.

The first of the 16-bit microprocessors was the PACE from National Semiconductor, released in 1974. It was followed by the following major 16/32-bit processors:
- 9900 from Texas Instruments in 1976
- CP-1600 from General Instrument in 1976
- 8086 from Intel in 1978
- Z8000 from Zilog in 1979
- 68000 from Motorola in 1979/1980
- 32016 from National Semiconductor in 1982

Perhaps as a surprise, the winners of the battle for market shares with 8-bit microprocessors, Zilog with their Z-80 in the 8080 family and MOS Technology with their 6502 in the 6800 family, have not emerged as strong contenders in the new competition with 16-bit and 32-bit microprocessors. Rather, the founders of the two 8-bit families, Intel and Motorola, have emerged as the leaders with new 16-bit and 32-bit processors that are logical extensions to their earlier 8-bit families. As a late arrival, the 16032 family from National Semiconductor is also becoming a major contender (later renamed as the 32016 family). In addition to the Intel, Motorola and National Semiconductor families that started as 16-bit families and evolved into 32-bit families, some new 32-bit families have also arrived, without 16-bit predecessors, such as the Bellmac-32A from Bell Telephone and the "no-name" microprocessor from Hewlett-Packard.

One key factor in explaining why Zilog and MOS Technology were unable to transform their commercial success with 8-bit microprocessors into success with 16-bit microprocessors may be that the two key designers, Masatoshi Shima of Zilog and Chuck Peddle of MOS Technology, who originally transfered know-how from Intel to Zilog and from Motorola to MOS Technology, left Zilog and MOS Technology before the age of 16-bit and 32-bit microprocessors. (Masatoshi Shima did design the early Z8000 microprocessor before leaving Zilog to return to Intel. Chuck Peddle switched from designing microprocessors to designing microcomputers, such as the popular PET microcomputer for Commodore, later for Victor, and now for Tandon.)

However, it is less surprising that both Intel and Motorola are most successful in the respective market areas where their 8-bit product families were most successful. The preliminary conclusions in the middle of this race appear to be that:

– Intel is leading the race in the market for commercial systems, but with the single standard operating system of MS-DOS from Microsoft rather than the CP/M family of 16-bit operating systems from Digital Research, for the same reasons why Zilog led this race for 8-bit microprocessors. The commercial success of the IBM PC and compatibles falls within this framework.

– Motorola is leading the race:

where the more demanding UNIX operating system is used, for scientific applications where higher performance is required (such as in workstations for graphics and artificial intelligence – particularly for systems that work with or compete against the large VAX minicomputers from DEC) and for personal computers with advanced graphics capabilities (such as the Macintosh from Apple, the 520 ST from Atari, and the Amiga from Commodore, – all companies with strong commitments to the earlier 8-bit 6502 microprocessor).

Again, there appears to be more major operating systems for the Motorola family than the Intel family, for the same reasons.

In the long term, the Intel family appears to be suffering more from its self-imposed upward compatibility to earlier 4-bit and 8-bit microprocessors. In particular, the limited abilities of the Intel microprocessors to directly address large memory areas is imposing an increasing burden. It is difficult to address more than 640 kilobytes of memory directly through the MS-DOS operating system with the Intel family of microprocessors, whereas the Motorola family provides simple direct access to at least 16 megabytes of memory. Complicated tricks are required to address more than 1 megabyte with the Intel family.

This limitation continues to grow in importance as the demands for better graphics continue to grow. For example, if you want to work with a picture that has a resolution of $1024 * 1024$ pixels, the picture contains 1 megapixels. If you allow 256 colors per pixel, this requires a frame buffer with 1 megabyte of memory and if you allow 24 bit planes for 16 million different colors per pixel (TV and motion-picture quality), you need 3 megabytes for a frame buffer. A program that transforms one such picture into another, without overwriting, requires simple high-speed access to 6 megabytes of memory for the two frame buffers alone. It is relatively easy to handle both the program and data for such tasks with the Motorola family but it is significantly more difficult with the Intel family.

The 8008 microprocessor was designed to address a maximum of only 16 kilobytes of memory. Several years later, while the Z-80 and 6502 8-bit microprocessors dominated the market, very few people realized that microprocessors would ever need to address more than 64 kilobytes of memory. One of the most important lessons of history is that the demands for memory have nearly always grown faster than anticipated. Although the first processor in the M68000 family, the 68000 microprocessor, has only 24 address lines and can directly address a linear memory space of 16 megabytes of memory, all microprocessors in this family have identical 32-bit internal address registers. It has, therefore, been possible to introduce new processors in this family later with up to 32 address lines that can directly address a memory space of $256 * 16$ megabytes ($= 4$ gigabytes) of memory – without any changes in the basic architecture. The future of the M68000 family is not limited by this barrier that limits many other families of processors.

1.2.4 The History of 32-bit Microprocessors

The first of the true 32-bit microprocessors, with 32-bit internal and external data paths, include

– the 68020 (and 68030 in 1987) from Motorola,
– the 32032 and 32332 from National Semiconductor,
– the VL86C010 RISC microprocessor from VLSI Technology,

- the 80386 from Intel,
- the 32100 and 32200 Series from AT & T,
- the Clipper from Fairchild and
- the Transputer from INMOS.

At the time that this is written, this market is still very young. Estimates for total sales up to the end of 1986 are approximately 475,000 units for the 68020, 250,000 for the 32032, 100,000 for the RISC microprocessor from VLSI and 90,000 for the 80386. However, as the relatively new 80386 goes into full production in 1987, it will certainly capture a significant share of this market. Therefore, it is expected that Motorola and Intel will ultimately capture the largest shares of this market, with National Semiconductor close behind. The other processors should also be successful in other more specialized markets. The 32100 and 32200 series from AT & T are focused upon implementing the UNIX operating system from AT & T; the Clipper appears to be the fastest microprocessor available, and it is aimed at specialized markets that require this speed; the RISC microprocessor from VLSI is aimed at large OEM customers, and the Transputer has an entirely different architectural approach for supporting large numbers of Transputers communicating with one another in multiprocessor systems, such as for graphics applications. When the prices for these 32-bit processors drop to less than $ 50 per unit by the end of 1987, the resulting price-to-performance ratios will open new opportunities for new applications.

The increased power and speed of these new 32-bit microprocessors places increasingly more complex demands upon the designers of systems that use them. Otherwise, the surrounding systems will prevent these processors from delivering their full performance and advantages over earlier microprocessors. In particular, the flow of data and instructions between the main memory and these processors has become increasingly critical, since the low-cost VLSI memory devices have not become faster at the same rate as the microprocessors. This is leading to the use of multiple paths from processors to memory and different paths for main memory (no interrupts allowed) and peripheral-device interfaces (interrupts allowed). Variations of the Harvard architecture (with separate buses and main memories for instructions and data) are appearing, such as with separate caches for instructions and data (as in the 68030 microprocessor) as well as separate memory-management units for instructions and data. Although it may be relatively easy to modify a system with a 16-bit or 16/32-bit microprocessor to accept a full 32-bit microprocessor, the increase in performance may be dissappointing if the system itself is not redesigned to allow the faster 32-bit microprocessor to operate at full speed with a minimum of wait states.

The historical trend from the first 4-bit microprocessors to 8-bits, to 8/16 bits, to 16 bits, to 16/32 bits and now to 32 bits seems to imply a continuation on to 32/64 bits, 64 bits, 64/128 bits, etc. However, a point of diminishing returns occurs when the processor is designed to process operands as data in sizes larger than naturally needed.

For word processing with one 8-bit byte for each character, using a 16-bit processor with a 16-bit bus to main memory does not help much. However, once the 16-bit processor and 16-bit bus are available, it becomes feasible to include attributes with each character, such as by using a 16-bit word for each character (including attributes).

For mathematical operations on floating-point numbers, the standard format for "single-precision" uses 32-bit operands, and it is possible to use 64-bit operands for "double-precision". However, if single-precision operations are used nearly all of the time, a 64-bit processor with a 64-bit bus to memory would not be cost effective for performing such 32-bit operations. Except for the most critical applications, it will probably be more cost effective to use a 32-bit processor and bus that will require 2 to 4 times as long for an exceptional 64-bit floating-point operation as for its standard 32-bit floating-point operations. Super computers often use 80-bit operands for floating-point operations and this appears to be the upper limit for the near future.

For color graphics, there is no perceived need for using more than 24 bits per pixel to define the color (over 16 million different colors) although one does occassionally use up to 32 bits per pixel, to store other attributes for each pixel in the same word of data. Although one needs to move 24 to 32-bit words of data quickly in such applications, one only needs to calculate with three 8-bit bytes at one time, since the 24 bits for color are partitioned into 8 bits for 256 intensity levels for each of the 3 primary colors (there is no "carry" from the 8 bits for one primary color to the 8 bits for the next primary color).

It is, of course, possible that other types of operations will evolve that require larger word sizes for efficient operations, such as for "artifical intelligence".

Millions of units need to be produced and sold of each new microprocessor in order to bring its unit price to an acceptable level for it to compete with earlier predecessors. It appears very unlikely, therefor, that the current trend in the size of microprocessors will continue rapidly beyond the most recent 32-bit size. Rather, we can expect continued improvement in the performance of 32-bit microprocessors, such as the improvements in the 68030 microprocessor over the earlier 68020 microprocessor from Motorola as well as increased use of multiprocessor architectures.

1.2.5   The Controversy Between RISC and CISC Philosophies

There has been an important ideological struggle in the background – between the RISC and CISC philosophies. The philosophy behind a RISC (reduced instruction-set computer) is that a computer should have as few instructions as possible (roughly 30 to 40), and each instruction should execute in one cycle of the system clock. The philosophy behind a CISC (complex instruction-set computer) is that a computer should have powerful instructions for implementing the concepts of modern high-level languages and operating systems which results in large instruction sets (several hundred to a thousand) and where each instruction takes a different number of cycles of the system clock to execute, depending upon its complexity. One argument from the RISC enthusiasts is the 20-80 rule. This rule claims that most programmers use 20% of the instruction set of a CISC computer 80% of the time and the remaining 80% of the instruction set 20% of the time – at least partially because it is difficult for a human to remember the details for several hundred different instructions. The CISC enthusiasts counter by claiming that most computer code is written by high-level compilers rather than by human programmers in assembler. The RISC enthusiasts claim that a smaller number of simpler instructions enables programmers to implement complex concepts that execute faster because each instruction is simpler and faster. However, the CISC enthusiasts claim that the richer set of more complex tailor-made instructions enables programmers to implement complex concepts that execute faster. Emotions run high on both sides of this controversy, and there is no clear winner at this time.

Probably without having had a strategic plan to do so at that time, Intel became an accepted leader in the CISC camp with their 8-bit 8080 microprocessor and Motorola became an accepted leader in the RISC camp with their 8-bit 6800 microprocessor (both in 1974). Both the 6800 microprocessor and the 6502 microprocessor (from MOS Technology) have 56 instructions whereas the 8080 has 75 instructions. However, the later Z-80 microprocessor expanded the instruction set of the 8080 microprocessor to 158 instructions. This placed Intel under competitive pressure to develop their 8085 with a substantially larger instruction set than the 8080. Together with their general strategy of maintaining upwards compatibility, these two factors automatically launched Intel on the path towards increasingly larger and more complex instruction sets. By contrast, Motorola took a more relaxed position on upwards compatibility when climbing from 8-bit to 16-bit processors than Intel, which allowed Motorola to start with a reasonably lean set of instructions for its M68000 family.

Although the processors in the M68000 family are not true RISC processors (for example, individual instructions use more than one cycle of the system clock), they do follow the general philosophy of RISC. These processors achieve a delicate compromise between using a small number of basic instructions (that a programmer must remember) and a large number of permutations of addressing modes (that are more or less obvious from the context) in order to simultaneously achieve basic goals from both the RISC and CISC camps.

Even at the level of the early 8-bit microprocessors, the difficulty in comparing processors with different philosophies became apparent. As mentioned above, benchmark tests with comparable programs have shown that the 6502 microprocessor at 2 MHz is usually about 20% faster than the Z-80 microprocessor at 4 MHz. However, this is not in itself a complete proof that the RISC philosophy of the 6502 microprocessor is faster than the CISC philosophy of the Z-80 microprocessor. The difference in the definition of the clock signals and, therefore, the clock rates of "2 MHz" versus "4 MHz" is such that these two clock rates should be considered to be roughly equivalent, rather than one being twice that of the other. Also, as mentioned above, the extra instructions of the Z-80 microprocessor have seldom been used in practice. As an example, the popular BASIC-80 compilers from Microsoft contain a Z-switch than enables the user to optionally compile using only the instruction set of the 8080 microprocessar as the default when this switch is not used and with the expanded instruction set of the Z-80 microprocessor when this flag is set. Setting this flag results in compiled programs that are somewhat faster and smaller in size than with 8080 code. However, the library of routines that is linked to these compiled programs is obviously in 8080 code, in order to be compatible for both options.

One of the unfortunate consequences of this debate between RISC and CISC philosophies, applied to the M68000 family, is that authors from the RISC camp tend to distort their descriptions of the M68000 family as far as possible in the direction of the RISC philosophy whereas authors from the CISC camp tend to distort their descriptions of the M68000 family as far as possible in the direction of the CISC philosophy. As we will see in Chapters 3, 4 and 8 below, this leads to very confusing counts of such simple specifications as the number of instructions in a given instruction set and the number of addressing modes – depending on how you decide to count. You will, therefore, encounter claims in different articles that appear to be contradictory to one another. You will also find that it is extremely difficult to compare microcomputers from different manufacturers, based upon the number of instructions or addressing modes, without counting them yourself to be certain that you are counting in the same way in order to obtain comparable results. Also, as the debate between RISC and CISC itself indicates, the number of different instructions does not in itself tell you which of two microprocessors is the more powerful.

The microcomputers that were designed with the 8-bit microprocessors were relatively small systems that challenged the existing market for computer systems from the bottom up. As low cost stand-alone systems, they opened new market areas that were not economically feasible with the more expensive minicomputers and mainframe computers. In the case of the existing market for multi-user systems, the new microcomputers:

- replaced the multi-user systems with multiple stand-alone systems in most cases where the only justification for the multi-user aspect was to share computational resources and
- distributed intelligence down to intelligent workstations of multi-user systems, where the multi-user aspect was justified by the need to share a common base of data as well as hardware resources (such as expensive disk drives and printers).

Although attempts were made, microcomputers based upon 8-bit microprocessors were not competitive as multi-user systems themselves.

In advancing from 8-bit microprocessors to 16-bit and 32-bit microprocessors, goals were set to cover a larger share of the total computer market. This meant that microcomputers based upon these newer microprocessors should also be able to implement competitive multi-user systems as well as provide more powerful stand-alone systems and intelligent terminals or work-stations. However, the philosophy for achieving these goals is different, depending upon the application. For scientific applications that require heavy number crunching, it is necessary to keep the design of both the hardware and the operating system as lean and simple as possible – in order to minimize any unessential overhead. For commercial applications with many users working at lower levels of complexity, the hardware and the operating system tend to become more complex while the application programs are relatively simple. Therefore, the commonly stated goal of supporting high-level languages and modern operating systems can have different interpretations for different designers.

1.2.6   The Design Philosophy of the M68000 Family

When the team at Motorola began to design the M68000 family of 16-bit and 32-bit microprocessors, they defined the following design goals:

1   Consistent Architecture for a Family

The result should be one single architecture, with various implementations of various subsets of the common architecture. The first version, the 68000 microprocessor, implements only a subset of the defined architecture. The top-down design of the complete architecture at the beginning provides both upward and cross compatibility for individual implementations later.

2   Flexibility and Effectiveness

A clean and simple design is required that is easy to program without bending over backwards to accomodate for unnatural complications. This goal implicitly includes the goals of the RISC philosophy for a symmetrical and regular set of instructions.

3   Broad Area of Applications

The M68000 family should be a general-purpose family that can be used for a broad variety of applications.

4   Expandability

The architecture must specify many capabilities from the beginning, such as for floating-point arithmetic and string operations that are not implemented in the first M68000 microprocessor but can be implemented in later versions. In addition, unused address areas in memory must be reserved for new functions that are expected with additional advances in technology.

5   Support for High-Level Languages

The architecture must contain functions that support and simplify the implementation of advanced operating systems and high-level languages. Motorola agreed, as a matter of policy, to support the development of high-level languages.

This design team, including Tom Gunter, Edward Stritter, John Zolnowski and Nick Tredennick, began in 1977, and their first prototype, the XC68000, came onto the market in 1979. For the first time, this microprocessor offered 32-bit registers, direct addressing of up to 16 megabytes and a set of instructions that are equivalent to those of a modern minicomputer system. This microprocessor had an equivalent of 68000 transistors or 13000 logical gates (compared to the 4 gates on the SN 7400 mentioned above) on a chip of silicon with an area of only 6.2 ∗ 7.1 mm. In order to achieve this performance, Motorola had to develop the new HMOS Technology (High-density NMOS) that provides twice the density of circuits and an improvement by a factor of 4 in the speed/power product (see Figure 1-3 below). As an illustrative example, if the first XC68000 had been implemented in normal NMOS technology, the chip size would have exceeded the economically feasible maximum size, and it would have consumed approximately 6 watts, instead of 1.5 watts in HMOS.

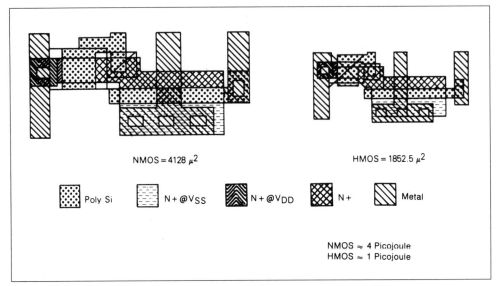

Figure 1-3: NMOS/HMOS Technology

The original goals for this new architecture were met for the first prototype model, and they continue to be met with the latest versions, as explained in the second volume of this book. The large addressing range opens new applications, such as for color graphics. Special functions, such as for protective measures, support the implementation of multi-user, multi-processing systems. Other functions, such as the LINK and UNLK instructions (see Chapter 4), support the implementation of high-level languages. The use of microcode and prefetching of instructions optimizes both the flexibility and performance of the architecture for the first time in a microprocessor (see Chapters 2.1 and 6).

In this context, we might conclude that engineers who design computer systems for scientific applications would more often prefer the RISC philosophy and that engineers who design computer systems for commercial applications would more often prefer the CISC philosophy. We might also conclude that the priorities within the design philosophy of the M68000 family favor the requirements of scientific applications, whereas the corresponding priorities within the design philosophy of the Intel family favor the requirements of commercial applications. Although this creates an important bias, microcomputers based upon the M68000 family will be used successfully for commercial applications, and microcomputers based upon the Intel family will be used successfully for scientific applications.

1.3   The M68000 Family and its Producer

Whenever a user selects a component, whether a microprocessor or another component, it is important that there should be at least one, if not more, second sources. This is important, first, because it increases the competition, and second, because a user is no longer completely dependent upon a single manufacturer (who may not be able or willing to deliver in quantity at all times for various reasons).

There are usually differences between second sources. Therefore, it is important for the user to know whether the second sources use duplicate copies of the original masks. If this is the case, then the resulting microprocessors are usually exchangeable with one another. In some cases, the user may have to compare the data sheets of the different manufacturers, as well as the different version numbers of the masks that are used (see Chapter 5).

A second criterion is whether a second source conducts its own development work, such as to develop support devices, and whether the second source exchanges these masks with the original source and other second sources. Fortunately, these criteria are all fullfilled for the M68000 family, as shown in Table 1.4 below. (See also Chapter 7 on support devices in Volume II.)

Company	Product Name	Exchange of Masks	Sampling or Production	R&D for Support Devices
Motorola	MC68000	Yes	Yes	Yes
Signetics/Valvo/Philips	SC68000	Yes	Yes	Yes
Hitachi	HD68000	Yes	Yes	Yes
	(HD63000 CMOS)	–	–	–
Thomson CSF	EF68000	Yes	Yes	Yes
Rockwell	R68000	Yes	Yes	Yes

Figure 1-4: The 68000 Microprocessor and its Manufacturers

The M68000 microprocessors are among the few microprocessors that are produced by several manufacturers as second sources. This implies that other experts have found this product line to have technological excellence. The 68000 microprocessor is well on its way towards becoming an industrial standard in the area of 16-bit microprocessors. Companies such as Motorola and Hitachi are already planning to produce the M68000 family in CMOS technology. This will open new markets for this processor.

Figure 1-5 below gives a summary of when second source contracts were signed.

Mostek	September, 1981
Signetics/Valvo/Philips	January, 1981
Hitachi	1980
Thomson CSF	1982
Rockwell	1981

Figure 1-5: Signing of Second-Source Contracts

1.4   The New Programming Techniques

In recent years, one has heard frequently about the "software crisis". Where does it come from? At the beginning of the computer age, programming was accomplished by entering binary control bits into a computer. Assemblers and compilers were not yet conceived. In addition, a developer was concerned primarily with the question of whether his system would work at all – rather than to be concerned with user friendliness. The user had to be satisfied with a very limited system memory since semiconductor memory components were not available at all in the beginning, and when they did first arrive, they were very expensive. Therefore, it was not so important that code be efficient and easy to understand – since it was more important that the code could fit into the available memory.

The situation was similar when the first microprocessors arrived on the market. They were originally conceived and designed as replacements for discrete logic. No one foresaw at that time that microprocessors would ever serve as the central processors of complete computer systems and thereby edge into the domain of minicomputers. It was in fact hobbyists, who wanted to build computers of their own, who designed, built and marketed the first microcomputers based upon microprocessors.

Microprocessors were programmed nearly exclusively with assembler languages at the beginning. These low-level languages differ from machine languages primarily in the use of mnemonics (short abbreviations) as names for commands – that are easier for human beings to remember and use than the binary words that a processor uses and understands. In some cases, single macro commands replaced complete sequences of simpler commands – which greatly simplified the programming. A very good understanding of the hardware and how it operates is necessary for this type of programming – even if not as much as was orginally required for programming directly in the machine language. Programs that are written this way are usually not transportable to other computers and are very difficult for the user to read and understand.

For the many programs that were written in an assembler language and are still being written in assembler languages, it is necessary to write a new and separate program for each computer or processor used for the given application. The programmer has to reinvent the same wheel each time. In addition, it is very easy to write a program in an assembler language with a style that is practically unreadable and incomprehensible for anyone other than the orginal programmer. These factors all contribute to making the practical problems associated with programming in assembler languages difficult to solve.

There are many methods that are used today to overcome these problems.

Orginally, the designers of microprocessors were not concerned with the question of how easy and elegant it would be for a programmer to program their microprocessors. Rather, designers were only concerned that programmers could solve real problems in some way with their microprocessors. However, for modern processors, such as the M68000 microprocessors, designers place a very high priority upon designing their microprocessors with a set of instructions that is clearly structured and easy to use. Therefore, the design of the first 68000 microprocessor was influenced significantly by software developers. The results are evident in the regular structure of instructions that simplify programming both in assembler language and high-level languages. Earlier, one measured the power of a microprocessor by the number of different instructions that it could execute. One forgot, thereby, that a programmer had to remember all of these instructions in order to be able to use them effectively. As a result, most programmers only used part of the available instructions since they could not remember all of them in detail. The rule-of-thumb developed that most programmers used 20% of the instructions 80% of the time and the remaining 80% of the instructions only 20% of the time. Therefore, a large and impressive set of instructions does not automatically bring a corresponding advantage in practice.

The designers of the M68000 family used a different strategy. The first M68000 microprocessor, the 68000, has "only" 56 different basic instructions. However, the 68000 microprocessor also has 12 basic modes for addressing (19 modes when all variations are included) that are applied systematically to this set of 56 different basic instructions to form all useful permutations. (This implements the concept of orthogonality that is required in the theory for RISC computers.) The result is a set of over 1000 permutations of basic instructions with addressing methods that is extremely powerful – while remaining well structured and easy to remember and understand. In addition, the set of registers of the 68000 supports simple and understandable programming.

In recent years, the new strategy of "structured programming" has become popular. Before structured programming, programs were praised that had a complex "spaghetti" structure of jumps in all directions – that may have been efficient in the use of memory (an important criterion in the early days of programming) but were very difficult for anyone to understand, including the programmer himself. The goals of structured programming include dividing a program into well-defined modules that can be designed, written and tested separately as modules before they are integrated into a complete program. Jumps are only allowed from the ends of modules to the beginnings of modules. Modules can be nested and subroutines are used when duplicate code is required at different places in a program. In order to write programs with the technique of structured programming, a programmer must first design a flowchart or a structogram that clearly shows what the program will do. Then, the programmer must write the individual modules of code in such a way that they are both reentrant and relocatable.

A reentrant module of code can be stopped in its execution by an interrupt, can be reentered and used during the interrupt and can continue without losing its original data after the interrupt. Such modules can be shared by several different programs at the same time.

A relocatable module of code executes properly at any location in memory, without having to be reassembled and relinked. In practice, this means that a program in EPROM does not have to be burned into another EPROM each time that the address space of the EPROM is changed in the hardware. As an example, a relocatable monitor program should run properly independent of whether its starting address happens to be at $ 1000 or $ 8000.

The M68000 microprocessors have several very important functions that support the development of reentrant and relocatable modules of code. Examples include the LINK and UNLINK instructions, as well as the MOVEM instruction. The LINK and UNLINK instructions allow the user to easily create an individual stack area for each module of code. The MOVEM instruction assists the user in temporarily storing and later retrieving the contents of the register before and after subroutines and interrupt routines. The TRAP instruction simplifies the inclusion of calls to the operating system from an application program. The addressing modes of the M68000 microprocessors for addresses that are relative to the program counter assist the user in writing relocatable modules of code. In addition, the M68000 microprocessors have a large number of features for identifying error conditions – that simplify the testing of programs. There are a large number of other features of the M68000 microprocessors that simplify the writing of good programs – that you will recognize while reading this book.

Another important factor in solving the software crisis is the use of intermediate-level programming languages (such as "C") and high-level programming languages (such as BASIC and PASCAL) – that are much easier for the user to read and understand than low-level languages like assembler languages. If the high-level language is also standardized (such as is the case for FORTRAN V, Standard Wirth PASCAL, ADA, etc.), then application programs are relatively portable from one computer to another. This means that programs written for a given application, but for use on different computers, do not have to be rewritten from the beginning for each computer. It also implies that a programmer does not have to know the hardware details of how each individual computer works in order to write application programs that will be used on different computers. Another advantage of writing programs in a high-level language is that they are much more transparent and easier to read than programs that are written in an assembler language – which are, in turn, much easier to read than programs that are written directly in a machine language. Both compilers and interpreters for high-level languages use the features of the respective processor for creating reentrant and relocatable modules of code. The M68000 microprocessors are, therefore, ideal for supporting high-level languages as well as low-level languages.

The trend in programming microprocessors is continuing strongly in the direction of creating modular, transparent, portable and universal programs. The tools for supporting this trend are developing on both the hardware side (microprocessors and emulators) and the software side. The programmer, himself, can contribute to this trend by using the available tools and methods, such as:

– flow charts
– structograms
– modular programming
– reentrant and relocatable programs
– high-level languages
– good in-line documentation of programs (a good rule-of-thumb calls for using as many lines for documentation in a program as for lines of code).

1.5   Foundations of Operating Systems

In the days when the computer age was beginning, concepts such as "operating system", "multiprocessing", etc. had not yet been invented. The typical user of a computer in those days had to know much more about the hardware of the computer than is the case today. The user was confronted with the naked hardware and had to control every action of the computer from his program. This meant that the user had to organize the way his program used the available memory space, load the program into memory (that was coded in machine language – since assemblers and high-level languages were not yet available), set the program counter at the beginning of the program and then start the program. The program had to manage all of the details of input and output with terminals, the communication with external memory if used and other organizational aspects. The user worked practically at the bit level through the hardware. Therefore, the user had to have a very detailed knowledge of all components of the hardware. Functions such as multitasking and multi-user capabilities were simply not feasible with this approach, and the hardware, itself, could not be used efficiently.

The modern concept of an operating system evolved out of this set of practical problems. An operating system establishes a standard interface between the hardware and application programs. It includes standard functions, such as for input and output to various peripheral devices, so that these functions do not have to be duplicated in each application program. This simplifies the task of a programmer in creating an application program.

Following are a few examples of the functions that a typical operating system performs:

– control over the execution of the various programs that are running in the system,
– management and optimal assignment of the common system resources, such as the central processor, printer, background memory, special input/output devices and internal memory,
– communications with input/output devices,
– storing and management of data (libraries, protection against loss of data such as by saving copies in background memory, file management, and organization and
– providing tool programs for the programmer (compilers, assemblers, linker, etc.) and maintenance programs (that test the hardware itself).

In the schema that is illustrated in Figure 1-4 above, the application program no longer has a direct contact to the hardware of the system. The application program leaves the control over the hardware to the operating system. When the application program wants to use a function of the hardware, it gives a request to the operation system, and the operating system then performs this task. The programmer no longer needs to know the details of the hardware but only needs to know how to make requests to the operating system to use this hardware. Such a request could typically be to display a character on the screen of a

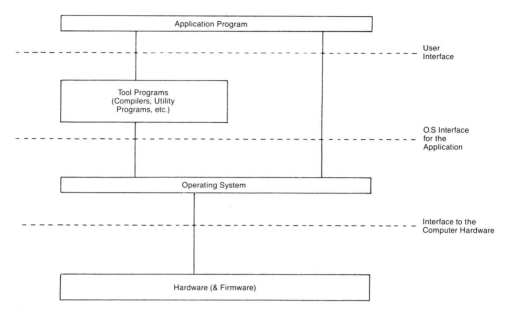

Figure 1-6: Roles of Tool Programs and an Operating System

terminal or to print a character on a printer. Multi-programming and multi-user functions only became feasible after this approach for delegating requests to the operating system was defined – since it gives the operating system the capability for determining whether a particular request can actually be performed at a given moment in time.

Following are a few of the concepts related to operating systems:

Single-User Operating System

This type of operating system only allows one user to work with the computer at one time. Such an operating system may or may not have capabilities for managing disk drives. It takes over the tasks of input and output as well as memory management for the application program, debugging and file management if there is a background memory device.

Multi-User Operating System

This type of operating system allows more than one user to work with the computer at the same time. The allocation of the computer to different users can occur with time sharing or with interrupts according to priorities. This type of operating system also performs all of the functions of a single-user operating system, plus the management of the system memory and other resources (background memory, printer, etc.) for the competing requests from different users.

Multi-Tasking or Multi-Programming Operating System

These two types of operating systems are the same in principle. The distinction between a task and a program is that a program may consist of several tasks that also execute in parallel. A program can also consist of a single task. A task can be a program or a part of a program. A multi-tasking system manages the execution of several tasks at the same time, using the same general techniques of time sharing and interrupts as used by a multi-user operating system.

Multi-Processor Operating System

This type of operating system coordinates the use of more than one processor at the same time. The individual processors usually have a mixture of private memory and shared memory that allows them to run nearly independently of one another when using their private memory but allows communications through the shared memory. The operating system assigns tasks to the individual processors and synchronizes their activities. The relatively low cost of powerful microprocessors, such as from the M68000 family, make very powerful multi-processor systems practical for demanding applications.

Real-Time Operating System

This type of operating system responds to external requests (such as interrupts from the control of external processes). The response times for such requests must be kept very short—so short that it appears to be "instantaneous" for the external process. By contrast, a batch-mode operating system processes tasks in a fixed order, with no flexibility for responding dynamically to external events. Examples, from Motorola for the M68000 family of microprocessors, include
– RMS68K–multi-tasking real-time operating system and
– VERSAdos – multi-user, multi-tasking, real-time operating system.
RMS68K is the kernel of VERSAdos and VERSAdos has additional capabilities.

Batch-Mode Operating System

This type of operating system runs all programs or tasks sequentially – in contast to a real-time operating system. Therefore, it is not possible for these programs or tasks to react to external events. In the early days of computers, all operating systems were batch-mode operating systems. The user inserted one deck of punched cards after the other on the input tray for the card reader, where each deck of cards contained control cards for running and data. The computer processed one deck of cards after the other. There was very little dialogue with the user, other than error messages.

Job Scheduling or Dispatching

Job scheduling refers to the assignment of resources (such as the processor or memory) to individual programs or tasks that currently have the highest priority. In systems with time sharing, jobs are rescheduled after each time slice (such as every 10 milliseconds or 1 second).

Spooling

For the simplest mode of operations with a printer, a program starts the printing and then waits until the printing operation is finished before the user can do anything else with the program. With spooling, the program does not start the printing but rather writes everything that needs to be printed into a file in the background memory. This operation proceeds much faster than actual printing since the background memory is many times faster than a mechanical printer. As soon as this spooling operation is complete, the program can continue with other activities. The spool file can then be printed with a lower priority when the resources of the computer are not being used directly by the users. Since users working at computer terminals do not use all of the capability of a computer continuously all of the time, the actual printing takes place in parallel, in the brief moments while the computer has free capacity.

Task

A task is either a complete program or a part of a program that is currently executing in a computer. It is nothing other than a running program. The primary characteristics of a task are the current status of the registers in the processor while it is running, its priority and its current state. The different states that a task can be in at any given moment are:
- non-existant,
- waiting for a particular event, such as an interrupt,
- ready for execution, but waiting for other tasks with higher priorities that are currently executing and
- executing.

Segment

A segment is a continuous part of a memory area that a program can address by specifying the starting address of the segment and an offset within the segment. A memory-management unit requires the starting address and the length of a segment in order to declare and use the part of a memory area as a segment.

Mailbox

It can occur in a multi-tasking or multi-processor system that one task needs to send a message to another task. A mailbox is a shared area of memory where all tasks can write messages that other tasks can read. This enables tasks (as well as users and processors) to communicate with one another.

Semaphor

Access to a segment of memory or a printer must be protected in a multi-tasking or multiprocessor system – otherwise serious conflicts and errors would occur. This protection of access is provided most often in an operating system by semaphores. A semmaphore is usully a single bit in memory that is assigned to a particular segment of memory or device, such as a printer. If this bit is set equal to 1, then its segment of memory or device is currently reserved for exlusive use by one task or processor. If this bit is reset equal to 0, then its segment of memory or device is free for a new request. Each task or processor can reserve a segment of memory or device for its exclusive use by changing the status of its bit from 0 to 1. The complexity of an operating system grows according to the size of the computer hardware and the variety of different functions that it provides. Figure 1.7 below illustrates the different levels of complexity. The more complex the operating system is, the more powerful the hardware must be – in order to provide all of the necessary functions and to perform with a realistic response time. It would certainly be impossible to implement a complex operating system such as UNIX on a 4-bit microprocessor that can only adress 16 kilobytes of memory. However, UNIX is an appropriate operating system for use with a microprocessor from the M68000 family. With an M68000 microprocessor, the choice of whether to use UNIX or not is determined by the limitations of UNIX rather than the hardware. In particular, UNIX does not support real-time interrupts, and there it can not be used for applications of process control (controlling equipment in a factory) or online direct booking (such as for airlines or banks). However, other operating systems are available for the M68000 family of microprocessors that do support real-time interrupts and are suitable for such demanding applications (such as RMS68K and VERSAdoes from Motorola). Other

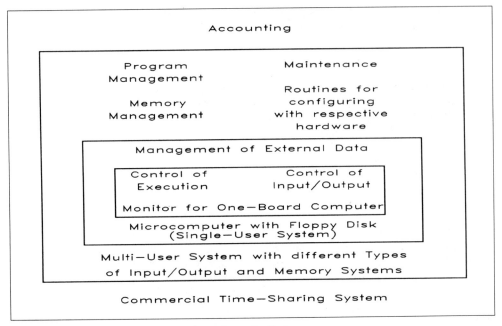

Figure 1-7: Different Levels of Complexity for an Operating System

operating systems and tools are listed in the "Motorola Microprocessor Software Catalog" that is available from Motorola.

The dream of every user is to have one single operating system that can do everything that the user needs. However, practise shows that different applications demand different capabilities from an operating system. Such a general-purpose operating system that contained all capabilities that any user might ever need would be too large and unwieldy for actual individual applications, since they would only use a small part of the total capabilities available. It is, therefore, a practical necessity to develop and work with more specialized operating systems that are optimized for use with specific categories of applications. Several articles and books are cited in the bibliography to this book that describe operating systems in general as well as individual operating systems in detail.

2
Organization of the
M68000 Microprocessors

The hardware of the M68000 family of microprocessors is described in this chapter.

2.1 Technology and Architecture of Processors in the M68000 Family

This section presents a physical model that explains how a microprocessor from the M68000 family is designed and operates. By contrast, the rest of this manual presents a functional model for these processors that explains how these processors work from the perspective of typical users, rather than from the perspective of designers of processors. Most users will not need to know or understand the physical model presented in this section of this chapter. However, a general understanding of this model will help all users to understand why the M68000 microprocessors behave the way they do.

2.1.1 Microcode Versus Combinatorial Logic

There are two basically different ways to design the architecture of a modern microprocessor:
– with combinatorial logic or
– with microcode.
All of the early microprocessors used combinatorial logic. This means that all of the instructions in the instruction set are implemented in space as logical circuitry. The result is a separate set of circuitry for each instruction that appears to be a random maze of AND (or NAND), OR (or NOR) and NOT logical gates where several transistors are used for each logical gate. A controller decodes the instruction, to identify which instruction is involved, and then sends the appropriate operands and parameters to the circuitry for the given instruction.
Some of the more recent microprocessors, such as the early PACE 16-bit microprocessor from National Semiconductor and later the M68000 family of microprocessors from Motorola, use microcode instead of combinatorial logic. These processors have a "processor within a processor". The innermost "processor" has a simpler architecture and a more-primitive set of instructions than the microprocessor itself. The simpler architecture is implemented with combinatorial logic, as before, but it uses a smaller amount of combinatorial-logic circuitry. The translation between the instruction set of the microprocessor and the more-primitive instruction set of its inner "processor" is implemented with firmware, ie. simple programs that are stored as "microcode" in ROM.
In Chapter 1.2 above, it was explained that the first microprocessors were designed to replace combinatorial-logic circuitry with a more flexible and programmable standard device. The use of

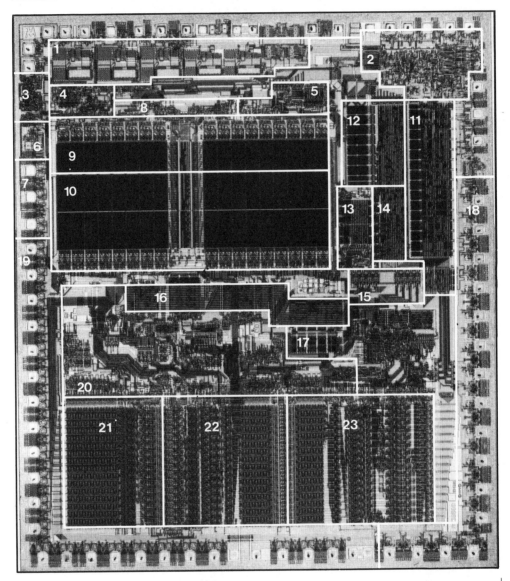

1	Clock Generator	9	Microcode ROM	17	Controller of Execution Units
2	Bus Control Logic	10	Nanocode ROM	18	Data-Bus Drivers
3	Interrupt Logic	11	Decoder for A1	19	Address-Bus Drivers
4	Timer Logic	12	Decoding for A2 – A3	20	Control Unit & Sequencer
5	Decoder for A0	13	Branching Logic (PLA)	21	Execution Unit (MSW –
6	Function-Code Logic	14	TRAP & Illegal Inst. (PLA)		Addresses and Data
7	Function-Code Drivers	15	Instruction Register	22	Execution Unit (LSW – Addr.)
8	Decoder Drivers	16	Instruction Decoder	23	Execution Unit (LSW – Data)

Figure 2-1: Photograph of the 68000 Microprocessor Chip

Figure 2-2: Photograph of a Combinatorial-Logic Microprocessor

microcode and a more-primitive processor within the microprocessor to replace combinatorial-logic circuitry of the microprocessor itself is, therefore, an example of applying the same general strategy a second
time, at a deeper hierarchical level.

The advantages of microcode over combinatorial logic include:
- The instruction set of the microprocessor can be changed or expanded by the relatively simple task
  of changing the microcode, ie. the contents of a ROM, rather than redesigning combinatorial logic.
- The design and layout of circuitry on the chip requires less area, has a simpler and clearer structure
  and is less complex.
- The time for designing and developing a new microprocessor is reduced since more design activities
  can be performed in parallel, rather than sequentially.
- The inevitable errors that are made in any large project are fewer in number, less serious in their effects
  upon the overall structure and easier to correct.

The advantages of combinatorial logic over microcode include:
- The speed in executing instructions is usually higher since fewer steps or levels of logic are required.
- It is more difficult for competitors to make illegal copies or compatible versions.

These differences, and the practical consequences, can be seen graphically by comparing the chip
photographs of two microprocessors, one with each architectural approach. (See Figures 2-1 and 2-2
below.) It is easy to see that the chip of the 68000 microprocessor is organized in clearly defined blocks
or areas on the chip, whereas the other chip, with combinatorial logic, is a complex maze of transistor
equivalents. Not only the logic itself is simplied, but the internal interconnections are also simplified.

In the case of the M68000 family of microprocessors, flexibility was a major criterion for the design. The
philosophy was to design the architecture for a family of microprocessors first and then to introduce the
first members of this family before all of the other members have been designed in detail.

The area of the ROM containing microcode covered only 23% of the chip for the first 68000
microprocessor, compared with up to 60% of the area on the chip for the equivalent functions of a
combinatorial-logic microprocessor. Therefore, only a small part of the chip had to be changed in order
to change the functionality of the microprocessor – and these changes involved only a mask for the
microcode that is stored in this ROM.

In addition, the first 68000 microprocessor left approximately 1/4 of the ROM for microcode unused and
approximately $1/8$ of the possible opcodes for instructions unused. This left a relatively large reserve for
adding additional instructions later, as has been the case for the 68010, 68012, 68020 and 68030
microprocessors that were developed later in this family.

2.1.2   Internal Versus External Storage of Microcode

The microcode of a microprocessor that uses microcoding can be stored in ROM either:
- on the chip of the microprocessor or
- externally in a separate ROM chip.

In principle, it is very attractive to store the microcode externally. In this case, one single chip for a
"microprocessor engine" (microprocessor minus the microcode that defines how it operates) can be used
with different ROM chips to redefine the capabilities of the processor. A "new processor", with different
or additional instructions, would consist of a new and inexpensive ROM chip that would be used with the
same chip for the standard microprocessor engine. Another set of arguments in this direction includes
the factor that area can be saved on the chip of the microprocessor – that can be used either to lower production costs or for adding other functions, such as additional registers, cache memory, etc. at the same costs.

The early LSI-11 microprocessor chip from Digital Equipment Corporation used microcoding with the
microcode stored in an external ROM. Due to practical limitations on the number of pins for interconnections to an integrated circuit at that time, the LSI11 microprocessor used microcode that is only 22 bits

wide. As shown in Section 2.1.3 below, such microcode is more efficient and executes much faster if it is wider. Therefore, this practical limitation severely limited the speed of the LSI-11 in a fundamental way that is difficult to overcome.

As a result of several factors, an M68000 microprocessor stores its microcode on the same chip as the microprocessor itself. Although this reduces the area available for other functions and reduces the flexibility for changes in the instruction set, it offers several important advantages that outweigh the dissadvantages, including:

– a significantly smaller package with a smaller number of pins (without having to resort to complex multiplexing – where each pin is used for different purposes),
– lower packaging costs,
– lower costs for the user due to a single-chip solution and
– faster execution times.

2.1.3   Horizontal Versus Vertical Microcode

The microcode for a microcoded microprocessor can be configured with trade-offs for expansion in either the:
– horizontal or
– vertical
direction.

Expanding horizontally means that each word of microcode is decoded so that it can drive each individual logic line of the execution unit with a minimum of additional decoding. The consequence is that each word of microcode must be quite wide (horizontal), ie. have a large number of bits. Microcode that is expanded horizontally also requires more total memory space since the wide word length is not always fully used and decoded information uses more space than encoded information.

One method for expanding vertically consists of using the maximum amount of encoding that combines bits logically, whenever feasible, to shorten the width of each word of microcode and reduce the total amount of memory space required. The consequence is that several levels of decoding (vertical) are required, with combinatorial logic, in order to convert each word into signals that can drive individual logic lines of the execution units. Microcode that is expanded vertically usually requires more words of microcode.

In summary, microcode that is optimized by horizontal expansion is substantially faster than microcode that is optimized by vertical expansion. However, microcode that is optimized vertically requires substantially less ROM space. Storing the microcode in an external ROM requires vertical expansion, to minimize the number of input/output pins on the chip, whereas storing microcode internally in ROM on the same chip as the processor allows horizontal expansion since no input/output pins are needed.

The M68000 family of microprocessors uses a compromise that provides most of the benefits from both horizontal and vertical optimization of microcode. This compromise consists of using two levels of microcode, where the first level is expanded vertically, and the second level is expanded horizontally. The two levels are called
– microcode (expanded vertically) and
– nanocode (expanded horizontally).

Somewhat simplified, this two-level architecture works, as follows, in the M68000 family of microprocessors:

A single instruction from the instruction set of the microprocessor, or a part thereof (such as an accessing mode – see Chapter 3 below), is defined to be a macro instruction. Each such macroinstruction is coded as a sequence of micro instructions. Each such micro instruction is coded to contain either:
– the address of one single nano instruction or

– the address of the next micro instruction in the sequence (only in the case of a jump to a micro instruction that is out of the normal linear sequence).
Therefore, one sequence of short micro instructions defines a sequence of long nano instructions.

Each such nano instruction is 70 bits wide and contains low-level coded information that requires a maximum of 3 levels of decoding to obtain signals that drive the approximately 180 control points in the execution units directly. Theoretically, 2^{70} different 70-bit words exist that could potentially be used as nano instructions. Fortunately, practice shows that less than 512 of these 2^{70} potential nano instructions are actually useful and needed. Therefore, the M68000 family of microprocessors are designed for a maximum capacity of 512 such nano instructions in the nanocode ROM – which requires a 9-bit address for selecting one of these nano instructions.
The microcode ROM is designed with a maximum capacity of 1024 micro instructions – which requires a 10-bit address for selecting one of these micro instructions. There are two formats for one word of microcode, depending upon whether the word contains a 9-bit address for a nano instruction or a 10-bit jump address for a micro instruction that is out of the normal linear sequence. If it contains a 9-bit address for a nano instruction, then it also contains a 1-bit jump flag that specifies whether the next word in the linear sequence contains:
– another 9-bit address for a nano instruction or
– a 10-bit jump address for a micro instruction.
Therefore, both formats use exactly 10 bits per word and the microcode ROM has a width of 10 bits. These two formats are illustrated in Figure 2-3 below.

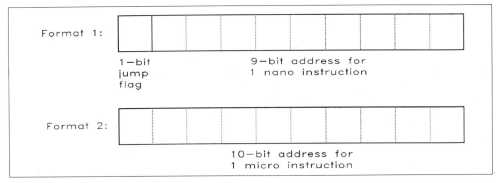

Bild 2.3 Two Formats for Micro Instructions

There is no duplication of nano instructions in the nanocode ROM. As a result, the nanocode ROM behaves like a simple "look-up table" with 9-bit addresses and 70-bit operands. However, there is some duplication of micro instructions in the microcode ROM since some different macro instructions are often similar and use the same nano instructions. The capability for jumping to addresses in the microcode ROM is necessary in order to allow the use of subroutines that minimize the amount of duplicated microcode. The first 68000 microprocessor used approximately 640 10-bit micro instructions, out of the potential 1024 micro instructions allowed with a 10-bit address. It used 280 70-bit nano instructions, out of the potential 512 instructions allowed with a 9-bit address. This used a total of approximately 26,000 bits (slightly over 3 kilobytes) of ROM, out of the 46,080 bits (slightly less than 6 kilobytes) allowed with this combination of 9-bit and 10-bit addresses. This left a substantial reserve of nearly 50% for later microprocessors in the same family, with larger instruction sets and functionality – without any need for changes in the architectural framework.

By contrast, design estimates for the alternative of using only one level of microcode indicated that over 45 kilobits would have been required for the first 68000 microprocessor – compared to 26,000 bits with two levels of microcode. This substantial savings illustrates the practical efficiency of the two-level approach.

2.1.4 Custom Microprocessors in the M68000 Family

The technical option has been available from the beginning for the first 68000 microprocessor to allow users to change the mask for either the microcode ROM or both the microcode ROM and nanocode ROM on the microprocessor chip – in order to create a customized version. In particular, users could change and expand upon the instruction set by changing the contents of only the microcode ROM, without having to change the nanocode ROM. However, Motorola has not decided to allow customers to change the microcode for customized version, except in one individual case.

Following are a few of the arguments that have reasoned against allowing customers to design their own custom versions by changing the ROM mask on the microprocessor chips:

– This would reduce the number of standard units sold at the beginning, thereby increasing the unit costs for the standard units.
– This could encourage the development of a confusing variety of non-compatible assemblers, disassemblers, compilers and cross compilers.
– This could discourage the development of standard emulators and analysers.
– This would only be feasible for large quantities for each custom version, due to the costs for developing and testing different masks and the results.

All of these arguments were more valid at the beginning when Motorola first introduced the M68000 family. With time, these arguments have become weaker, and it is increasingly more likely that at least one of the manufacturers of the M68000 family could offer this option to their customers in the future.

The most efficient and economical solution up to now has been to place both the microcode and nanocode on the same chip with the rest of the microprocessor. However, advances in the technology for making larger and more complex chips less expensively may open the door for one or several of the following alternatives in the near future, by placing the microcode in

– an external ROM or RAM (requires extra pins),
– an internal PROM or EPROM (requires programming and erasing capabilities) or
– an internal RAM (requires bootstrap loading capabilities).

These alternatives would provide flexibility for creating customized microprocessors with a M68000 microprocessor engine. In particular, these alternatives to changing the mask for the ROM on the chip would involve low costs for low quantities–since one single chip as a standard microprocessor engine would be required. However, special software tools may be necessary for creating and testing the several hundred 10-bit words of microcode required to define a custom microprocessor that is based upon an M68000 microprocessor engine.

2.1.5 Architecture of the Control Unit

The architecture for the control unit of a microprocessor from the M68000 family is shown in Figure 2-4 below.

An instruction is copied from memory into the instruction register. The instruction decoder decodes it into macro instructions and then divides each macro instruction into two parts:

– information that is constant in time for the macro instruction and
– information that changes from one cycle of the system clock to the next cycle.

The instruction decoder sends the constant information directly to the execution units and holds this information valid on these signal lines for the duration of the macro instruction. For the variable information, the instruction decoder defines the starting address for a program of micro instructions in the microcode ROM and acts as a sequencer to manage this program. If the 1-bit jump flag is not set in a micro instruction, then the instruction decoder increments the address to the microcode by 1 address after each such instruction in order to execute one instruction after the other in a linear sequence. If the 1-bit jump flag is set in a micro instruction, then the sequencer reads the next word in the microcode ROM and uses it as the jump address for the next micro instruction.

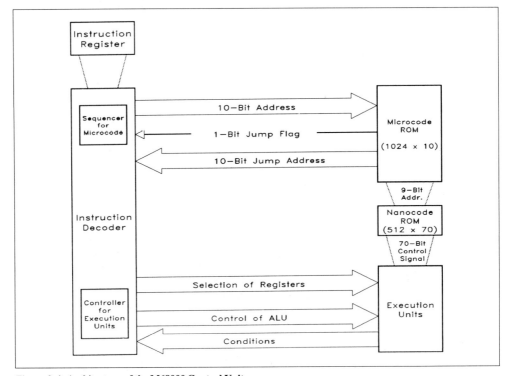

Figure 2-4: Architecture of the M68000 Control Unit

As shown in the photograph of Figure 2-1 above, the architecture of the M68000 control unit contains 3 execution units (shown collectively as only one block in Figure 2-4 above). They are for:
– the least-significant 16-bit words of data,
– the least-significant 16-bit words of addresses and
– the most-significant 16-bit words of data and addresses.
A limited address ALU (Arithmetic-Logic Unit) is included in each execution unit for addresses and a more powerful data ALU is included in each execution unit for data. Both ALUs are included in the combined execution unit for data and addresses. The execution unit for the least-significant 16-bit words of data also has another ALU for special functions, such as manipulating bits and packing and unpacking data.
Each execution unit is connected to two internal buses, one for addresses and the other for data. Each of these two internal buses is partitioned into 3 sub-buses and the 3 sub-buses of each bus are joined by switches that connect or disconnect them for bi-directional communications. Therefore, the data ALU in the

execution unit for the least-significant words of data can carry out an operation on data while the address ALU in the execution unit for the least-significant words of addresses can carry out a different operation on an address–simultaneously and independently of one another. Such simultaneous operations, parallel in time, are performed automatically by the microprocessor, without the user having to know about them. When the sub-buses are joined together, there are carry signals from the execution unit for least-significant words of data to the execution unit for most-significant words of data.

The architectural relationships among these three execution units and the two internal buses are illustrated in Figure 2-5 below.

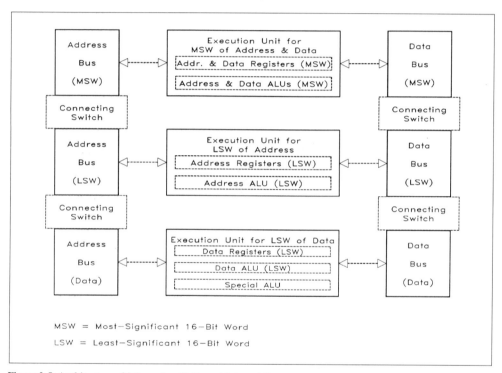

Figure 2-5: Architecture of 3 Execution Units and Internal Buses

2.1.6   Parallel Processing, Pipelining and Prefetch

Although the microprocessors of the M68000 family appear to be classical von-Neumann processors from the outside, with one processor doing one thing at a time, their internal operations are quite different. The most important ingredient of a non von-Neumann-architecture is the use of several different processors in parallel, at the same time. There are two different dimensions in which multiple processors can be arranged, as illustrated in Figures 2-6 and 2-7 below.

Figure 2-6: Pipeline Architecture – Parallel Processing Along Time Axis

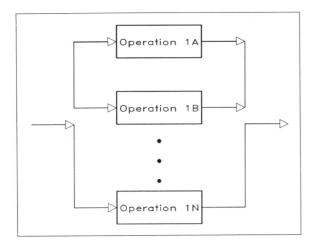

Figure 2-7: Vector Architecture – Parallel Processing Along Space Axis

In a pipeline architecture, the individual processors are usually of different types and perform different functions – much like the work-stations along an assembly line in a factory. One example of this architecture within the M68000 microprocessors is for the "prefetch technique" of fetching the next instruction while the current instruction is still being decoded and executed. This is illustrated in Figure 2-8 below:

```
        ┌─────────┐      ┌─────────┐      ┌─────────┐
   ─────▷│  Fetch  │─────▷│ Decode  │─────▷│ Execute │▷
        └─────────┘      └─────────┘      └─────────┘
```

Time:	Instructions:		
t1	1	—	—
t2	2	1	—
t3	3	2	1
t4	—	3	2
t5	—	—	3

Figure 2-8: The Prefetch Technique

While the 1st instruction is being decoded in time interval t_2, the 2nd instruction is being fetched (loaded into the instruction register). While the 1st instruction is being executed in time interval t_3, the 2nd instruction is being decoded and the 3rd instruction is being fetched. The M6800/08/10/12 microprocessors use a two-stage pipeline for prefetch, whereas the 68020/30 microprocessors use a three-stage pipeline for prefetch. However, this is not apparent to the user, other than in different execution times.

The processor that is executing instruction n and the processor that is fetching instruction n+2 both compete in the same time interval in using the buses and memory. These competing activities must, therefore, be closely coordinated. The M68000 microprocessors are "tightly coupled" to solve these problems so that no time is wasted with one processor waiting for the other processor to finish using the buses and memory.

In the case of a branch or interrupt, the instructions after the current instruction that have already been fetched and decoded are not used. Rather, a new sequence is started at the new jump, branch or interrupt address. No execution will occur until the first instruction at this new address is fetched and decoded.

A vector architecture usually uses identical processors that perform the same operation on different operands at the same time. The M68000 microprocessors use a more general version where the processors are different and perform different operations at the same time and phase along the pipeline. An example is the use of 3 execution units that can do different things at the same time. Therefore, it is possible to perform a register-to-register add in one execution unit and to increment the program counter in another execution unit – both at the same time. The combination of these two types of parallelism is shown in Figure 2-9 below. In this case, both the fetch and decode "processors" are implemented within the instruction-decoder unit.

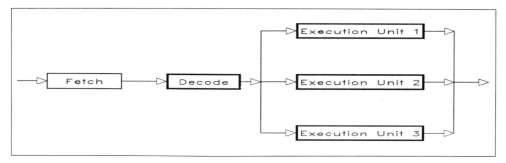

Figure 2-9: Combination of Pipeline and Vector Techniques

The M68000 family of microprocessors uses both types of parallel processing whenever technically feasible. The result is a family of microprocessors that is very fast and efficient for the given clock speeds. The gains in speed due to parallel processing more than compensate for the loss in speed due to the use of microcoding (that provides flexibility and other advantages).

2.2   Architectures of Systems

2.2.1   Block Diagram for a Typical System

The block diagram for a typical system with an M68000 microprocessor is shown in Figure 2-10 below. In particular, there is:
– an asynchronous bus for communicating with the newer 16-bit M68000 support devices and
– a synchronous bus for communicating with the older 8-bit M6800 support devices.

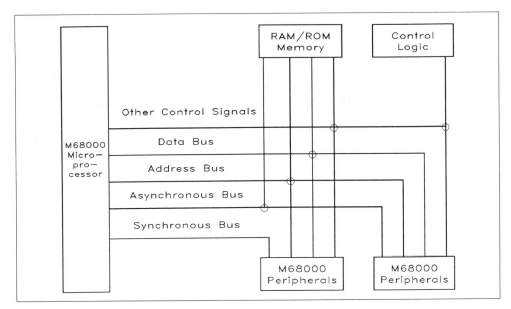

Figure 2-10: Block Diagram for a Typical System

2.2.2   Definition of the Pins on a 68000 Microprocessor

Figure 2-11 below shows the pins of a 68000 microprocessor, organized in logical groups. (The 68010, 68012, 68020 and 68030 microprocessors have additional control signals – see Chapter 8 for details.) The M68000 family of microprocessors uses a single 5-volt power supply, Vcc. There are two pins each for Vcc and ground. However, you only need to use one pin for each. There is only one clock input signal. Since the internal registers are dynamic, rather than static, it is necessary to maintain a minimum clock rate to refresh the internal registers.

There are separate pins for the address signals A1–A23 that directly address 8 megawords of 16 bits each (equivalent to 16 megabytes) – without segmentation or paging. The 68000 microprocessor can access 16-bit words or 8-bit bytes over a 16-bit data bus. Therefore, the least-significant address signal, A0, (that is required for directly addressing 16 megabytes) is already decoded as two enable strobe signals, LDS and UDS, for even and odd byte addresses respectively. For byte operations, only one enable signal is used. For word operations, both enable signals are used simultaneously. Words must always begin at an even address. This is explained in more detail in Section 2.5 below.

There are separate pins for the bi-directional data-bus signals, D0–D15. For some operations, such as for bytes, this bus can be partitioned into a lower and upper half by the enable strobe signals LDS and UDS. The M68000 family of microprocessors has two separate buses for communicating with peripheral-interface devices:

– a synchronous bus for use with older 8-bit M6800 peripheral-interface devices and
– an asynchronous bus for use with newer 16-bit M68000 peripheral-interface devices.

The synchronous bus is described in more detail in Section 2.8 below and the asynchronous bus is described in more detail in Section 2.6 below.

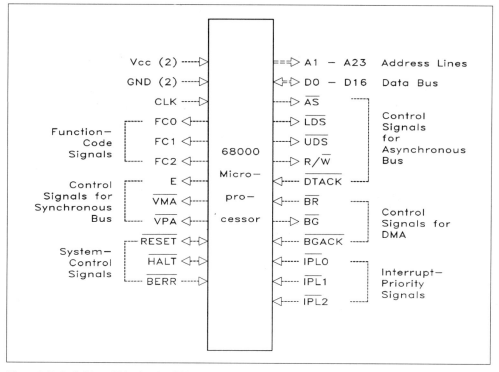

Figure 2-11: Definition of Pins for the 68000 Microprocessor

The other groups of signals are described elsewhere in more detail as follows:
- function-code signals – Section 2.7
- system control signals (RESET, HALT, and BERR) – Section 2.10
- control signals for DMA – Section 2.11
- interrupt-priority signals – Section 2.9

The actual assignment of pins depends upon the microprocessor in the package and the package used. You should refer to the data sheet for the particular combination that you are using for details. For illustrative purposes, the package forms for the 68000 microprocessor are shown in Figure 2-12 below. The pin assignments for the 68000 microprocessor are shown for:
- the dual-in-line package in Figure 2-13,
- quad pack in Figure 2-14,
- chip-carrier package in Figure 2-15 and
- pin-grid package in Figure 2-16.

Figure 2-12: Package Forms for the 68000 Microprocessor

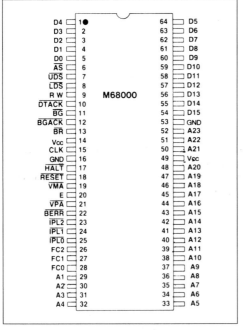

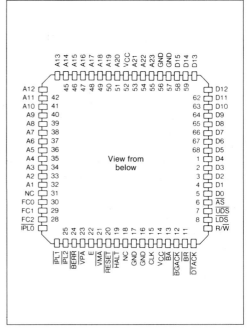

Figure 2-13: 68000 Pin Assignments for Dual-In-Line Package

Figure 2-14: 68000 Pin Assignments for Quad Pack

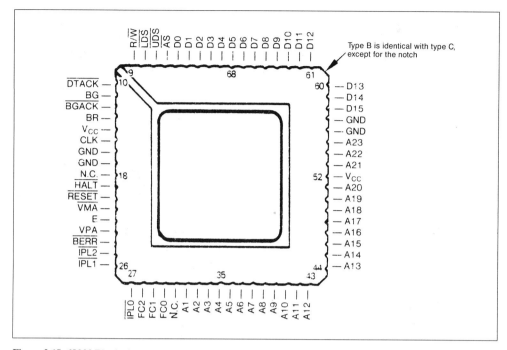

Figure 2-15: 68000 Pin Assignments for Chip-Carrier Package

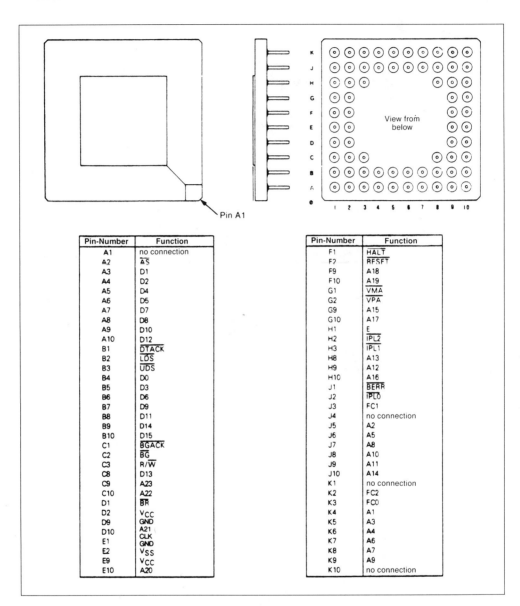

Pin-Number	Function
A1	no connection
A2	$\overline{AS}$
A3	D1
A4	D2
A5	D4
A6	D5
A7	D7
A8	D8
A9	D10
A10	D12
B1	$\overline{DTACK}$
B2	$\overline{LDS}$
B3	$\overline{UDS}$
B4	D0
B5	D3
B6	D6
B7	D9
B8	D11
B9	D14
B10	D15
C1	$\overline{BGACK}$
C2	$\overline{BG}$
C3	$R/\overline{W}$
C8	D13
C9	A23
C10	A22
D1	$\overline{BR}$
D2	V_{CC}
D9	GND
D10	A21
E1	CLK
	GND
E2	V_{SS}
E9	V_{CC}
E10	A20

Pin-Number	Function
F1	$\overline{HALT}$
F2	$\overline{RESET}$
F9	A18
F10	A19
G1	$\overline{VMA}$
G2	$\overline{VPA}$
G9	A15
G10	A17
H1	E
H2	$\overline{IPL2}$
H3	$\overline{IPL1}$
H8	A13
H9	A12
H10	A16
J1	$\overline{BERR}$
J2	$\overline{IPL0}$
J3	FC1
J4	no connection
J5	A2
J6	A5
J7	A8
J8	A10
J9	A11
J10	A14
K1	no connection
K2	FC2
K3	FC0
K4	A1
K5	A3
K6	A4
K7	A6
K8	A7
K9	A9
K10	no connection

Figure 2-16: 68000 Pin Assignments for Pin-Grid Package

The individual signals of the 68000 microprocessor are described in Figure 2-17 below. The pin numbers are also given, for the DIP package.

Name	Pins (DIP)	Input or Output	Active High/Low	Tristate	Function
A1–A23	29–49, 50–52	O	H	Yes	Address lines
D0–D15	5–1, 64–54	I/O	–	Yes	Data lines
AS	6	O	L	Yes	Address Strobe
R/W	9	O	H/L	Yes	Read/Write
UDS,LDS	7, 8	O	L	Yes	Upper/Lower Data Strobe
DTACK	10	I	L	No	Data Acknowledge
BR	13	O	L	No	Bus Request
BGACK	12	I	L	No	Bus-Grant Acknowledge
IPL0,IPL1,IPL2	25,24,23	I	L	No	Interrupt-Priority Level
BERR	22	I	L	No	Bus Error
RESET	18	I/O	L	No*	Reset
HALT	17	I/O	L	No*	Halt
E	20	O	H	No	Enable
VMA	19	O	L	Yes	Valid Memory Address
VPA	21	I	L	No	Valid Peripheral Address
FC0,FC1,FC2	28,27,26	O	H	Yes	Function Codes 0–2
CLK	15	I	H	No	Clock
Vcc	14 & 19	–	–	–	5 V Power (2 pins)
GND	16 & 53	–	–	–	Ground
* = open drain					

Figure 2-17: Description of Signals and Pin Connections for DIP Package

2.2.3   Definition of a Minimal System

A minimal system, based upon a microprocessor from the M68000 family, contains the following components:

- microprocessor
- clock generator
- RESET logic
- address decoder

- DTACK logic
- ROM/EPROM
- RAM
- parallel I/O plus timer

In addition, the following components may also be desirable, depending upon the application:
- serial I/O
- bus drivers
- logic for acknowledgement of interrupts
- watchdog timer (to monitor the bus)

A block diagram is presented in Figure 2-18 below:

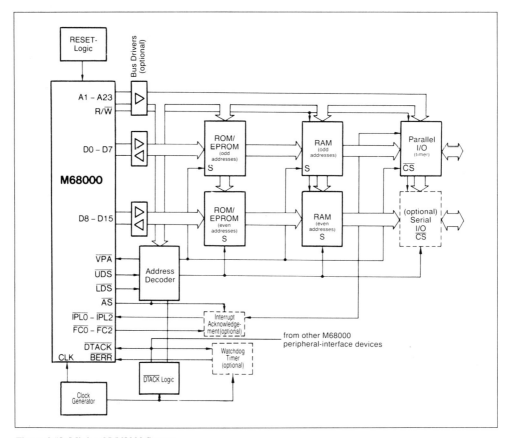

Figure 2-18: Minimal M68000 System

The most important tasks are performed by the DTACK logic and the address decoder. The address decoder generates the chip select signal, CS, for the memory and peripheral-interface devices, as well as the valid-peripheral-address signal, VPA, for synchronous peripheral-interface devices. The address decoder combines the upper-data-strobe signal, UDS, lower-data-strobe signal, LDS, and the chip-select signal, CS, to create the enable signals for odd and even memory as well as peripheral-interface devices. You can use these separate enable signals to create separate DTACK signals for each memory device or peripheral-interface device – even when separated for read and write cycles. This would allow you to mix slow EPROM and fast RAM devices with an optimization of the respective access times.

If the peripheral-interface devices fail to generate a DTACK signal after being accessed then the system will "hang up" and the processor will simply wait until it receives a DTACK signal. You can avoid this problem by including a "watchdog timer" that monitors bus activities. It can identify a situation where a memory device or a peripheral-interface device is accessed and no DTACK signal returns as a response after a given time interval. In such cases, it generates a bus-error signal, BERR, that initiates exception handling – so that you can recover from this situation with an exception routine and then continue working. The timer in the parallel-interface and timer circuit, MC68230, can perform this watchdog-timer function.

There are no special requirements for the clock generator. A single-phase clock signal at TTL levels is adequate. It also clocks the DTACK logic and bus surveillance logic. Since the internal registers are dynamic, rather than static, the clock generator must always maintain a minimum clock speed to provide adequate refreshing for these dynamic registers.

If you work with interrupts, it is advisable to include logic for acknowledging interrupts, as described in Section 2.9.4 below.

Depending upon the loads that are attached to the buses, it may be advisable and necessary to include bus drivers. It the bus loads are larger than specified for the particular microprocessor, the result can be erroneous signals – converting the system into a "random-number generator".

2.3   Data Formats and Registers

2.3.1   Data Formats

The M68000 family of microprocessors can process the 5 data formats that are shown in Figure 2-19 below:

Name	Length	Processing
bit	1 bit	bit-manipulation instructions
BCD	4 bits	BCD instructions (packed, with 2 BCD numbers in one byte)
byte	8 bits	various instructions and external data
word	16 bits	various instructions and external data long
word	32 bits	various instructions and external data

Figure 2-19: Data Formats of an M68000 Microprocessor

The standard data format is for words since the data bus is 16 bits wide. These formats are shown in more detail in Figure 2-20 below that also illustrates how they are stored in memory. (These data formats are extended for the 68020 and 68030 microprocessors – see Chapter 8, Vol. II for details.)

The first microprocessor in the M68000 family, the 68000, uses 24-bit addresses. However, the internal address registers are 32 bits wide and addresses use 32 bits when stored in memory. When storing a 16-bit word in an address register, its most-significant bit, bit 15, is repeated for the remaining high-order bits, from bit 16 to bit 31. When an address is copied from an address register to a location in memory, it occupies 4 bytes = 32 bits in memory, where at least the 9 high-order bits, from bit 23 to bit 31 will be identical. Since the most-significant bit of a data word is often used to store the sign, this is sometimes referred to as "sign extending". This architectural design has allowed later microprocessors in the M68000 family to use up to 32-bit addresses that can linearly address up to 256 x 16 megabytes of memory (= 4 gigabytes), without any changes in the architecture (see Chapter 8 below). This is illustrated in Figure 2-21 below.

If you do not use an address register when writing an address into memory, you must be careful to perform "sign extending" manually.

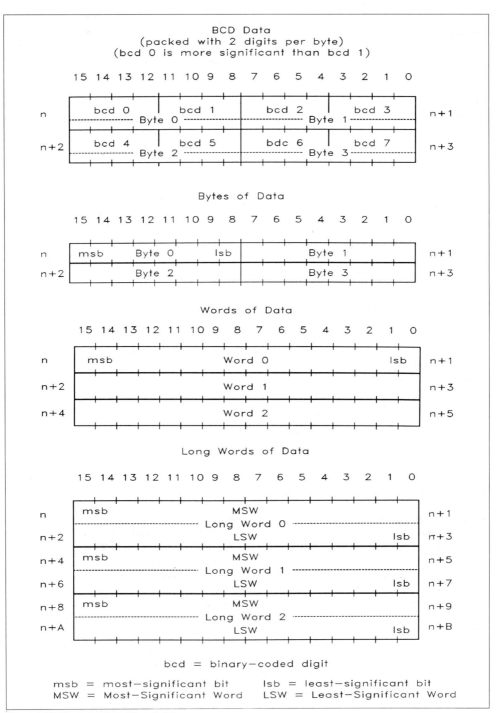

Figure 2-20: Organization of Data in Memory

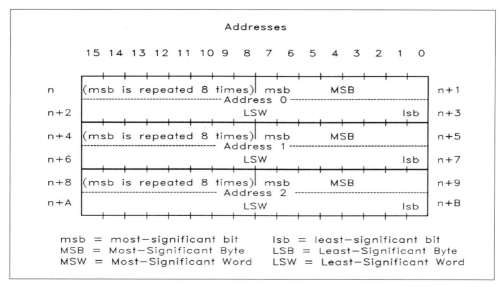

Figure 2-21: Organization of Addresses in Memory for the 68000 Microprocessor

The microprocessors of the M68000 family are oriented in bytes with respect to memory – sometimes referred to as "byte oriented" or as "byte machines". Although the data bus is 16-bits wide and it can read and write 2 bytes at a time, separate consecutive addresses are used for each byte in a 16-bit word. The following rules, therefore, apply for accesses to these byte addresses:

– Words and long words always begin at even addresses.
– Bytes can begin at either an even or an odd address.
– Opcodes (16-bits long) always begin at even addresses.

For the 68000, 68010 and 68012 microprocessors, the address signal A0 is only available in the decoded form of UDS (Upper Data Strobe) and LDS (Lower Data Strobe). These strobes allow the system to transmit a byte to or from an even or odd address upon either the most-significant half or least-significant half of the data bus. If both strobes are active, then a 16-bit word is communicated on both halves of the data bus. If only the UDS strobe is active, then a byte is communicated on the most-significant half of the data bus. If only the LDS strobe is active, then a byte is communicated on the least-significant half of the data bus. This is explained in Section 2.6 below in more detail.

Therefore, the remaining 23 address signals, A1–A23, that are available explicitly for the 68000/10/12 microprocessors, direct address 8 megawords of memory. The size of the operands for memory operations is usually specified by the programmer with an extension of .B, .W, or .L to the mnemonic for the instruction (for Byte, Word or Long word respectively – see Chapter 4 below). From the combination of the internal address signal of A0 (not available at a pin of the chip for the 68000, 68010 and 68012 microprocessors) and the size of the operand, the processor generates the two strobe signals UDS and LDS.

For the 68000/10/12 microprocessors, the two strobes UDS and LDS determine whether the whole word is used (for word and long-word operations) or only one half is used (for byte operations). Although it is possible that the address stored in memory, an address register or the program counter, could be an odd number, the processor can not generate signals on the lines A1 to A23 plus UDS and LDS for an odd address for a word or long-word operation. Therefore, when this situation occurs, the processor initiates exception handling, due to an address error, as explained in Section 2.5.1 below.

This concept for the 68000/10/12 microprocessors, where even addresses to words are defined by the address lines (minus the A0 line), and the byte or whole word is selected by UDS and LDS, is illustrated in Figure 2-22 below. The logic table for the decoder that generates UDS and LDS inside of the microprocessor is given in Figure 2-23 below. (See also Figures 2-47 and 2-48 in Section 2.6 below.) By contrast, the 68008, 68020 and 68030 microprocessors bring out the A0 address signal explicitly and do not use the decoded UDS and LDS strobe signals. The reasons are different however. The 68008 has a data bus that is only 8-bits wide and therefore there is no distinction between even and odd bytes being transfered over it. The 68020 and 68030 microprocessors use bus sizes that are dynamically determined.

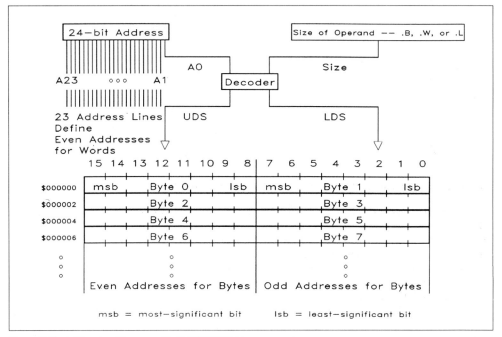

Figure 2-22: Addressing Memory with 68000/10/12 Microprocessors

Input		Output	
A0	Size	UDS	LDS
Even	Byte	High	Low
Even	Word	High	High
Even	Long Word	High	High
Odd	Byte	Low	High
Odd	Word	*	*
Odd	Long Word	*	*

* = Illegal Input → Exeption Handling

Figure 2-23: Logic Table for Decoding UDS and LDS

2.3.2 Registers

In comparison with other 16-bit microprocessors, the microprocessors of the M68000 family have a large number of registers that are accessible to the user. This feature is particularly important for adapting high-level languages, the intermediate-level language C and operating systems for use with these processors. In addition, it reduces the response times of user programs since the values for a larger number of variables can be kept in registers.

Although there is a distinction between data registers and address registers in the M68000 family of microprocessors, you can store data in address registers and you can store addresses (such as for indexes) in data registers. Therefore, if you run out of registers of a given type, you can flexibly substitute registers of the other type that happen to be free.

The M68000 microprocessors have the following registers that are accessible to the user:
- eight 32-bit data registers,
- nine 32-bit address registers (only 24 bits are used by the first 68000 microprocessor, but all bits are used by later microprocessors),
- one 32-bit program counter (only 24 bits are used by the first 68000 microprocessor, but all bits are used by later microprocessors),
- one 16-bit status register.

Seven of the nine 32-bit address registers are for general purposes but the last two 32-bit address registers are for:
- the user stack pointer and
- the supervisor stack pointer.

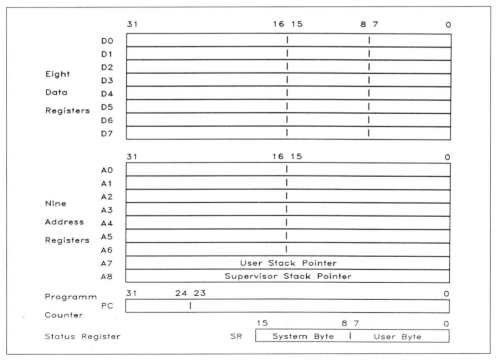

Figure 2-24: Register Model for M68000 Family of Microprocessors

However, both stack pointers have the same number, A7, and the processor automatically selects the appropriate stack pointer, depending upon whether the processor is in the user mode or the supervisor mode (see Section 2.4 below). The status register is divided into two halves, a system byte and a user byte. The system byte is generally accessible only from the supervisor mode, and the user byte is generally accessible from both the supervisor mode, and the user mode (with some exceptions).

In addition to these basic registers of the 68000 and 68008 microprocessors, the 68010, 68012, 68020 and 68030 have additional registers, as explained in Chapter 8 below.

These basic registers are summarized in a register model that is presented as Figure 2-24 below.

The differences between data registers and address registers are summarized in Figure 2-25 below:

Characteristics	Data Registers	Address Registers
Size	32 bits	32 bits
Operands	bit, 2xbcd, byte word, long word	word, long word
Sign Extending	No (except EXT, MOVEQ instruction)	Yes
Affect Flags in CCR	Yes	No

Figure 2-25: Comparison Between Data and Address Registers

Both data registers and address registers are 32 bits long. However, the first 68000 microprocessor uses only 24-bit addresses. This means that the option was already built in for later processors in this family to use up to 32-bit addresses that can linearly address up to $256 * 16$ megabytes $= 4$ gigabytes of memory. You can use a bit, a pair of digits encoded in BCD format that are packed into one byte, a byte, a 16-bit word or a 32-bit long word as an operand with data registers. With address registers, you can only use a word or a long word as operand.

When reading or writing a byte or word, from or to a data register, the least-significant byte or word will always be used. However, you can rotate or shift more-significant bytes or words into the position of the least-significant byte or word in order to operate on them. You can also use the SWAP instruction to swap the most-significant half of a data register with its least-significant half. Using the BSET and BCLR instructions (see Chapter 4 below), you can set or clear any individual bit of the 32 bits in a data register.

When writing a word into an address register, the processor will automatically "sign extend" the word, by copying the most significant bit, bit 15, into all of the more significant positions of the address register, bits 16 to 31. The whole address register is therefore changed whenever it is written to, even with a word as the operand. However, it is possible to read just the least-significant word in an address register – which does not change the rest of the register.

When writing an operand into a data register, the flags in the condition-code register are changed (see below). However, these flags are not changed when writing into an address register.

The two stack pointers are two physically-separate address registers. However, both the user stack pointer and the supervisor stack pointer have the same register number, A7. The processor automatically uses the appropriate stack pointer, depending upon whether the processor is in the user mode or the supervisor mode (see the next Section below). You can read the contents of the user stack pointer and change the contents while you are in the user mode. However, this is a dangerous operation, if you make an inappropriate change – it can easily cause a "system crash".

The current value in the user stack pointer is the address in memory for the top of the user stack. The user stack contains return addresses for subroutines. Each time that an additional subroutine is called, another return address is "pushed" onto the stack. Each time that a return from a subroutine occurs, the relevant return address is "popped" from the stack. Therefore the size of the stack grows and shrinks dynamically, depending upon the current level of nested subroutines. The two stack pointers contain the address in memory of the active ends of the two stacks. Both stacks grow in size in the direction of decreasing addresses in memory.

The program counter, PC, contains the current address for the program that is executing. However, due to pipelining in the microprocessors of the M68000 family, the current value in the program counter is usually the address of the instruction being executed plus two, since the processor is already fetching and decoding the next instruction. For the 68000 microprocessor, only 24 of the 32 bits are actually used (leaving room for expansion in later processors). Bits 1 to 23 drive the address signal lines, A1 to A23, directly. Bit 0 is decoded further, together with the size of the operand, to create the UDS and LDS data strobes, as illustrated in Figures 2-22 and 2-23 above. (See Chapter 8 below for the differences for the other microprocessors in the M68000 family.)

The status register, SR, contains two bytes, a system byte and a user byte. In general, the system byte is only accessible from the supervisor mode whereas the user byte is accessible from the user mode. The user byte is also refered to as the condition-code register, CCR. Both bytes are only partially used by current microprocessors in the M68000 family, leaving room for expansion in later processors. (If you read the contents of the unused bits 5–7, the result will always be 0.) The structure of the status register is shown in Figure 2-27 below:

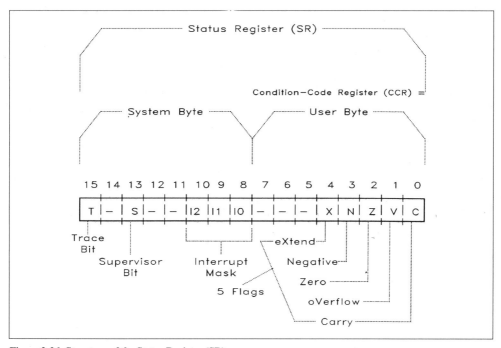

Figure 2-26: Structure of the Status Register (SR)

The user byte (condition-code register – CCR) contains 5 flags as follows:
– the carry flag (C),
– the overflow flag (V),
– the zero flag (Z),
– the negative flag (N) and
– the extend flag (X).
Details are given in Chapter 4 below on how each instruction uses and changes these flags.

The microprocessor will set the carry flag equal to 1 whenever a carry bit is generated from an operation (such as add or shift) on bytes, words or long words. It will also set the carry flag if it used a borrow (such as for subtraction).

The microprocessor will set the overflow flag equal to 1 whenever the result of an operation lies outside of the allowed range. For example, if two positive numbers are added and the result is a negative number in two's complement form, then the processor would set this flag. The DIV instruction also uses this flag when the dividend is too large or the quotient would be larger than 16 bits.

The microprocessor will set the zero flag equal to 1 whenever the result of an operation is zero or the result of a compare operation is such that both operands have the same value.

The microprocessor will set the negative flag equal to 1 whenever the result of an operation is a negative number, ie. whenever the most-significant bit in two's complement form is equal to 1.

The extend flag is unique to the M68000 family of microprocessors, and it is very similar to the carry flag. However, there are some instructions that set the carry flag but do not set the extend flag. You can use the extend flag to remember earlier settings of the carry flag in some cases.

The system byte contains:

- the trace bit
- the supervisor bit and
- the interrupt mask (3 bits).

If you set the trace bit, bit 15, then the processor will automatically switch to the supervisor mode and a fixed vector address after each instruction is executed from a program in the user mode (see Section 2.5.1 below). After executing the subroutine at that address, the processor can return to the user mode and execute the next instruction. This allows you to write or use a system program, at the vector address, that documents the status of the system after each instruction. In this way, you can "trace" the execution of a program, one instruction at-a-time, until you turn the trace bit off. The trace operation is illustrated in Figure 2-27 below.

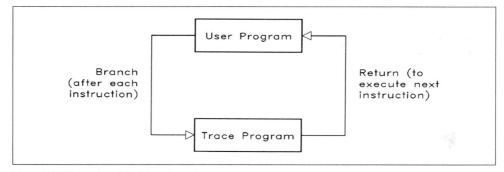

Figure 2-27: Operation of the Trace Function

The supervisor bit defines the mode that the processor is in (see Section 2.4 below). If it contains a 1, then the processor is in the supervisor mode. If it contains a 0, then the processor is in the user mode. You can read this bit but can not change it directly.

The interrupt mask contains 3 bits. The microprocessors in the M68000 family have seven levels of interrupts. If a given interrupt that arrives at the processor has a higher priority level than contained in this interrupt mask, then the processor will process the interrupt. Otherwise, the processor will not process the interrupt. This is explained in more detail in Section 2.9 below.

2.4   The User Mode and the Supervisor Mode

A distinction between a user mode and a supervisor mode is particularly useful in multi-user systems and other systems where the functions of the operating system should not be available automatically to all users at all times. This distinction comes from experience with large mainframe computer systems and helps to make multi-user systems more reliable.

Microprocessors in the M68000 family have both:

– normal instructions that can be used in both the user mode and the supervisor mode and

– privileged instructions that can be used only in the supervisor mode.

Using a privileged instruction while in the user mode results in a privilege error and initiates exception handling (see Section 2.5 below). The table in Figure 2-28 below shows the functions that are available in both the user mode and the supervisor mode.

Function	**User Mode**	**Supervisor Mode**
normal instructions	Yes	Yes
privileged instructions	No	Yes
8 data registers	Yes	Yes
1st 7 address registers	Yes	Yes
user stack pointer	No	Yes
supervisor stack pointer	No	Yes
program counter	Yes	Yes
read system byte of SR	Yes	Yes
change system byte of SR	No	Yes
read user byte of SR	Yes	Yes
change user byte of SR	Yes	Yes

Figure 2-28: Comparison of Functions Available in User/Sup Modes

Privileged instructions are those that use functions or resources that are not allowed from the user mode (see Figure 2-28 above). These privileged instructions are summarized in Figure 2-29 below. Details on these, as well as all other instructions, are given in Chapter 4 below.

Instruction	**Availability and Comments**
RESET	
STOP	
RTE	modified for 68010/012/020/030 but compatible
ANDI to SR	
EORI to SR	
ORI to SR	
MOVE from CCR	available only for 68010/012/020/030
MOVE to SR	
MOVE from SR	privileged for 68010/012/020/030, but not for other processors
MOVE USP	
MOVEC	available only for 68010/012/020/030
MOVES	available only for 68010/012/020/030

Figure 2-29: Privileged Instructions (only in Supervisor Mode)

As a simple example, it is usually not desirable to allow every user in a multi-user system to reset the system. (This would give each user the power to stop the programs of all other users and destroy the intermediate results of those programs!) If a user program that is running in the user mode uses the RESET instruction, the microprocessor will not simply execute the RESET instruction. Rather, since this is a violation of the privilege, the microprocessor will switch to exception handling in the supervisor mode, using a particular exception vector that starts a particular exception routine. This routine can check whether the particular user has the right password, whether other programs are running, etc. before deciding whether to allow the user to actually reset the system or not.

The microprocessor switches from the supervisor mode to the user mode whenever it:
- encounters the RTE (Return from Exception) instruction or
- the S-bit is reset equal to 0, such as with
  - MOVE #0,SR or
  - ANDI #$DFFF,SR.

The microprocessor switches from the user mode to the supervisor mode
- only when an exception occurs (such as from a TRAP instruction to generate a particular exception).

Whenever an exception occurs, it generates a specific exception vector that allows the designer of the system to control precisely what happens for each type of exception (see Section 2.5 below). The switching back-and-forth between these two modes is illustrated in Figure 2-30 below:

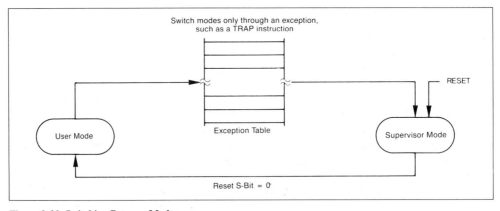

Figure 2-30: Switching Between Modes

A typical application for switching between modes occurs when user programs use common resources, such as the software driver for an input/output peripheral or other functions of the operating system. Therefore, the use of a TRAP instruction is sometimes refered to as a "system call". The RMS68K realtime operating system from Motorola is a good example where such system calls are used frequently. The principle of such applications is illustrated in Figure 2-31 below.

In addition to the software aspects of the user mode and supervisor mode, the function-code signal FC2 can communicate the current status of the mode to the external hardware. For example, you can use this signal, together with a memory-management device, to restrict access to subsets of memory while in the user mode – or even to use two separate 16 megabyte address ranges for user programs and supervisor programs. This is explained in more detail in Chapter 7.7 below – where the use of the 68451 MMU (memory-management unit) is explained.

The distinction between a user mode and a supervisor mode is very useful for multi-user systems but is not always necessary or useful for simpler single-user sytems, such as for an intelligent graphics terminal.

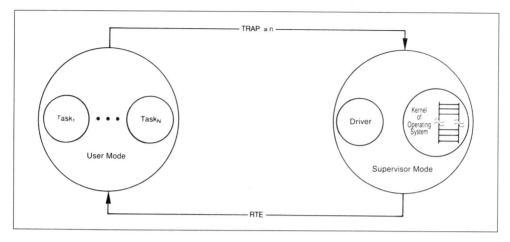

Figure 2-31: Typical Application for Switching Modes

Since the capabilities of the supervisor mode form a superset and the capabilities of the user mode form a subset, you can design a system that uses only the supervisor mode. In this case, you would use the RTS instruction at the end of exception routines instead of the RTE instruction.

The distinction between a user mode and a supervisor mode is particularly useful for implementing the UNIX operating system – since they correspond quite closely to the user and kernel modes of UNIX. This is one of several reasons why the M68000 family has been the most popular family of microprocessors for implementing UNIX systems.

2.5   Handling of Exceptions and Exception Vectors

A microprocessor from the M68000 family is always in one of the following three processing states:

Normal State

This is the normal state of the processor for processing instructions (including the STOP instruction). The processor can operate in both the user mode and the supervisor mode while in the normal state (see Section 2.4 above for a definition and description of these privilege modes).

Exception State

This is the state of the processor while handling exceptions, such as for interrupts, traps and the trace mode. The processor is always in the supervisor mode while in the exception state.

Halt State

This is the state when the processor is stopped because of a catastrophic hardware failure for which the processor can not compensate, such as a double bus error or the HALT signal line. The only way to restart the processor is with an external reset.

What are Exceptions?

Exceptions are deviations that can occur as the result of either instructions or error conditions. They can be generated either internally or externally, as illustrated in Figure 2-32 below.

generated internally	instructions (TRAP, TRAPV, CHK, DIV) address errors, trace mode
generated externally	interrupts bus errors, RESET

Figure 2-32: Examples of Exceptions

We distinguish between the following categories of exceptions:

Traps

Traps are interrupts for exceptions that are usually generated internally by the processor itself, such as due to overflow in an operation, division by zero, a bus error, an address error, a privilege violation, tracing, undefined opcodes and special instructions such as TRAP and TRAPV. Most of the first 64 exception numbers are reserved for such traps. These traps are defined in more detail in this section of this chapter.

Hardware Interrupts

Hardware interrupts are exceptions that are usually generated by input/output peripheral-interface devices. The purpose of an interrupt is to temporarily stop the processor from whatever it is doing in order to do something else, such as to respond to an input/output device. An M68000 microprocessor checks between the execution of each instruction whether valid interrupt requests are present. An M68000 microprocessor has provisions for two types of hardware interrupts:

Autovector Interrupts
Particularly for small and simple systems, you can design the hardware to use autovector interrupts. In this case, the peripheral-interface device communicates both the priority and the number of the interrupt as one identical number (from 1 to 7) over the 3 input lines of IPL0, IPL1 and IPL2. The processor then automatically adds 23 to this number in order to create the number of the exception (from decimal 24 to 30, ie. from hexadecimal $19 to $1F). See Section 2.9.3 below for more details.

Non-autovector Interrupts (User Interrupts)
For larger systems, you can design the hardware to use non-autovector interrupts or a combination of both types. In the cas of non-autovector interrupts, the peripheral-interface device also communicates the priority of the interrupt to the processor over the 3 input lines of IPL0, IPL1 and IPL2. However, it communicates the number of the interrupt (exception number) over the least-significant half of the data bus. Microprocessors from the M68000 family have $256-64 = 192$ possible exception numbers available for non-autovector interrupts. See Section 2.9.4 below for more details.

What are Exception Programs and Exception Vectors?

We distinguish between exception programs, exception vectors, exception-vector addresses and exception-vector numbers as follows:

Exception Program

An exception program is a routine or program that is resident in memory and performs appropriate functions when an exception occurs.It is written by the user. Exception programs always run in the supervisor mode.

Exception Vector

An exception vector is a pointer to the address where an exception program begins for handling a particular exception. Since each exception vector is in itself an address, each vector is 4 bytes long.

Exception-Vector Address

An exception-vector address is the address in a table in memory that contains the exception vector (address of the beginning of the routine). This table is located at the beginning of memory and contains 1024 bytes or 256 long words at addresses from 0 to 1023 for the individual bytes.

Exception-Vector Number

An exception-vector number is the number of a particular exception, from 0 to 255.

Exception-vector numbers are related to exception-vector addresses by the simple formula:

Exception-Vector Address $= 4 *$ Exception-Vector Number

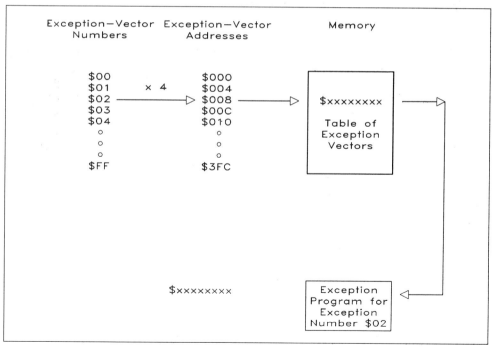

Figure 2-33: Exception-Vector Numbers and Addresses

A microprocessor from the M68000 family always works with exception-vector numbers and converts them into exception-vector addresses when appropriate. (Multiplication by 4 is simple in binary arithmetic and involves only a shift to the left by 2 binary places.)

The use of vector numbers is also important for non-autovectors (see chapter 2.9). These vector numbers are generated externally, rather than internally, and they are communicated over the least-significant 8-bit half of the data bus to the processor. This 8-bit data path can only communicate numbers from 0 to 255 and therefore multiplying by 4 is necessary later in order to be able to scan the address range from 0 to 1023 bytes for the table of exception vectors. For this reason, the interrupt-vector registers of the peripheral-interface devices in the M68000 family are only 8 bits wide.

These relationships are illustrated in Figure 2-33 below (using hexadecimal numbers).

What Exceptions Can the M68000 Microprocessors Recognize?

M68000 microprocessors have a larger number of possibilities for detecting error conditions than most other microprocessors or even minicomputers.

A specific exception vector is assigned to each exception, independent of whether it is generated internally or externally.

In order to compare exceptions with conventional microprocessors, you can think of each individual exception as corresponding to an individual type of interrupt.

Figure 2-34 below presents a table that shows the vector number, vector address, the type of exception vector and whether a supervisor program or data is involved.

Vector Number (hex.)	Vector Address (hex.)	Type of Exception Vector	Affects
00	000	beginning address of the supervisor stack pointer (for RESET)	SP[1]
01	004	beginning address of the program counter (for RESET)	SP
02	008	bus error	SD[2]
03	00C	address error	SD
04	010	non-implemented instruction	SD
05	014	division by zero	SD
06	018	CHK instruction also CHK 2 for 68020/30	SD
07	01C	TRAPV instruction also cpTRAPcc and TRAPcc for 68020/030	SD
08	020	violation of privilege	SD
09	024	trace mode	SD
0A	028	non-implemented instruction beginning with 1010 (emulation)	SD
0B	02C	non-implemented instruction beginning with 1111 (emulation)	SD
OC[3]	030	reserved for future use	SD
OD	034	Coprocessor Protocol Violation (only 68020/030)	SD

Vector Number (hex.)	Vector Address (hex.)	Type of Exception Vector	Affects
OE[3]	038	illegal format (only 68010/012/020/030)	SD
0F	03C	non-initialized interrupt	SD
10–17	04C–05	reserved for future use	SD
18	060	spurious interrupt	SD
19	064	level 1 autovector interrupt	SD
1A	068	level 2 autovector interrupt	SD
1B	06C	level 3 autovector interrupt	SD
1C	070	level 4 autovector interrupt	SD
1D	074	level 5 autovector interrupt	SD
1E	078	level 6 autovector interrupt	SD
1F	07C	level 7 autovector interrupt	SD
20–2F	080–0BC	vectors for TRAP instructions	SD
30–3F	0C0–0FC	reserved for future use	SD
40–FF	100–3FC	user interrupt vectors (non-autovectors)	SD

1 SP = Supervisor Program
2 SD = Supervisor Data
3   These vector numbers aur reserved for future use. You ahould not use them, auch as for non-autovectors.

Figure 2-34: Exception Vectors

One long word with 32 bits is reserved for each vector address, even though only 24 address lines are used by the first 68000 microprocessor. This maintains upward compatibility with the later microprocessors that now use up to 32 address lines. Extensions to the table of exception vectors will be possible by replacing existing vectors or using the reserved vectors. Each exception vector has the following format:

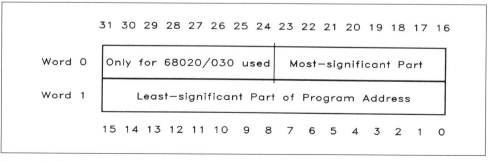

Figure 2-35: Format for each Exception Vector

As a special case, two long words are reserved for the RESET exception vector. An M68000 microprocessor loads the supervisor stack pointer (SSP) from the first long word and it loads the program counter (PC) from the second long word.

2.5.1   Descriptions of the Exceptions

RESET (SSP)

Vector Address:	$000–$003	Vector Number: $00

Description: The processor will load the contents at this address into the Supervisor Stack Pointer (SSP) during a hardware RESET. (See Chapter 2.10).
Application: Loading the initial value of the supervisor stack from this vector address.

RESET (PC)

Vector Address:	$004–$007	Vector Number: $01

Description: The processor will load the contents at this address into the Program Counter (PC) during a hardware RESET. (See Chapter 2.10).
Application: Loading the starting address of the first program from this vector address.

Bus Error

Vector Address:	$008–$00B	Vector Number: $02

Description: If the BERR signal line of an M68000 microprocessor is active (logical 0), then the microprocessor gets this vector and starts the exception program specified by this starting address. (See Chapter 2.10).
Application: A bus error is always initiated from an external device. As an example, a parity generator can initiate a bus error when it identifies a parity error. The activities of the BERR signal line are used for other applications with the so-called "Watchdog Timer". This timer controls whether the asynchronous DTACK signal is always generated and whether it is generated in the defined time. If this is not the case, then this timer initiates a bus error in order to avoid a "hang up". The Memory-Management Unit (MMU) can also initiate a bus error. It has a FAULT output signal line for this purpose. These errors can occur when the processor attempts to perform an illegal access to a protected area of memory or to non-existing memory. (See Chapters 2.10 and 7.7.)
The possible sources of bus errors are illustrated in Figure 2-36 below.

Address Error

Vector Address:	$00C–$00F	Vector Number: $03

Description: This exception occurs whenever access would otherwise occur to an uneven address when working with words or long words (nor for the 68020/030). In particular, this can occur during indirect

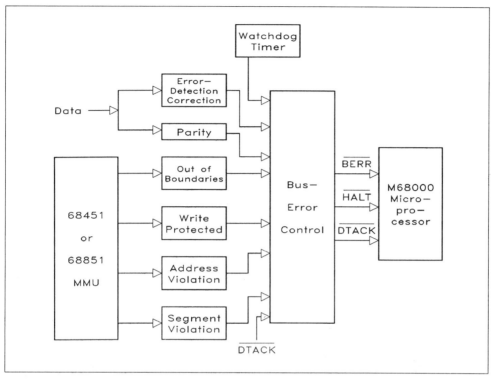

Figure 2-36: Possible Sources of Bus Errors

addressing (see Chapter 3.5.1) and when other errors occur, such as an incorrect address due to a spike or a glitch. It can also occur when fetching operands, such as from the stack and after the RTE instruction. *Application:* This exception is useful for identifying attempted accesses to uneven addresses while working with words or long words. This is particularly relevant for identifying errors in the calculation of addresses while a program is running. An assembler can not recognize this type of error in the calculation of addresses, such as when the contents of an address register are loaded later while the program is running. As in the case of a bus error, additional information is stored on the supervisor stack, to provide the possibility for a diagnosis later. It is left for the user, however, to get and use this information. This could be done, for example, in the exception program for processing the address error. As shown in Figure 2-37 below, the 68000 microprocessor inserts approximately 8 idle cycles after identifying an address error and before storing its status on the stack.

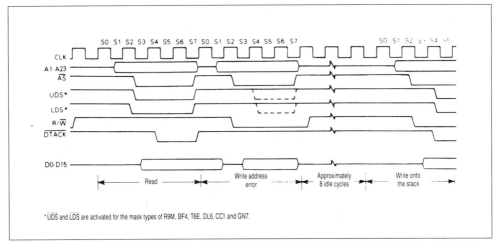

Figure 2-37: Clock Timing Diagram for Address Error

Illegal Instruction

Vector Address:	$010–$013	Vector Number: $04

Description: An M68000 microprocessor generates this exception when it decodes an instruction into an opcode that is not defined. Potential causes include spikes or glitches on the signal lines or defective memory components. Several bit combinations lead to this exception, such as $4AFA, $4AFB and $4AFC. However, the user should only use the bit combination $4AFC deliberately – otherwise, the user may lose compatability with future products in the M68000 family. Motorola uses the other two bit comb in its development systems, such as to set break points in its emulators. Two additional bit patterns, $Axxx and SFxxx, are also not yet defined and are reserved for future use, but they lead to separate exceptions, as defined below.

Application: This exception is used to identify opcodes that have not yet been implemented in hardware or for the user to implement custom opcodes and functions in software. They also allow the user to set breakpoints in a program.

Division by Zero

Vector Address:	$014–$017	Vector Number: $05

Description: This exception occurs when the divisor in the instruction DIVU or DIVU is equal to 0.

CHK Instruction

Vector Address:	$018–$01B	Vector Number: $06

Description: This exception occurs when the contents of a data register are outside of the range specified in a CHK instruction. (See the CHK instruction in Chapter 4 for more details.)

TRAPV Instruction

Vector Address:	$01C–$01F	Vector Number: $07

Description: This exception occurs if the overflow bit, V, is set at the time when the TRAPV instruction is executed. (See the TRAPV instruction in Chapter 4 for more details.)

Violation of Privilege

Vector Address:	$020–$023	Vector Number: $08

Description: This exception occurs when a program uses a privileged instruction (that is only allowed in the supervisor mode) while an M68000 microprocessor is in the user mode.
Application: This feature is useful as a protective measure in multi-user and multi-tasking operating systems.

Trace Mode

Vector Address:	$024–$027	Vector Number: $09

Description: This exception occurs after each instruction of a program while the trace bit is set in the status register. This implements tracing or single-stepping in software, rather than hardware, since an M68000 microprocessor goes to a trace program, the exception program of this exception, after each instruction.
Application: The trace program (exception program), that the processor calls each time that this exception occurs, can display information on the screen after each instruction, such as some or all of the contents of the registers. This provides a programmer with a powerful and flexible tool in software for testing a program. (See Figure 2-27 above.)

Non-implemented Instructions (Opcodes $Axxx)

Vector Address:	$028–$02B	Vector Number: $0A

Description: Non-implemented instructions lead to exceptions. Two categories of non-implemented instructions have their own special exceptions. One category is the set of opcodes beginning with "1010" = "A" and the other category is the set of opcodes beginning with "1111" = "F". This exception, with the vector number $0A, is for the first category.
Application: This exception, with the vector number $0A, is used for identifying the accidental use of an opcode that has not been defined and to allow the user to define custom opcodes that are implemented in software.

Non-implemented Instructions (Opcodes $Fxxx)

Vector Address:	$02C–$02F	Vector Number: $0B

Description: Non-implemented instructions lead to exceptions. Two categories of non-implemented instructions have their own special exceptions. One category is the set of opcodes beginning with "1010"

= "A" and the other category is the set of opcodes beginning with "1111" = "F". This exception, with the vector number $0B, is for the second category.

Application: This exception, with the vector number $0B, is used for identifying opcodes for the floating-point coprocessor 68881. If the coprocessor is not physically present in the system, the vector number of this exception switches to an emulation of the opcodes for the floating-point coprocessor in software. Other coprocessor instructions that are already implemented in the 68020 microprocessor lead to this exception for earlier microprocessors.

Illegal Format (only for the 68010/12/20/30 microprocessors)

Vector Address:	$038–$03B	Vector Number: $0E

Description: The 68010/12/20/30 microprocessors store more information than the 68000 microprocessor after a bus error. The stack pointer should not be changed since this information could be important for the return jump. Therefore, the 68010/10/20/30 microprocessors examine the depth of the stack when they reread this stored data. If this does not agree with the stored value then the processor generates this exception (see Chapter 8.2).

Non-initialized Interrupt

Vector Address:	$03C–$03F	Vector Number: $0F

Description: When M68000 peripheral-interface devices use the non-automatic vector principle (see Chapter 2.9.2) and are not programmed, they will generate an exception with this vector number.
Application: This exception identifies unexpected interrupts and interrupt-vector registers in M68000 peripheral-interface devices that are not programmed.

Spurious Interrupt

Vector Address:	$060–$063	Vector Number: $18

Description: This exception occurs when a bus error occurs during the acknowledgment of an interrupt (FC0–FC2 = 111, AS = 0). See Chapter 2.9.2.

Autovector Interrupts

Vector Addresses	Priority Level	Vector Number	Priority
$64–$67	1 (lowest)	$19	lowest
$68–$6B	2	$1A	
$6C–$6F	3	$1B	
$70–$73	4	$1C	
$74–$77	5	$1D	
$78–$7B	6	$1E	
$7C–&7F	7 (NMI)	$1F	highest

Description: These are the interrupt vectors that are initiated externally and are communicated to the processor by the signals appearing on the IPL0–IPL2 signal lines. The processor itself then generates the actual exception vector. The VPA signal line of a 68000 microprocessor (or AVEC signal line of the 68020/030) determines the difference between an autovector and a non-autovector (see Chapter 2.9.1).
Application: You can use these exceptions to assign autovector interrupts to peripheral devices that do not have interrupt-vector registers of their own (such as M6800 peripheral-interface devices).

TRAP Instruction

Vector Addresses	Instruction	Vector Number
$80–$83	Trap #0	$20
$84–$87	Trap #1	$21
$88–$8B	Trap #2	$22
$8C–$8F	Trap #3	$23
$90–$93	Trap #4	$24
$94–$97	Trap #5	$25
$98–$9B	Trap #6	$26
$9C–$9F	Trap #7	$27
$A0–$A3	Trap #8	$28
$A4–$A7	Trap #9	$29
$A8–$AB	Trap #10	$2A
$AC–$AF	Trap #11	$2B
$B0–$B3	Trap #12	$2C
$B4–$B7	Trap #13	$2D
$B8–$BB	Trap #14	$2E
$BC–$BF	Trap #15	$2F

Description: When the processor decodes this instruction, it goes into the exception mode, reads the vector and jumps to the exception program that begins at this vector address (see the description of this instruction in Chapter 4).
Application: The TRAP instruction allows a desired switch from the user mode to the supervisor mode, such as in a "software interrupt" or for a call to a system function.

Non-autovectors

Vector Addresses:	Vector Numbers:
$100–$103	$40
$104–$107	$41
.	.
.	.
.	.
$3FC–$3FF	$FF

Description: These are the interrupt vectors that are generated externally and are communicated directly in decoded form over the data-bus lines D0–D7. The DTACK signal line determines whether non-autovectors or autovectors are involved (see Chapter 2.9.2). A total of 192 vectors are available for use in this category.

Application: Most of the M68000 peripheral-interface devices use this approach with non-autovectors for processing interrupts.

Every exception is executed as illustrated in the flow chart of Figure 2-38. First, the processor makes a temporary internal copy of the status register – in its original condition, before the exception occurred. Then, the processor sets the S-bit = 1 and the T-bit = 0 in the status register. This means that every exception automatically switches the processor into the supervisor mode and turns the trace off (if it was on). However, if you want to use tracing within an exception program, you can turn tracing on (or back on) by setting the T-bit from within the exception program. If the exception was an interrupt, then the processor will set the priority mask in the status register equal to the priority of the current interrupt. This prevents the same interrupt from interrupting itself.

Next, the processor gets the vector number and converts it into the corresponding vector address (by multiplying by 4). (See Figure 2-17 for details.) Only after this point in time does the processor save the contents of the program counter (PC) and the current contents of the status register (SR) on the supervisor stack. (See Chapter 2.5.4 for details.)

The processor loads the vector address into the program counter and thereby starts the exception program that is stored at that address. The RTE instruction (Return from Exception) is usually used at the end of the exception program to return control to the original program, in the user mode, where the exception occurred. This does all of the necessary housekeeping so that the program counter will be at the address of the next instruction after the instruction where the exception occurred in the original program and the status register will have the same contents as it had before the exception occurred.

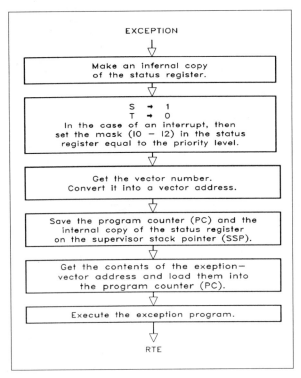

Figure 2-38: General Flow of an Exception

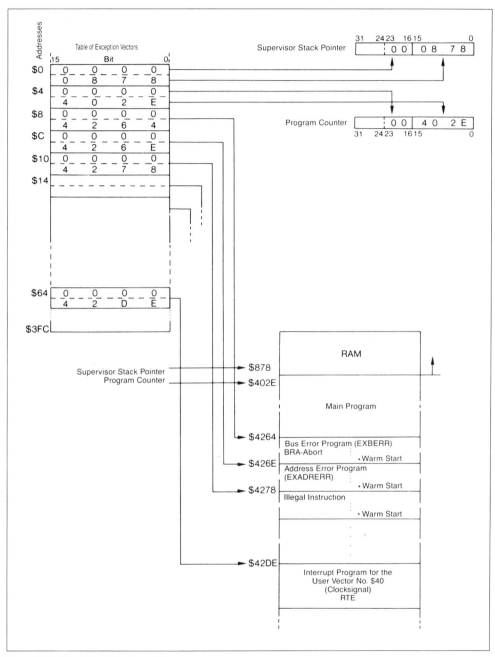

Figure 2-39: Handling of an Exception

2.5.2   Handling of Exceptions

Exceptions not only give the user an opportunity to identify the fact that an error or exceptional situation has occurred, but also give the user the opportunity to react to this situation. You can decide yourself what you want your system to do when such an exception occurs. In the simplest case, you can make the system present an error message to the user. Such an error message can be presented directly on the screen of a terminal or can be directed to the operating system. Comfortable operating systems for M68000 microprocessors usually have an "Exception Handler" for this purpose.

While developing software for an M68000 system, you will be confronted by the question of what to do when an exception arises. For some types of exceptions, such as interrupts, it is relatively clear how the system should respond. In other cases, it is not so clear as to what the system should do. Some actions, that may be appropriate in some cases, depending upon the application, would include: resetting peripheral-interface devices, clearing areas of memory or only giving an error message to the user. The following two general guidelines can be recommended:

- Every exception should have an exception vector that leads to an exception program. Even the exceptions that you think will never occur under unexpected circumstances. Therefore, you can send all of these exception vectors to one single exception program that gives the user a simple message, such as "Undefined Exception".
- **You should at least consider the possibility of storing exception vectors in RAM, in order to have "dynamic" vectors.** Exception vectors are normally stored in a "bootstrap" ROM orEPROM since the exception vectors for resetting the system are included in the block of exception vectors. However, you may want to use both ROM an RAM for the bottom address area in memory, where the ROM has the hardware priority during a reset operation and then the RAM has the priority for other operations. In this case, you may want to copy the exception vectors from the ROM into RAM at the same addresses with a block move. (M68000 microprocessors do not care whether the exception vectors are in ROM or RAM, as long as they are at the addresses from \$000-\$3FF.) Such a block move isimplemented in the minimal system that is described in Chapter 9 (see Figure 2-39 below) and an additional possibility is described in reference [51]. Once the exception vectors are in RAM, you can change them "dynamically" from your programs to meet changing requirements.

2.5.3   Exception Priorities

"Multiple exceptions" refers to the case where several exceptions occur at the same time. What does the CPU do in such a case ? The CPU handles the exceptions according to their priorities, as explained in Figure 2-40 below:

Exceptions in group 0 of Figure 2-40 have the highest priority an exceptions in group 2 have the lowest priority. If a bus error occurs during a trace operation, then the processor will interrupt the trace operation and go into the exception state in order to start the exception program for a bus error. Afterr returning from this exception program, the processor can continue with the trace operation. The priorities also apply to the order in which the exceptions occur in the table above within each group. For example, if a bus error and an address error occur simultaneously, then the bus error will have the priority.

The beginning of th exception handling is also important, since small shifts in the priorities can occur from different starting points.

Group	Exception	Exception Handling begins:
0	RESET Bus Error Address Error	At the end of a clock cycle
1	Trace Interrupt	At the end of an instruction cycle
	Illegal Instruction Nonimplemented In- struction (Opcode $Axxx,$Fxxxx) Violation of Privilege	At the end of a bus cycle
2	Instructions: TRAP TRAPV, and CHK Division by Zero	Within an in- struction cycle

Figure 2-40: Exception Groups and Exception Handling

2.5.4   Saving Important Information on the Stack

There are two cases for the ways that an M68000 microprocessor saves important information on the stack, as shown below. In addition, the format of this information on the stack is different for
− the 68000 and 68008 microprocessors,
− the 68010 and 68012 microprocessors and
− the 68020 and 68030 microprocessors.
The structure of this information is presented in this Chapter for the 68000 and 68008 microprocessors. The difference for the other microprocessors are presented in Chapter 8. (These differences are the source of the problem encountered by owners of an Atari 520ST who have unsuccessfully attempted to replace the original 68000 microprocessor with a 68010 microprocessor. This problem is also discussed in more detail in Chapter 8.) Following are the two cases:

Case 1: Bus Errors and Address Errors (from Group 0)

In this case, more information is saved than in case 2. Since the processor stops normal operations in the middle of a clock cycle of ethe current instruction, there are two subcases as follows:

Subcase a: The error occurs BEFORE the processor prefetches the next instruction. In this subcase, the processor saves the program counter that contains the address of the instruction within which the error occurred.

Subcase b: The error occurs DURING or AFTER the processor has prefetched the next instruction. In this subcase, the processor saves the program counter that contains an address that may be 2 to 20 bytes higher than the address of the instruction within which the error occurred, depending upon how much of the next instruction has already been prefetched by the processor.

Because of the need to overcome this ambiguity in a later diagnosis of the problem, the processor saves not only the standard information, consisting of:
− the contents of the program counter and
− the contents of the status register, but also the following additonal information in this case:
− the address at which an access was attempted when the bus error or address error occurred and
− a "super status word".

The format of this "super status word" is given in Figure 2-41 below. The stucture of the stored information on the supervisor stack is given in Figure 2-42 below.

Case 2: All other exceptions (from Groups 1 and 2). In this case, the standard information, constisting of:
- the contents of the program counter and
- the contents of the status register, is stored on the supervisor stack. For all exceptions in group 1, except trace and interrupt, the program counter contains the address of the instruction where the error occurred. For the exceptions of trace and interrupt in group 1 and all exceptions in group 2, the program counter contains the address of the next instruction.

The structure of the stored information for this case is illustrated in Figure 25-43 below. (Please note that the 68010 and 68030 microprocessors store FOUR words instead of two words – see Chapter 8.2.5, Vol.II for more detail.)

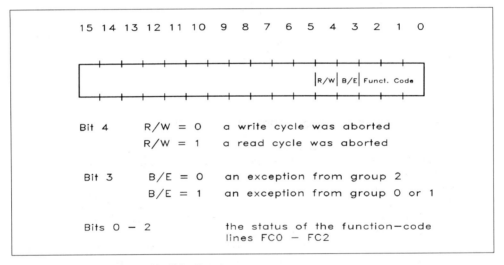

Figure 2-41: The "Super Status Word" for Case 1

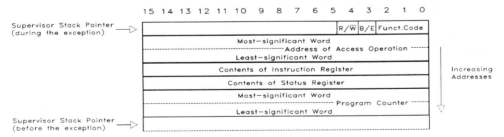

Figure 2-42: Structure of Supervisor Stack Data (for bus errors and address errors) for 68000/008

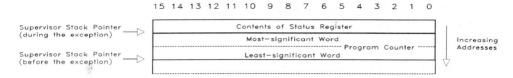

Figure 2-43: Structure of Supervisor Stack Data (for all errors other than bus errors and address errors) for 68000/008

2.5.5 Execution Times for Exceptions

Exception	Cycles
Address Error	50 (4/7)
Bus Error	50 (4/7)
CHK Instruction*	44 (5/4)[+]
Division by Zero	42 (5/4)
Nonimplemented Instruction	34 (4/3)
Interrupt**	44 (5/3)
Violation of Privilege	34 (4/3)
Reset***	40 (6/0)
Trace	34 (4/3)
TRAP Instruction	38 (4/4)
TRAV Instruction	34 (4/3)

[+]   Add the number of cycles for the respective addressing mode as given in Figure 2-45 below (also see Chapter 4).

*   means the maximum value.

**   4 clock cycles are assumed for the acknowledgment of the interrupt.

***   means the time from when RESET and HALT are first stored until the time when the execution of instructions begins.

Figure 2-44: Execution Times for Exceptions

The table in Figure 2-44 below gives the execution times for the exceptions for the 68000 microprocessor. The first number given before the parentheses is the number of clock cycles. The first number within the parentheses is the number of read bus cycles and the second number within the parantheses is the number of write bus cycles.

The table in Figure 2-45 below gives the access times for the various addressing modes that must be added to the execution times for some exceptions, as described in Figure 2-44 above. The values in these two tables are only valid for the 68000 microprocessor. Corresponding tables are given in Chapter 8 below for the other M68000 microprocessors.

Addressing Mode		Byte	Word	Long Word
	Register			
Dn	Data-register direct	0(0/0)	0(0/0)	0(0/0)
An	Address-register direct	0(0/0)	0(0/0)	0(0/0)
(An)	Memory			
(An)+	Address-register indirect (ARI)	4(1/0)	8(2/0)	16(4/0)
	ARI with postincrement	4(1/0)	8(2/0)	16(4/0)
–(An)	ARI with predecrement	6(1/0)	10(2/0)	18(4/0)
d16(An)	ARI with offset	12(3/0)	16(4/0)	24(6/0)
d8(An, Rx)*	ARI with index and offset	14(3/0)	18(4/0)	26(6/0)
$xxxx	Short-address absolute	12(3/0)	16(4/0)	24(6/0)
$xxxxxxxx	Long-address absolute	20(5/0)	24(6/0)	32(8/0)
d16(PC)	PC relative, with offset	12(3/0)	16(4/0)	24(6/0)
d8 (PC, Rx)	PC relative, with index & offset	14(3/0)	18(4/0)	26(6/0)
#xxx	Immediate data	8(2/0)	8(2/0)	16(4/0)

*The size of the index register has no influence on the time.

Figure 2-45: Maximum Times for the Different Addressing Modes

2.6   The Asynchronous Bus-Signals and Timing Diagrams

The microprocessors MC 68000/008/010/012 have two buses:

Asynchronous Bus

The M68000 microprocessors use the asynchronous bus primarily for communications with memory and 16-bit peripheral devices. A data-transfer bus cycle with a 68000 microprocessor operating at 8 MHz can take from 500 ns to indefinitely longer, depending upon the time required by the other device. Therefore, memory devices and other devices with arbitrary access times can be attached to this bus. This bus is described in this section of this chapter.

Synchronous Bus

The M68000 microprocessors use the synchronous bus primarily for communications with 8-bit peripheral devices. This bus is described in Section 2.8 of this chapter.

The Asynchronous Bus has 3 Components:

– an address bus (with lines A1 to A23),
– a data bus (with lines D0 to D15) and
– the control signals:
  AS (Address Strobe)
  LDS (Lower Data Strobe)
  UDS (Upper Data Strobe)
  R/W (Read/Write)
  DTACK (Data Transfer ACKnowledge)
It is illustrated in Figure 2-46 below.

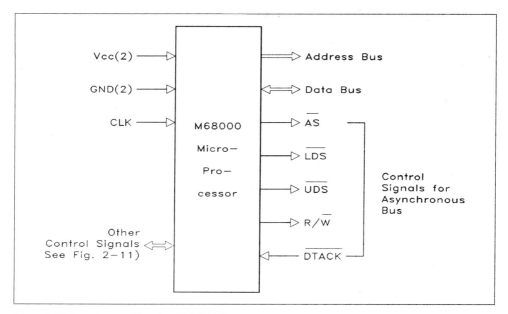

Figure 2-46: Asynchronous Bus of an M68000 Microprocessor

The address bus and the data bus are not multiplexed on top of each other, as for some other processors, but rather have separate pins on M68000 microprocessors. This separation makes life much easier for the hardware designer since it eliminates the need for extra external latches for each of these lines. Even more important, it is much easier to test both the hardware and software of the resulting system – using both logic analyzers and oscilloscopes. Using one single point for the trigger, you can then observe both the address information and data information – without needing extra circuits for demultiplexing.

The 68000 microprocessor has 24 address lines for 24-bit addresses, and it can therefore directly address up to 16 megabytes of memory as one linear block of memory, without segmenting as is required by many other processors. The upper 23 address lines, from A1 to A23, are directly available as pins of the microprocessor. The least-significant address line, A0, is "hidden" behind the two signal lines UDS and LDS, as explained below.

The M68000 microprocessors (except the 68008) have a 16-bit bidirectional data bus. The R/W signal line determines the direction on this data bus, ie. whether it is a read or a write operation. If the R/W signal contains a logical 1 (high), then it is a read operation. If the R/W signal contains a logical 0 (low), then it is a write operation.

The AS signal line of the asynchronous bus indicates whether a valid address appears on the address lines of the M68000 microprocessor. A value of logical 0 (low) on this line indicates that the address is valid.

A 68000 microprocessor can operate on bytes (8 bits), words (16 bits) and long words (32 bits) as operands. It can transfer a byte on either the lower or upper half of its 16-bit data bus. It uses the LDS (Lower Data Strobe) and UDS (Upper Data Strobe) lines to select whether to transmit:
– a byte with an odd address on the lower half of the data bus (LDS set low),
– a byte with an even address on the upper half of the data bus (UDS set low) or
– a 16-bit word on both halves of the data bus (both LDS and UDS set low).

Since the least-significant bit of a 24-bit address, line A0, would determine whether the location is even or odd, this combination of the LDS and UDS lines carries the information of an A0 line implicitly. This use of the LDS and UDS lines is illustrated for the case of read bus cycles for a word, an odd byte and an even byte in Figure 2-47 below. (See also Figures 2-23 and 2-24 in section 2.3.1 above.)

Bild 2-47 einsetzen

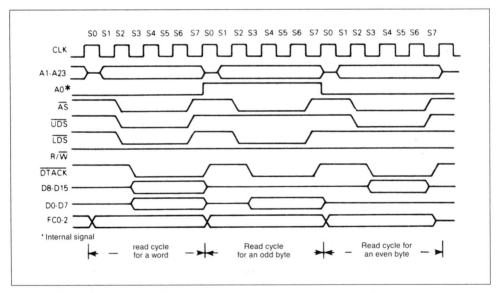

Figure 2-47: Read Bus Cycles for a Word, Odd Byte and Even Byte (only for the 68000 microprocessor)

Odd bytes are always transmitted on the lower half of the data bus (D0–D7), using LDS as their select signal, and even bytes are always transmitted on the upper half of the data bus (D8–D15), using UDS as their select signal. Therefore, you can divide the total available memory into two separate 8-bit areas when you are working with bytes rather than words or long words. The lower half of the data bus services the half of memory with odd addresses and the upper half of the data bus services the other half of memory with even addresses. For operations with words (or long words), both halves of the data bus and both halves of memory can be used simultaneously. This architecture is illustrated in Figure 2-48 below:

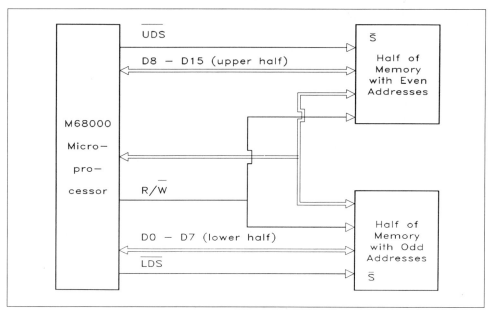

Figure 2-48: Independent Memory Areas for Even/Odd Addresses (only for 68000, 68010, and 68012 micro-processors)

The DTACK signal line (Data Transfer ACKnowledge) reports back from the memory or peripheral devices to an M68000 microprocessor that it is ready to receive or send requested data by setting the signal on this line to low. If the microprocessor does not receive the DTACK answer during a read or write bus cycle, then the microprocessor will automatically insert idle clock cycles until it does receive this signal. This mechanism allows the 68000 microprocessor to work with slow memory and peripheral devices. An M68000 microprocessor freezes the address lines for a read operation and both the address lines and the data lines for a write operation until it receives this acknowledgment. The M68000 does nothing else while waiting. If the system designer forgets to include provisions for the hardware to provide this signal, then the microprocessor will stop working and wait forever. However, the designer could include a "watch-dog timer" to limit the time that the microprocessor waits for a DTACK signal that never comes. It could also be useful under some circumstances to create this situation deliberately, so that a test engineer can statically examine the status of the frozen address and data lines.

In general, every bus cycle of an M68000 microprocessor must be acknowledged with a DTACK signal, independent of whether it is a read bus cycle or a write bus cycle. In the case of an error, the BERR signal should be generated by the hardware – in order to complete the bus cycle. The effects of a BERR signal are described in more detail in Sections 2.5 and 2.11. The timing for the DTACK signal is described in more detail in the descriptions of the read bus cycle and write bus cycle below, as well as in Section 2.12.

2.6.1 The Read Bus Cycle

An M68000 microprocessor reads data from memory or a peripheral-interface device during a read bus cycle. The microprocessor can read either one byte (8 bits) or one word (16 bits) in one read bus cycle. It can read one long word (32 bits) in two consecutive read bus cycles. The selection between reading one byte, one word or one long word is determined by the opcode of the instruction. (The 68008 can only read one byte per read bus cycle, and it requires 2 bus cycles for one word and 4 bus cycles for one long word.) When a 68000, 68010 or 68012 microprocessor reads one byte of data, it uses the LDS or UDS signal line for the least-significant bit of the address, as explained above. If the byte is at an odd address, the microprocessor sets LDS low and reads the byte from the lower half of the data bus. If the byte is at an even address, the microprocessor sets UDS low and reads the byte from the upper half of the data bus. In both cases, the microprocessor places the byte in the correct position of the data register, ie. the lowest 8 bits of the data register. When reading one word, the microprocessor also places it in the lower half of a data register or an address register.

A timing diagram is presented for the 68000 microprocessor in Figure 2-49 below that assists in the following explanation of the timing for a read bus cycle. The times S0, S1, etc. in this diagram refer to half cycles of the system clock.

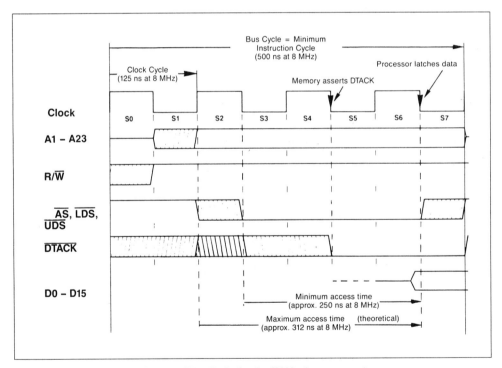

Figure 2-49: Timing Diagram for a Read Bus Cycle (for the 68000 microprocessor)

All of the control signals are inactive at the time of S0, including the address bus that is still in the high-impedance state. As the single exception, the function-code outputs could be set during S0, depending upon the following bus cycle. They would select the area of memory in which the rest of the bus cycle should apply.

In the half clock cycle S1, the address lines go from the high-impedance state to the active state and present the address for the read bus cycle. If it hasn't already done so, the R/W line goes high at this time to indicate that this is a read bus cycle and not a write bus cycle.

In the half clock cycle S2, the AS signal goes active to low, indicating that valid address information currently appears on the address lines. For the 68000 microprocessor, LDS and UDS go active at the same time, as appropriate, to indicate whether it is reading an odd byte, an even byte or a word. The selected memory device or peripheral-interface device should now present the requested data as quickly as possible and confirm having presented the requested data by sending the DTACK signal. This informs the microprocessor that valid data is currently available on the data lines.

The DTACK signal must appear no later than the falling flank of S4 in order to avoid idle clock cycles. Otherwise, the M68000 microprocessor will insert idle cycles until either it or the BERR signal does appear (see Figure 2-50). In other words, an M68000 microprocessor checks the value of the DTACK signal every clock signal after the falling flank of S4, while holding all of the other signals constant, until the DTACK or BERR signal appears. This makes it easy for you to attach slow memory devices and slow peripheral devices to an M68000 microprocessor.

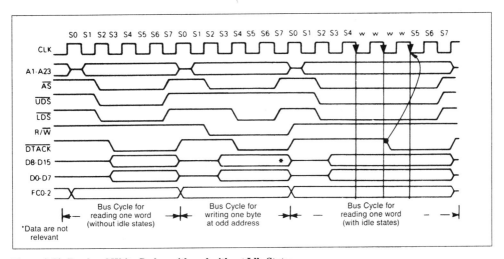

Figure 2-50: Read and Write Cycles, with and without Idle States

An M68000 microprocessor does not activate any additional control signals during the half clock cycles S3 and S4.

If the DTACK signal arrives in time, then the M68000 microprocessor will latch the data from the data bus into the internal data register.

During the half clock cycle S7, a 68000 microprocessor deactivates the AS, UDS and/or LDS signals. However, the signals on the address bus remain valid during this half cycle – to allow static operations and to avoid signal distortions. The R/W and function-code outputs also remain valid during S7 – to allow a transfer of data without errors. The selected memory device or peripheral device must hold both its data and the DTACK signal valid until the processor deactivates either the AS or respective LDS or UDS signals. As soon as one of these data strobes is inactive, the memory device or peripheral device has one clock cycle to remove its DTACK and data signals. It is possible therefore that the DTACK and data signals are still valid from the previous operation through S0 and S1 of the following operation.

It is very important that the selected memory device or peripheral-interface device remain active as long as the AS signal is valid. This is a prerequisite for an error-free read-modify-write bus cycle, as described in the next section of this chapter.

2.6.2   The DTACK Signal and Memory-Access Times of a Processor

If you examine the timing diagram for a bus cycle, you will determine that the maximum access time for a 68000 microprocessor, without idle states, is 2 complete clock cycles (ie. 250 ns at 8 MHz). This is the time from when the address lines have valid information at the end of the half cycle S2 until the microprocessor has finished latching the data from the data bus at the end of the half cycle S6. Of course, this calculation is only valid when the selected device delivers the DTACK signal to the microprocessor by the falling flank of S4.

If all memory devices and peripheral-interface devices in a system have an access time of 250 ns or less, you might want to consider holding the DTACK signal low statically, independent of the operation and timing. This is actually possible, as long as all peripheral devices have access times of less than 250 ns. However, this is seldom the case in reality.

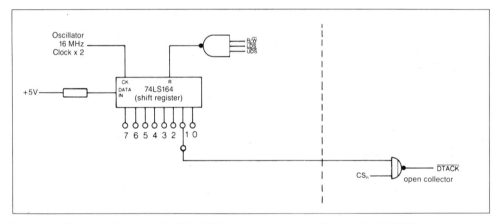

Figure 2-51:Circuit for Generating the DTACK Signal   **Figure 2-52:DTACK Connection**

All of the 16-bit peripheral-interface devices in the M68000 family provide the DTACK signal automatically. However, the DTACK signal must be generated separately in hardware for memory devices and 8-bit peripheral-interface devices. Figure 2-51 below presents a possible approach for generating the DTACK signal separately in hardware. You can use plug contacts with this circuit to select from 0 to 6 idle states ("wait states") that will be inserted into the read or write bus cycle. Figure 2-52 below shows how different sources can be connected together into one DTACK signal line. Figure 2-53 shows the different possible sources for DTACK and how they can be connected. The "Watchdog Timer" can detect both defective peripheral-interface devices and areas of memory that are not implemented and decoded. It generates the BERR signal to prevent the processor from becoming permanently locked when no DTACK signal arrives for a long period of time. (Non-decoded addresses have no physical devices and therefore can not generate a DTACK signal!.)

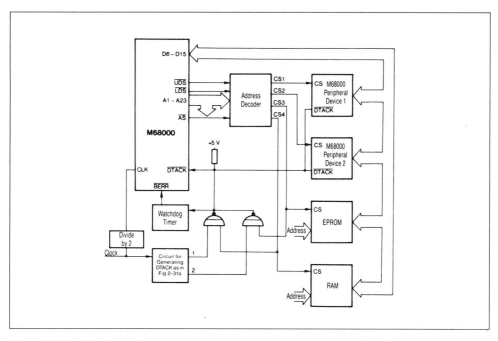

Figure 2-53: Possible Sources for DTACK

2.6.3 The Write Bus Cycle

An M68000 microprocessor writes data to either a memory device or a peripheral-interface device in a write bus cycle. The microprocessor can write one byte (8 bits) or one word (16 bits) in one bus cycle, and it can write one long word (32 bits) in two consecutive write bus cycles. (The 68008 microprocessor can only write one byte in one write bus cycle.) The size of the data that is written is specified in the opcode of the instruction.

When writing a byte, a 68000, 68010 or 68012 microprocessor uses the implicit A0 address signal that is "hidden" behind the LDS and UDS signals to select whether to transmit the byte to an odd address over the lower half of the data bus (lines D0 to D7) or to an even address over the upper half of the data bus (lines D8 to D15). In both cases, the microprocessor will send the byte from the 8 least-significant bits of the data register.

A timing diagram for the 68000 microprocessor is presented in Figure 2-54 below, that assists in the following explanation of the timing for a write bus cycle. The times S0, S1, etc. in this diagram refer to half cycles of the system clock.

All of the control signals are inactive at the time of S0, including the address bus that is still in the high-impedance state. As the single exception, the function-code outputs could be set during S0, depending upon the following bus cycle. They would select the area of memory in which the rest of the bus cycle should apply.

In the half clock cycle S1, the address lines go from the high-impedance state to the active state and present the address for the write bus cycle.

In the half clock cycle S2, the AS signal goes active to low, indicating that valid address information currently appears on the address lines. The R/W line goes low at this time see p. 33 to indicate that this is

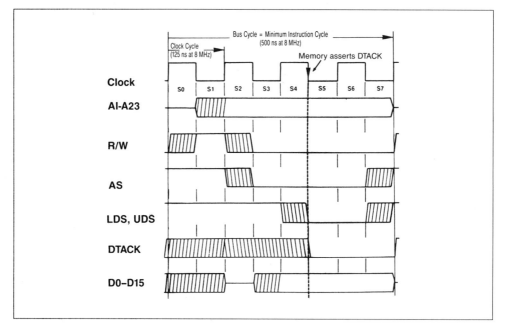

Figure 2-54: Timing Diagram for a Write Bus Cycle (for the 68000 microprocessor)

a write bus cycle and not a read bus cycle. (For a read bus cycle, the R/W line goes high during the half clock cycle S1.) This difference assures that no conflict will occur with a preceding read operation. If you use bus drivers for the data bus, you can use the R/W line for selecting the direction of the bus. The 68000 microprocessor switches the R/W line to high during the half clock cycle S0 between two consecutive write bus cycles – in order to keep them separate from each other.

In the half clock cycle S3, the 68000 microprocessor presents the data on the data bus, thereby giving the drivers enough time to switch directions in S2.

With the rising flank of S4, the 68000 microprocessor activates the LDS and UDS line, as appropriate, to indicate whether an odd byte, an even byte or a word is being written. The selected memory device or peripheral-interface device should send the DTACK signal to the processor by the falling flank of S4 in order to avoid idle states. Otherwise, the microprocessor will insert idle states until a DTACK or BERR signal arrives and will hold its other signals constant while waiting.

In the half clock cycle S7, the 68000 microprocessor deactivates the AS, LDS and UDS signals (assuming no idle cycles in between). Therefore, the selected memory device or peripheral-interface device must have accepted the transmitted data by this time. However, the microprocessor still maintains valid signals on the address lines and data lines to assure reliable operations and to avoid signal distortions. It also holds the R/W line and function-code outputs active during S7. The selected memory device or peripheral-interface device must hold DTACK active until either the AS, LDS or UDS signals go inactive. Once one of these data strobe lines goes inactive, the selected device has one clock cycle of time to remove the DTACK signal from the processor. The 68000 microprocessor deactivates the data bus at the end of the half cycle S7. However, the DTACK signal from one operation may still be present during the half cycles S0 and S1 of the following operation.

With a few minor exceptions, such as for the R/W line and the data strobes, the write bus cycle is practically the same as for the read bus cycle. Therefore, the access times and the use of the DTACK signal are essentially the same.

2.6.4 The Read-Modify-Write Bus Cycle

In a read-modify-write bus cycle, an M68000 microprocessor:
- reads data from a memory device or peripheral device,
- modifies the data within the microprocessor itself and
- writes the results back to the same device and address.

An M68000 microprocessor has two types of read-modify-write bus cycles as follows:

1 The first type applies to instructions such as the ROL, ROR, LSL and LSR instructions. In this case, the microprocessor reads the operand, shifts the operand, and writes the results at the same address. It does not change any of its data registers or address registers. This type of read-modify-write bus cycle behaves like a simple read operation that is followed by a simple write operation. The AS (Address Strobe) is inactive for a short time between the read and write operations, and therefore, **this type of read-modify-write bus cycle can be interrupted between the read and write operations.**

2 The second type applies only to the TAS (Test and Set) instruction (that serves for communications between processors in multi-processor systems). This instruction operates only on bytes (see the detailed description in Chapter 4). The AS (Address Strobe) is active continuously through both the read and write operations. **This type of read-modify-write bus cycle can not therefore be interrupted between the read and write operations.**

Only the second type of read-modify-write bus cycle is described in detail here (since the first type is essentially the same as separate read and write bus cycles). The timing is shown in Figure 2-55 below for a 68000 microprocessor. The flow of actions is shown in Figure 2-56 in more detail than in the text that follows.

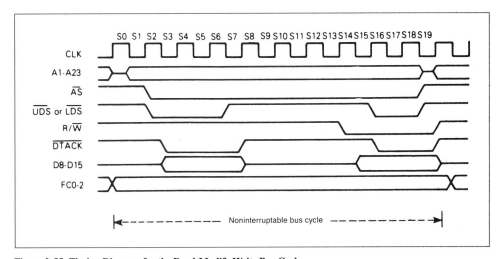

Figure 2-55: Timing Diagram for the Read-Modify-Write Bus Cycle

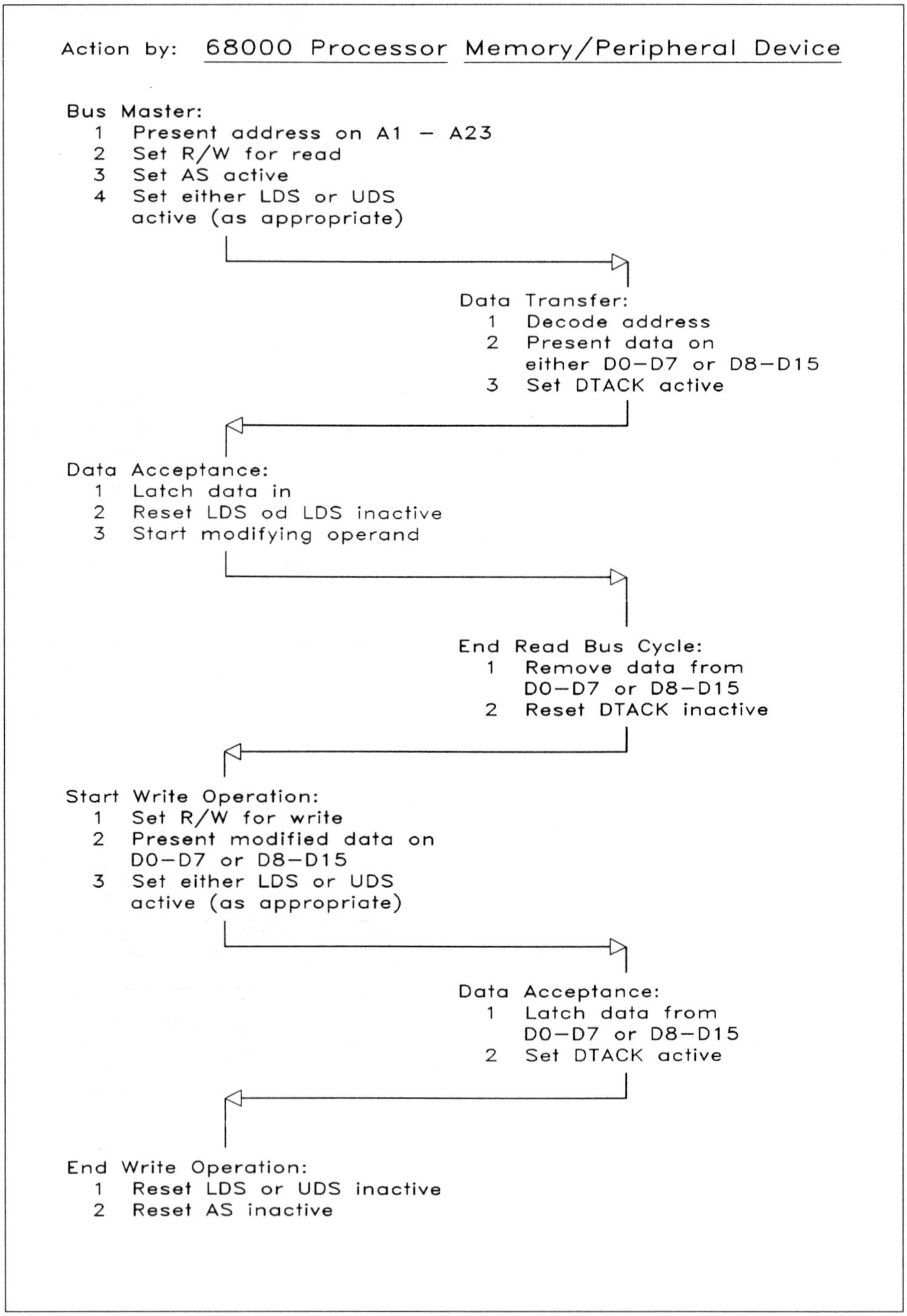

Action by: 68000 Processor Memory/Peripheral Device

Bus Master:
1   Present address on A1 – A23
2   Set R/W for read
3   Set AS active
4   Set either LDS or UDS
    active (as appropriate)

Data Transfer:
1   Decode address
2   Present data on
    either D0–D7 or D8–D15
3   Set DTACK active

Data Acceptance:
1   Latch data in
2   Reset LDS od LDS inactive
3   Start modifying operand

End Read Bus Cycle:
1   Remove data from
    D0–D7 or D8–D15
2   Reset DTACK inactive

Start Write Operation:
1   Set R/W for write
2   Present modified data on
    D0–D7 or D8–D15
3   Set either LDS or UDS
    active (as appropriate)

Data Acceptance:
1   Latch data from
    D0–D7 or D8–D15
2   Set DTACK active

End Write Operation:
1   Reset LDS or UDS inactive
2   Reset AS inactive

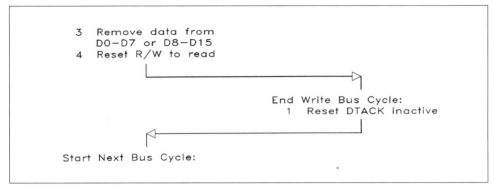

Figure 2-56: Flowchart for Read-Modify-Write Bus Cycle

The second type of read-modify-write bus cycle behaves exactly the same as a read bus cycle up through the half clock cycle S7. The 68000 microprocessor keeps the same values for the address lines (A1–A23), the address strobe line (AS), the R/W line and the function codes as in the preceding read bus cycle. However, the memory device or peripheral-interface device that is selected must remove its data from the data bus and its DTACK signal after the processor removes the data strobe.

The microprocessor uses the half clock cycles from S8 until S11 to modify the data. During this time interval, the microprocessor makes no changes in its output signals.

From the half clock cycle S12 on, there is a normal write bus cycle in which the processor writes the modified results back to the same address from which it read the original operand.

This second type of read-modify-write bus cycle is the same as a normal read bus cycle followed by a normal write bus cycle except that

– the write address and the function codes are exactly the same as for the read address,
– the address strobe (AS) remains active throughout both bus cycles and
– the double bus cycle can not be interrupted in the middle because the address strobe remains active.

However, this read-modify-write bus cycle can be interrupted by a BERR signal, instead of a DTACK signal, to the M68000 microprocessor. This makes the M68000 microprocessor abort the bus cycle and continue with an exception of the type "bus error" (see Sections 2.5 and 2.10 for more details).

2.7 Function-Code Outputs FC0–FC2

A 68000 microprocessor has 24 address lines (LDS & UDS equivalent to A0 in decoded form and explicit lines from A1 to A23) and therefore it can directly address 16 megabytes of memory. Other M68000 microprocessors can directly address up to 4 gigabytes of memory. This address range should be sufficient for most applications. However, M68000 microprocessors have an additional capability for managing address space. An M68000 microprocessor has 3 function-code outputs, FC0–FC2, to indicate which address area it is working with. However, you could also use them to extend the total address range of memory, as explained below.

The pins of the function-code outputs are illustrated in Figure 2-57 below. The logical interpretation of the potential combinations of these signals is given in Figure 2-58 below. A simple circuit for decoding these 3 outputs into the 8 logical states is given in Figure 2-59 below.

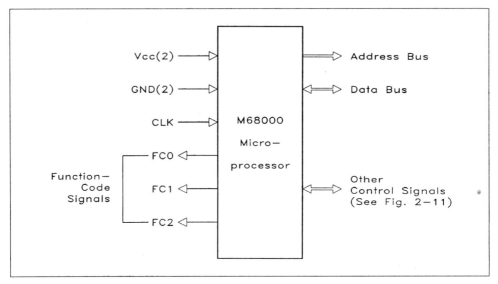

Figure 2-57: Function-Code Pins of an M68000 Microprocessor

Function–Code Signals			Address Area
FC2	FC1	FC0	
0	0	0	Undefined (Reserved)
0	0	1	User Data
0	1	0	User Program
0	1	1	Undefined (Reserved)
1	0	0	Undefined (Reserved)
1	0	1	Supervisor Data (SD)
1	1	0	Supervisor Program (SP)
1	1	1	Interrupt Acknowledgement

Figure 2-58: Logic Table for Function-Code Signals

The function-code signals are used by both the MMU (Memory Management Unit) and the DMA (Direct Memory Access) Controller of the M68000 family. In the case of the MMU, the processor uses them to inform the MMU whether an access to memory is to data or to a program and whether the data or program is in the supervisor area or the user area of memory.

The AS (Address Strobe) signal determines the timing for both the function-code signals and the address signals in exactly the same way.

The M68000 uses the current value of the supervisor bit in its status register to generate the function-code signal FC2. Therefore, when this bit is high, it always refers to the supervisor area of memory, and when

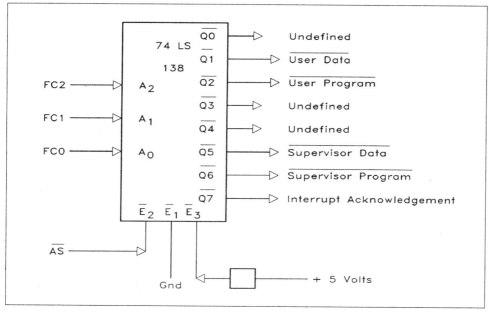

Figure 2-59: Circuit for Decoding Function-Code Signals

it is low, it always refers to the user area of memory. The M68000 uses FC0 to identify when an access is to data and it uses FC1 to identify when an access is to a program. The combinations of FC0 and FC1 corresponding to neither data nor a program are not used at this time but are reserved for possible later use. The combination of FC0 and FC1 corresponding to both being set, is not used in the user area but is used in the supervisor area (for an interrupt acknowledgment). (This last case is described in more detail in Section 2.9 below on handling interrupts.) The other 3 combinations that are not defined and are not used are reserved for future use. An M68000 microprocessor will never generate these combinations. Therefore, the logic circuit for decoding these 3 signals, in Figure 2-59 above, will never generate signals on the lines Q0, Q3 and Q4.

The criteria, used by an M68000 microprocessor to determine whether to set FC0 (access to data) or FC1 (access to program) high, is whether it is using the contents for the program counter (PC) as the source for the address (FC1 = 1) or if not (FC0 = 1). The microprocessor will set FC1 high when reading a reset vector, indicating access to program. Therefore, FC0 will be high while the microprocessor is writing operands, getting all vectors except the reset vector and reading most operands. (In all of these cases, the program counter is never the source of the address.) The reservation that FC0 will be high while the M68000 microprocessor is reading most but not all operands, is for the special cases where the operand is included in the opcode, such as for MOVEQ, ADDQ and SUBQ.

These three function-code signals are used primarily together with a memory-management unit for managing and protecting memory. This ability to partition the memory into a user area and a supervisor area, as well as to distinguish between accesses to data and programs, can be powerful tools for increasing the reliability of a system.

However, you can use these three function-code signals to expand the address space of the M68000 with a simple memory-management system that does not use a memory-management unit. To do this, you can use these signals directly as address lines to create, for example, separate 16-megabyte address spaces for:

- user data,
- user programs,
- supervisor data and
- supervisor programs,

using the circuit illustrated in Figure 2-59 above.

One well known alternative to the "von-Neumann architecture" is the "Harvard architecture". It has separate memories for data and programs, rather than one general-purpose memory for both data and programs. Therefore, you can easily implement a Harvard architecture with M68000 microprocessors, using these function-code signals as select signals to distinguish between a data memory and a program memory. But you still do not have the full advantage of a Harvard architecture with the earlier M68000 microprocessors since there is only one external bus and therefore the processor can only access memory sequentially, either data or program memory, but not both in parallel. However, the later 68030 microprocessor allows you to take nearly full advantage of this feature with a modified Harvard architecture. The 68030 microprocessor still has only one external bus connecting it to memory, and therefore appears like a von-Neumann architecture to software but internally it has separate buses and caches so that it can access both opcodes and operands simultaneously over separate buses from its separate cache memories.

2.8 The Synchronous Bus-Signals and Timing Diagrams

The M68000 microprocessors have two buses:
- **Asynchronous Bus** (described in section 2.6 above)
- **Synchronous Bus** (described in this section)

Although Motorola was the pioneer in developing and releasing both a microprocessor and several peripheral-interface devices at the same time (for the 8-bit M6800 microprocessor family in 1974), it was not practically feasible for any of the producers of 16-bit and 32-bit microprocessors to develop and release a complete set of peripheral-interface devices at the same time that they released new 16-bit and 32-bit microprocessors. In the case of the first 68000 microprocessor, Motorola took advantage of the wide palette of 8-bit peripheral-interface devices that were already available in the 8-bit M6800 family from Motorola (and second sources) and the very similar 8-bit 6500 family from MOS Technology (and second sources, such as Rockwell). A listing of these 8-bit peripheral interface devices is given in chapter 7. Since releasing the first M68000 microprocessor in 1979, a large number of matching peripheral-interface devices have been developed and released, but it is still often economical to use the older 8-bit devices for some applications.

Motorola created three special signals to enable the M68000 family of microprocessors to work together with 8-bit peripheral interface devices:

–	VPA	(Valid Peripheral Address)
–	E	(Enable)
–	VMA	(Valid Memory Address)

With these three signals, you can use 8-bit peripheral-interface devices without needing extra hardware. (See Figure 2-60 and 2-61 below).

As you can see in Figure 2-61 above, the VPA signal is a "fallout" product from the address decoder that must be available as a chip-select signal within any system when creating addresses for peripheral-interface devices. This chip-select signal is combined with AS, using the logical AND operation and fed back to the M68000 microprocessor as the VPA signal.

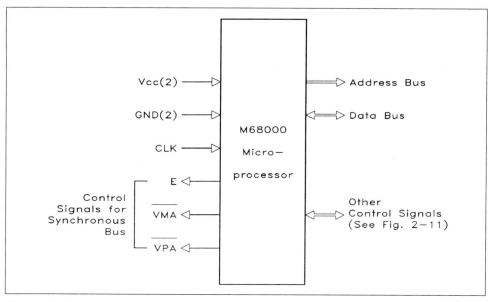

Figure 2-60: Synchronous Bus Signals of an M68000 Microprocessor

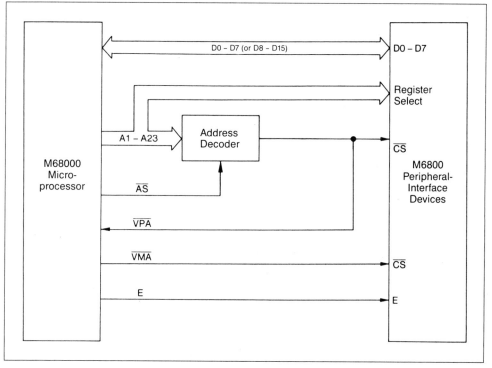

Figure 2-61: Connecting 8-bit Peripheral-Interface Devices

The enable signal, E, is the synchronizing signal that gives this bus its name of synchronous bus. (It is sometimes called the 02 signal.)

The transfer of data must occur synchronously in both directions. Most 8-bit peripheral-interface devices have an input for this signal for the purpose of synchronization. For example, the 6821 PIA (Parallel Interface Adapter) sets and resets flags in the status register. Also, the 8-bit peripheral-interface devices from the M6800 family usually have a maximum clock speed of 2 megahertz, whereas the first 68000 microprocessor has a maximum clock speed of 8 megahertz in its slowest version. This requires a division of the system clock and a factor of 1/10 was chosen. Therefore, when the system clock is running at 8 megahertz, the E signal will appear at exactly 800 kilohertz during a synchronous access to a peripheral-interface device (see Figure 2-62). The auto-vector interrupts (see section 2.9.1 below) use the same timing since VPA is used as the criterium for generating an auto vector after recognizing an interrupt.

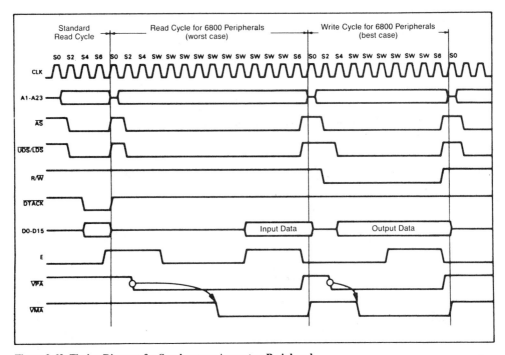

Figure 2-62: Timing Diagram for Synchronous Access to a Peripheral

As the sequence of events, the processor begins a "normal" read and write bus cycle. The VPA signal tells the processor that it must use a synchronous cycle.

In order to create time for the E signal within a bus cycle, the processor inserts 10 idle clock cycles (20 idle half cycles) after the 6th clock cycle (S5). The E signal remains at zero for 6 clock cycles and then at one for 4 clock cycles.

During the 5th idle half cycle after the processor ascertains that E is at zero; the processor will set VMA active (zero). This guarantees that the peripheral-interface device will be selected at the correct time. VMA will be connected with the chip select either at the peripheral-interface device or the address decoder.

As you can see from Figure 2-62 above, two cases can arise since the signal E is asynchronous:

1 Best Case: VPA will become active 3 clock cycles before E goes to logical "1" (or 3 cycles after E goes to logical "0").
2 Worst Case: VPA will become active 2 clock cycles before E goes to logical "1" (or 4 cycles after E goes to logical "0").

Otherwise, it would not be possible to use the full speed without the possibility of using the asynchronous connection (see reference [23]). Then the maximum speed of the peripheral interface-devices can be used. Four TTL IC's are required for the realisation. Synchronization and the generation of the DTACK signal can be achieved with flip flops or with buffers for the data (see Figure 2-63 below).

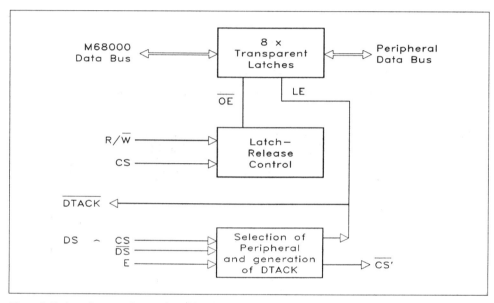

Figure 2-63: Asynchronous Connection of Synchronous Peripherals

2.9 Handling of Interrupts

An interrupt is merely a special case for an exception where the exception is generated externally from the microprocessor. The M68000 family of microprocessors has an elegant and flexible structure for interrupts. Altogether, 199 interrupt vectors are available for the user. They are divided into:
– 7 autovectors and
– 192 non-autovectors, in 7 priority levels.
Interrupts are initiated by a signal on one or more of the 3 interrupt lines IPL0, IPL1 or IPL2, that also defines the priority level of the interrupt. In principle, these 3 lines can be decoded into 8 levels. However, the 8th level, with 111, does not exist and does not generate an interrupt. These signals are illustrated in Figure 2-64 below:

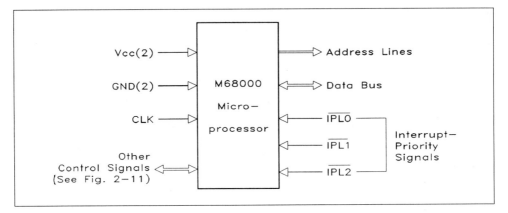

Figure 2-64: Interrupt-Priority Signals of M68000 Microprocessors

The priority levels and the interactions with the interrupt-mask bits of the status register are shown in Figure 2-65 below:

Priority	Interrupt-Mask Bits in the status register			Interrupt Signal Lines			Rank of Priority
	10	9	8	$\overline{IPL2}$	$\overline{IPL1}$	$\overline{IPL0}$	
7	1	1	1	0	0	0	
6	1	1	0	0	0	1	
5	1	0	1	0	1	0	
4	1	0	0	0	1	1	
3	0	1	1	1	0	0	
2	0	1	0	1	0	1	
1	0	0	1	1	1	0	
–	0	0	0	1	1	1	none
Status Register (SR)							

Figure 2-65: Interrupt-Priorities and the Status Register

The priority levels from 1 to 6 are maskable. When the microprocessor receives a bit combination for a priority level from 1 to 6 on the interrupt lines, it will first check the interrupt mask in the status register (bits 10, 9 and 8 in the register). The microprocessor will only handle the interrupt if it has a higher priority than the priority specified in the mask. For example, if the interrupt mask is set at priority level 3 (bits I2, I1 and I0 = 011), then the microprocessor will only handle interrupts for the priority levels 4, 5, 6 and 7 (lines IPL2, IPL1 and IPL0 = 011, 010, 001 and 000).

The priority level 7 is nonmaskable. When the microprocessor receives the bit combination for priority level 7 on the interrupt lines, it will branch to the exception program without checking the status register. For example, this level can be used for promptly saving data into nonvolatile memory when a power failure occurs.

The differences at the hardware level are:

- Priority Levels 1–6:
  maskable interrupts
  triggering upon levels

- Priority Level 7 :
  nonmaskable interrupts
  triggering upon flanks

In both cases, the suppression is for 2 clock cycles. This minimizes spurious results from noise, glitches, etc.

2.9.1   Identification of Interrupts

You should follow two guidelines to be certain that the microprocessor will get the correct exception vector and start the exception program that you want:

1   The priority level of the incoming interrupt signal must be higher than the interrupt mask in the status register.
2   The interrupt signal lines (IPL0–IPL2) must hold the information for the priority level valid until the microprocessor acknowledges the interrupt by setting FC0–FC2 to logical "1" and resetting AS to logical "0". In addition, the microprocessor will present the priority level that it recognized on the address lines A1–A3. If, at this time, the incoming signal changes to that of a higher priority, the microprocessor will get the exception vector with the higher priority (see Section 2.9.2 below). This can be desirable, such as to identify and process interrupts or to combine interrupts of higher priorities faster. In this special case, it is sufficient to hold the signal on the interrupt signal lines for a minimum of 2 clock cycles.

2.9.2   Sequence of Steps for Handling an Interrupt

Figure 2-66 below shows the sequence of steps for handling an interrupt as a flow chart. It is followed by a discussion that enables you to calculate the length of an interrupt. The minimum setup time for an interrupt with a non-autovector is 44 clock cycles, not including idle cycles. This is the time from the request until the execution of the first instruction of the exception program (interrupt program).

The following sequence of steps occurs when the microprocessor identifies an interrupt. This sequence is the same for 68000 microprocessors with the masks DL6, CC1 and GN7 (see Section 2.9.5 below and Chapter 5):

1   A peripheral-interface device provides a bit combination for the priority level on the interrupt signal lines IPL0–IPL2.
2   The microprocessor checks the interrupt mask in the status register. If the requested priority level is 7 (NMI) or at least higher than the level set in the interrupt mask, then the microprocessor continues with step 3 below. Otherwise, the microprocessor will continue with the instruction that was next before it was interrupted by the interrupt signal lines.
3   The microprocessor saves the status register in an internal register that is not accessible from outside the microprocessor.
4   The microprocessor sets the S-bit (supervisor status) and clears the T-bit (trace mode). It sets the interrupt mask equal to the priority level of the interrupt that it is currently processing and presents this level on the address lines A1–A3. No other activities take place on the buses. (Steps 3 and 4 together use 6 clock cycles.)
5   The microprocessor saves the least-significant word of the program counter (PC) on the supervisor stack. (This uses 4 clock cycles – without idle cycles.)
6   At this point, the microprocessor has acknowledged the interrupt. It indicates this by setting the function-code ouputs FC0– FC2 = 111 and resetting AS = 0–this implies acknowledgement of the interrupt = IACK. There are 3 different cases at this point:
    Case 1: VPA arrives (autovector). The microprocessor will create an autovector with the same number as the priority level appearing on the interrupt signal lines IPL0–IPL2. **It is important that DTACK should never be active in this case** (see Section 2.9.3 below).

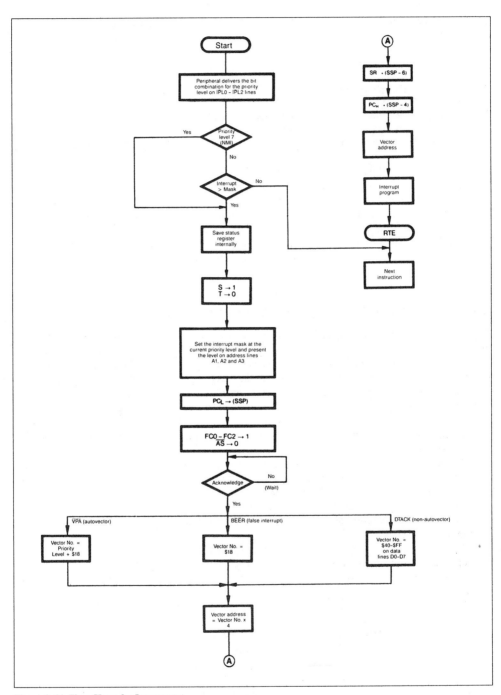

Figure 2-66: Flow Chart for Interrupts

Case 2: DTACK arrives (non-autovector). The vector number is generated externally and is communicated over the data lines D0–D7 after DTACK is active. This vector number is usually in the range from $30–$FF, but it can be a different number, as explained in Section 2.5 above. The peripheral-interface devices in the M68000 family have the capability to generate non-autovectors (see Section 2.9.4 below).

Case 3: BERR arrives (spurious interrupt). Even though the interrupt signal lines are synchronized and the interrupts are suppressed for 2 clock cycles, it can happen that an accidental interrupt signal will be sent to the microprocessor, especially due to spikes and glitches that occur in process-control applications. In this case, the peripheral-interface devices do not deliver either a VPA or DTACK signal to the microprocessor. However, a ''watchdog timer'' can be included in the hardware that sends a BERR signal to the processor after a given time interval when neither a VPA or DTACK signal is sent after an interrupt signal. The microprocessor then uses the exception-vector number $18 to branch to the exception program for false interrupts. You can supply appropriate steps in this exception program.

(The microprocessor uses 4 clock cycles, without idle cycles, for a non-autovector and from 10 to 18 clock cycles for an autovector.)

7 The microprocessor generates the exception-vector address from the exception-vector number (by multiplying by 4). (This uses 4 clock cycles – without bus activities.)

8 The microprocessor saves the contents of the status register that it saved temporarily in step 3 above, on the supervisor stack. (This uses 4 clock cycles, without bus idle cycles.)

9 The microprocessor saves the most-significant word of the program counter (PC) on the supervisor stack. (This uses 4 clock cycles – without idle cycles.)

10 The microprocessor reads the exception vector from the location specified by the exception-vector number in the table of exception vectors and loads it into the program counter (PC). (This uses 4 clock cycles each, without idle states, for the most-significant and least-significant words.)

11 The microprocessor fetches the first word of the first instruction of the exception program (interrupt program).

12 There are now two idle clock cycles, without bus activities.

13 The microprocessor fetches the second word of the exception program. At the same time, the microprocessor examines the interrupt signal lines. If a valid interrupt is present, with a higher priority than the priority of the current interrupt, then the microprocessor will branch to the exception program with the higher priority before branching to the exception program with the lower priority. Each exception program (interrupt program) ends with an RTE instruction (Return from Exception – see Chapter 4).

The supervisor stack pointer (SSP) will be decremented by the number of bytes that are stored on the stack by this sequence (see Figure 2-43, in Section 2.5.4 above). However, it is difficult to say at which point in time this will occur.

Normally, the microprocessor examines for the presence of interrupts at the end of each bus cycle. The MOVEM instruction is an exception however. It is the only instruction that uses a data prefetch (see chapter 6). If the program contains a MOVEM instruction followed by a DIVS instruction and an interrupt request arrives at the beginning of the MOVEM instruction, then the microprocessor will not recognize the interrupt until the end of the DIVS instruction. Since the DIVS instruction is the slowest instruction in the instruction set, this leads to the worst case for the time from when an interrupt request arrives until it is recognized:

MOVEM	146 clock cycles	(+ possible wait cycles)
DIVS	174 clock cycles	(+ possible wait cycles)
Interrupt acknowledgement	58 clock cycles	(for autovectors)
	378 clock cycles	(worst case)

(The worst-case times for the MOVEM and DIVS instructions for the 68000 microprocessor are used in this calculation.)

2.9.3   Autovector Interrupts

External hardware sends a VPA signal to an M68000 microprocessor to initiate an autovector interrupt. Therefore, the microprocessor continues on through one clock cycle, as if communicating with a synchronous peripheral-interface device. For this reason, autovector interrupts take longer than non-autovector interrupts.

Autovector interrupts are particularly useful when a peripheral-interface device does not have the capability for generating exception numbers (interrupt numbers) itself. This is the case for the peripheral-interface devices of the M6800 family as well as for peripheral-interface devices from other manufacturers.

The sequence of steps for handling an interrupt in general are described in Section 2.9.2 above. We will therefore only discuss a few hardware aspects for the special case of autovector interrupts in this section.

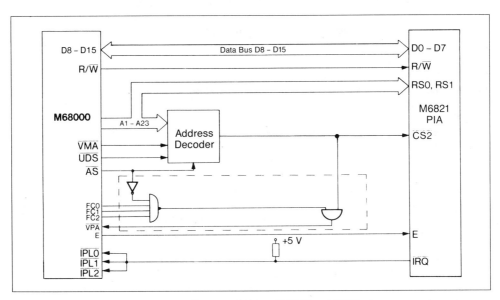

Figure 2-67: Simple Autovector Interrupt Structure (using a 6821 PIA and 68000 microprocessor)

Figure 2-67 above shows the connection of a 6821 PIA (Parallel Interface Adapter) to the synchronous bus of an M68000 microprocessor. The PIA is located at an even address that is at the most-significant byte in a data word and on the data bus (lines D8–D15). For the case of a 68000 microprocessor, the UDS (Upper Data Strobe) line goes into the address decoder. (As an alternate design, the PIA could be attached to the least-significant half of the data bus (D0–D7) and the LDS (Lower Data Strobe) line could be connected to the address decoder – which would place the PIA at an uneven address.)

So far, this figure is practically the same as Figure 2-61 above (Section 2.8). However, the 3 additional gates in the dotted box enable the use of autovector interrupts. The VPA signal can be generated either from a normal read/write cycle or from the acknowledgement of an interrupt (when FC0–FC2 = 111 and AS = 0). The request for an interrupt comes from one of the two halves of the 6821 PIA, ie. either IRQA or IRQB. The request automatically generates both the interrupt priority 7 and the autovector number 7 since the input lines IPL0–IPL2 are connected together. If you have more than 3 different interrupt sources that need to be distinguished from one another, then you will need an encoder (such as 74LS148) in front of the IPL0–IPL2 inputs to the microprocessor. An interrupt acknowledgement is not necessary in this example, but the interrupt request, IRQ, must be reset by software.

Following is a summary of the steps:

1 The peripheral-interface device requests an interrupt (IRQ is active).

2 The microprocessor recognizes a valid interrupt and stops at the end of the current instruction.

3 The microprocessor sends IACK (Interrupt Acknowledge = FC0–FC2 = 111 and AS = 0) and the identified priority level (on the address lines A1–A3) and waits for a confirmation.

4 The 3 additional gates generate VPA from the relevant signals from the microprocessor.

5 The microprocessor receives VPA and branches to the selected exception program (interrupt program).

6 The exception program must clear the interrupt request and perform "polling" if necessary.

Remark: If more than 7 different peripheral-interface devices are used with this principle some of them will have to be connected together ("wired OR") and requests at these priority levels may need to be checked by cyclical polling.

2.9.4 Non-autovector Interrupts

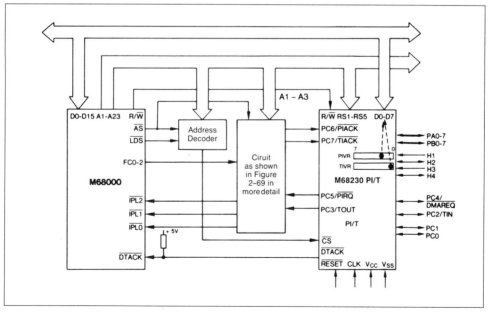

Figure 2-68: Non-autovector Interrupt Structure (using an 68230 PI/T)

Nearly all of the peripheral-interface devices in the M68000 family generate non-autovectors. For this purpose, these devices contain one or more 8-bit vector registers (see Chapter 7). You can enter a vector number, from $40 to $FF, in these vector registers. When the device sends an interrupt request to the microprocessor, it also sends this vector to the microprocessor over the data bus. Vector registers that have no vector assigned to them automatically send the vector number $0F (corresponding to a non-initialized interrupt).

Figure 2-68 above shows a simple example of connecting a 68230 PI/T (Parallel Interface / Timer) to an M68000 microprocessor. Very little extra hardware is required. One reason is that support devices such as a priority encoder and address decoder are always present in a system. The DTACK signal that is needed for this application is generated by the peripheral-interface device itself. As a typical example, we selected the 68230 PI/T (see Chapter 7.5 for more details on this device). The additional hardware that you need for acknowledging a request for an interrupt is shown as a single block in Figure 2-68 above, but it is expanded in detail in Figure 2-69 below.

Peripheral-interface devices in the M68000 family have:

- an IRQ (Interrupt ReQuest) input and
- an IACK (Interrupt ACKnowledge) output.

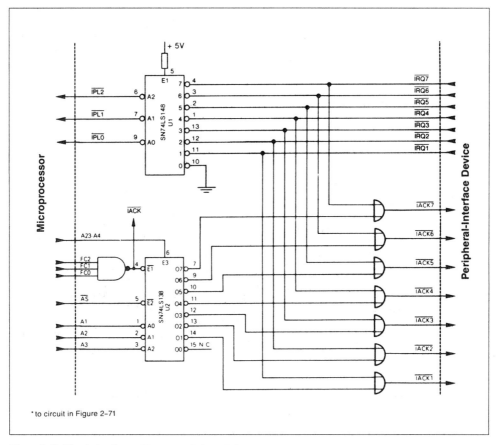

Figure 2-69:Circuit for General Interrupt Acknowledgements

The IACK signal is derived from the address lines A1–A3 since the microprocessor presents the current priority level on these lines. A circuit that generates interrupt acknowledgments for all 7 priority levels, IACK1–IACK7, is shown in Figure 2-69 below.

A 3-to-8 decoder (74LS138) decodes the 7 priority levels from the 3 address lines, on the condition that FC0–FC2 = 111 and AS = 0. The peripheral-interface device holds its IRQ signal active until it receives the IACK signal. Then the device sends the vector number from its vector register over the data bus and finally sends the DTACK signal. The DTACK signal informs the microprocessor that the interrupt request is for a non-autovector, and this vector is now present on the data bus, ready for the microprocessor to read.

If you want to attain compatibility with the 68010, 68020 and 68030 microprocessors, then you must combine the address signals A4–A23 and enter the result into the E3 input of the 74LS138. The reason is for this that these two microprocessors can also generate special breakpoint sequences and the 68020 can generate coprocessor sequences – in addition to interrupt acknowledgements. These are also presented on the address lines (see Chapter 8, Sections 8.1 and 8.2).

Non-autovectors can be created with extra circuitry for peripheral-interface devices that do not possess this capability themselves. Figure 2-70 below shows an example with a mixture of autovectors and non-autovectors.

In this example, priority level 3 is assigned to autovectors and the M6800 family of peripheral-interface devices. Priority level 5 is reserved for non-autovectors. The control logic that is enabled by IACK5 has the task of generating the DTACK signal and releasing the vector number, such as from a PROM.

Following is a summary of the steps:

1 The peripheral-interface device requests an interrupt (IRQ is active).

2 The microprocessor recognizes a valid interrupt and stops at the end of the current instruction.

3 The microprocessor sends IACK (Interrupt Acknowledge = FC0–FC2 = 111 and AS = 0) and the identified priority level (on the address lines A1–A3) and waits for a confirmation.

4 The external circuitry generates IACKn from IACK and the address lines A1–A3 for the peripheral-interface device that initiated the request.

5 The requesting peripheral-interface device receives IACKn and it then presents the contents of the appropriate vector register on the data bus (line D0–D7), activates DTACK and deactivates IRQ.

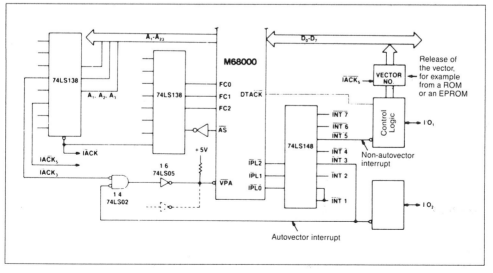

Figure 2-70:External Generation of Non-autovectors

6   The microprocessor recognizes DTACK, reads the vector number from the data bus and branches to the appropriate exception program (interrupt program).

Remark: If more than 7 different peripheral-interface devices are used with this principle, some of them will have to be connected together with daisy chaining or the autovector principle must be used with polling.

2.9.5   Polling and Daisy Chaining of Interrupts

In systems that require more than 7 priority levels, you must create the additional levels. This is possible either:
- with the software, using cyclical polling or
- with the hardware, using daisy chaining.

Daisy chaining has the advantage that it is faster but the disadvantage that you must use extra hardware.

For polling, the exception program (interrupt program) polls the peripheral-interface devices by reading the interrupt flags in their registers. This information informs the system which device or devices have requested interrupts.

For daisy chaining, several peripheral-interface devices can share one priority level, but hardware only allows an interrupt request from one device to pass through a chain to the microprocessor if no other devices in the chain have already requested interrupts with a higher priority. This principle is illustrated with Figure 2-68 above. We will assume that 3 peripheral-interface devices share the priority level 4. The circuit in Figure 2-71 below shows how the interrupt requests from these 3 devices can be daisy chained together. The priority within the chain is determined by the hardware and therefore it is impossible for two devices to generate interrupts with the same priority.

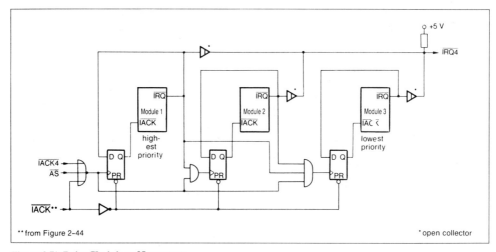

Figure 2-71: Daisy Chaining of Interrupts

Whenever an interrupt is recognized by the microprocessor with a priority level of 4, then the microprocessor sets FC0–FC2 = 111 and AS = 0. This resets the D-type flip-flops in the circuit above to their starting values, ie. Q = 1. The circuit in Figure 2-69 generates the interrupt acknowledgement,

IACK4. At this time, the interrupt request, IRQ, is clocked in, ie. temporarily saved. This temporary saving is only possible for a device with higher priority. The AND gate, U3, is responsible for this.

2.9.6 Interrupt Synchronization for Older Processor Types

The different mask versions of the 68000 microprocessor are described in Chapter 5. One small irregularity in the handling of interrupts by different mask versions will be discussed briefly here in advance, together with a practical solution.

This section refers only to processors that were produced before April 1980, ie. mask types R9M, BF4 and T6E. In addition, these mask types were never put into production – they were only released in sample quantities. However, if you still have some of these sample processors, you should use the extra circuitry shown in Figure 2-72 below.

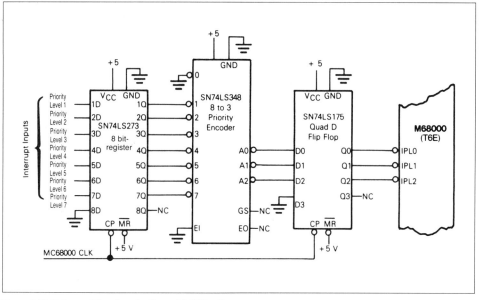

Figure 2.72: Interrupt Synchronization with Older Types

The older mask types mentioned above do not suppress interrupts for 2 clock cycles – as all later types do. Therefore, the internal synchronization does not work properly. As a result, it is possible that 2 interrupt requests can be presented simultaneously. This circuit solves this problem.

2.10 RESET, HALT and Bus Error (BERR)

Each microprocessor of the M68000 family has 3 system-control signals:
- RESET,
- HALT and
- BERR.

All 3 signals are available at pins of the microprocessor in their complemented forms. A unique feature of the M68000 family is that the RESET signal is a bidirectional input/output line of the processors. (See Figure 2-73 below.)

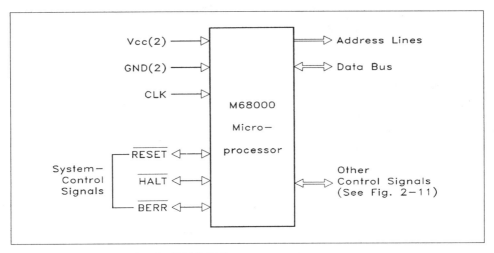

Figure 2-73: System-Control Signals of M68000 Microprocessors

2.10.1   RESET

Every microprocessor requires a RESET input line – as the only way to initialize the microprocessor in a predefined starting condition.

Errors, particularly when developing new systems software, can occur that place the microprocessor out of control – such as by reading an area of memory that contains data as if it contained a program. The worst-case solution is always to turn the power off and to start over again with a "cold restart". However, with this approach, the contents of memory are lost – including all programs, all data and clues as to what happened to generate this condition. Therefore, the RESET input line provides a better solution for such a problem by providing a "warm restart" that initializes the microprocessor but leaves the contents of memory intact.

The conditions for a reliable restart of the system are different, depending upon whether

1   the power has just been turned on, and the power-supply voltages have not yet stabilized,

2   the system has already been running, with stable power-supply voltages or

3   the system has just been reset, and you want to reset it again.

In the first case, both the RESET and the HALT inputs must be held low for a minimum of 100 milliseconds. In the second case, only the RESET input must be held low for a minimum of 10 clock cycles. In the third case, only the RESET input must be held low for a minimum of only 4 clock cycles. In all cases, the microprocessor will obtain both the supervisor stack pointer and the starting address for the reset program from the addresses beginning at $000000. It will also set the interrupt level in the status register at level 7, set the trace bit T to null, set the supervisor bit to 1 and then start the reset program.

A circuit diagram is presented in Figure 2-74 below that you can use for driving the complemented RESET input line. The upper half of the circuit diagram automatically generates a RESET when the power is turned on and the lower half of the circuit diagram generates a RESET when the RESET key is depressed. The CMOS timer (MC1455) in the upper half pulls the complemented RESET and HALT lines down for the required length of time after this timer is powered up. The NAND gates in the lower half debounce the RESET key and thereby hold the complemented RESET line down for the required length of time. Both circuits generate the RESET signal for both the microprocessor and other components.

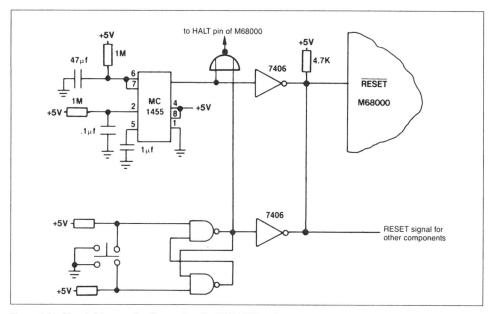

Figure 2-74: Circuit Diagram for Generating the RESET Signal

As mentioned above, the RESET pin of microprocessors in the M68000 family is a bidirectional input/output pin. These processors have a RESET instruction in their instruction sets that makes the processor itself use this pin as an output to pull this signal line down to low for 124 clock cycles. This allows a program to reset all other components that are attached to this signal line, without resetting the microprocessor itself. The microprocessor does nothing during these 124 clock cycles, and it can not be interrupted during this period of time. At the end of the 124 clock cycles it continues where it left off.

Following is a typical application for this bidirectional feature. The microprocessor attempts to send data to a peripheral-interface device, such as the 68120, and this device responds with an error signal. The microprocessor can then jump to an exception program that includes the RESET instruction to reset the peripheral-interface device. The microprocessor can then try again.

2.10.2 HALT

The HALT pin of a microprocessor in the M68000 family is also a bidirectional input/output pin, and the HALT signal is in the complemented form at this pin.

When external circuitry pulls this complemented signal down to low, the microprocessor performs the following actions:

– The microprocessor stops and waits. If it was in the middle of processing an instruction, it completes the current bus cycle before stopping and waiting.

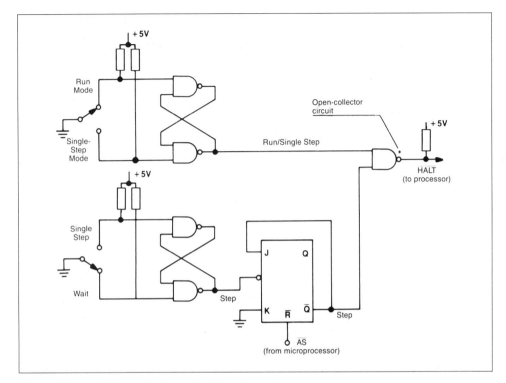

Figure 2-75: Circuit Diagram for Single-Step Operations

- The microprocessor places the address-bus lines, data-bus lines and function-code lines in the tri-state condition.
- The microprocessor inactivates the AS, UDS and LDS signals for controlling the asynchronous bus, leaving only the control signals for DMA functional.
- The microprocessor then waits until the complemented HALT signal returns to high.

You can use an external HALT signal to implement a single-step mode for a system, as illustrated in Figure 2-75 below. The upper half of the circuit diagram selects between the run mode and the single-step mode. The lower half of the circuit diagram initiates each individual step – but only if the upper half is in the single-step mode. Since the HALT, RESET and BERR signals are functionally related, you must be careful in the combined circuit that you do not allow the single-step switch to also influence the other signal lines.

Single stepping with an external switch and the HALT signal allows you to trace a program one single bus cycle at-a-step. As an alternative, you can use the trace function in software to trace a program one single instruction at-a-step. The choice usually depends upon whether you want to see bus cycles or whole instructions in each step.

The timing diagram in Figure 2-76 below shows the timing of various signals when you use the circuit from Figure 2-75 above. Each time that the AS signal indicates that a new valid address is available, the external circuit pulls the complemented HALT signal line down to low. After the bus cycle is complete, the microprocessor stops and waits. The user must use the external switch to reset the complemented HALT signal to high, so that the microprocessor can start the next bus cycle.

As mentioned above, the HALT pin of microprocessors in the M68000 family is a bidirectional input/output pin. The processor itself can pull the complemented HALT signal down to low in order to indicate that it has stopped. Therefore, you may want to attach an LED to this line, to indicate to the user that the microprocessor has stopped. Conditions where the microprocessor itself stops include serious errors from which the microprocessor can not recover, such as

- the double-bus-error condition,
- the address-error condition and
- a condition with the BERR signal that is described below.

2.10.3   Bus Error (BERR)

In complex systems, it is necessary to include the capability for identifying a variety of different kinds of error conditions. The BERR input signal, in complemented form, allows you to design external circuits that identify such errors. When the complemented BERR signal goes low, this informs the microprocessor that a problem has arisen in the current bus cycle. Figure 2-76 below shows a block diagram for handling such errors and also presents a listing of typical errors that you may want to consider.

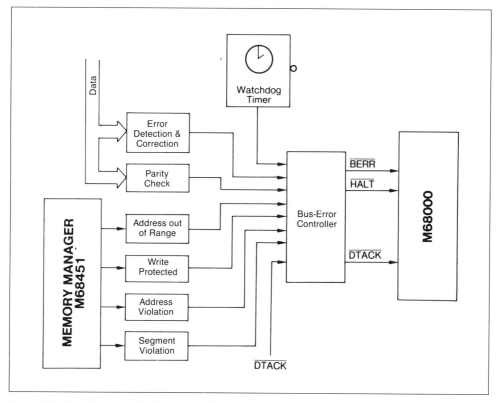

Figure 2-76: Block Diagram with Summary of Potential Errors

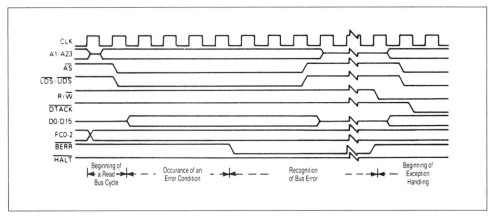

Figure 2-77: Timing Diagram for Bus-Error Exception Handling

When the complemented BERR signal goes low, the microprocessor has two potential courses of action:
1 The microprocessor can initiate exception handling, with the exception vector for a bus error.
2 The microprocessor can repeat the current bus cycle.
The microprocessor selects:
– Case 1 if only the complemented BERR signal goes low and
– Case 2 if the complemented BERR and HALT signals both go low together.
For case 1, the microprocessor interrupts the current bus cycle (read or write) when the complemented BERR signal goes low. It holds the address and data lines in the tri-state condition as long as the complemented BERR signal remains low. When the complemented BERR signal returns to high, the microprocessor begins exception handling, consisting of the following steps:
– saving the contents of the program counter and status register on the stack,
– storing information concerning the error on the stack,
– getting the exception vector for a bus error and
– executing the exception program at that address.
The exception program may be able to use the information concerning the error that is now on the stack to analyze and correct the error. The timing for this case is presented in Figure 2-77 below. (See Section 2-5 above for more detailed information on the handling of exceptions.)
For case 2, the microprocessor interrupts the current bus cycle. It places the address and data lines in the tri-state condition. The microprocessor waits until the complemented HALT and BERR signals return to high, whereby the HALT signal should change exactly one clock cycle before the BERR signal changes. Then, the microprocessor repeats the previous bus cycle that was interrupted by the error condition. All of the other signals from the microprocessor will be the same as for the first attempt to perform the bus cycle. The timing for this case is shown in Figure 2-78 below.
There is one important exception for case 2. The TAS instruction (Test and Set – See Chapter 4) uses a special read-modify-write bus cycle. The microprocessor can not interrupt this double bus cycle and therefore can not repeat it. Therefore, the microprocessor will treat this situation the same as in case 1 above, ie. initiate exception handling – even though the complemented HALT and BERR signals both go low. The flowchart in Figure 2-79 below shows the handling of case 2, including the special exception for the TAS instruction.

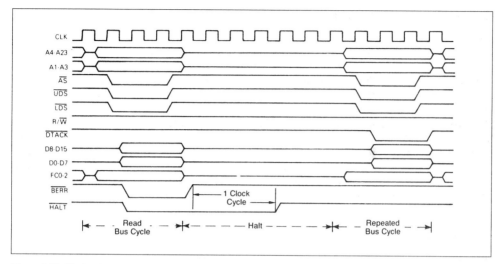

Figure 2-78: Timing Diagram for Repeating a Bus Cycle

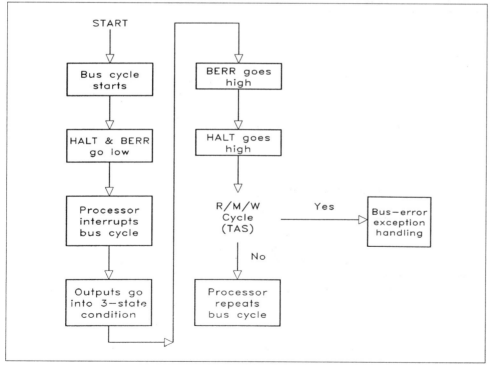

Figure 2-79: Flowchart for Repeating a Bus Cycle

2.10.4   Double Bus Error

At the beginning of bus-error exception handling, the microprocessor saves various data on the stack (program counter, status register, etc.). A double bus error is defined to be the situation where a second bus error (or address error) occurs while this data is being saved on the stack. Since the microprocessor could not save the data from the first bus error, a double bus error stops the microprocessor completely. An external reset is necessary to restart the microprocessor (the complemented RESET signal must go low and then high again).

The first error does not have to be a bus error. Whenever the complemented BERR signal goes low or the microprocessor encounters an address error while the microprocessor is getting an exception vector from the exception-vector table, the result will be a double bus error and the microprocessor will stop.

If the first bus error initiates a rerun bus cycle, no exception handling is involved and therefore a double bus error can not occur. Therefore, the microprocessor will repeat a bus cycle as many times as the external hardware pulls both of the complemented signals for HALT and BERR down to low.

2.10.5   Summary

The table in Figure 2-80 below gives a summary of the different results and uses for the different combinations of external signals on the complemented RESET, HALT and BERR signal lines.

RESET	HALT	BERR	Result and Use
low	low	high	cold restart (power-on reset)
low	high	high	warm restart
high	low	high	stop the processor
high	low	low	repeat a bus cycle
high	high	low	bus-error exception handling
high	high	high	normal operations

Figure 2-80: Summary for the RESET, HALT and BERR Signals

2.11   Direct Memory Access (DMA)

Direct memory access (DMA) is the operation of transfering data directly from one unit to another unit within a system – over the data bus but without using the microprocessor. Therefore, the unit that wants to transfer data to another unit must first inform the microprocessor that it needs the data bus. Otherwise, conflicts would occur with both the microprocessor and the other unit trying to use the system buses (data bus and address bus) at the same time.

The microprocessors of the M68000 family use 3 signals for this control over its system buses:

– BR (bus request),
– BG (bus grant) and
– BGACK (bus-grant acknowledge).

All 3 of these signals are in complemented form at the pins of the microprocessor. The microprocessor and an external DMA controller use a three-wire handshake for negotiating use of the system buses. They are illustrated in Figure 2-81 below.

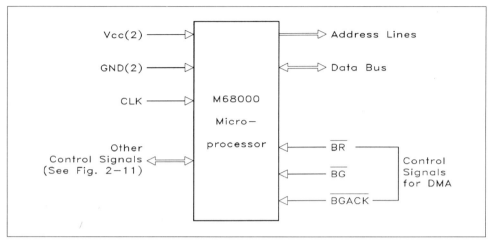

Figure 2-81: DMA Control Signals of M68000 Microprocessors

You can use more than one DMA controller (such as the 6844 or 68450 DMA controllers) in a system, but will then need to, either use extra hardware to resolve priorities, or use a bus-arbitration module (such as the 68452 bus-arbitration module of the M68000 family). You can also use several processors, in a multi-processor system, that compete for using the same buses.

Each microprocessor assigns the lowest priority to itself. Therefore, if any external units request the buses from the microprocessor, the microprocessor will grant the request and wait until the buses are free again. The flowchart in Figure 2-82 below shows the sequential steps for transfering control of the system buses. When an external unit, such as a DMA controller, wants to obtain control over the system buses, it pulls the complemented BR signal down to low. This transition can be synchronous with the system clock. However, it must be active before the falling flank of S4 in order for the microprocessor to recognize it in the current bus cycle. Otherwise, the external unit will have to wait until the end of the next bus cycle. When several external units may request direct memory access, then each of these devices can be connected to the complemented BR pin of the microprocessor. When the signal on this pin goes low, the microprocessor knows that some unit is requestin use of the system buses, but the microprocessor does not know which unit is making the request. The microprocessor will then surrender control ot the system buses to this unknown unit, as soon as the microprocessor complets its current bus cycle.

The microprocessor responds as quickly as possible, ater internal synchronization of the incoming BR signal, by pulling the complemented BG signal down to low. This usually takes two cycles of the system clock. The only exception occurs when the microprocessor has already started the next bus cycle but has not yet activated the address strobe signal (AS). In this case, the activated BG signal occurs one cycle, at the earliest, after the address strobe is active – in order to inform the requesting unit that the microprocessor is still completing a bus cycle. The timing diagram for the standard case ist shown in Figure 2-83 below and the timing diagram for the exception, where the address strobe is not yet active, is shown in Figure 2-84 below.

If several units can request direct memory access, you can send the complemented BG signal from the microprocessor to a bus-arbitration module (such as the 68452) or another module for decoding the priority. This is necessary so that the requesting simultaneously. The microprocessor is not involved in this process of selecting the unit with highest priority. The microprocessor is only concerned that a partner responds with the predefined sequence of signals.

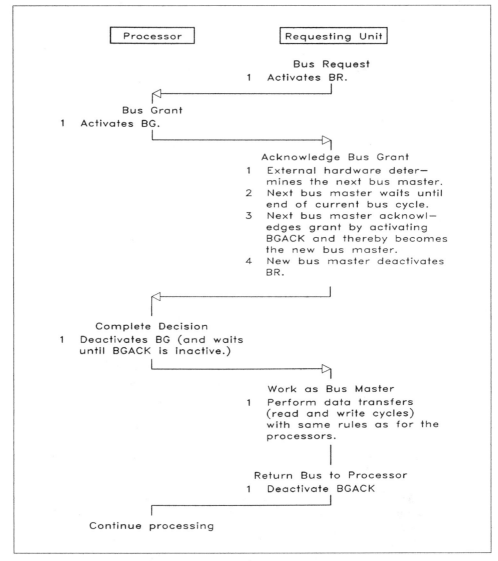

Figure 2-82: Flowchart for Transfering Control over Buses

Once the requesting unit received the BG signal, it must wait until the address strobe (AS), data-transfer acknowledge (DTACK) and bus-grand acknowledge (BGACK) signals are inactive before it can send its own complemented BGACK signal back to the microprocessor. The deactiviation of the AS signal indicates to the rest of the system that the current bus master has completed its current bus cycle. No other unit can interrupt a bus cycle as long as AS is active. The deactivation of the BGACK signal indicates to the rest of the system that the previous bus master has surrendered control over the system buses. The new bus master retains control over the buses from the time that it presents its own active BGACK signal until

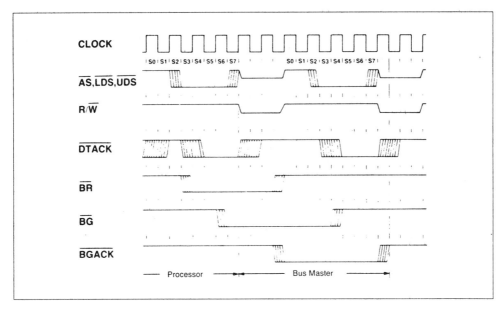

Figure 2-83:Timing Diagram for Bus Transfer (normal case)

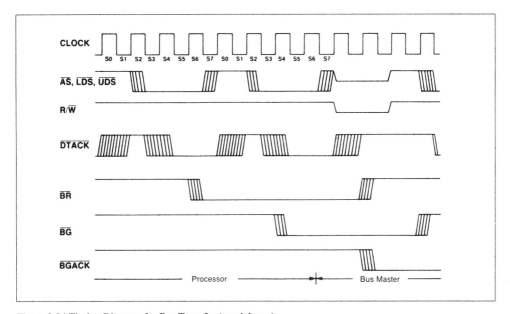

Figure 2-84:Timing Diagram for Bus Transfer (special case)

it deactivates its BGACK signal. The new bus master must complate all of its bus cycles before it deactivates its BGACK signal, bu pulling the complemented signalj line down to low.

IF the active BR signal disappears before the microprocessor receives an active BGACK signal from a requesting unit, the micorprocessor will not surrender control over the buses and will continue with its own operations. This feature protects the system from spurious or glitches that may occur on the complemented BR signal line.

If the BR signal remains active after the BGACK signal has been deactivated, the microprocessor will assume that a new request has arrived from either the same or a different requesting unit. Therfore, the microprocessor will proceed in granting this new request, without using the system buses itself. It is possible therfore that several external units may be waiting with simultaneous bus requests and that they will receive the system buses sequentially according to a priority scheme.

3
Addressing Modes

During the pioneering days of microprocessors, when microprocessors were designed for the single purpose of replacing random logic, the concept of addressing modes was far in the background. The goal of providing a microprocessor with a powerful set of addressing modes only became relevant when microprocessors were designed for use as central processing units (CPU's) in complete computer systems. Addressing modes are very important for the users of computer systems who write software for their systems.

The different addressing modes of a processor are the different ways that an instruction can address locations in memory. These different modes are very helpful when the programmer wants to:

- calculate the address in memory at run time, rather than while writing the program, such as for data structures with dynamic dimensions,
- calculate addresses in the same way that a mathematician expresses vectors, matrices, etc.,
- calculate addresses relative to the given instruction, so that the resulting code will be relocatable and
- use shorter addresses for commonly used addresses in order to shorten the time of execution and length of code.

3.1   General Principles of Addressing Modes

Before describing each addressing mode in detail, in Section 3.2 below, we will first define a few of the relevant concepts.

3.1.1   General Types of Addressing Modes

The M68000 family of microprocessors supports the following general types of addressing modes:
- immediate
- absolute
- register direct
- register indirect
- relative

With **immediate-addressing modes, the operand is specified explicitly** in the instruction itself. This operand is stored either in the next word or words **"immediately"** after the opcode for the instruction or in the opcode itself.

With **absolute-addressing modes, the address of the operand in memory is specified explicitly** in the instruction itself. This **absolute address** is stored in the next word or words after the opcode for the instruction.

With the **register direct-addresing modes,** the operand is in a data register or an address register, and **the register with the operand is specified explicitly** in the instruction. The number of the register is usually stored in the opcode of the instruction.

With the **register indirect-addressing modes,** the address of the operand in memory is stored in an address register. **The register with this address is specified explicitly** in the instruction. The number of the register is usually stored in the opcode of the instruction.

With the **relative-addressing modes,** the address is calculated relative to the current contents of the program counter, ie. where the current instruction is located. In this case, **the offset and/or index for calculating the distance from the current position is specified** in the instruction.

For both the register indirect-addressing modes and the relative-addressing modes, it is possible to use either:
- an offset,
- an index or
- both.

An **offset** is a distance, forwards or backwards, from an already given address. It is specified immediately in the instruction, and it is stored either in the opcode or immediately after the opcode. An **index** is an offset that is stored in an "index register" that can be either a data register or an address register. This index register is specified in the instruction, and it is usually stored in the next word after the opcode. The name "index" comes from its typical use for specifying the index of a value in a table for a vector or a matrix. In a typical application, the offset is used to define the position of the beginning of a table, relative to a given address, and the index is used to specify a particular entry within the table. The actual address is the sum of the given address plus offset plus index.

Each addressing mode is explained in detail, with at least one short example, in Section 3.2 below. The 68020 and 68030 microprocessors add an additional set of addressing modes that is presented in Section 3.8 below.

3.1.2 Definition of an "Effective Address"

We distinguish between:
- a source address,
- a destination address and
- an effective address.

The **source address** is the address from which the processor obtains an operand for an operation. The destination address is the address to which the processor sends the operand that results from an operation. Both the source address and the destination address can refer to either a location in memory or a particular register of the processor. In addition, the source operand can be provided directly as a part of the instruction. We use angle brackets, < >, to refer to the contents stored at an address. Therefore, <source> refers to the operand stored at the source address, rather than the address itself. Likewise, <destination> refers to the operand stored at the destination address.

For a unitary operation, the source address and the destination address are often the same, meaning that the processor obtains the operand from an address, operates upon that operand and returns the result to the same address. In this case, it is common practice to refer to both addresses as the destination address.

For a binary operation, the processor often obtains the first operand from a source address and the second operand from the same address that will later become the destination address for the result of the operation. In this case, it is common practice to refer to the source address for the second operand as the destination address.

An **effective address** can be either the source address or the destination address for an operand. It is calculated by the processor, using the addressing mode that is specified, together with the parameters that are provided for that addressing mode. We will use the notation:

− <ea> to refer to the addressing mode, plus parameters, and

− <ea> to refer to the calculated value of an effective address in memory.

The addressing mode for calculating an effective address is specified by a special syntax that includes parameters, in an instruction of an assembler language. Examples are (A3)+ and $5(A1). The assembler specifies the effective address as a 6-bit field in the opcode for an instruction that is divided further into two 3-bit subfields with the names

− effective-address mode and

− effective-address register.

For the first 7 effective-address modes, the contents of the effective-address register contain the number of the data register or address register used (from 0 to 7). The 8th effective-address mode is subdivided into 8 cases by the entry of a number from 0 to 7 in the subfield for the effective-address register.

This structure for defining the effective address gives the M68000 microprocessors 15 potential addressing modes, but only 12 are used by the 68000 microprocessor. They are illustrated in Figure 3-1 below for the 68000, 68808, 68010 and 68012 microprocessors (the addressing modes are expanded for the 68020 and 68030 microprocessors − see Section 3.8 below).

| Effective Address | | Addressing Mode | Mnemonic |
Mode	Register		
000	Reg. No.	Data-Register Direct	Dn
001	Reg. No.	Address-Register Direct	An
010	Reg. No.	Address-Register Indirect (ARI)	(An)
011	Reg. No.	ARI with Postincrement	(An)+
100	Reg. No.	ARI with Predecrement	−(An)
101	Reg. No.	ARI with Offset	d16(An)
110	Reg. No.	ARI with Index and Offset	d8(An,Rx)
111	000	Short-Address Absolute	$XXXX
111	001	Long-Address Absolute	$XXXXXXXX
111	010	PC Relative with Offset	d16(PC)
111	011	PC Relative with Index and Offset	d8(PC,Rx)
111	100	Immediate Data, Status-Register Im.	#,SR,CCR
111	101	(not used)	
111	111	(not used)	

Figure 3-1: Summary of the Addressing Modes

Different authors usually list more than 12 addressing modes for the 68000, 68008, 68010 and 68012 microprocessors, using different variations of these 12 basic addressing modes to obtain 2 or 3 additional addressing modes. We will use 19 addressing modes in this book. (The 68020 and 68030 have additional addressing modes, as explained in Section 3.8 below.)

First, by splitting the mode for immediate data (effective address = 111 100) as follows, we obtain 3 additional modes:

− immediate byte data

− immediate word data

− immediate long-word data

− immediate quick (special case)

Second, by including separate register direct-addressing modes for the status register and condition-code register, this group is expanded from 2 to 4 addressing modes, as follows:

- data-register direct
- address-register direct
- status-register direct
- condition-code-register direct

Finally, by including the branch instructions as a relative addressing mode (relative to the program counter), there are two more addressing modes, for

- branching with an 8-bit offset and
- branching with a 16-bit offset.

Some authors also refer to:

- quick immediate (using inherent or implied data) and
- implied register (using SR, USP, SP and PC registers)

as additional addressing modes. (As you can see from the difficulty in counting the number of addressing modes for the 68000 microprocssor, it is difficult to compare processors in a table by simply comparing the number of addressing modes that they supposedly have. You should also consider the power of the individual addressing modes and how they are broken down into submodes for the purpose of counting.)

3.1.3   Syntax for Instructions

Instructions appear differently:

- as an "opcode" in the machine language of a processor and
- as an "instruction" in an assembler language.

It is the task of an assembler or disassembler to translate between these two formats. Even though a programmer usually works only with the instructions of an assembler language (or a high-level language), it is often useful to know how the opcodes appear in the machine language. If you need to examine the assembled code, such as for debugging a program that is running, you will need to understand the structure of the opcodes. Therefore, both formats are presented in this book, usually side-by-side.

An M68000 microprocessor can process bytes (8 bits), words (16 bits) and long words (32 bits) as operands. Therefore, whenever a particular operation can process different sizes of operands, it is necessary to specify the actual size in both the instruction of the assembler language and the opcode of the machine language.

Each opcode for an M68000 microprocessor has 16 bits, ie. one word. It can also be followed by one or more words of data or parameters, before the next opcode. Each opcode has a general syntax or structure with 3 fields, as illustrated in Figure 3-2 below:

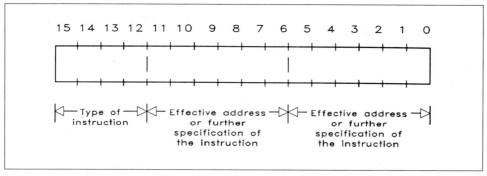

Figure 3-2: General Syntax of an Opcode

For most opcodes, the first field (bits 15–12) defines the type of instruction, whereby several different instructions may have the same type. The second field (bits 11–6) then specifies further which instruction is involved from this set and provides other parameters for the instruction. The third field (bits 5–0) usually contains an effective address but may contain further specifications and parameters for the instruction. If the second and third fields both contain an effective address, then the first field must specify one instruction without ambiguity, the second field will specify the destination address for an operand, and the third field will specify the source address for an operand. If only the third field contains an effective address, it can be for either a source address or a destination address.

However, there are some exceptions to this general structure that are described in detail in Chapter 4 for those particular instructions.

The general syntax or structure of an instruction in the assembler language is shown in Figure 3-3 below:

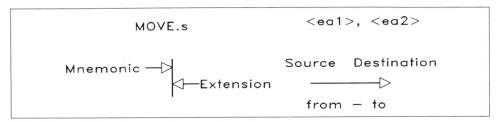

Figure 3-3: General Syntax of an Instruction

The mnemonic is a simple abbreviation for the instruction that is easy to remember. The extension specifies whether the operands are bytes, words or long words – when the instruction can use more than one size of operand. There are only 3 values for w as follows:

B	–	operand size is one byte (8 bits)
W	–	operand size is one word (16 bits)
L	–	operand size is one long word (32 bits)

If the instruction only uses one size of operand, you can omit the extension. If you omit the extension when two or more sizes are allowed, the assembler will usually use W for word size as the default value.

The M68000 microprocessors are true two-address machines. Therefore, you can specify an effective address for each of two operands of a binary operation. The first address is usually the source address and the second address is usually the destination address. For binary operations, the second address is used both as the source address for the second operand and the destination address for the result, but it is usually refered to as the destination address.

The most commonly-used instruction of the M68000 microprocessors is the MOVE instruction, illustrated in Figure 3-4 below. Merely by reversing the source and destination addresses, you can use it to load an operand from memory into a register or to store an operand from a register into memory. Therefore, it replaces the more limited LDA and STA instructions in the instruction sets of some other processors. You can also use it for reading from and writing to input/output ports of peripheral interface devices. You should note that the source address is specified **before** the destination address in the syntax of an assembler language, but the source address usually occurs **after** the destination address in the opcode of the machine language.

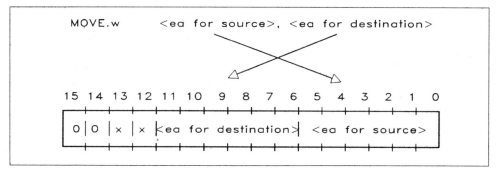

Figure 3-4: Comparison Between Instruction and Opcode Syntaxes

3.1.4   A Model for Representing Addressing Modes

A model is presented in Figure 3-5 below for representing the effects of addressing modes. This same model will appear in the detailed description of each individual addressing mode in the rest of this chapter. It shows the status of the processor (program counter and registers that are used) as well as both the program memory and data memory – both before and after the processor executes an instruction.

The contents of the registers and locations in memory are shown as hexadecimal numbers. Only those registers are shown in each model that are relevant to the given example. The difference in the program counter, before and after the operation, is shown and depends upon the number of bytes used by the opcode and any immediate operands that may follow the opcode. This can be expressed by the following formulas:

Increment of PC (in bytes) = 2 + 2 x number of operand words
0 ≤ number of operand words ≤ 4
1

Restated, each opcode has exactly one word in size (2 bytes) and it can be followed by a maximum of 4 immediate words of data (2 bytes each) for a maximum of 5 words in size (10 bytes) exception: 68020 and 68030. The choices for the starting addresses in program memory and data memory are usually arbitrary. The syntax for each instruction and its opcode is given in detail in Chapter 4.

A short description of each example follows as text in a standard format after each picture with the model. More detailed programming examples for the addressing modes are given in Chapter 6.

3.1.5   Addressing Modes and Addressing Categories

The addressing modes of the M68000 microprocessors can be divided into the following main types:
– immediate (data)
– absolute (address)
– register direct
– address-register indirect
– relative (to the program counter)

A summary listing of the 12 main addressing modes for these types is given in Figure 3-6 below. Detailed examples are given in the next section of this chapter for each of the addressing modes in each of these groups.

Some authors also define 4 addressing categories in order to give a name to the combinations of instruc-

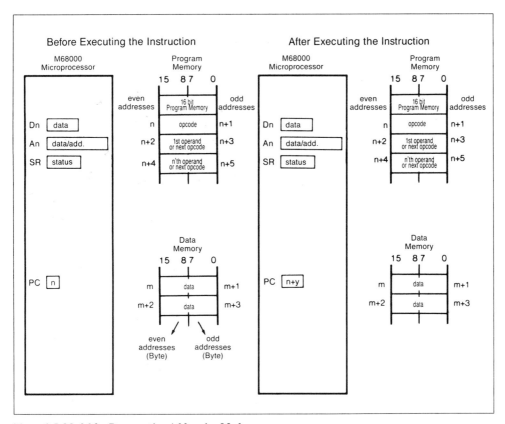

Figure 3-5: Model for Representing Addressing Modes

Addressing Modes	Addressing Categories			
	Data	**Memory**	**Control**	**Alterable**
Dn	X			X
An				X
(An)	X	X	X	X
(An)+	X	X		X
−(An)	X	X		X
d16(An)	X	X	X	X
d8(An,Rx)	X	X	X	X
$XXXX	X	X	X	X
$XXXXXXXX	X	X	X	X
d16(PC)	X	X	X	
d8(PC, Rx)	X	X	X	
# , SR,CCR	X	X		

Figure 3-6: Addressing Modes and Categories

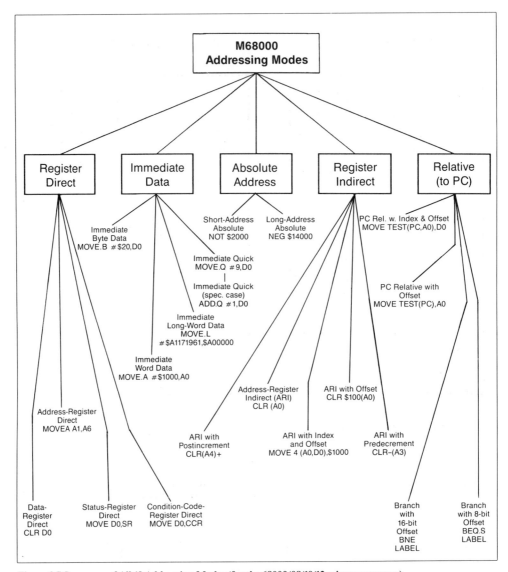

Figure 3-7:Summary of All 19 Addressing Modes (for the 68000/08/10/12 microprocessors)

tions and the 12 main addressing modes that are allowed and not allowed. (It is not useful or allowed to use every instruction with every combination of addressing modes for source and destination addresses.) These categories are not necessary in this book because tables show all allowed combinations explicitly for each instruction in Chapter 4. They are presented briefly here only to make this presentation complete. These 4 addressing categories are: data, memory, control and variable. Figure 3-6 below presents a matrix of the 12 main addressing modes and these 4 addressing categories.

Even more limited subcategories can be derived from these categories. Only those addressing modes are allowed for a category that are listed under the category in Figure 3-6 above.

Figure 3-7 below presents a summary of all 19 addressing modes, together with appropriate examples.

3.2   Register Direct-Addressing Modes

The register direct-addressing modes specify a register directly, that contains the operand, by giving the number of the data register or address register or the name of another register. We distinguish between the following different register direct-addressing modes, by the type of register involved:

– data-register direct
– address-register direct
– status-register direct
– condition-code-register direct

Each of these addressing modes is described separately in detail below.

3.2.1   Data-Register Direct-Addressing Mode

Assembler Notation:

Dn $(0 \leq n \leq 7)$

<ea> in Opcode:

Mode	Register
0 0 0	Reg. No.

The bit pattern 000 appears in the subfield for the mode and the number of the data register appears in the subfield for the register number.

Example 1:

CLR D0		
CLR.W D0		(equivalent notation)
Instruction	= CLR	
Length of Operand	= W	(optional, W = default)
Effective Address	= D0	(destination address)

Model for Operation:

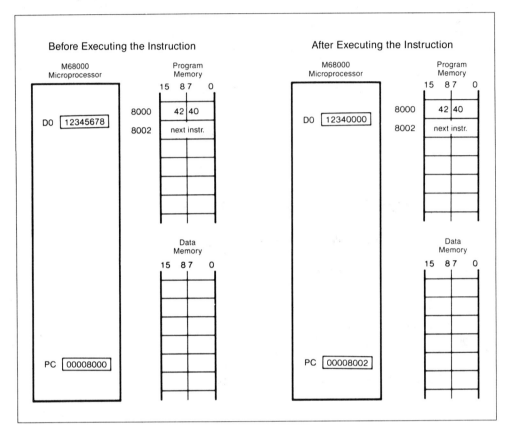

Description:

This instruction clears the contents of data register D0 by filling D0 with zeros. Since the register contains 32 bits and this particular example is for a word operation, it will only clear the least-significant half of the register.

For this example, we have used the arbitrary address of $8000 for the location of the opcode. Since the opcode is 2 bytes long, the program counter must be at $8000 + $2 = $8002 after executing the instruction.

In order to clear the whole register, it is necessary to specify that the operand is a long word with 32 bits as follows:

CLR.L D0
This is illustrated in example 2 below.

Example 2:

CLR.L D0
Instruction   = CLR
Length of Operand   = L   (optional, W = default)
Effective Address   = D0   (destination address)

Model for Operation:

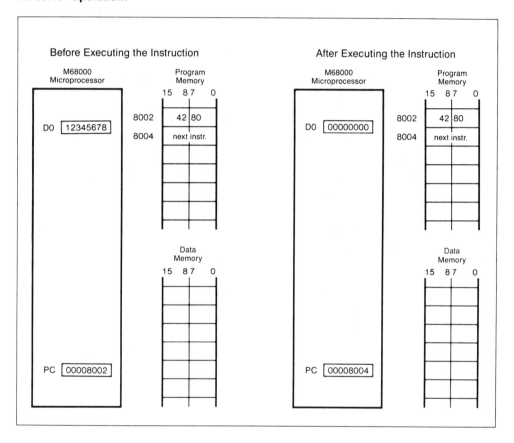

Description:

This instruction clears all 32 bits in the data register D0 by filling D0 with zeros.

In the two examples above, the CLR instruction performs a unitary operation and uses only one address. In the following example, the MOVE instruction is also a unitary operation, but it uses both a source address and a destination address – illustrating the M68000 microprocessors as two-address machines.

Example 3:

MOVE D0,D3		
MOVE.W D0,D3		(equivalent notation)
Instruction	= MOVE	
Length of Operand	= W	(optional)
Effective Address	= D0	(source address)
Effective Address	= D3	(destination address)

Model for Operation:

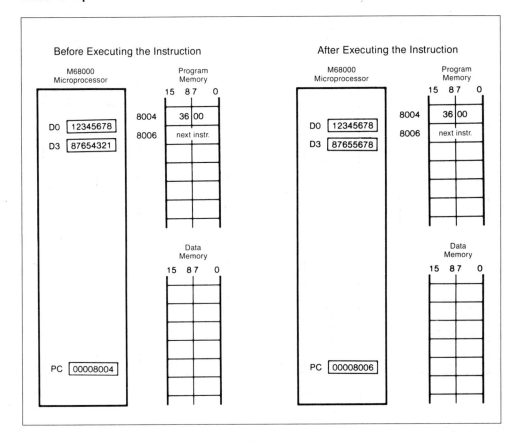

Description:

This instruction copies the contents in the least-significant half of data register D0 into the least-significant half of data register D3. It leaves all of the contents in D0 unchanged, and it also leaves the most-significant half of D3 unchanged. It has a one-word opcode that does not have any extra data words attached to it. To copy all 32 bits of data from one data register to another data register, you must use the extension .L, as follows:

```
MOVE.L D0,D3
```

To copy only the least-significant byte from one data register to another data register, you must use the extension .B.

Application:

This addressing mode is used for a large variety of uses, such as loading, storing, saving, shifting and copying data as well as loop counters and index registers.

3.2.2 Address-Register Direct-Addressing Mode

Assembler Notation:

```
An (0 ≤ n ≤ 7)
```

< ea > in Opcode:

Mode	Register
0 0 1	Reg. No.

The bit pattern 001 appears in the subfield for the mode and the number of the data register appears in the subfield for the register number.

Example:

```
MOVEA.L D3,A1
MOVE.L D3,A1                      (equivalent notation for some assemblers)
Instruction          = MOVEA
Length of Operand    = W          (optional)
Effective Address    = D3         (source address)
Effective Address    = A1         (destination address)
```

Model for Operation:

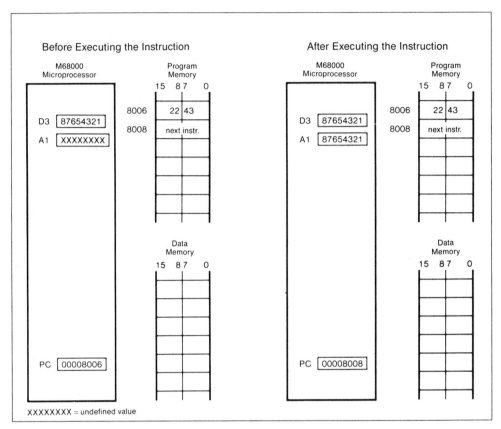

Description:

This instruction copies all 32 bits of the contents of data register D3 into address register A1. The contents of D3 remain unchanged.

Remark: When you want to use the MOVE instruction address register as the destination address, it is necessary to use the special MOVEA instruction for most assemblers. The result is the same opcode as for the MOVE instruction, except that it is limited to only word and long-word operands. When you copy a word (16 bits) into an address register, it will automatically be expanded to a 32-bit value, with the correct sign (see Section 3.4.2 below for an explanation of this expansion).

Application:

This addressing mode is used for a large variety of uses, such as loading, storing, saving, shifting and copying data as well as index registers.

3.2.3 Status-Register (and Condition-Code-Register) Direct-Addressing Mode

Assembler Notation:

SR	(all 16 bits of the Status Register) or
CCR	(the least-significant 8 bits of the Status Register – called the Condition-Code Register)

< ea > in Opcode:

Mode	Register
1 1 1	1 0 0

The bit pattern 111 appears in the subfield for the mode, and 100 appears in the subfield for the register number.

Example 1:

MOVE D3,SR		
MOVE.W D3,SR		(equivalent notation)
Instruction	= MOVE	
Length of Operand	= W	(optional)
Effective Address	= D3	(source address)
Effective Address	= SR	(destination address)

Model for Operation:

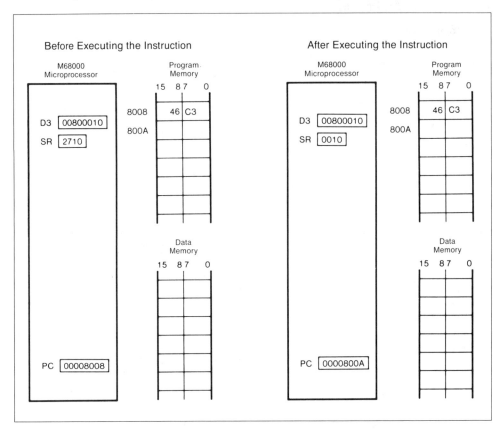

Description:

This instruction copies the least-significant 16 bits of the contents of data register D3 into the status register. The contents of D3 remain unchanged.

Remark: This is a privileged instruction that is only allowed in the supervisor mode. When an M68000 microprocessor encounters this instruction while in the user mode, it will initiate exception handling.

Example 2:

MOVE D3,CCR		
MOVE.W D3,CCR		(equivalent notation)
Instruction	= MOVE	
Length of Operand	= W	(optional)
Effective Address	= D3	(source address)
Effective Address	= CCR	(destination address)

Model for Operation:

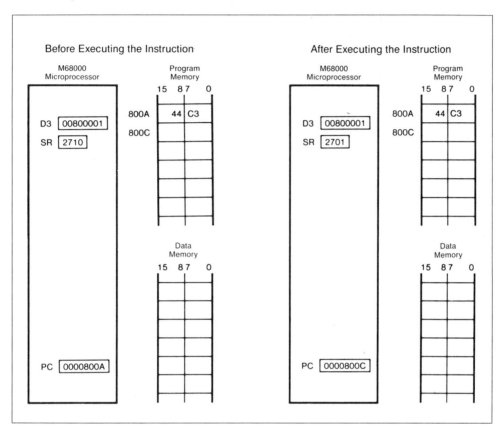

Description:

This instruction copies the least-significant 8 bits of the contents of data register D3 into the condition-code register (the least-significant half of the status register). The contents of D3 remain unchanged.

Remark: This is not a privileged instruction, as is the case for MOVE D3,SR, and therefore it is allowed in both the user and the supervisor modes. The length of the operand is word (16 bits), even though only the least-significant byte (8 bits) is copied – actually only 5 of these bits, corresponding to flags, are actually copied.

3.3 Absolute-Addressing Modes

The absolute-addressing modes specify an address in memory directly, by including the explicit address as an extra word or pair of words after the opcode. We distinguish between the:

– short-address absolute-addressing mode (using one 16-bit word after the opcode for the address) and
– long-address absolute-addressing mode (using 24 bits of 2 16-bit words after the opcode for the address).

The 68000 microprocessor can address a memory space of 16 megabytes linearly. To do so requires a 24-bit address. With only 16 bits for the address, the short absolute-addressing mode can only address a 64-kilobyte memory space.

Addresses for 68000 microprocessors are always signed numbers. Therefore, the most-significant bit of a 16-bit address defines whether the address is at the top or the bottom of the 16-megabyte address space. The remaining 15 bits in the address define the address within these two blocks of 32 kilobytes each. This is illustrated in Figure 3-8 below:

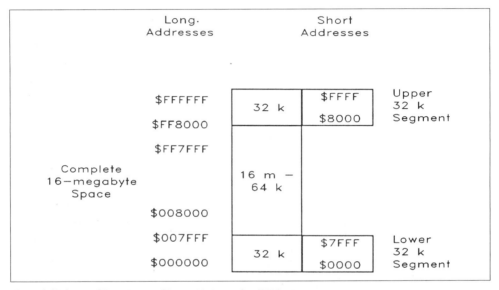

Figure 3-8:Memory Map (short and long addresses) (for 68000 microprocessor)

The long-address absolute-addressing mode is therefore all that is needed. However, the short-address absolute-addressing mode has advantages in requiring two bytes less of code and being faster in its execution – whenever it is not necessary to address the complete 16 megabytes of memory space.

This chapter contains not only examples of absolute addressing but also for processing bytes, words and long words of data as well as writing one byte at-a-time at even and uneven addresses.

3.3.1   Short-Address Absolute-Addressing Mode

Assembler Notation:

$xxxx	(can also be written as $FFxxxx)
	$0 \leq \$xxxx \leq \$7FFF$
	$0 \leq xxxx \leq 32767$

<ea> in Opcode:

Mode	Register
1 1 1	0 0 0

The bit pattern 111 appears in the subfield for the mode, and the bit pattern 000 appears in the subfield for the register.

Example 1:

```
NOT.L $2000
Instruction              = NOT
Length of Operand        = L        (optional, W = default)
Effective Address        = $2000    (destination address)
```

Model for Operation:

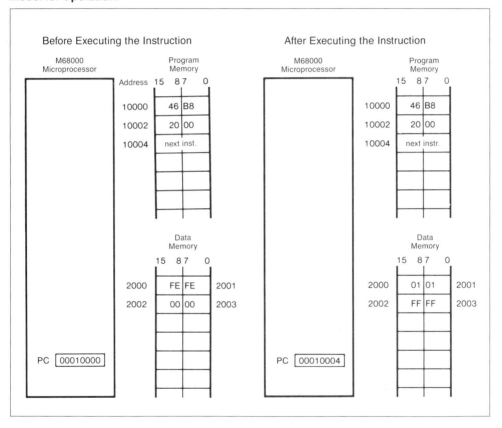

Description:

This instruction inverts the contents of the effective address, beginning at the address $2000 in memory. The extension ".L" in the assembler notation specifies the operation for long words, ie. for the 4 bytes starting at the address $2000 and continuing up to and including the 4th byte at $2003. (If the extension were ".W", then the opcode would be different and it would only operate on 2 bytes at $2000 and $2001. If the extension were ".B", then it would only operate on 1 byte at $2000.) Although the 68000 microprocessor can operate with words, it can also operate with bytes and therefore it addresses data as bytes in memory.

The opcode for this instruction uses two words (4 bytes) as illustrated above.

Example 2:

MOVE $1000,$2000		
MOVE.W $1000,$2000		(equivalent notation)
Instruction	= MOVE	
Length of Operand	= W	(optional, W = default)
Effective Address	= $1000	(source address)
Effective Address	= $2000	(destination address)

Model for Operation:

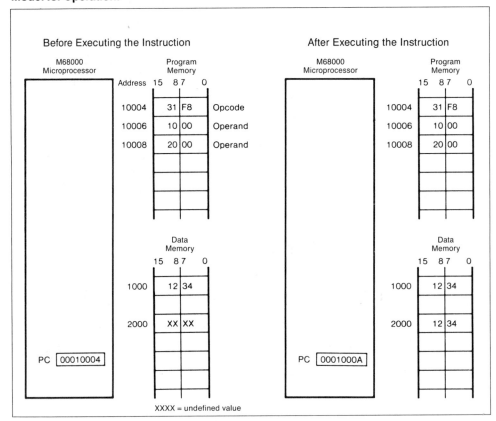

Description:

The MOVE instruction copies data from one location to another location. In this case, the lack of an extension specifies the default case for operating upon a word (2 bytes). Therefore, it copies the two bytes located at $1000 and $1001 (the source address) into the locations $2000 and $2001 (the destination address) without changing the orginal contents at $1000 and $1001.

The opcode plus 2 extra words for the two addresses in this example of the MOVE instruction uses 3 words (6 bytes) as illustrated above.

Example 3:

```
MOVE D0,$1F00
MOVE.W D0,$1F00                    (equivalent notation)
Instruction            = MOVE
Length of Operand      = W         (optional, W = default)
Effective Address      = D0        (source address)
Effective Address      = $1F00     (destination address)
```

Model for Operation:

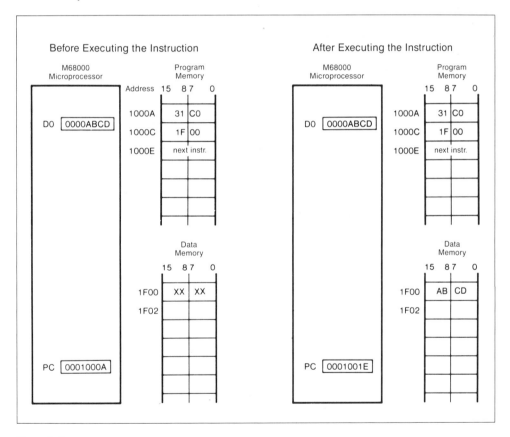

Description:

The MOVE instruction copies data from one location to another location. In this case, the lack of an extension specifies the default case for operating on a word (2 bytes). Therefore, it copies the two least-significant bytes located in the lower half of the data register D0 (the source address) into the locations $1F00 and $1F01 (the destination address) without changing the orginal contents of D0. In this case, two different addressing modes are used, the data-register direct-addressing mode for the source address and the short-address absolute-addressing mode for the destination address.

The opcode plus 1 extra word for the one absolute short address in this example of the MOVE instruction uses 2 words (4 bytes) as illustrated above.

Note:

The 68000 microprocessor can read and write words and long words starting only at even addresses. If you attempt to read or write words or long words at uneven addresses, the M68000 will switch to exception handling (using the exception vector for an address error).

Example 4:

MOVE.B D0,$1F00
Instruction   = MOVE
Length of Operand   = B   (optional, W = default)
Effective Address   = D0   (source address)
Effective Address   = $1F00   (destination address)

Model for Operation:

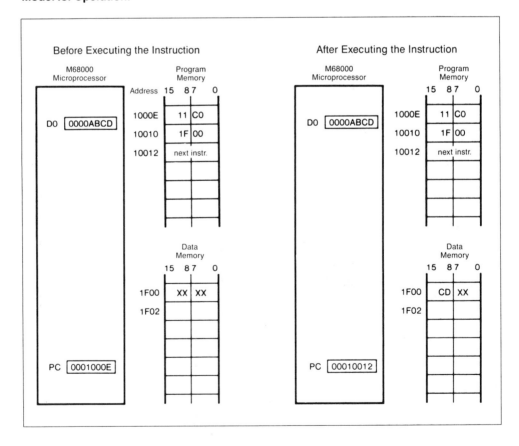

Description:

This example is the same as Example 3 above, except that it copies one byte instead of one word.

The MOVE instruction copies data from one location to another location. The extension ".B" specifies operations on a byte of data. Therefore, it copies the least-significant byte in the data register D0 (the source address) into the location $1F00 (the destination address) without changing the orginal contents of D0.

Note: In order to copy bytes other than the least-significant byte out of a register, you must first use either a shift instruction or a rotate instruction, to place the desired byte at the bottom of the register.

Example 5:

```
MOVE.B D0,$1F01
Instruction            = MOVE
Length of Operand      = B        (optional, W = default)
Effective Address      = D0       (source address)
Effective Address      = $1F01    (destination address)
```

Model for Operation:

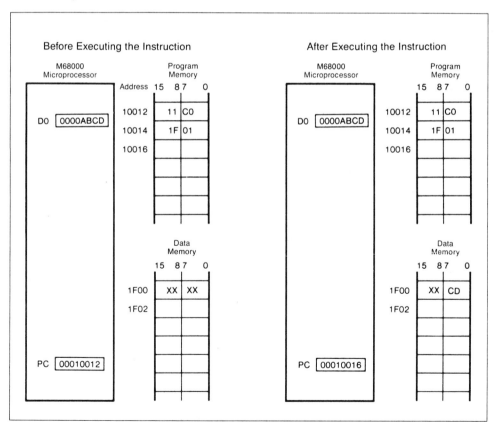

Description:

This example is the same as in Example 4 above, except that it uses an odd address in memory.

The MOVE instruction copies data from one location to another location. The extension ".B" specifies operations on a byte of data. Therefore, it copies the least-significant byte in the data register D0 (the source address) into the location $1F01 (the destination address) without changing the orginal contents of D0.

Note: In order to copy bytes other than the least-significant byte out of a register, you must first use either a shift instruction or a rotate instruction to place the desired byte at the bottom of the register.

Example 6:

```
MOVE.L D0,$1F00
Instruction          = MOVE
Length of Operand    = L        (optional, W = default)
Effective Address    = D0       (source address)
Effective Address    = $1F00    (destination address)
```

Model for Operation:

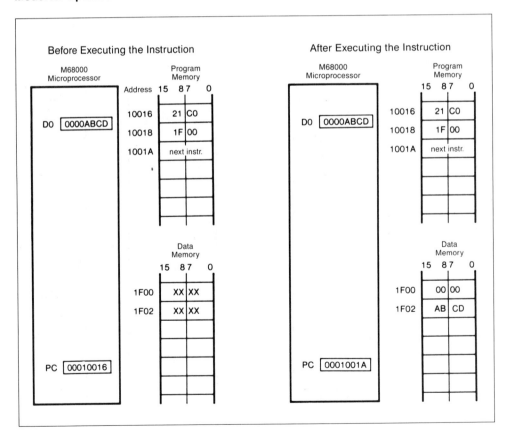

Description:

This example is the same as in Example 3 above, except that it uses a long word.
The MOVE instruction copies data from one location to another location. The extension ".L" specifies operations on a long word of data. Therefore, it copies the whole contents of the data register D0 (the source address) into the locations from $1F00 to $1F03 (the destination address) without changing the orginal contents of D0.

Application:

Using the short-address absolute-addressing mode, whenever possible, instead of the more general long-address absolute-addressing mode, saves both time for execution and bytes of code for the program. (The processor only requires one access to memory to construct a 16-bit short address.) Therefore, you can optimize a program by identifying variables or addresses that the program uses often and locating them in the 64-kilobyte segment of memory that this efficient addressing mode can address. You can also use the physical partition of this 64-kilobyte segment into two 32-kilobyte segments at the top and bottom of memory to distinguish logically and physically between different types of addresses, such as by using RAM in the lower segment and peripheral-port addresses in the upper segment.

3.3.2 Long-Address Absolute-Addressing Mode

Assembler Notation:

```
$xxxxxxxx          0 ≤ $xxxxxxxx ≤ $FFFFFFFF
0 ≤ xxxxxxxx ≤ 4,294,967,295
```

This full range of values is only useful for manipulating data and registers. For addresses with only 24 address lines, the following practical range applies:

```
0 ≤ $xxxxxxxx ≤ $FFFFFF
0 ≤ xxxxxxxx ≤ 16,777,215
```

<ea> in Opcode:

Mode	Register
1 1 1	0 0 1

The bit pattern 111 appears in the subfield for the mode, and the bit pattern 001 appears in the subfield for the register.

Example 1:

```
NEG $14000
NEG.W $14000              (equivalent notation)
Instruction        = NEG
Length of Operand  = W    (optional, W = default)
Effective Address  = $14000  (destination address)
```

Model for Operation:

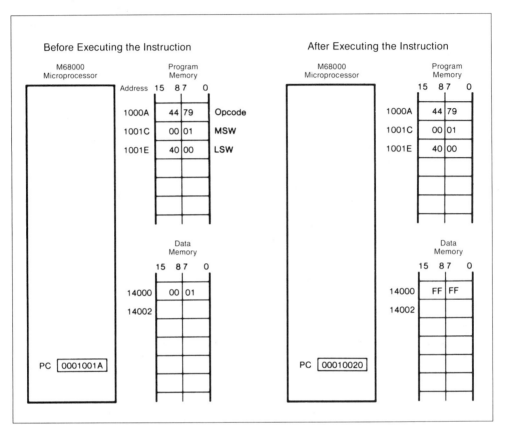

| MSW | = most-significant word |
| LSW | = least-significant word |

Description:

The NEG instruction makes the two's complement out of an operand, ie. converts a positive number into a negative number and vice versa. If no extension is given, then the default value is "W" for operating upon one word of data. Therefore, this instruction complements the word stored at the addresses $14000 and $14001 and places the results back into the same addresses.

The opcode for this instruction uses 3 words (6 bytes). The opcode itself uses 1 word and the next two words contain the absolute long address, with the most-significant half first and the least-significant half second.

Example 2:

MOVE.L $100000,$200000
Instruction	= MOVE	
Length of Operand	= L	(optional, W = default)
Effective Address	= $100000	(source address)
Effective Address	= $200000	(destination address)

Model for Operation:

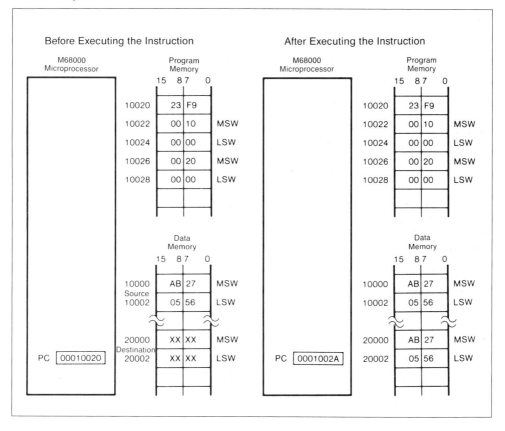

Description:

The MOVE instruction copies data from one location to another location. The extension ".L" specifies operations on a long word of data. Therefore, it copies the long word starting at address $100000 (source address) into the location starting at $200000 (destination address) without changing the contents at $100000. By specifying both addresses absolutely, it does not use any address registers or data registers. This is one of the longest instructions when coded, since it uses 4 words after the opcode, for a total of 5 words (10 bytes).

Application:

You can use this instruction whenever you need to use an address in memory that lies outside of the two 32-kilobyte segments at the top and bottom of memory that you can address with the short-address absolute-addressing mode.

3.4   Immediate-Addressing Modes

For the immediate-addressing modes, the data follows immediately after the opcode. (By contrast, for the absolute-addressing modes, the address follows immediately after the opcode.) The notation, depending upon the size of the operand is as follows:

# x	quick (special case of byte)
# xx	byte
# xxxx	word
# xxxxxxxx	long word

< ea > in Opcode:

Mode	Register
1 1 1	1 0 0

As a special case, the immediate operand for the MOVEQ instruction is contained in the opcode itself, rather than immediately after the opcode.

Some instructions (such as ADD, AND and SUB) have special mnemonics when using an immediate-addressing mode. For example:

ADD # $20,D6 should be written as ADDI # $20,D6

Most assemblers will accept both notations and use the correct opcode.

The bit combinations in the effective address are the same for all of the immediate-addressing modes. The only difference is in other bits that specify the size of the operands.

3.4.1   Immediate-Addressing Mode for Bytes (and Quick)

Assembler Notation:

# xx	$80 ≤ $xx ≤ $7F	
	$-128 ≤ xx ≤ +128$	

< ea > in Opcode:

Mode	Register
1 1 1	1 0 0

There are two submodes, depending upon whether the byte is included in the opcode or follows as the least-significant half of the next word. They are called:

– immediate-addressing mode quick (byte is in opcode) and
– immediate-addressing mode byte (byte is after opcode).

Example 1:

MOVEQ #$5A,D3
Instruction   = MOVEQ
Length of Operand   = W   (optional, L = default)
Immediate Operand   = $5A
Effective Address   = D3   (destination address)

From its functions, this instruction is equivalent to:

MOVE.L #$5A,D3

but MOVEQ is both shorter and faster in its execution.

Model for Operation:

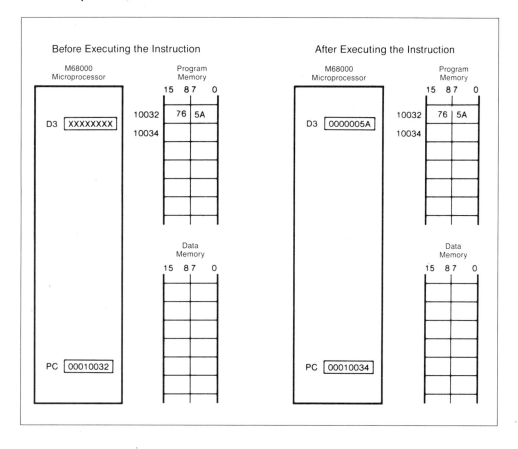

Description:

The MOVEQ instruction expands the immediate value of $5A into a long word and copies the result into the data register D3 (destination address). Since the most-significant bit in $5A is zero, this expansion will fill the rest of the register with zeros.

Remark: This instruction can only copy to data registers.

Example 2:

MOVEQ #$84,D3		
Instruction	= MOVEQ	
Length of Operand	= W	(optional, L = default)
Immediate Operand	= $84	
Effective Address	= D3	(destination address)

Model for Operation:

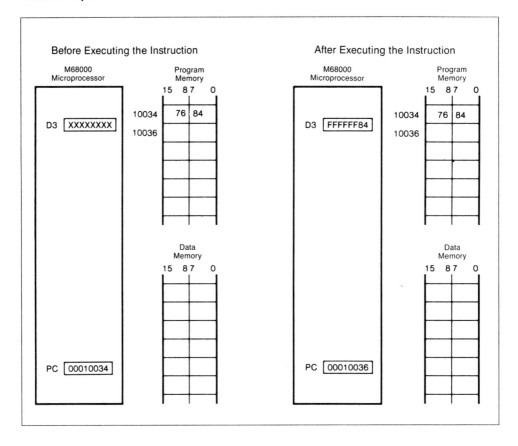

Description:

This example is the same as in Example 1 above, except that the constant is greater than $80.
In this case, the expansion of the constant fills bits 8–31 of the data register with ones, instead of zeros.

Application:

You can use this instruction and addressing mode when you need to load a constant with a value from –128 to +127 into a data register for use as a loop counter or a flag (such as for managing different tasks).

3.4.2   Immediate-Addressing Mode for Words

Assembler Notation:

# xxxx	$0 \leq \$xxxx \leq \$FFFF$
	$0 \leq xxxx \leq 65,535$

This range of values applies only when the destination address is a data register. The following range applies for addresses:

$$\$8000 \leq \$xxxx \leq \$7FFF$$
$$-32,768 \leq xxxx \leq + 32,767$$

<ea> in Opcode:

Mode	Register
1 1 1	1 0 0

The immediate constant is in the word immediately after the opcode.

Example 1:

MOVEA #$1000,A0		
MOVE.W #$1000,A0		(equivalent for some assemblers)
Instruction	= MOVEA	
Length of Operand	= W	(optional, W = default)
Immediate Operand	= $1000	
Effective Address	= A0	(destination address)

Model for Operation:

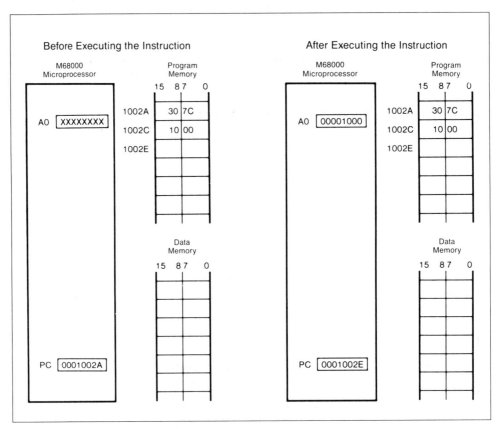

Description:

The MOVEA instruction expands the operand $1000 into a 32-bit double word and writes the result in the address register A0.

Remark: When a MOVE instruction writes a word into a register, it expands the word by repeating the most-significant bit of the word if the register is an address register–but not if the register is a data register (as shown in the following example).

Example 2:

MOVE #$1000,D0		
MOVE.W #$1000,D0		(equivalent notation)
Instruction	= MOVE	
Length of Operand	= W	(optional, W = default)
Immediate Operand	= $1000	
Effective Address	= D0	(destination address)

Model for Operation:

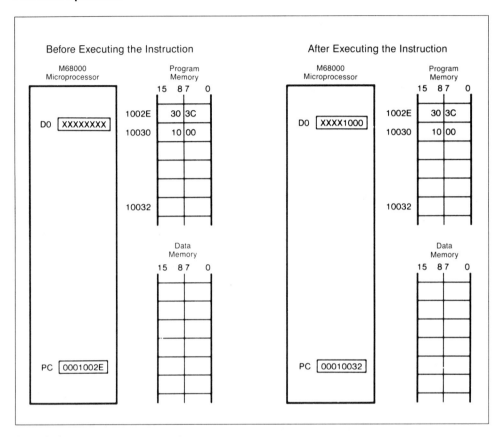

Description:

This example is the same as in Example 1 above, except the the immediate word of $1000 is written into the data register D0, instead of the address register A0. In this case, with a data register, the MOVE instruction does not expand the word. Therefore, this instruction does not change the most-significant half of the data register D0.

Remark: The table in Figure 3-9 below illustrates the differences in the effect of the immediate-addressing modes upon the MOVE instruction when the destination address is an address register or a data register.

```
MOVE #$1000,DO          <DO> = $xxxx1000
MOVE #$1000,AO          <AO> = $00001000
MOVE #$8000,DO          <DO> = $xxxx8000
MOVE #$8000,AO          <AO> = $FFFF8000

MOVE.L #$1000,DO        <DO> = $00001000
MOVE.L #$1000,AO        <AO> = $00001000
MOVE.L #$8000,DO        <DO> = $00008000
MOVE.L #$8000,AO        <AO> = $00008000
```

Figure 3-9: Examples of Immediate Operations

3.4.3   Immediate-Addressing Mode for Long Words

Assembler Notation:

# xxxxxxxx	$0 \leq \$xxxxxxxx \leq \$FFFFFFFF$
	$0 \leq xxxxxxxx \leq 4,294,967,295$

< ea > in Opcode:

Mode	Register
1 1 1	1 0 0

The immediate constant is in the two words immediately after the opcode.

Example 1:

MOVE.L # $B1021958,$A00000		
MOVE.L # $B1021958,$0A00000		(equivalent notation)
Instruction	= MOVE	
Length of Operand	= L	(optional, W = default)
Immediate Operand	= $B1021958	
Effective Address	= $A00000	(destination address)

Model for Operation:

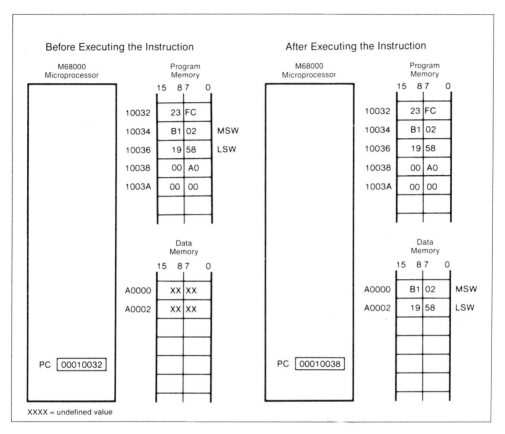

Before Executing the Instruction

After Executing the Instruction

XXXX = undefined value

Description:

The MOVE instruction loads the immediate constant $B1021958 into memory, starting at the location $A00000.

Application:

Processing immediate constants that are greater than 65,535.

General Applications for the Immediate-Addressing Modes: You can use the immediate-addressing modes whenever you need to load, store, add, subtract, compare or test with constants.

Another use is to create instructions for incrementing or decrementing the contents of a register or location in memory, since the M68000 microprocessors do not have unique mnemonics or opcodes for these functions. This situation is advantageous in that you do not have to learn additional mnemonics for these functions. For example, the instruction

```
ADDQ #2,D4
```

increments the contents of data register D4 by 2. By contrast, the instruction

SUBQ #3,D4

decrements the contents of data register D4 by 3. There are many more such possibilities. These possibilities are explained for each instruction in more detail in Chapter 4 below.

3.5 Address-Register Indirect-Addressing Modes

The address-register indirect-addressing modes specify an address in memory indirectly, by specifying the number of an address register that contains the actual address in memory. There are several variants of these modes, with options for:
- incrementing the contents of the address register before using the contents as the address,
- decrementing the contents of the address register after using the contents as the address,
- adding an offset (constant) to the address contained in the address register and
- adding both an index (contents of another address register or data register) and an offset (constant) to the address contained in the address register.

These addressing modes are summarized below, with their names and one typical example of the mnemonic for each:

address-register indirect	(A0)
address-register indirect, with post increment	(A0)+
address-register indirect, with predecrement	−(A0)
address-register indirect, with offset	$100(A0)
address-register indirect, with index and offset	$50(A0,D0)

3.5.1 Address-Register Indirect-Addressing Mode

Assembler Notation:

(An) $0 \leq n \leq 7$

<ea> in Opcode:

Mode	Register
0 1 0	Reg. No.

Example 1:

MOVE (A0),D0		
MOVE.W (A0),D0		(equivalent notation)
Instruction	= MOVE	
Length of Operand	= W	(optional, W = default)
Effective Address	= (A0)	(source address)
Effective Address	= D0	(destination address)

Model for Operation:

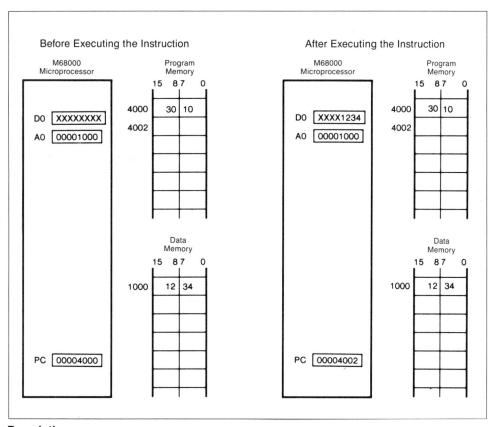

Description:

The MOVE instruction copies data from one location to another location. The default value for the extension is ".W", for operations on words. Therefore, it reads the address of $1000 contained in the address register A0 (source address) and copies the two bytes of data located at this address in memory into the least-significant half of the data register D0 (the destination address) without changing the original contents at $1000 or in A0.

Application:

A common application for this addressing mode is for indirect jumps, such as JMP (A1) or JSR (A1). You can use such jumps to process a table of jump addresses after loading the appropriate jump address into the address register before the jump instruction. A practical example would be for the emulation of a coprocessor, such as the 68881, or the floating-point instructions of the 68020 microprocessor, in software with the 68000 microprocessor.

Remark: This instruction has a one-word opcode.

3.5.2   Address-Register Indirect-Addressing Mode, with Postincrement

Assembler Notation:

(An)+ 0 ≤ n ≤ 7

<ea> in Opcode

Mode	Register
0 1 1	Reg. No.

After reading and using the contents of the address register, the processor increments the contents of the address register. The size of the increment is to the next byte, word or long word in memory, depending upon the size of the operands used (.B, .W, or .L).

Example 1:

MOVE (A4)+,$2000		
MOVE.W (A4)+,$2000		(equivalent notation)
Instruction	= MOVE	
Length of Operand	= W	(optional, W = default)
Effective Address	= (A4)+	(source address)
Effective Address	= $2000	(destination address)

Model for Operation:

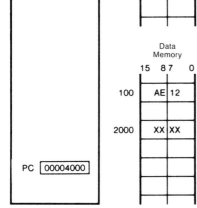

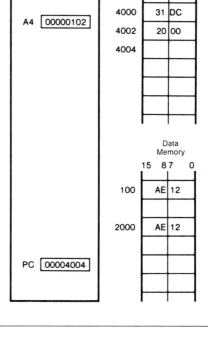

Before Executing the Instruction

After Executing the Instruction

Description:

The MOVE instruction copies data from one location to another location. The default value for the extension is ".W", specifying words as operands. Therefore, it reads $100 as the effective address in address register A4 (source address) and copies the word of data, located at the starting address of $100 in memory, into the location starting at the address $2000 in memory (destination address). Then, it increments the address in A4 by 2 bytes, from $100 to $102, since the operand of the instruction is a 2-byte word. (If the operand were a byte, it would have incremented the address by 1. If the operand were a 4-byte long word, it would have incremented the address by 4.)

Application:

You can use this addressing mode to move blocks of data or code as well as to read or write into tables. Each time that you use an instruction, the address in the address register is automatically incremented to be ready for the next use of the same instruction without requiring intermediate instructions for incrementing the address. It is particularly useful in program loops and for using address registers as user stacks (pull from stack).

Remark: When you use the system stack pointer (address register A7) while working with bytes, this addressing mode will increment the address in A7 by 2, to maintain an even address, rather than by 1, as would be the case for other address registers during byte operations.

3.5.3   Address-Register Indirect-Addressing Mode, with Predecrement

Assembler Notation:

−(An) 0 ≤ n ≤ 7

<ea> in Opcode:

Mode	Register
1 0 0	Reg. No.

Before reading and using the contents of the address register, the processor decrements the contents of the address register. The size of the decrement is to the next byte, word or long word in memory, depending upon the size of the operands used (.B, .W, or .L).

Example 1:

MOVE −(A3),$4000		
MOVE.W -(A3)+,$4000		(equivalent notation)
Instruction	= MOVE	
Length of Operand	= W	(optional, W = default)
Effective Address	= −(A3)	(source address)
Effective Address	= $4000	(destination address)

Model for Operation:

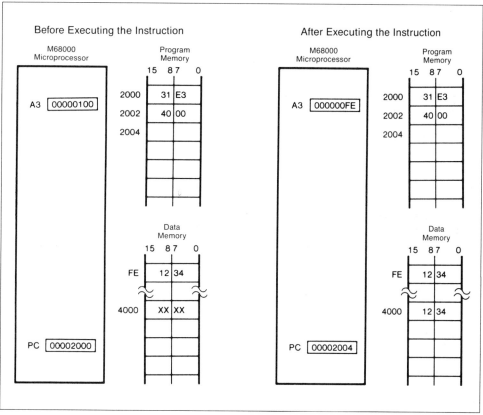

Description:

The MOVE instruction copies data from one location to another location. The default value for the extension is ".W", specifying words as operands. Therefore, it reads $100 as the effective address in address register A4 (source address) and decrements this address by 2 to $FE (since the operand size is for a 2-byte word). (If the operand had been a byte, it would have decremented the address by 1. If the operand had been a 4-byte long word, it would have decremented the address by 4.)

Then, it copies the word of data, located at the starting address of $FE in memory, into the location starting at the address $4000 in memory (destination address).

Application:

You can use this addressing mode to move blocks of data or code as well as to read or write into tables. Each time that you use an instruction, the address in the address register is automatically decremented to be ready for the next use of the same instruction without requiring intermediate instructions for decrementing the address. It is particularly useful in program loops and for using address registers as user stacks (push onto the stack).

Remark: When you use the system stack pointer (address register A7) while working with bytes, this addressing mode will decrement the address in A7 by 2, to maintain an even address, rather than by 1, as would be the case for other address registers during byte operations.

3.5.4   Address-Register Indirect-Addressing Mode, with an Offset

Assembler Notation:

d16(An) $0 \leq n \leq 7$

<ea> in Opcode:

Mode	Register
1 0 1	Reg. No.

After reading the contents of the address register, the processor adds an offset to these contents before using them as an address–but without changing the original contents in the address register. This offset can be specified with a maximum of 16 bits, and it is a signed number. The effective address is calculated as follows:

<ea> = <An> + d16	$-32{,}768 \leq d16 \leq +32{,}767$
	$\$8000 \leq d16 \leq \$7FFF$

Example 1:

MOVE $100(A0),$3000		
MOVE.W 256(A0),$3000		(equivalent notation)
Instruction	= MOVE	
Length of Operand	= W	(optional, W = default)
Effective Address	= $100(A0)	(source address)
Effective Address	= $3000	(destination address)

Model for Operation:

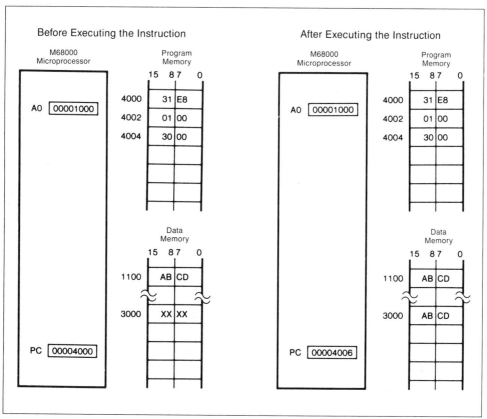

Description:

The MOVE instruction copies data from one location to another location. The default value for the extension is ".W", for a 2-byte word as operand.

It reads the address of $1000 stored in address register A0 and then adds $100 (= #256) as the offset to it, to obtain an effective address <ea> of $1100. This does not change the original contents of A0.

Then, the MOVE instruction copies the 2-byte word of data starting at $1100 (source address) into the locations starting at $3000 (the destination address) without changing the original contents at $1100.

Remark: This instruction requires 3 words when assembled. The first word is for the opcode, the second word for the offset and the third word for the destination address.

Example 2:

MOVE.L $100(A0),$3000		
Instruction	= MOVE	
Length of Operand	= L	(optional, W = default)
Effective Address	= $100(A0)	(source address)
Effective Address	= $3000	(destination address)

Model for Operation:

Description:

This example is the same as Example 1 above, except that it copies a 4-byte long word rather than a 2-byte word.

The MOVE instruction reads the address of $1000 stored in address register A0 and then adds $100 (= #256) as the offset to it, to obtain an effective address <ea> of $1100. This does not change the original contents of A0.

Then, the MOVE instruction copies the 4-byte long word of data starting at $1100 (source address) into the locations starting at $3000 (the destination address) without changing the original contents at $1100.

Application:

You can use this addressing mode when you want to work with a table or stack (reading or writing) that is stored in memory. The contents of the address register usually specify the starting address for the table and the offset usually specifies the particular entry within the table (the reversed roles are also possible). These two possible combinations are illustrated in Figure 3-10 below. You can also use it to specify which register a peripheral device should use.

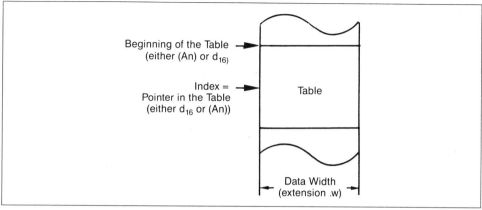

Figure 3-10: Indirect Addressing with Offset

3.5.5 Address-Register Indirect-Addressing Mode, with an Index and with or Without an Offset

Assembler Notation:

$$
\begin{array}{ll}
\text{d8(An,Rx.w)} & 0 \le n \le 7 \\
& 0 \le x \le 7 \\
& \text{Rx} = \{A,D\} \\
& \text{w} = \{W,L\}
\end{array}
$$

<ea> in Opcode:

Mode	Register
1 1 0	Reg. No.

After reading the contents of the address register, An, the processor adds both:
- an index, contained in the register Rx and
- an offset, specified as d8,

before using the result as an address–but without changing the original contents in either the address register or the index register. The index can use either a word or long word from the index register. The offset can be specified with a maximum of 8 bits, and it is a signed number. The effective address is calculated as follows:

$$
\begin{array}{lll}
\text{<ea>} = \text{<An>} + \text{<Rx.w>} + & & \\
\text{d8} & & \\
-32{,}768 \le & \text{<Rx.W>} & \le +32{,}767 \\
\$8000 \le & \text{<Rx.W>} & \le \$7\text{FFF} \\
0 \le & \text{<Rx.L>} & \le 4{,}294{,}967{,}295 \\
0 \le & \text{<Rx.L>} & \le \$\text{FFFFFFFF} \\
-128 \le & \text{d8} & \le +127 \\
\$80 \le & \text{d8} & \le \$7\text{F}
\end{array}
$$

Example 1:

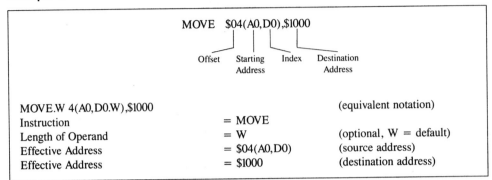

MOVE.W 4(A0,D0.W),$1000   (equivalent notation)
Instruction   = MOVE
Length of Operand   = W   (optional, W = default)
Effective Address   = $04(A0,D0)   (source address)
Effective Address   = $1000   (destination address)

Model for Operation:

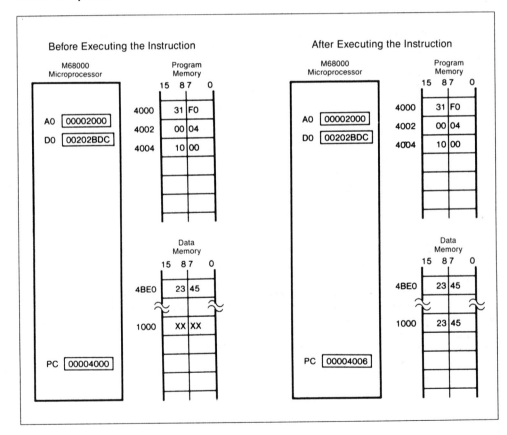

Description:

The MOVE instruction copies data from one location to another location. The extension ".W" specifies operations on a word of data.

This instruction calculates the effective source address by adding the following three components:

–	contents of address register A0	=	$00002000
–	contents of index register D0.W	=	$00002BCD
–	address offset d8	=	$00000004
	effective source address < ea >	=	$00004BE0

It then copies the 2-byte word of data starting at $00004BE0 into the destination address starting at $1000.

Example 2:

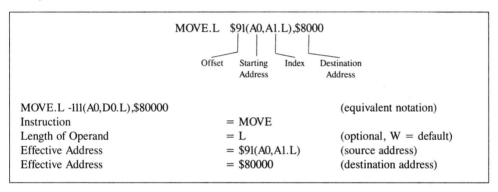

MOVE.L -111(A0,D0.L),$80000			(equivalent notation)
Instruction	= MOVE		
Length of Operand	= L		(optional, W = default)
Effective Address	= $91(A0,A1.L)		(source address)
Effective Address	= $80000		(destination address)

Model for Operation:

Before Executing the Instruction

M68000 Microprocessor		Program Memory

AO 00011111
A1 00022222

Program Memory
15 8 7 0

4000 23 F0
4002 98 91
4004 00 08
      00 00

Data Memory
15 8 7 0

332C4 25 02
333C6 19 50

80000 XX XX
80002 XX XX

PC 00004000

After Executing the Instruction

M68000 Microprocessor

AO 00011111
A1 00022222

Program Memory
15 8 7 0

4000 23 F0
4002 98 91
4004 00 08
4006 00 00

Data Memory
15 8 7 0

332C4 25 02
332C6 19 50

80000 25 02
80002 19 50

PC 00004006

Description:

This example is very similar to the previous example, except that this example uses long words for both the operand that is copied and the index register.

This instruction calculates the effective source address by adding the following three components:

– contents of address register A0	=	$00001111
– contents of index register D0.W	=	$00022222
– address offset d8	=	$FFFFFF91
effective source address <ea>	=	$000332C4

It then copies the 4-byte long word of data starting at $000332C4 into the destination address starting at $80000.

Application:

You can use this addressing mode for a conversion program that has several tables, one after the other. In a typical application, you could use the address register to specify where the set of tables begins, use the offset to specify a particular table and use the index register to specify the location within any table.

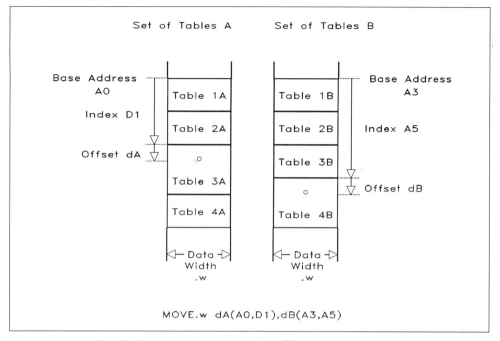

Figure 3-11: Typical Use of Indirect Addressing with Index and Offset

This is illustrated graphically in Figure 3-11 below for the case of copying an operand from one set of tables to another set of tables.

In Figure 3-11 above, one single MOVE instruction copies an operand from the set of tables A to the set of tables B. Both sets of tables must have the same data width.

The effective source address for the operand in the set of tables A is calculated as $<source> = <A0> + <D1> + dA$. The effective destination address for the operand in the set of tables B is calculated as $<destination> = <A3> + <A5> + dB$.

Remark: The instruction in Example 2 uses 3 words when assembled. The first word, with the opcode, contains only the addressing mode and one register. Since two registers are used in this instruction, the second word contains the second register and the address offset. The third word contains the absolute destination address.

The second word, with both the extra register and the address offset is structured as follows:

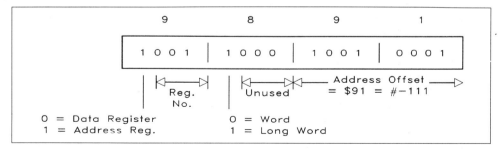

Figure 3-12: Format for Index Register and Offset

3.6   Relative-Addressing Modes

Relative-addressing modes define an effective address relative to the program counter, ie. the location of the instruction that uses this addressing mode. We will distinguish between two types:
- program-counter relative-addressing modes and
- branch instructions (for jumps relative to the program counter).

The program-counter relative-addressing modes are similar to the address-register indirect-addressing modes. The main difference is that the effective address is calculated relative to the program counter rather than relative to the contents of an address register. There are two variants, with options for:
- adding an offset and
- adding an index (contents of an address register or data register) with or without an additional offset

to the current contents of the program counter. These addressing modes are summarized below, with their names and the mnemonic for each:

program-counter relative, with/without offset	d16(PC)
program-counter relative, with index and offset	d8(PC,Rx.w)

The concept of addressing, relative to the program counter, may be new for users who have not worked with processors that have relative-addressing modes (such as the branch instructions for the 8-bit 6802 microprocessor) or program-counter relative-addressing modes (such as with the 8-bit 6809 microprocessor). A typical application is for a multi-user system where several users share the same processor and operating system. All users share the same global memory space and the operating system dynamically allocates memory to each user as appropriate. When a user wants to work with a particular program, the operating system must search for free memory space, load the program in that space and allow the user to run the program. This implies that such programs must be relocatable, in that they will run from any location in memory. This may sound simple and obvious, but it is extremely difficult to implement with many processors. The program-counter relative-addressing modes of the M68000 microprocessors make this task relatively easy.

The problem of relocatability occurs frequently in low-cost systems that do not use a MMU (memory-management unit). A typical example is the MVME319 VME system from Motorola. It uses a 68000 microprocessor and the VERSAdos operating system, with the RMS68K real-time kernel (see Chapter 2.4 above). This operating system uses TRAP instructions to implement calls to the system. This does not cause any difficulties as long as it is not necessary to pass parameters simultaneously.

Figure 3-13 below shows such a non-relocatable program and Figure 3-14 below shows a relocatable version of the same program. This program displays a string of text from a buffer in memory onto the screen, using the IOS (Input-Output System) call (TRAP #2) when the logon terminal is used. However, the beginning and ending addresses must be specified in the parameter block. This is accomplished as constants for the non-relocatable version and as reserved memory locations in the relocatable version. These addresses must be loaded into address register A0 before executing the system call. The non-relocatable program in Figure 3-13 will only work properly when:
- the system contains a MMU or
- the program is located by the assembler/linker at an address that is physically available in memory and is not otherwise used.

This program must be modified slightly for a system without a MMU. The beginning and ending addresses of the buffer must be calculated first by the program (depending upon where the program is located) and only then stored in the parameter block. Therefore, a label is set at the location in the parameter block where the beginning and ending addresses should be inserted. Therefore, these addresses are calculated first and then stored in the parameter block. At this time, the address of the parameter block can be loaded into address register A0 (of course PC relative). At this time, the system call can take place. The resulting program will execute correctly, independently of where it is located.

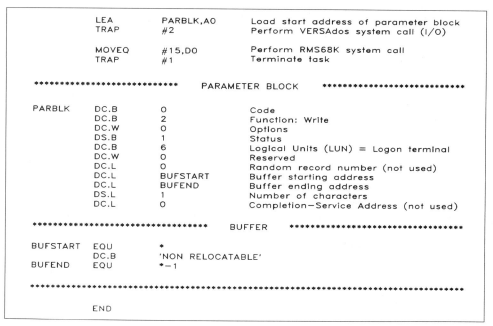

```
            LEA       PARBLK,A0     Load start address of parameter block
            TRAP      #2            Perform VERSAdos system call (I/O)

            MOVEQ     #15,D0        Perform RMS68K system call
            TRAP      #1            Terminate task

    **************************** PARAMETER BLOCK ****************************

PARBLK      DC.B      0             Code
            DC.B      2             Function: Write
            DC.W      0             Options
            DS.B      1             Status
            DC.B      6             Logical Units (LUN) = Logon terminal
            DC.W      0             Reserved
            DC.L      0             Random record number (not used)
            DC.L      BUFSTART      Buffer starting address
            DC.L      BUFEND        Buffer ending address
            DS.L      1             Number of characters
            DC.L      0             Completion—Service Address (not used)

    ********************************* BUFFER *********************************

BUFSTART    EQU       *
            DC.B      'NON RELOCATABLE'
BUFEND      EQU       *—1

    *************************************************************************

            END
```

Figure 3-13: Non-relocatable Program (with MMU)

```
            LEA       BUFST(PC),A0        Load destination address for p.block
            LEA       BUFSTART(PC),A1     Load starting address of buffer
            MOVE.L    A1,(A0)             Fill the parameter block

            LEA       BUFEND(PC),A0       Load destination address for p.block
            LEA       BUFEND(PC),A1       Load ending address of buffer
            MOVE.L    A1,(A0)             Fill the parameter block

            LEA       PARBLK(PC),A0       Load starting address for p.block
            TRAP      #2                  Perform VERSAdos system call (I/O)

            MOVEQ     #15,D0              Perform RMS68K system call
            TRAP      #1                  Terminate task
    **************************** PARAMETER BLOCK ****************************
PARBLK      DC.B      0             Code
            DC.B      2             Function: Write
            DC.W      0             Options
            DS.B      1             Status
            DC.B      6             Logical Unit (LUN = logon terminal)
            DC.W      0             Reserved
            DC.L      0             Random record number (not used)
BUFST       DS.L      1             Buffer starting address
BUFEN       DS.L      1             Buffer ending address
            DS.L      1             Number of characters
            DC.L      0             Cmpletion—Service Address (not used)
    ********************************* BUFFER *********************************
BUFSTART    EQU       *
            DC.B      'RELOCATABLE'
BUFEND      EQU       *—1
    *************************************************************************
            END
```

Figure 3-14: Relocatable Program (without MMU)

3.6.1   Program-Counter Relative-Addressing Mode, with or Without an Offset

Assembler Notation:

d16(PC) (different notation for different assemblers)

<ea> in Opcode:

Mode	Register
1 1 1	0 1 0

The processor reads the contents of the program counter, adds two to this address and then adds the value of the offset (if given) in order to calculate the effective address. It increments the program counter by the number of bytes used by the particular instruction. This calculation is illustrated below:

$$<ea> = <PC> + 2 + dl \qquad -6\text{-}32{,}768 \leq d16 \leq +32{,}767$$
$$\$8000 \leq d16 \leq \$7FFF$$

Example 1:

MOVE TEST(PC),D0		
MOVE.W TEST(PC),D0		(equivalent notation)
Instruction	= MOVE	
Length of Operand	= W	(optional, W = default)
Effective Address	= TEST(PC)	(source address)
Effective Address	= D0	(destination address)

Model for Operation:

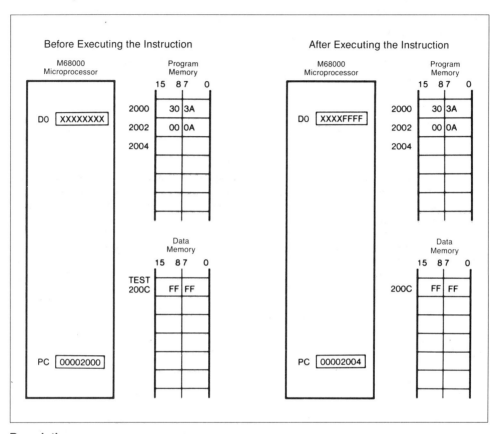

Description:

The MOVE instruction copies data from one location to another location. The default value for the extension is ".W", for a 2-byte word as operand. Therefore, it copies the operand stored at the label TEST in memory into the data register D0.

The assembler calculates the offset distance from the opcode for the MOVE instruction to the label TEST and stores this offset distance in the first word after the opcode. (In this case, this offset is $000A.) Later, when the M68000 microprocessor executes this instruction, it reads the offset as the next word after the opcode and adds it to the current value of the program counter (plus 2) to obtain the effective address where the operand is stored. (In this case, $2000 + $2 + $000A = $200C as the effective address for the source operand.) This offset can be positive or negative, corresponding to an offset forwards or backwards in memory from the opcode of the instruction. Since this address is relative to the program counter while executing the MOVE instruction, it does not matter where the program is loaded in memory–since the MOVE instruction and label will still be separated by the same distance.

3.6.2 Program-Counter Relative-Addressing Mode, with an Index and with or Without an Offset

Assembler Notation:

d8(PC,Rx.w)	(different notation for different assemblers)
	R = {A,D} w = {W,L} 0 ≤ x ≤ 7

<ea> in Opcode:

Mode	Register
1 1 1	0 1 1

The processor reads the contents of the program counter, adds two to this address, adds the value stored in the register (index) and finally adds the value of the offset (if given) in order to calculate the effective address. It increments the program counter by the number of bytes used by the particular instruction. This calculation is illustrated below:

$$<ea> = <PC> + 2 + <Rx.w> + d8 \qquad -\#128 \le d8 \le +\#127$$

$$\$80 \le d8 \le \$7F$$
$$-32{,}768 \le <Rx.W> \le +32{,}767$$
$$\$8000 \le <Rx.W> \le \$7FFF$$
$$0 \le <Rx.L> \le 4{,}294{,}967{,}295$$
$$\$0 \le <Rx.L> \le \$FFFFFFFF$$

Example 1:

MOVE TEST(PC,A0),D0		
MOVE.W TEST(PC,A0.W),D0		(equivalent notation)
Instruction	= MOVE	
Length of Operand	= W	(optional, W = default)
Effective Address	= TEST(PC,A0.W)	(source address)
Effective Address	= D0	(destination address)

Model for Operation:

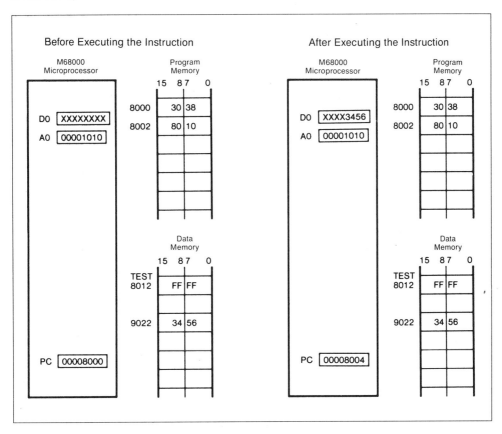

Description:

The MOVE instruction copies data from one location to another location. The default value for the extension is ".W", for a 2-byte word as operand. Therefore, it copies the operand stored at an index value past the label TEST in memory into the data register D0.

The assembler calculates the offset distance from the opcode for the MOVE instruction to the label TEST and stores this offset distance in the first word after the opcode. (In this case, this offset is $10.) Later, when the M68000 microprocessor executes this instruction, it reads the offset as the next word after the opcode and adds it to the current value of the program counter (plus 2). Then, it adds the contents of the index register (address register A0 containing $00001010 in this case) to obtain the effective address where the operand is stored. (In this case, $8000 + $2 + $10 + $1010 = $9022 as the effective address for the source operand.) The index and offset can be positive or negative, corresponding to displacements forwards or backwards in memory from the opcode of the instruction. Since this address is relative to the program counter while executing the MOVE instruction, it does not matter where the program is loaded in memory – since the MOVE instruction and label will still be separated by the same distance.

Application:

You can use this addressing mode when you work with a table in a program that should be relocatable in memory. You can use the offset to define the beginning of the table, relative to the program counter and the index to define the position within the table (from the beginning of the table). This is illustrated in Figure 3-15 below.

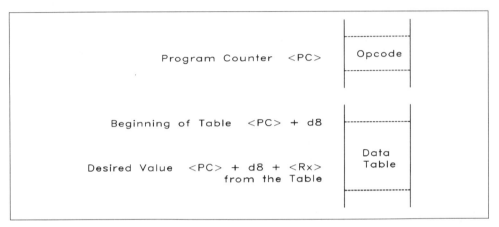

Figure 3-15: Relocatable Table

Remark: The first word after the opcode of the instruction has the same format as in Figure 3-15 of Example 2 in Section 3.5.5 above. It contains the type of index register (address or data), number of the index register, size of the operand from the index register and the offset.

3.6.3 Branch Instructions (Conditional and Unconditional Jumps)

Although both conditional and unconditional jumps are instructions and are therefore presented in detail in Chapter 4 below, they are presented briefly here due to their behavior as control mechanisms relative to the program counter.
There are two cases, with an:
– 8-bit "short" jump distance and
– 16-bit "long" jump distance.
– 32-bit is also available for 68020/030
The default case is long and therefore the short case must be specified explicitly as an extension of ".S" after the mnemonic for the instruction.

Example: BNE.S Label

The M68000 microprocessors process 14 different conditions for conditional jumping. All of these conditions are derived as logical combinations of the bits (flags) in the condition-code register. These flags have the names N, Z, V and C. The logical conditions are listed in Figure 3-16 below:

Conditional Jumps		
Mnemonic	Name	Logical Condition
BEQ	Equal	Z = 1
BNE	Not equal	Z = 0
BPL	Plus	N = 0
BMI	Minus	N = 1
BGT *	Greater	Z + (N & V) = 0
BLT *	Less	N & V = 1
BGE *	Greater or equal	N & V = 0
BLE *	Less or equal	Z + (N & V) = 1
BHI	Higher	C + Z = 0
BLS	Lower or same	C + Z = 1
BCS	Carry set	C = 1
BCC	Carry cleared	C = 0
BVS *	Overflow	V = 1
BVC *	No overflow	V = 0

* = 2's—complement arithmetic
+ = logical OR
& = exclusive OR

Unconditional Jumps	
Mnemonic	Name
BRA	Branch Always
BSR	Branch to Subroutine

Figure 3-16: Conditional and Unconditional Jump Instructions

3.6.3.1 Branch Instructions with an 8-bit Jump Distance

Example 1:

The BEQ instruction is used in the following simple program:

```
              ORG           $4FFA
        PIA   EQU           $1000
              MOVEQ         #5,D1
              MOVE.W        PIA,D0
              BEQ.S         NULL
              CLR.L         D1
NULL          ADDQ          #2,D1
              .             .
              .             .
              END
```

Description:

The contents of memory at address $1000 are copied into the data register D0. The processor then loads a value of 5 into the data register D1. There are two cases, depending upon the value of the operand in D0, tested with BEQ.S:

Case 1: Contents of D0 = 0

BEQ.S will cause a jump to the label NULL, since Z = 1. Therefore, 2 will be added to the contents of D1, leaving a result of 7 in D1 at the end.

Case 2: Contents of D0 > 0

BEQ.S will not do anything, since Z = 0. Therefore the next instruction will clear the data register D1 before the following instruction adds 2. The result in D1 will be 2 at the end.

Model for Operation:

Case 1 (Contents of D0 = 0)

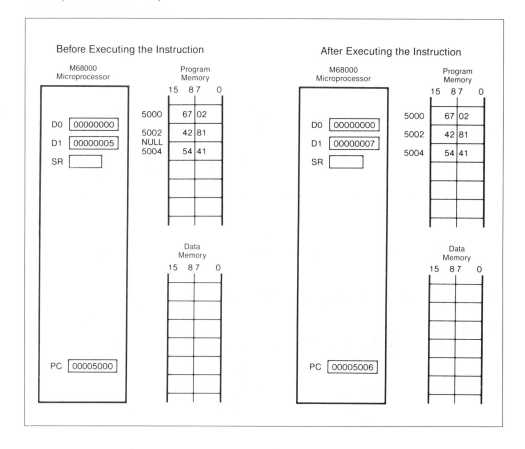

Model for Operation:

Case 2 (Contents of D0 > 0)

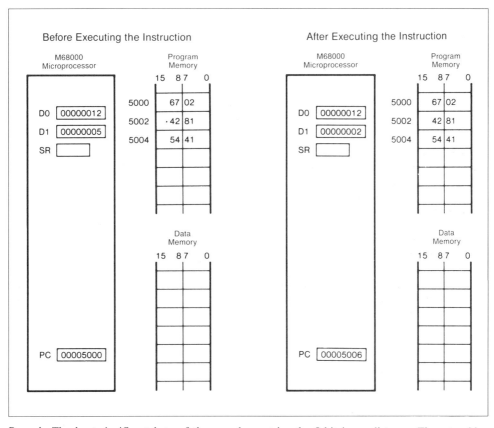

Remark: The least-significant byte of the opcode contains the 8-bit jump distance. The assembler calculates this distance during assembly, using the formula:

d = <ea>–<PC> + 2

where <ea> is the effective address of the target of the jump (the label NULL in this case) and <PC> is the contents of the program counter. In this particular example:

d = $5004–$5000–$2 = $0002

Application:

You can use such sequences of instructions to create loops and to skip over segments of code.

3.6.3.2 Branch Instructions with a 16-bit Jump Distance

Example 1:

The BNE instruction is used in the following simple program:

$8000		MOVEQ	#100,D0
$8002	LABEL	MOVE.W	A0,D1
	.	.	.
	.	.	.
	.	.	.
$9000		SUBQ	#1,D0
$9002		BNE	LABEL

Description:

This program loads the value of 100 into the data register D0. Then, it has a loop from $8002 to $9000. Each time through the loop, the SUBQ instruction decrements the value in D0 by 1. As long as this value is greater than 0, the BNE instruction repeats the loop. Therefore, this loop will be repeated 100 times. The assembler calculates the jump distance as:

d16 = <ea>(LABEL)−<PC>−$2
d16 = $8002−$9002−$2 = $EFFD

This distance is negative and exceeds the negative value of −128 that is allowed for an 8-bit jump distance. Therefore, the assembler writes zeros in the least-significant half of the opcode and uses another word for the 16-bit address.

3.7 Addressing Modes that Sign Extend

Some of the addressing modes expand the operand automatically, by repeating the most-significant bit of the operand to fill the format of a larger operand. These addressing modes are:
- absolute short
  A word as an address is sign extended into a long word.
- address-register indirect (only as destination address)
  A word as an address is sign extended into a long word.
- address-register indirect, with an offset
  A word as an offset is sign extended into a long word.
- address-register indirect, with index
  A word or byte as an index is sign extended into a long word.
- program-counter relative, with offset
  A word as an offset is sign extended into a long word.
- program-counter relative, with index
  A word or byte as an index is sign extended into a long word.

3.8 Extra Addressing Modes of the 68020 and 68030 Microprocessors

Special attention was given to increasing the addressing capabilities of the 68020 microprocessor (and the later 68030 microprocessor with the same addressing capabilities as the 68020). Whereas offsets (address displacements) were limited to values that can be defined with 8 bits or 16 bits with the 68000/08/10/12 microprocessors, the 68020/30 microprocessors allow you to use offsets defined with 32 bits (scanning 4 gigabytes).

The new addressing modes are designed specifically to provide many additional options for addressing data in tables flexibly. In the case of a table that is stored in memory, we speak of a base address as the starting address in memory (where the table begins) and an offset or index (selection of one entry from the table) that specifies how far to go into the table from the base address in order to obtain a particular value. In the case of multiple tables (such as for multi-dimensional arrays), we speak of a base address for the beginning of the set of tables, an index that advances to the beginning a particular table in the set of tables, and an offset that advances to a particular entry in that table (see Figure 3-11 above as an good example). A base address is always a long word but an index or offset can often be either a short word or a long word.

For such addressing of tables, one distinguishes between:
– based addressing (where a base address is contained in a base register and an offset from the base address is specified directly in the instruction) versus
– indexed addressing (where a base address is specified directly in the instruction and an index as offset is contained in an index register.

The new addressing modes of the 68020/30 microprocessors define a more general set of addressing modes that combine both features whereby:
– the base address can be specified either as
   the contents of a base register (an address register, data register or the program counter),
   a value specified directly in the instruction, bd (base displacement) or
   both (the two are added together) and
– the offset can be specified either as
   the contents of an index register (an address register or data register),
   a value specified directly in the instruction, od (outer displacement) or
   both (the two are added together).

This gives you complete flexibility in selecting whether to specify all or part of both the base address and the offset explicitly in the instruction before assembly or to allow all or part of the base address and the offset to be calculated later at run time. It also gives you flexibility for using several offsets for multi-dimensional arrays. In addition, you can:
– specify a scale factor of 1, 2, 4 or 8 that is multiplied by the contents of the index register and
– specify the width of the index register that is used (16 bits or 32 bits).

Finally, you can place square brackets, []'s, around different parts of the resulting expression. The processor will then evaluate the expression within the brackets and use it as an effective address for indirect addressing in memory. The processor then uses one read bus cycle to obtain the value stored at this location in memory and then uses this value for the rest of the calculation of the effective address using this new addressing mode. A distinction can be drawn in the terminology between:
– pre-indexed indirect-addressing modes, where the indirect access to memory occurs AFTER the index (offset) is evaluated and
– post-indexed indirect-addressing modes, where the indirect access to memory occurs BEFORE the index (offset) has been evaluated.

The result is one new generalized addressing mode that you can customize to meet the specific requirements of a given problem. According to the RISC philosophy, there is only one new addressing mode that you need to learn in order to use these new possibilities and according to the CISC philosophy, you can solve a wide variety of complex addressing problems with a large number of different customized versions of this one generalized addressing mode.

Therefore, we do not attempt to assign names to each of the many customized versions that are possible. An assembler will assemble any of these customized versions into one of the basic addressing modes. You should check the user's manual for the assembler that you are using for the notation that it accepts for these customized versions.

Figure 3-17 below illustrates how customized versions are constructed from the one generalized model.

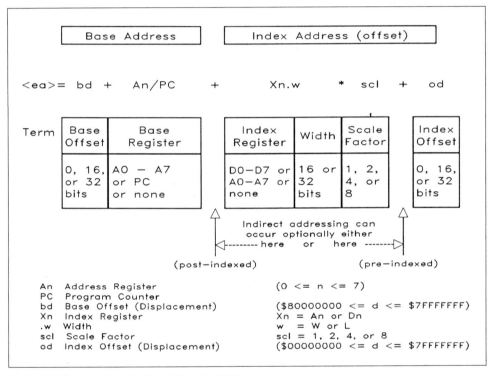

Figure 3-17: Construction of the New Addressing Modes

Any combination of the terms for the effective address can be omitted or set equal to 0. However, it would not be useful to set all of them equal to 0. One interesting example is in the case of the following addressing mode:

(bd,An,Xn.s*scl)

when the value for bd = 0, An is suppressed, Xn = Dn and scl = 1. The resulting simplified expression is simply:

(Dn)

ie. a data-register indirect-addressing mode. This mode was not available in the set of addressing modes for the 68000/08/10/12 microprocessors. Adding it here, even in this indirect way, completes the symmetry of the addressing modes.

The scale factor allows you to access different tables without disturbing the index pointer.

Many of the new addressing modes are useful for compilers that must frequently access tables (arrays or pointers). They are also useful for operating systems and peripheral-interface devices (such as disk controllers), such as when they use a tree structure to address data areas with a table.

Following is an illustrative example for one of these new addressing modes. The problem consists of adding a value from one table in a set of tables to the contents of D5. The syntax for the instruction with effective addresses is:

ADD ([Base,A1,D3*4],Offset),D5

The calculation of the first effective address and the result is illustrated in Figure 3-18 below:

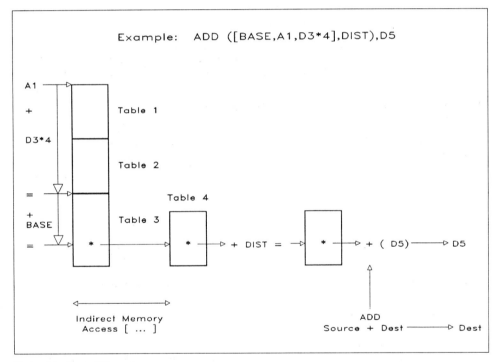

Figure 3-18: Typical Example

At the hardware level, the opcodes (first 16 bits) remain the same, and the distinctions that lead to "different" addressing modes or variants thereof are mainly in the extension words that follow the first opcode. At the software level, the "different" addressing modes result in different mnemonics that are assembled by an assembler into the basic opcodes and extension words.

The new addressing modes are extensions to the two types of:

– indirect-addressing modes and
– program-counter relative-addressing modes.

Two new subtypes, "memory indirect" and "register indirect", are added to both of these two types of addressing modes. These new additions are presented in different formats in this Section.

The 68020 and 68030 microprocessors have the same addressing modes as the 68000, 68008, 68010 and 68010 microprocessors plus several extra addressing modes. The exact number of additional addressing modes is difficult to specify, depending upon how you choose to count addressing modes. Motorola claims an increase of 2 basic types (from 7 to 9) and an increase of 6 basic addressing modes (from 14 to 18), as illustrated in Figure 3-19 below:

Type of Mode	Addressing Mode	Motorola Mnemonic	New
Register Direct	Data-Register Direct	Dn	
	Address-Register Direct	An	
Address-Register Indirect (ARI)	ARI	(An)	
	ARI, with Postincrement	(An)+	
	ARI, with Predecrement	–(An)	
	ARI, with Displacement	(d16,An)	
Memory Indirect	Memory Indirect Post-Indexed	([bd,An],Xn,od)	(New)
	Memory Indirect Pre-Indexed	([bd,An,Xn],od)	New
			New
Programm-Counter Relative, with Displacement	Relative, with Displacement		
	PCR, with Displacemen)	(d16,PC)	
Program-Counter Relative, with Index	PCR, with Index (8-bit Displacement)	(d8,PC,Xn)	
	PCR, with Index (Base Displacement)	(bd,PC,Xn)	New
Program-Counter Memory Indirect	PC Memory Indirect Post-Indexed	([bd,PC],Xn,od)	(New)
	PC Memory Indirect Pre-Indexed	([bd,PC,Xn],od)	New
			New
Absolute	Short-Address Absolute	$xxxx	
	Long-Address Absolute	$xxxxxxxx	
Immediate	Immediate	# <data>	

Figure 3-19: Comparison of Official Addressing Modes (68000/08/10/12 versus 68020/30 microprocessors)

Motorola then distinguishes between:
- basic addressing modes and
- generic addressing modes.

There is one basic addressing mode that appears uniquely in the opcode (first 16 bits) of an instruction. There may be several generic addressing modes for one basic addressing mode, where different mnemonics for generic addressing modes are assembled to the same opcode for one single basic addressing mode. Therefore, basic addressing modes correspond to the viewpoint of the microprocessor and generic addressing modes correspond to the viewpoint of the programmer. An assembler assembles a generic addressing mode into the optimal basic addressing mode when several options are available. With all permutations of possibilities, there are 73 generic addressing modes, as defined by Motorola.

In Figure 3-7 earlier in this Chapter, we listed 19 addressing modes for the 68000/08/10/12 microprocessors. Eliminating the special cases for special-register direct (2), immediate (3) and branching (2) gives the same 12 basic addressing modes defined by Motorola for these processors.

Using the notation of this book, we obtain 50 new generic addressing modes for the 68020/30 microprocessors, for a total of 62 generic addressing modes for these microprocessors. These relationships are illustrated in Figure 3-20 below. The following abbreviations are used in the column for the 68020/30 microprocessors of Figure 3-20 below:

d	a displacement defined with 8, 16 or 32 bits
Xn	an index register that can use 16 or 32 bits of any data register or address register.
scl	a scaling factor of 1, 2, 4 or 8.

Types of Addressing Modes	68000/008/ 010/012	Added for 68020/30 Microprocessors
Register Direct	Dn An	None
Address-Register Indirect (ARI)	(An) (An)+ −(An) d16(An)	(bd,An) (Xn∗scl) (bd,Xn∗scl) (An,Xn∗scl) (bd,An,Xn∗scl)
Data-Register Indirect	None	(bd,Dn), (Xn∗scl) (bn,Xn,∗scl)
Address-Register Indirect, with Index	d8(An,Xn)	None
Memory Indirect	None	([bd]) ([bd],od) ([An]) ([bd,An]) ([An],od) ([bd,An],od) ([Xn∗scl])
Memory Indirect, with Pre-Index	None	([bd,Xn∗scl]) ([Xn∗scl,od]) ([bd,Xn∗scl],od) ([An,Xn∗scl]) ([bd,An,Xn∗scl]) ([An,Xn∗scl],od) ([bd,An,Xn∗scl],od)
Programm-Counter Relative	d16(PC) d8(PC,Xn)	(bd,PC) (Xn∗scl) (bd,Xn∗scl) (PC,Xn∗scl) (bd,PC,Xn∗scl)
Program-Counter Memory Indirect	None	([bd]) ([bd],od) ([PC]) ([bd,PC]) ([PC],od) ([bd,PC],od) ([Xn∗scl])
Program-Counter Memory Indirect, with Pre-Index		([bd,Xn∗scl]) ([Xn∗scl],od) ([bd,Xn∗scl],od) ([PC,Xn∗scl]) ([bd,PC,Xn∗scl]) ([PC,Xn∗scl],od)([bd,PC,Xn∗scl],od)
Programm-Counter Memory Indirect, with Post-Index		([bd],Xn∗scl) ([bd],od,Xn∗scl) ([PC],Xn∗scl)
Absolute	$xxxx $xxxxxxxx	None
Immediate Data	#	None

Figure 3-20: New and Old Addressing Modes for 68020/30 Microprocessors

Figure 3-21 on the next page shows a summary of all addressing modes of the 68020 and 68030 microprocessors. All of the changes from the earlier 68000, 68008, 68010 and 68012 microprocessors are in the blocks with dashed lines. Each of these blocks with dashed lines is expanded in detail in Figures 3-22 to 3-25 on the following pages.

The new features of these new addressing modes are explained in the text that follows after these 5 figures.

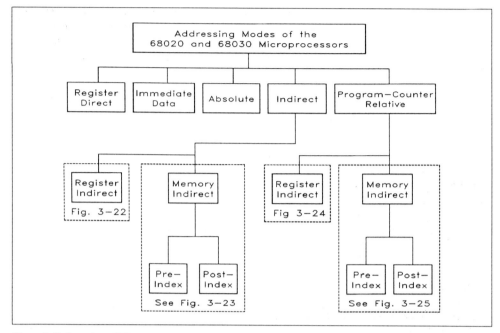

Figure 3-21:Overview of Hierarchy of addressing Modes (68020 and 68030 microprcessors)

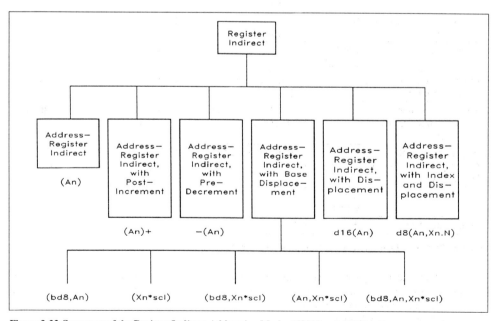

Figure 3-22:Summary of the Register Indirect-Addressing Modes (68020 and 68030 microprocessors)

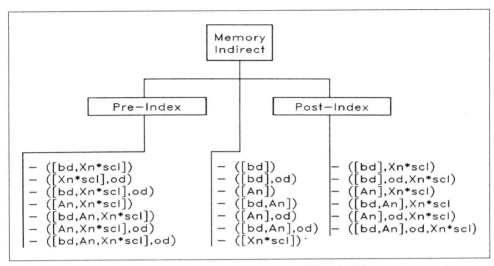

Figure 3-23: Summary of the Memory Indirect-Addressing Modes (68020 and 68030 microprocessors)

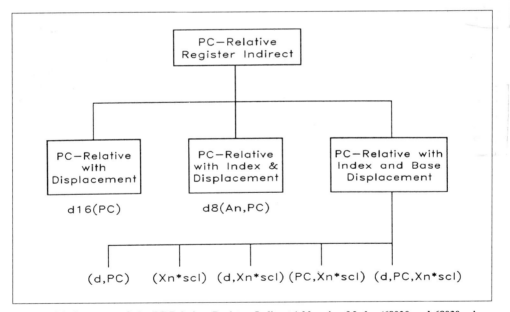

Figure 3-24: Summary of the PC-Relative, Register, Indirect-Addressing Modes (68020 and 68030 microprocessors)

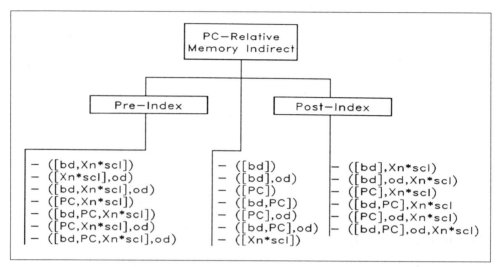

Figure 3-25: Summary of the PC-Relative, Memory, Indirect-Addressing Modes (68020 and 68030 microprocessors)

As you can see from Figure 3-21 above, the 3 groups of "Register Direct", "Immediate" and "Absolute" are the same as for the 68000/08/10/12 microprocessors. Four additional pictures are presented above, Figures 3-22 to 3-25, that display the 2 groups of "Indirect" and "PC-Relative" in more detail. Only the subgroup of "Register Indirect" was available for the earlier processors and the new subgroup of "Memory Indirect" has been added for the 68020/30 microprocessors. (This fulfills an outstanding wish of 6809 programmers who had this capability for the 8-bit 6809 microprocessor and missed it for the 16-bit 68000/08/10/12 microprocessors.) However, with the 68020/30 microprocessors, this variant is even more flexible than it was for the 6809 microprocessor.

4
Instructions of the M68000 Microprocessors

This chapter contains a detailed description of each instruction in the instruction sets of the 68000, 68008, 68010 and 68012 microprocessors. They are presented in alphabetical order by their mnemonic names, for easy reference. The instruction sets for the 68000 and 68008 microprocessors are identical. The instruction sets for the 68010 and 68012 microprocessors are also identical with each other but contain two changes and four additions from the instruction set for the 68000 and 68008 microprocessors. These changes and additions are clearly labeled in this chapter.

The last section of this chapter, 4.3, presents a comparison of the instruction sets for the different microprocessors in the M68000 family including the instruction sets of the 68020 and 68030 microprocessors. However, detailed descriptions of the additions and changes in the instructions sets for the 68020 and 68030 microprocessors are given in Chapter 8, in the respective sections for these two microprocessors.

The beginning of this chapter contains a summary of these instructions, by different categories – also for easy reference. There is also a table with the beginnings of the opcodes, for easy reference in the reverse direction, (from the opcode to the instruction).

The beginning of this chapter also contains a definition of the abbreviations that are used in the chapter.

4.1 Summary of the Instruction Sets for 68000/08/10/12 Microprocessors

This section contains:
- one table that shows all instructions for the 68000, 68008, 68010 and 68012 microprocessors in summary form,
- a set of tables for the different categories of instructions and
- a table with the beginnings of the opcodes.

The detailed descriptions for each instruction are given in the next section (Section 4.2).

The summary table in Figure 4-1 below lists all of the instructions by their mnemonic names, together with their effects upon the flags (X, N, Z, V and C) in the condition-code register.

	X	N	Z	V	C		X	N	Z	V	C		X	N	Z	V	C
ABCD	★	u	★	u	★	EORI to CCR	★	★	★	★	★	OR	–	★	★	0	0
ADD	★	★	★	★	★	EXG	–	–	–	–	–	ORI	–	★	★	0	0
ADDA	–	–	–	–	–	EXT	–	★	★	0	0	ORI to CCR	★	★	★	★	★
ADDI	★	★	★	★	★	JMP	–	–	–	–	–	PEA	–	–	–	–	–
ADDQ	★	★	★	★	★	JSR	–	–	–	–	–	RESET	–	–	–	–	–
ADDX	★	★	★	★	★	LEA	–	–	–	–	–	ROL,ROR	–	★	★	0	★
AND	–	★	★	0	0	LINK	–	–	–	–	–	ROXL,ROXR	★	★	★	0	★
ANDI	–	★	★	0	0	LSL,LSR	★	★	★	0	★	RTD	–	–	–	–	–
ASL,ASR	★	★	★	★	★	MOVE	–	★	★	0	0	RTE	★	★	★	★	★
Bcc	–	–	–	–	–	MOVE from CCR	–	–	–	–	–	RTR	★	★	★	★	★
BCHG	–	–	★	–	–	MOVE from SR	–	–	–	–	–	RTS	–	–	–	–	–
BCLR	–	–	★	–	–	MOVE to CCR	★	★	★	★	★	SBCD	★	u	★	u	★
BRA	–	–	–	–	–	MOVE to SR	★	★	★	★	★	Scc	–	–	–	–	–
BSET	–	–	★	–	–	MOVE USP	–	–	–	–	–	STOP	★	★	★	★	★
BSR	–	–	–	–	–	MOVEA	–	–	–	–	–	SUB	★	★	★	★	★
BTST	–	–	★	–	–	MOVEC	–	–	–	–	–	SUBA	–	–	–	–	–
CHK	–	★	u	u	u	MOVEM	–	–	–	–	–	SUBI	★	★	★	★	★
CLR	–	0	1	0	0	MOVEP	–	–	–	–	–	SUBQ	★	★	★	★	★
CMP	–	★	★	★	★	MOVEQ	–	★	★	0	0	SUBX	★	★	★	★	★
CMPA	–	★	★	★	★	MOVES	–	–	–	–	–	SWAP	–	★	★	0	0
CMPI	–	★	★	★	★	MULS	–	★	★	0	0	TAS	–	★	★	0	0
CMPM	–	★	★	★	★	MULU	–	★	★	0	0	TRAP	–	–	–	–	–
DBcc	–	–	–	–	–	NBCD	★	u	★	u	★	TRAPV	–	–	–	–	–
DIVS	–	★	★	★	0	NEG	★	★	★	★	★	TST	–	★	★	0	0
DIVU	–	★	★	★	0	NEGX	★	★	★	★	★	UNLK	–	–	–	–	–
EOR	–	★	★	0	0	NOP	–	–	–	–	–						
EORI	–	★	★	0	0	NOT	–	★	★	0	0						

Codes: – = not affected, u = undefined, 0 = reset to 0, 1 = set to 1, ★ = set, depending upon the results

Figure 4-1: Instructions and their Effects upon Flags

The following tables, in Figures 4-2 to 4-8, summarize the instructions of the 68000, 68008, 68010 and 68012 microprocessors in the following categories:

4-2	arithmetic operations with integers
4-3	arithmetic operations with BCD numbers
4-4	logical operations
4-5	shifting and rotating
4-6	manipulating bits
4-7	transfering data
4-8	program control

Mnemonic	Title of Instruction
ADD	binary addition – without extend (for carry)
ADDA	binary addition – address register as destination
ADDI	binary addition – immediate (with a constant)
ADDQ	quick binary addition – immediate (small constant)
ADDX	binary addition – with extend (for carry)
CLR	clear an operand
CMP	compare two operands
CMPA	compare an operand with an address register

Mnemonic	Title of Instruction
CMPI	compare an operand immediate (with a constant)
CMPM	compare contents of two memory locations
DIVS	signed division
DIVU	unsigned division
EXT	extend register with sign
MULS	multiply with sign
MULU	multiply withwout signs
NEG	negate binary number
NEGX	negate binary number with extend
SUB	binary subtraction – without extend (for borrow)
SUBA	binary subtraction – address register as destin.
SUBI	binary subtraction – immediate (with a constant)
SUBQ	quick binary subtraction – immediate (small c.)
SUBX	binary subtraction – with extend (for borrow)
TST	test the contents of an operand

Figure 4-2: Instructions for Arithmetic Operations with Integers

Mnemonic	Title of Instruction
ABCD	addition of BCD number
NBCD	negate BCD number with extend
SBCD	subtraction of BCD numbers

Figure 4-3: Instructions for Arithmetic Operations with BCD Numbers

Mnemonic	Title of Instruction
AND	ligical AND immediate (with a constant)
ANDI to CCR	logical AND immediate to condition-code register
ANDI to SR	logical AND immediate to status register
EOR	exclusive OR
EORI	exclusive OR immediate (with a constant)
EORI to CCR	exclusive OR immediate to condition-code register
EORI to SR	exclusive ORimmediate to status register
NOT	logical complement
·OR	logical inclusive OR
ORI	logical inclusice OR immediate (with a constant)
ORI to CCR	inclusive OR immediate to condition-code register

Figure 4-4: Instructions for Logical Operations

Mnemonic	Title of Instruction
ASL	arithmetic shift left
ASR	arithmetic shift right
LSL	logical shift left
LSR	logical shift right
ROL	rotate left (without extend)
ROR	rocate right (without extend)
ROXL	rotate left (with extend)
ROXR	rotate right (with extend)

Figure 4-5: Instructions for Shifting and Rotating

Mnemonic	Title of Instruction
BCHG	test and change one bit
BCLR	test and clear one bit
BSET	test and set one bit
BTST	test one bit

Figure 4-6: Instructions for Manipulating Bits

Mnemonic	Title of Instruction
EXG	exchange register contents
LEA	load effective address in address register
LINK	link stack area for subroutine
MOVE	move data from source to destination
MOVE fr CCR*	move from condition-code register
MOVE to CCR	move to condition-code register
MOVE to SR	move to status register
MOVE fr SR*	move from status register
MOVE USP	move user stack pointer
MOVEA	move into address register
MOVEC*	move into and out of control register
MOVEM	move multiple registers
MOVEP	move data for peripherals
MOVEQ	move constant quickly into data register
MOVES*	move data between memory areas
PEA	push effective address onto stack
SWAP	swap halves of data register
UNLK	unkink and retrieve the stack pointer

* = different for 68010/12 than 68000Y/08 microprocessors

Figure 4-7: Instructions for Transferring Data

Mnemonic	Title of Instruction
Bcc	conditional branch
BRA	unconditional branch
BSR	branch to subroutine
CHK	check whether data register is out of range
DBcc	test condition, decrement, and branch
JMP	jump
JSR	jump to a subroutine
NOP	no operation
RESET	reset external peripherals
RTD*	return and delete temporary parameters
RTE*	return from exception handling
RTR	return and restore flags
RTS	return from subroutine
Scc	set or clear a byte conditionally
STOP	load the status register and stop
TAS	test and set a bit in an aperand
TRAP	trap
TRAPV	trap upon overflow

* = different for 68010/12 than 68000/08 microprocessors

Figure 4-8: Instructions for Program Control

The following table in Figure 4-9 presents all combinations for the first 4 bits of an opcode, followed by a description of the subset of instructions that uses this beginning. Starting with an opcode, you can use this table as the first step in identifying which instruction is involved.

Beginnings of Opcodes	Subsets of Instructions
0000	bit-manipulation/MOVEP/immediate
0001	MOVE byte
0010	MOVE long word
0011	MOVE word
0100	miscellaneous instructions
0101	ADDQ/SUBQ/Scc/DBcc
0110	Bcc/BSR
0111	MOVEQ
1000	OR/DIV/SBCD
1001	SUB/SUBX
1010	not used
1011	CMP/EOR
1100	AND/MUL/ABCD/EXG
1101	ADD/ADDX
1110	shifting & rotating instructions
1111	reserved for extensions

Figure 4-9: Beginnings of Opcodes

4.2 Detailed Description of the Instruction Set of the 68000/08/10/12 Microprocessors

Each of the instructions from the instruction set of the M68000 microprocessor is described in detail in the rest of this chapter. They are listed alphabetically, by the mnemonic names that are used by most assemblers. A standard format is used to describe each instruction that is summarized in Figure 4-10 below. In particular, the use of tables in a standard format simplifies the quick visual comparison between instructions. It is particularly easy to see which combinations of addressing modes are allowed for source addresses and destination addresses.

This information is presented at an appropriate level for both a beginner who has no experience with the instruction set of the M68000 as well as a professional who has already worked with the M68000 family of processors.

Title	Description of Block that Follows
Mnemonic	This is the mnemonic name for the instruction, followed by a longer title in clear text.
Assembler Syntax	This is the syntax used by most assemblers.
Operation	This illustrates the operation of the instruction in a concise symbolic notation.
Flag Changes	This explains any changes that the instruction makes to the flags.
Operand Sizes	This defines the sizes that are allowed for the operands.
Description of Instruction	This explains the function and operation of the instruction in detail, in clear text but with illustrations where appropriate.
Format of Opcode	This present the format of the opcode, together with a detailed explanation for each field.
Addressing Modes	This presents all of the combinations of addressing modes that are allowed for the source and destination addresses.
Execution Times	This gives the number of clock cycles required for executing the instruction (including getthe opcode and any operands) as well as the number of read and write bus cycles required.
No. of Bytes per Instruction	This gives the number of bytes that are requirin the object code for the instruction, including the opcode and immediate operands that follow the opcode.
Examples	This gives one or two short illustrative examples. Larger axamples, with mor typical programming styles are given in Chapter 6.
Applications	This gives typical uses and applications for instruction.

Figure 4-10: Format for Describing Each Instruction

The symbols that are used in the descriptions of instructions are presented in Figure 4-11 below.

Symbol	Interpretation
X	X-flag in the condition-code register
N	N-flag in the condition-code register
Z	Z-flag in the condition-code register
V	V-flag in the condition-code register
C	C-flag in the condition-code register
Rs	arbitrary source register (s = 0–7)
Rd	arbitrary destination register (d = 0–7)
Ds	arbitrary source data register (s = 0–7)
Dd	arbitrary destination data register (d = 0–7)
D0–D7	data registers 0 to 7
As	arbitrary source address register (s = 0–7)
Ad	arbitrary destination address register (0–7)
A0–A7	address registers 0 to 7
CCR	condition-code register
SR	status register
PC	program counter
SP	stack pointer (either user or supervisor)
SSP	supervisor stack pointer
USP	user stack pointer
ea	effective address
<ea>	opperand at effective address
<address>	operand at address
+	addition
−	aubtraction
*	multiplication
/	division
^	logical AND
v	logical OR (inclusive)
⊕	logical OR (exclusive)
$xxxx	hexadecimal number
#xxxx	decimal number
@	indirect-addressing mode

Figure 4-11: Explanation of Symbols

ABCD   Addition of BCD Numbers (with Carry)

Assembler Syntax:

```
ABCD.w Ds,Dd
ABCD.w −(As), −(Ad)
```

Operation:

$$< Source > \ + \ < Destination > \ \rightarrow \ < Destination >$$

Flag Changes:

X   Set equal to 1 if a decimal overflow (carry) occurs, otherwise reset to 0.
N   Undefined after the operation.
Z   Set equal to 0 if the result is not equal 0, otherwise unchanged.
V   Undefined after the operation.
C   Set equal to 1 if a decimal overflow (carry) occurs, otherwise reset to 0.

It is a good practice to set the Z-flag equal to 1 before this operation. You can then read this flag after multiple-precision operations – to determine whether the result was 0 for all of them. You should also reset the X-Flag equal to 0 before this operation – to avoid adding a carry that may have been left in this flag.

Operand Sizes:

This instruction operates on single bytes. Therefore, a statement of ABCD or ABCD.B (for most assemblers) will lead to the same result.

Description of Instruction:

The ABCD instruction adds an operand from the source address, an operand from the destination address, and a carry bit (X-Flag) together using BCD arithmetic. It writes the result at the destination address and sets both the X-Flag and C-Flag equal to 1 if there was a carry and otherwise equal to 0. Since this is a byte instruction, it operates on bytes that contain up to 2 digits each in the packed BCD format. If you need to add numbers with more than two digits, you can repeat this instruction, as illustrated in the examples below.

If the operands contain data in the hexadecimal format, problems may arise. You will obtain the correct result in some cases, such as when you add $0A to 13, but incorrect results in other cases, such as when you add $FE to 88 since the resulting carry can not be processed properly. Therefore, you should check whether only BCD numbers will be added before you use the ABCD instruction.

Format of Opcode:

15	14	13	12	11	10	9	8	7	6	5	4	3	2	1	0
1	1	0	0	Register Rd			1	0	0	1	0	R/M	Register Rs		

Bits 15–12. These bits indicate that this instruction belongs to the set of instructions {ABCD,AND, MUL,EXG}. Other bits in the opcode select this particular instruction from this set.

Register Field Rd, Bits 11–9. Depending upon the contents of the R/M field, this field contains the number of either the destination data register that contains the operand (R/M = 0) or the destination address register for the address-register indirect-addressing mode, with predecrement (R/M = 1).

R/M Field, Bit 3. This field determines whether the registers Rs and Rd are data registers for the data-register direct-addressing mode (R/M = 0) or address registers for the address-register indirect-addressing mode, with predecrement (R/M = 1).

Register Field Rs, Bits 2–0. Depending upon the contents of the R/M field, this field contains the number of either the source data register that contains the first operand (R/M = 0) or the source address register for the address-register indirect-addressing mode, with predecrement (R/M = 1).

Execution Times (Cycles):

(Operations on Bytes and Words)

The first number is the number of clock cycles required to: get the operands, execute the instruction, store the results and get the next opcode. The second pair of numbers are the number of read cycles and the number of write cycles respectively.

These values are only valid for the 68000 microprocessor. See the condensed tables in Chapter 8 for calculating times for the other microprocessors in the M68000 family.

Source	Destination											
	Dn	An	(An)	(An)+	−(An)	d(An)	d(An,Rx)	$xxxx	$xxxxxxxx	d(PC)	d(PC,Rx)	#
Dn	6 1/0											
An												
(An)												
(An)+												
−(An)					18 3/1							
d(An)												
d(An,Rx)												
$xxxx												
$xxxxxxxx												
d(PC)												
d(PC,Rx)												
#												

Number of Bytes per Instruction for Different Addressing Modes:

Source	Destination											
	Dn	An	(An)	(An)+	−(An)	d(An)	d(An,Rx)	$xxxx	$xxxxxxxx	d(PC)	d(PC,Rx)	#
Dn	2											
An												
(An)												
(An)+												
−(An)					2							
d(An)												
d(An,Rx)												
$xxxx												
$xxxxxxxx												
d(PC)												
d(PC,Rx)												
#												

Example:

Adding two BCD numbers, with more than 2 digits each, in memory.

	1st number	= 225713
	2nd number	= 504345

Before the operations:
Contents in Memory:

	1st number	2nd number
	$1007 13	$2007 45
	$1006 57	$2006 43
	$1005 22	$2005 50

MOVE #4,CCR	Clear the X-Flag to avoid adding any carry that may already be in this flag and setting the Y-Flag to distinguish later whether the whole result is 0.
MOVE #$2008,A1	Load the address registers with starting addresses.
MOVE #$1008,A0	
ABCD −(A0),−(A1)	The result 58 is stored at location $2007.
ABCD −(A0),−(A1)	The result 00 is stored at location $2006.
ABCD −(A0),−(A1)	The result 73 is stored at location $2005.

After the operations:
Contents in Memory:

	1st number	2nd number
	$1007 13	$2007 58
	$1006 57	$2006 00
	$1005 22	$2005 73

Applications:

In the case of a system that presents its results with BDC displays, it is often practical to store and process the data in the BCD format. The ABCD instruction performs the operation of addition on such BCD numbers.

ADD   Binary Addition, Without Extend (for Carry)

Assembler Syntax:

```
ADD.w <ea>,Dd
ADD.w Ds,<ea>
```

Operation:

```
<Source> + <Destination> → <Destination>
```

Flag Changes:

X	Set equal to 1 if a carry occurs, otherwise reset to 0.
N	Set equal to 1 if result is negative, otherwise reset to 0.
Z	Set equal to 1 if result equals 0, otherwise reset to 0.
V	Set equal to 1 if an overflow occurs, otherwise reset to 0.
C	Set equal to 1 if a carry occurs, otherwise reset to 0.

Operand Sizes:

This instruction operates on bytes, words and long words. The .w in the syntax refers to .B, .W or .L respectively.

Description of Instruction:

The ADD instruction reads the first operand from the source address and the second operand from the destination address. Either the first operand or the second operand must already be in a data register. It adds the two operands together, using binary addition, and it stores the result at the destination address, ie. either an extended address or a data register. This operation does not include the addition of a carry bit from a previous add operation. If you want to add numbers that are longer than long words (32 bits), then you will need to use the ADDX instruction after the ADD instruction in order to add the carry from each previous operation.

Format of Opcode:

15	14	13	12	11	10	9	8	7	6	5	4	3	2	1	0
1	1	0	1	\multicolumn{3}{Register Ds/Dd}			Opmode			Effective Address \<ea\>			
											Mode			Register	

Bits 15–12. These bits indicate that this instruction belongs to the set of instructions {ADD,ADDX}. Other bits in the opcode select this particular instruction from this set.

Register Ds/Dd, Bits 11–9. Either the source address or the destination address of the ADD instruction must be a data register. The number of this register is specified in this field.

Opmode, Bits 8–6. The first bit, bit 8, determines whether the source address or the destination address of the instruction is a data register. If this bit is 0, then the destination address is a data register. If it is 1, then the source address is a data register. The remaining 2 bits, 7 and 6, specify the length of the operands as follows:

00	–	8-bit bytes as operands
01	–	16-bit words as operands
10	–	32-bit long words as operands

Effective Address, Bits 5–0. There are two different cases for the effective address, depending upon whether the source address or the destination address is defined by this effective address:

Case 1: The effective address defines the source address. The effective address has two components, mode and register, that are defined in the table below:

Effective Address <ea>		Mnemonic for Addressing Mode
Mode	Register	
000	Register Number n	Dn
001	Register Number n	An
010	Register Number n	(An)
011	Register Number n	(An)+
100	Register Number n	−(An)
101	Register Number n	d(An)
110	Register Number n	d(An,Rx)
111	000	$xxxx
111	001	$xxxxxxxx
111	010	d(PC)
111	011	d(PC,Rx)
111	100	#

For the address-register direct-addressing mode, An, operands are only allowed with words and long words–since processing with bytes is not allowed in an address register.

Case 2: The effective address defines the destination address. The effective address has two components, mode and register, that are defined in the table below:

Effective Address <ea>		Mnemonic for Addressing Mode
Mode	Register	
*	*	Dn
*	*	An
010	Register Number n	(An)
011	Register Number n	(An)+
100	Register Number n	−(An)
101	Register Number n	d(An)
110	Register Number n	d(An,Rx)
111	000	$xxxx
111	001	$xxxxxxxx
*	*	d(PC)
*	*	d(PC,Rx)
*	*	#

* means that this addressing mode is not allowed

For the case where an address register is used as the destination address there is a separate mnemonic, ADDA. (It is described in more detail as the next instruction below.)

Execution Times (Cycles): (Operations on Bytes and Words)

The first number is the number of clock cycles required to: get the operands, execute the instruction, store the results and get the next opcode. The next pair of numbers is for the number of read cycles and the number of write cycles respectively.

These values are only valid for the 68000 microprocessor. See the condensed tables in Chapter 8 for calculating times for the other microprocessors in the M68000 family.

Source	Destination											
	Dn	An	(An)	(An)+	−(An)	d(An)	d(An,Rx)	$xxxx	$xxxxxxxx	d(PC)	d(PC,Rx)	#
Dn	4 1/0	12 2/1	12 2/1	14 2/1	16 3/1	18 3/1	16 3/1	20 4/1				
An	4 1/0											
(An)	8 2/0											
(An)+	8 2/0											
−(An)	10 2/0											
d(An)	12 3/0											
d(An,Rx)	14 3/0											
$xxxx	12 3/0											
$xxxxxxxx	16 4/0											
d(PC)	12 3/0											
d(PC,Rx)	14 3/0											
#	8 2/0											

Execution Times (Cycles): (Operations on Long Words)

The first number is the number of clock cycles required to: get the operands, execute the instruction, store the results and get the next opcode. The next pair of numbers is for the number of read cycles and the number of write cycles respectively.

These values are only valid for the 68000 microprocessor. See the condensed tables in Chapter 8 for calculating times for the other microprocessors in the M68000 family.

Source	Destination											
	Dn	An	(An)	(An)+	−(An)	d(An)	d(An,Rx)	$xxxx	$xxxxxxxx	d(PC)	d(PC,Rx)	#
Dn	8 1/0		20 3/2	20 3/2	22 3/2	24 4/2	26 4/2	24 4/2	28 5/2			
An	8 1/0											
(An)	14 3/0											
(An)+	14 3/0											
−(An)	16 3/0											
d(An)	18 4/0											
d(An,Rx)	20 4/0											
$xxxx	18 4/0											
$xxxxxxxx	22 5/0											
d(PC)	18 4/0											
d(PC,Rx)	20 4/0											
#	14 3/0											

Number of Bytes per Instruction for Different Addressing Modes:
(Operations on Bytes and Words)

Source	Destination											
	Dn	An	(An)	(An)+	−(An)	d(An)	d(An,Rx)	$xxxx	$xxxxxxxx	d(PC)	d(PC,Rx)	#
Dn	2		2	2	2	4	4	4	6			
An	2											
(An)	2											
(An)+	2											
−(An)	2											
d(An)	4											
d(An,Rx)	4											
$xxxx	4											
$xxxxxxxx	6											
d(PC)	4											
d(PC,Rx)	4											
#	4											

Number of Bytes per Instruction for Different Addressing Modes:
(Operations on Long Words)

Source	Destination											
	Dn	An	(An)	(An)+	−(An)	d(An)	d(An,Rx)	$xxxx	$xxxxxxxx	d(PC)	d(PC,Rx)	#
Dn	2		2	2	2	4	4	4	6			
An	2											
(An)	2											
(An)+	2											
−(An)	2											
d(An)	4											
d(An,Rx)	4											
$xxxx	4											
$xxxxxxxx	6											
d(PC)	4											
d(PC,Rx)	4											
#	4											

Examples:

1. Addition of bytes:

Before the operation:	
Contents of register D1:	$xxxxxx53
Contents of register D3:	$xxxxxx23
ADD.B D1,D3	Addition of D1 + D3
Result is stored in register D3:	$xxxxxx78
After the operation:	
The status of the flags:	X N Z V C
	0 0 0 0 0

2. Addition of short words:

Before the operation:	
Contents of register D1	: $xxxx1234
Contents at address $1000	: $5678
ADD.W $1000,D1	Addition of both numbers
After the operation:	
The status of the flags:	X N Z V C
	0 0 0 0 0
Contents of register D1:	$68AC

3. Addition of long words:

Before the operation:	
Contents of register D1	: $82345678
Contents at address $1000	: $84510213
ADD.L $1000,D1	Addition of both numbers
After the operation:	
The status of the flags:	X N Z V C
	1 0 0 1 1
Contents of register D1:	$0645888

Applications:

The ADD instruction can add binary words with a length of up to 32 bits. For binary words with a length of more than 32 bits, you must write a routine that can use the ADD instruction for the least-significant long word, but must use the ADDX instruction for the rest of the operations (to include the carry from less-significant operations).

ADDA   Binary Addition, with an Address Register as Destination

Assembler Syntax:

ADDA.w <ea>, Ad

Operation:

<Source> + <Destination> → <Destination>

Flag Changes:

None.

Operand Sizes:

This instruction operates only on words and long words–since only these data types can be processed in address registers. The .w in the syntax refers to .W or .L respectively.

Description of Instruction:

The ADDA instruction adds an operand from an extended address to the contents of an address register and stores the results in the address register, using binary addition. This operation does not include the addition of a carry bit from a previous add operation.

This instruction represent a mnemonic extension of the ADD instruction. There is no distinction between the ADD and ADDA instructions in most M68000 assemblers. Both ADD <ea>,An and ADDA <ea>,An are processed the same, whereas the assembler uses the ADDA opcode in both cases.

Format of Opcode:

15	14	13	12	11	10	9	8	7	6	5	4	3	2	1	0
1	1	0	1	Register Ad			Opmode			Effective Address <ea>					
										Mode			Register		

Bits 15–12. These bits indicate that this instruction belongs to the set of instructions {ADD,ADDX}. Other bits in the opcode select this particular instruction from this set.

Register,Bits 11–9. The ADDA instruction reads the second operand from an address register as the destination address and writes the result into the same address register. This field specifies the number of that register.

Opmode, Bits 8–6. This field determines the size of the operands for this instruction. The bit combination of 011 specifies words (16 bits). At the beginning of the operation, the 16-bit first operand is expanded into a 32-bit long word, with the correct sign, and added as a 32-bit long word to the 32-bit contents of the address register used as the destination address.

The bit combination of 111 specifies long words (32 bits). All 32 bits of the first operand are added to the 32 bits in the address register.

Effective Address,Bits 5–0. The effective address for the source address is stored in this pair of fields, one for the mode and the other for the register. The interpretation for this pair of fields is given in the table below:

Effective Address <ea>		Mnemonic for Addressing Mode
Mode	**Register**	
000	Register Number n	Dn
001	Register Number n	An
010	Register Number n	(An)
011	Register Number n	(An)+
100	Register Number n	–(An)
101	Register Number n	d(An)
110	Register Number n	d(An,Rx)
111	000	$xxxx
111	001	$xxxxxxxx
111	010	d(PC)
111	011	d(PC,Rx)
111	100	#

Execution Times (Cycles): (Operations on Words)

The first number is the number of clock cycles required to: get the operands, execute the instruction, store the results and get the next opcode. The next pair of numbers is for the number of read cycles and the number of write cycles respectively.

These values are only valid for the 68000 microprocessor. See the condensed tables in Chapter 8 for calculating times for the other microprocessors in the M68000 family.

Source	Destination											
	Dn	An	(An)	(An)+	–(An)	d(An)	d(An,Rx)	$xxxx	$xxxxxxxx	d(PC)	d(PC,Rx)	#
Dn		8 1/0										
An		8 1/0										
(An)		12 2/0										
(An)+		12 2/0										
–(An)		14 2/0										
d(An)		16 3/0										
d(An,Rx)		18 3/0										
$xxxx		16 3/0										
$xxxxxxxx		20 4/0										
d(PC)		16 3/0										
d(PC,Rx)		18 3/0										
#		12 2/0										

Execution Times (Cycles): (Operations on Long Words)

The first number is the number of clock cycles required to: get the operands, execute the instruction, store the results and get the next opcode. The next pair of numbers is for the number of read cycles and the number of write cycles respectively.

These values are only valid for the 68000 microprocessor. See the condensed tables in Chapter 8 for calculating times for the other microprocessors in the M68000 family.

Source	Destination											
	Dn	An	(An)	(An)+	–(An)	d(An)	d(An,Rx)	$xxxx	$xxxxxxxx	d(PC)	d(PC,Rx)	#
Dn		6 1/0										
An		8 1/0										
(An)		14 3/0										
(An)+		14 3/0										
–(An)		16 3/0										
d(An)		18 4/0										
d(An,Rx)		20 4/0										
$xxxx		18 4/0										
$xxxxxxxx		22 5/0										
d(PC)		20 4/0										
d(PC,Rx)		20 4/0										
#		14 3/0										

In the case where the first operand does not use a source address with a register direct-addressing mode (Dn or An), the time of execution is shorter for long words than for words. This is because of the conversion that is necessary for a short word.

Number of Bytes per Instruction for Different Addressing Modes:
(Operations on Bytes and Words)

Source	Destination											
	Dn	An	(An)	(An)+	−(An)	d(An)	d(An,Rx)	$xxxx	$xxxxxxxx	d(PC)	d(PC,Rx)	#
Dn	2											
An	2											
(An)	2											
(An)+	2											
−(An)	2											
d(An)	4											
d(An,Rx)	4											
$xxxx	4											
$xxxxxxxx	6											
d(PC)	4											
d(PC,Rx)	4											
#	4											

Number of Bytes per Instruction for Different Addressing Modes:
(Operations on Long Words)

Source	Destination											
	Dn	An	(An)	(An)+	−(An)	d(An)	d(An,Rx)	$xxxx	$xxxxxxxx	d(PC)	d(PC,Rx)	#
Dn	2											
An	2											
(An)	2											
(An)+	2											
−(An)	2											
d(An)	4											
d(An,Rx)	4											
$xxxx	4											
$xxxxxxxx	6											
d(PC)	4											
d(PC,Rx)	4											
#	6											

Example:

1. Addition of Words:

Before the operation:
Contents of register A1   : $00001234
Contents at source address   : $8123
ADDA.W #$8123,A1
The two numbers are added, after the first operand has been converted into a long word with the appropriate sign.

$$FFFF8123$$
$$+00001234$$

FFFF9357   Result in A1

After the operation:
The status of flags   : None are changed.
Contents of register A1   : $FFFF9357

2. Addition of Long Words:

Before the operation:	
Contents of register A1	: $12345678
Contents as source address	: $34512091
ADDA.L #$34512091,A1	
The two numbers are added.	
After the operation:	
The status of flags	: None are changed.
Contents of register A1	: $46857709

Applications:

The ADDA instruction is used for adding both words and long words, using binary addition, primarily for the calculation of addresses. After the address is calculated, the corresponding operand can be selected using the address-register direct-addressing mode.

ADDI Binary Addition, Immediate (with a Constant)

Assembler Syntax:

ADDI.w #Constant,<ea>

Operation:

<Source> + <Destination> → <Destination>

Flag Changes:

X	Set equal to 1 if an overflow occurs, otherwise reset to 0.
N	Set equal to 1 if result is negative, otherwise reset to 0.
Z	Set equal to 1 if result equals 0, otherwise unchanged.
V	Set equal to 1 if an overflow occurs, otherwise reset to 0.
C	Set equal to 1 if an overflow occurs, otherwise reset to 0.

Operand Sizes:

This instruction operates on bytes, words and long words. The .w in the syntax refers to .B, .W or .L respectively.

Description of Instruction:

The ADDI instruction adds a constant, as the first operand, to a second operand. It reads the second operand from the destination address, and it writes the results back into the destination address. A carry bit from a previous operation will not be added.

Format of Opcode:

15	14	13	12	11	10	9	8	7	6	5	4	3	2	1	0
0	0	0	0	0	1	1	0	Size		Effective Address \<ea\>					

										Effective Address \<ea\>					
0	0	0	0	0	1	1	0	Size		Mode		Register			
16-bit Constant										8-bit Constant					
32-bit Constant (including previous word)															

Bits 15–12. These bits indicate that this instruction belongs to the set of instructions {bit-manipulation,MOVEP,immediate}. Other bits in the opcode select this particular instruction from this set.

Bits 11–8. These bits select this particular instruction as ADDI.

SizeField,Bits 7–6. The size of the operands is stored in this field, defined as follows:

00	–	8-bit bytes as operands
01	–	16-bit words as operands
10	–	32-bit long words as operands

Effective Address, Bits 5–0. The effective address is stored in this pair of fields, one for the mode and the other for the register. The interpretation for this pair of fields is given in the table below:

Effective Address \<ea\>		Mnemonic for Addressing Mode
Mode	Register	
000	Register Number n	Dn
*	*	An
010	Register Number n	(An)
011	Register Number n	(An)+
100	Register Number n	–(An)
101	Register Number n	d(An)
110	Register Number n	d(An,Rx)
111	000	$xxxx
111	001	$xxxxxxxx
*	*	d(PC)
*	*	d(PC,Rx)
*	*	#

* means that this addressing mode is not allowed

When used with bytes, an extra word follows the opcode. The lower half of this word (bits 7–0) contains one byte as the constant. When used with words, the extra word contains one 16-bit word as the constant. When used with long words, there are two extra words after the opcode.

Execution Times (Cycles): (Operations on Bytes and Words)

The first number is the number of clock cycles required to: get the operands, execute the instruction, store the results and get the next opcode. The next pair of numbers is for the number of read cycles and the number of write cycles respectively.

These values are only valid for the 68000 microprocessor. See the condensed tables in Chapter 8 for calculating times for the other microprocessors in the M68000 family.

Source	Destination											
	Dn	An	(An)	(An)+	−(An)	d(An)	d(An,Rx)	$xxxx	$xxxxxxxx	d(PC)	d(PC,Rx)	#
Dn												
An												
(An)												
(An)+												
−(An)												
d(An)												
d(An,Rx)												
$xxxx												
$xxxxxxxx												
d(PC)												
d(PC,Rx)												
#	8 2/0	16 3/1	16 3/1	18 3/1	20 4/1	22 4/1	20 4/1	24 5/1				

Execution Times (Cycles): (Operations on Long Words)

The first number is the number of clock cyces required to: get the operands, execute the instruction, store the results and get the next opcode. The next pair of numbers is for the number of read cycles and the number of write cycles respectively.

These values are only valid for the 68000 microprocessor. See the condensed tables in Chapter 8 for calculating times for the other microprocessors in the M68000 family.

Source	Destination											
	Dn	An	(An)	(An)+	−(An)	d(An)	d(An,Rx)	$xxxx	$xxxxxxxx	d(PC)	d(PC,Rx)	#
Dn												
An												
(An)												
(An)+												
−(An)												
d(An)												
d(An,Rx)												
$xxxx												
$xxxxxxxx												
d(PC)												
d(PC,Rx)												
#	16 3/0	28 5/2	28 5/2	30 5/2	32 6/2	34 6/2	32 6/2	36 7/2				

Number of Bytes per Instructions for Different Addressing Modes:
(Operations on Bytes and Words)

Source	Destination											
	Dn	An	(An)	(An)+	−(An)	d(An)	d(An,Rx)	$xxxx	$xxxxxxxx	d(PC)	d(PC,Rx)	#
Dn												
An												
(An)												
(An)+												
−(An)												
d(An)												
d(An,Rx)												
$xxxx												
$xxxxxxxx												
d(PC)												
d(PC,Rx)												
#	4		4	4	4	6	6	6	8			

Number of Bytes per Instruction for Different Addressing Modes:
(Operations on Long Words)

Source	Destination											
	Dn	An	(An)	(An)+	−(An)	d(An)	d(An,Rx)	$xxxx	$xxxxxxxx	d(PC)	d(PC,Rx)	#
Dn												
An												
(An)												
(An)+												
−(An)												
d(An)												
d(An,Rx)												
$xxxx												
$xxxxxxxx												
d(PC)												
d(PC,Rx)												
#	6		6	6	6	8	8	8	10			

Example:

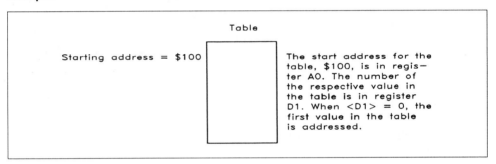

Table

Starting address = $100

The start address for the table, $100, is in register A0. The number of the respective value in the table is in register D1. When <D1> = 0, the first value in the table is addressed.

A program for addressing the values in the table above:

```
         CLR.L D1
         MOVE #(Number of values minus 1),D0
         LEA START,A0
LOOP     MOVE(A0,D1),(A5)+
         ADDI #2,D1
         DBRA D0,LOOP
```

Applications:

To give an example, you can use the ADDI instruction to increment a data register for calculating a table value that is addressed with a data register as an index register in a loop. This example is illustrated above:

ADDQ   Quick Binary Addition, Immediate (with a Small Constant)

Assembler Syntax:

ADDQ.w #Constant,<ea>

Operation:

<Source> + <Destination> → <Destination>

Flag Changes:

X   Set equal to 1 if an overflow occurs, otherwise reset to 0.
N   Set equal to 1 if result is negative, otherwise reset to 0.
Z   Set equal to 1 if result equals 0, otherwise unchanged.
V   Set equal to 1 if an overflow occurs, otherwise reset to 0.
C   Set equal to 1 if an overflow occurs, otherwise reset to 0.

If the destination address is an address register, then the flags will not be changed.

Operand Sizes:

This instruction operates on bytes, words and long words. However, the constant is limited to a small number, less than or equal to 8. The .w in the syntax refers to .B, .W or .L respectively.

Description of Instruction:

The ADDQ instruction is nearly identical to the ADDI instruction, except for minor differences. It is used to add a small constant to an operand that it reads from the destination address. It executes faster than the ADDI instruction, at the expense of limiting the constant to values less than or equal to 8. These differences are explained in the description of the opcode below.

Format of Opcode:

15	14	13	12	11	10	9	8	7	6	5	4	3	2	1	0
1	0	0	0		Data		0		Size		Effective Address <ea>				
											Mode			Register	

Bits 15–12. These bits indicate that this instruction belongs to the set of instructions {ADDQ,SUBQ, Scc,DBcc}. Other bits in the opcode select this particular instruction from this set.
Data Field, Bits 11–9. Direct data is stored in this field, with bit combinations from 000 to 111. The bit combination 001 corresponds to the integer 1, 111 corresponds to 7 and 000 corresponds to 8.
Size Field, Bits 7–6. The size of the operands is stored in this field, defined as follows:

00	–	8-bit bytes as operands
01	–	16-bit words as operands
10	–	32-bit long words as operands

Effective Address, Bits 5–0

The effective address is stored in this pair of fields, one for the mode and the other for the register. The interpretation for this pair of fields is given in the table below:

Effective Address <ea>		Mnemonic for Addressing Mode
Mode	Register	
000	Register Number n	Dn
001	Register Number n	An
010	Register Number n	(An)
011	Register Number n	(An)+
100	Register Number n	−(An)
101	Register Number n	d(An)
110	Register Number n	d(An,Rx)
111	000	$xxxx
111	001	$xxxxxxxx
*	*	d(PC)
*	*	d(PC,Rx)
*	*	#

* means that this addressing mode is not allowed

Execution Times (Cycles): (Operations on Bytes and Words)

The first number is the number of clock cycles required to: get the operand, execute the instruction, store the results and get the next opcode. The next pair of numbers is for the number of read cycles and the number of write cycles respectively.

These values are only valid for the 68000 microprocessor. See the condensed tables in Chapter 8 for calculating times for the other microprocessors in the M68000 family.

Source	Destination											
	Dn	An	(An)	(An)+	−(An)	d(An)	d(An,Rx)	$xxxx	$xxxxxxxx	d(PC)	d(PC,Rx)	#
Dn												
An												
(An)												
(An)+												
−(An)												
d(An)												
d(An,Rx)												
$xxxx												
$xxxxxxxx												
d(PC)												
d(PC,Rx)												
#	4 1/0	8 1/0	12 2/1	12 2/1	14 2/1	16 3/1	18 3/1	16 3/1	20 4/1			

Execution Times (Cycles): (Operations on Long Words)

The first number is the number of clock cycles required to: get the operand, execute the instruction, store the results and get the next opcode. The next pair of numbers is for the number of read cycles and the number of write cycles respectively.

These values are only valid for the 68000 microprocessor. See the condensed tables in Chapter 8 for calculating times for the other microprocessors in the M68000 family.

Source	Destination											
	Dn	An	(An)	(An)+	−(An)	d(An)	d(An,Rx)	$xxxx	$xxxxxxxx	d(PC)	d(PC,Rx)	#
Dn												
An												
(An)												
(An)+												
−(An)												
d(An)												
d(An,Rx)												
$xxxx												
$xxxxxxxx												
d(PC)												
d(PC,Rx)												
#	8 1/0	8 1/0	20 3/2	20 3/2	22 3/2	24 4/2	26 4/2	24 4/2	28 5/2			

Number of Bytes per Instruction for Different Addressing Modes:
(Operations on Bytes and Words)

Source	Destination											
	Dn	An	(An)	(An)+	−(An)	d(An)	d(An,Rx)	$xxxx	$xxxxxxxx	d(PC)	d(PC,Rx)	#
Dn												
An												
(An)												
(An)+												
−(An)												
d(An)												
d(An,Rx)												
$xxxx												
$xxxxxxxx												
d(PC)												
d(PC,Rx)												
#	2	2	2	2	2	4	4	4	6			

Number of Bytes per Instruction for Different Addressing Modes:
(Operations on Long Words)

Source	Destination											
	Dn	An	(An)	(An)+	−(An)	d(An)	d(An,Rx)	$xxxx	$xxxxxxxx	d(PC)	d(PC,Rx)	#
Dn												
An												
(An)												
(An)+												
−(An)												
d(An)												
d(An,Rx)												
$xxxx												
$xxxxxxxx												
d(PC)												
d(PC,Rx)												
#	2	2	2	2	2	4	4	4	6			

Example:

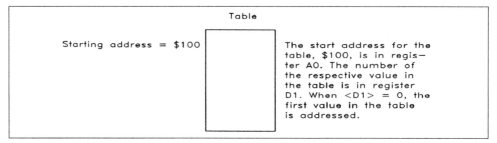

A program for addressing the values in the table above:

```
        CLR.L D1
        MOVE #(Number of values minus 1),D0
        LEA START,A0
LOOP    MOVE(A0,D1),(A5)+
        ADDQ #2,D1
        DBRA D0,LOOP
```

Applications:

To give an example, you can use the ADDQ instruction to increment a data register for calculating a table value that is addressed with a data register as an index register in a loop. This example is illustrated above. The choice between using the faster ADDQ instruction or the slower ADDI instruction depends upon the value of the constant being added. If this value is less than or equal to 8, then you should use the faster ADDQ instruction. Otherwise, you must use the slower ADDI instruction that can add larger constants.

ADDX   Binary Addition, with Extend Bit (for Carry)

Assembler Syntax:

```
ADDX.w Ds,Dd
ADDX.w -(As),-(Ad)
```

Operation:

$$<Source> + <Destination> + <X> \rightarrow <Destination>$$

Flag Changes:

X   Set equal to 1 if an overflow occurs, otherwise reset to 0.
N   Set equal to 1 if result is negative, otherwise reset to 0.
Z   Set equal to 0 if result not equal 0, otherwise unchanged.
V   Set equal to 1 if an overflow occurs, otherwise reset to 0.
C   Set equal to 1 if an overflow occurs, otherwise reset to 0.

As with the ABCD instruction, it is a good practice to set the Z-flag equal to 1 before this operation. You can then read this flag after multiple-precision operations – to determine whether the result was 0 for all of them.

Operand Sizes:

This instruction operates on bytes, words and long words. The .w in the syntax refers to .B, .W or .L respectively.

Description of Instruction:

The ADDX instruction uses binary addition to add two operands together, including the X-flag that may have a carry bit from a previous operation. It is therefore easy to add words with more than 32 bits with this instruction. It read the two operands from the source and destination addresses and it writes the result back into the destination address.

Format of Opcode:

15	14	13	12	11	10	9	8	7	6	5	4	3	2	1	0
1	1	0	1	Register Dd/Ad			1	Size		0	0	R/M	Register DS/As		

Bits 15–12. These bits indicate that this construction belongs to the set of instructions {ADD,ADDX}. Other bits in the opcode select this particular instruction from this set.

Register Field Dd/Ad, Bits 11–9. Depending upon the contents of the R/M field, this field contains the number of either the destination data register that contains the second operand (R/M = 0) or the destination address register for the address-register indirect-addressing mode, with predecrement (R/M = 1).

Size Field, Bits 7–6. The size of the operands is stored in this field, defined as follows:

00	–	8-bit bytes as operands
01	–	16-bit words as operands
10	–	32-bit long words as operands

R/M Field, Bit 3. This field determines whether the registers Rs and Rd are data registers (Ds and Dd) for the data-register direct-addressing mode (R/M = 0) or address registers (As and Ad) for the address-register indirect-addressing mode, with predecrement (R/M = 1).

Register Field Ds/As, Bits 2–0. Depending upon the contents of the R/M field, this field contains the number of either the source data register that contains the first operand (R/M = 0) or the source address register for the address-register indirect-addressing mode, with predecrement (R/M = 1).

Execution Times (Cycles): (Operations on Bytes and Words)

The first number is the number of clock cycles required to: get the operands, execute the instruction, store the results and get the next opcode. The next pair of numbers is for the number of read cycles and the number of write cycles respectively.

These values are only valid for the 68000 microprocessor. See the condensed tables in Chapter 8 for calculating times for the other microprocessors in the M68000 family.

Source	Destination											
	Dn	An	(An)	(An)+	−(An)	d(An)	d(An,Rx)	$xxxx	$xxxxxxxx	d(PC)	d(PC,Rx)	#
Dn	4 1/0											
An												
(An)												
(An)+												
−(An)				18 3/1								
d(An)												
d(An,Rx)												
$xxxx												
$xxxxxxxx												
d(PC)												
d(PC,Rx)												
#												

Execution Times (Cycles): (Operations on Long Words)

The first number is the number of clock cycles required to: get the operands, execute the instruction, store the results and get the next opcode. The next pair of numbers is for the number of read cycles and the number of write cycles respectively.

These values are only valid for the 68000 microprocessor. See the condensed tables in Chapter 8 for calculating times for the other microprocessors in the M68000 family.

Source	Destination											
	Dn	An	(An)	(An)+	−(An)	d(An)	d(An,Rx)	$xxxx	$xxxxxxxx	d(PC)	d(PC,Rx)	#
Dn	8 1/0											
An												
(An)												
(An)+												
−(An)				30 5/2								
d(An)												
d(An,Rx)												
$xxxx												
$xxxxxxxx												
d(PC)												
d(PC,Rx)												
#												

Number of Bytes per Instruction for Different Addressing Modes:
(Operations on Bytes and Words)

Source	Destination											
	Dn	An	(An)	(An)+	−(An)	d(An)	d(An,Rx)	$xxxx	$xxxxxxxx	d(PC)	d(PC,Rx)	#
Dn	2											
An												
(An)												
(An)+												
−(An)				2								
d(An)												
d(An,Rx)												
$xxxx												
$xxxxxxxx												
d(PC)												
d(PC,Rx)												
#												

Number of Bytes per Instruction for Different Addressing Modes:
(Operations on Long Words)

Source	Destination											
	Dn	An	(An)	(An)+	−(An)	d(An)	d(An,Rx)	$xxxx	$xxxxxxxx	d(PC)	d(PC,Rx)	#
Dn	2											
An												
(An)												
(An)+												
−(An)				2								
d(An)												
d(An,Rx)												
$xxxx												
$xxxxxxxx												
d(PC)												
d(PC,Rx)												
#												

Example:

Adding two numbers that are longer than 32 bits each.

Number 1:	$1234567801234567	
Number 2:	$8765432176543210	

Before the operation:
Contents in Memory:

Addresses:	Contents:
$100	$01234567
$104	$12345678
$200	$76543210
$204	$87654321

ADD.L $100,$200
ORI # $04,CCR   Set Z-flag = 1 to identify zero result.
ADDX.L $104,$204

After the operation:
Contents in Memory:

Addresses:	Contents:
$100	$01234567
$104	$12345678
$200	$77777777
$204	$99999999

The complete result is $9999999977777777

Applications:

The ADDX is used primarily for adding numbers with more than 32 bits. To avoid having to clear the X-flag before using the ADDX instruction, the simpler ADD instruction can be used first. This first ADD instruction sets the X-flag equal to 0 or 1, depending upon whether there is a carry bit from the first addition operation. The following ADDX instruction includes this X-flag with the carry bit in its addition. If you want to determine later whether the result of the ADDX instruction was 0, you should set the Z-flag equal to 1 before using the ADDX instruction. The instruction ORI $04,CCR sets the Z-flag equal to 1 without changing the other flags.

AND   Logical AND

Assembler Syntax:

AND.w <ea>,Dd
AND.w Ds,<ea>

Operation:

<Source> ˆ <Destination> → <Destination>

Flag Changes:

X   Not changed by the AND operation
N   Set equal to 1 if leading bit of result is 1, otherwise reset equal to 0.
Z   Set equal to 1 if result equals 0, otherwise reset to 0.
V   Always reset equal to 0.
C   Always reset equal to 0.

Operand Sizes:

This instruction operates on bytes, words and long words. The .w in the syntax refers to .B, .W or .L respectively.

Description of Instruction:

The AND instruction performs the logical AND operation on two operands, bit for bit. It reads the operands from the source and destination addresses and stores the results back into the destination address.

Format of Opcode:

15	14	13	12	11	10	9	8	7	6	5	4	3	2	1	0
										Effective Address <ea>					
1	1	0	0	Register Ds/Dd			Opmode			Mode			Register		

Bits 15–12. These bits indicate that this instruction belongs to the set of instructions {AND,MUL, ABCD,EXG}. Other bits in the opcode select this particular instruction from this set.
Register Field Ds/Ds, Bits 11–9. Either the source address or the destination address of the AND instruction must be a data register. The number of this register is specified in this field.
Opmode, Bits 8–6. The first bit, bit 8, determines whether the source address or destination address of the instruction is a data register. If this bit is 0, then the destination is a data register. If it is 1, then the source is a data register. The remaining 2 bits, 7 and 6, specify the size of the operands as follows:

00 –	8-bit bytes as operands
01 –	16-bit words as operands
10 –	32-bit long words as operands

Effective Address, Bits 5–0. There are two different cases for the effective address, depending upon whether the source address or the destination address is defined by this address:

Case 1: The effective address defines the source address. The effective address has two components, mode and register, that are defined in the table below:

Effective Address <ea>		Mnemonic for Addressing Mode
Mode	**Register**	
000	Register Number n	Dn
*	*	An
010	Register Number n	(An)
011	Register Number n	(An)+
100	Register Number n	–(An)
101	Register Number n	d(An)
110	Register Number n	d(An,Rx)
111	000	$xxxx
111	001	$xxxxxxxx
111	010	d(PC)
111	011	d(PC,Rx)
111	100	#

∗ means that this addressing mode is not allowed

Case 2: The effective address defines the destination address. The effective address has two components, mode and register, that are defined in the table below:

Effective Address <ea>		Mnemonic for Addressing Mode
Mode	**Register**	
*	*	Dn
*	*	An
010	Register Number n	(An)
011	Register Number n	(An)+
100	Register Number n	–(An)
101	Register Number n	d(An)
110	Register Number n	d(An,Rx)
111	000	$xxxx
111	001	$xxxxxxxx
*	*	d(PC)
*	*	d(PC,Rx)
*	*	#

∗ means that this addressing mode is not allowed

Execution Times (Cycles): (Operations on Bytes and Words)

The first number is the number of clock cycles required to: get the operands, execute the instruction, store the results and get the next opcode. The next pair of numbers is for the number of read cycles and the number of write cycles respectively.

These values are only valid for the 68000 microprocessor. See the condensed tables in Chapter 8 for calculating times for the other microprocessors in the M68000 family.

Case 1: The effective address defines the source address.

Source	Destination											
	Dn	An	(An)	(An)+	–(An)	d(An)	d(An,Rx)	$xxxx	$xxxxxxxx	d(PC)	d(PC,Rx)	#
Dn	4 1/0											
An	4 1/0											
(An)												
(An)+	8 2/0											
–(An)	10 2/0											
d(An)	12 3/0											
d(An,Rx)	14 3/0											
$xxxx	12 3/0											
$xxxxxxxx	16 4/0											
d(PC)	12 3/0											
d(PC,Rx)	14 3/0											
#	8 2/0											

Case 2: The effective address defines the destination address. (Bytes and Words)

Source	Destination											
	Dn	An	(An)	(An)+	–(An)	d(An)	d(An,Rx)	$xxxx	$xxxxxxxx	d(PC)	d(PC,Rx)	#
Dn			12 2/1	12 2/1	14 2/1	16 3/1	18 3/1	16 3/1	20 4/1			
An												
(An)												
(An)+												
–(An)												
d(An)												
d(An,Rx)												
$xxxx												
$xxxxxxxx												
d(PC)												
d(PC,Rx)												
#												

Execution Times (Cycles): (Operations on Long Words)

These values are only valid for the 68000 microprocessor. See the condensed tables in Chapter 8 for calculating times for the other microprocessors in the M68000 family.

Case 1: The effective address defines the source address.

Source	Destination											
	Dn	An	(An)	(An)+	–(An)	d(An)	d(An,Rx)	$xxxx	$xxxxxxxx	d(PC)	d(PC,Rx)	#
Dn	6 1/0											
An												
(An)	14 3/0											
(An)+	14 3/0											
–(An)	16 3/0											
d(An)	18 4/0											
d(An,Rx)	20 4/0											
$xxxx	18 4/0											
$xxxxxxxx	22 5/0											
d(PC)	18 4/0											
d(PC,Rx)	20 4/0											
#	14 3/0											

Execution Times (Cycles): (Operations on Long Words)

These values are only valid for the 68000 microprocessor. See the condensed tables in Chapter 8 for calculating times for the other microprocessors in the M68000 family.

Case 2: The effective address defines the destination address.

Source	Destination											
	Dn	An	(An)	(An)+	−(An)	d(An)	d(An,Rx)	$xxxx	$xxxxxxxx	d(PC)	d(PC,Rx)	#
Dn			20 3/2	20 3/2	22 3/2	24 4/2	26 4/2	24 4/2	28 5/2			
An												
(An)												
(An)+												
−(An)												
d(An)												
d(An,Rx)												
$xxxx												
$xxxxxxxx												
d(PC)												
d(PC,Rx)												
#												

Number of Bytes per Instruction for Different Addressing Modes:
(Operations on Bytes and Words)

Case 1: The effective address defines the source address.

Source	Destination											
	Dn	An	(An)	(An)+	−(An)	d(An)	d(An,Rx)	$xxxx	$xxxxxxxx	d(PC)	d(PC,Rx)	#
D	2											
An												
(An)	2											
(An)+	2											
−(An)	2											
d(An)	4											
d(An,Rx)	4											
$xxxx	4											
$xxxxxxxx	6											
d(PC)	4											
d(PC,Rx)	4											
#	4											

Number of Bytes per Instruction for Different Addressing Modes:
(Operations on Bytes and Words)

Case 2: The effective address defines the destination address.

Source	Destination											
	Dn	An	(An)	(An)+	–(An)	d(An)	d(An,Rx)	$xxxx	$xxxxxxxx	d(PC)	d(PC,Rx)	#
Dn			2	2	2	4	4	4	6			
An												
(An)												
(An)+												
–(An)												
d(An)												
d(An,Rx)												
$xxxx												
$xxxxxxxx												
d(PC)												
d(PC,Rx)												
#												

Number of Bytes per Instruction for Different Addressing Modes:
(Operations on Long Words)

Case 1: The effective address defines the source address.

Source	Destination											
	Dn	An	(An)	(An)+	–(An)	d(An)	d(An,Rx)	$xxxx	$xxxxxxxx	d(PC)	d(PC,Rx)	#
Dn	2											
An												
(An)	2											
(An)+	2											
–(An)	2											
d(An)	4											
d(An,Rx)	4											
$xxxx	4											
$xxxxxxxx	6											
d(PC)	4											
d(PC,Rx)	4											
#	4											

Number of Bytes per Instruction for Different Addressing Modes:
(Operations on Long Words)

Case 2: The effective address defines the destination address.

Source	Destination											
	Dn	An	(An)	(An)+	–(An)	d(An)	d(An,Rx)	$xxxx	$xxxxxxxx	d(PC)	d(PC,Rx)	#
Dn			2	2	2	4	4	4	6			
An												
(An)												
(An)+												
–(An)												
d(An)												
d(An,Rx)												
$xxxx												
$xxxxxxxx												
d(PC)												
d(PC,Rx)												
#												

Example:

Before the operation:	Contents of D3	= $XXXXFF00
	Data at $100	= $A0A0
	(X = don't care)	
	AND $100,D3	
Results after the operation:	Contents of D3	= $XXXXA000

Applications:

A typical application for this AND instruction would consist of examining the control register for a peripheral interface device with a mask to see whether a bit has been set (Yes/No as result). In reverse, you could set particular bits in the control register of a peripheral interface device with this instruction and a mask.

ANDI   Logical AND Immediate (with a Constant)

Assembler Syntax:

ANDI.w #Constant, <ea>

Operation:

#Constant ^ <Destination> → <Destination>

Flag Changes:

X   Not changed by the ANDI operation
N   Set equal to 1 if leading bit of result is 1, otherwise reset equal to 0.
Z   Set equal to 1 if result equals 0, otherwise reset to 0.
V   Always reset equal to 0.
C   Always reset equal to 0.

Operand Sizes:

This instruction operates on bytes, words and long words. The .w in the syntax refers to .B, .W or .L respectively.

Description of Instruction:

The ANDI instruction uses the logical operation of AND applied to a constant and an operand. It reads the operand from the destination address, and it stores the results back into the destination address.

Format of Opcode:

15	14	13	12	11	10	9	8	7	6	5	4	3	2	1	0
0	0	0	0	0	0	1	0	Size		Effective Address <ea>					

Effective Address <ea>: Mode, Register

8-bit Constant

16-bit Constant

32-bit Constant (including previous word)

Bits 15–12. These bits indicate that this instruction belongs to the set of immediate instructions. Other bits in the opcode select this particular instruction from this set.

Bits 11–8 These bits select this particular instruction as the ANDI instruction.

Size Field, Bits 7–6. The size of the operands is stored in this field, defined as follows:

00	–	8-bit bytes as operands
01	–	16-bit words as operands
10	–	32-bit long words as operands

Effective Address, Bits 5–0. The effective address for the destination address is stored in this pair of fields, one for the mode and the other for the register. The interpretation for this pair of fields is given in the table below:

Effective Address <ea>		Mnemonic for Addressing Mode
Mode	**Register**	
000	Register Number n	Dn
*	*	An
010	Register Number n	(An)
011	Register Number n	(An)+
100	Register Number n	–(An)
101	Register Number n	d(An)
110	Register Number n	d(An,Rx)
111	000	$xxxx
111	001	$xxxxxxxx
*	*	d(PC)
*	*	d(PC,Rx)
*	*	#

* means that this addressing mode is not allowed

Execution Times (cycles): (Operations on Bytes and Words)

The first number is the number of clock cycles required to: get the operand, execute the instruction, store the results and get the next opcode. The next pair of numbers is for the number of read cycles and the number of write cycles respectively. These values are only valid for the 68000 microprocessor. See the condensed tables in Chapter 8 for calculating times for the other microprocessors in the M68000 family.

Source	Destination											
	Dn	An	(An)	(An)+	–(An)	d(An)	d(An,Rx)	$xxxx	$xxxxxxxx	d(PC)	d(PC,Rx)	#
Dn												
An												
(An)												
(An)+												
–(An)												
d(An)												
d(An,Rx)												
$xxxx												
$xxxxxxxx												
d(PC)												
d(PC,Rx)												
#	8 2/0		16 3/1	16 3/1	18 3/1	20 4/1	22 4/1	20 4/1	24 5/1			

Execution Times (Cycles): (Operations on Long Words)

The first number is the number of clock cycles required to: get the operand, execute the instruction, store the results and get the next opcode. The next pair of numbers is for the number of read cycles and the number of write cycles respectively.

These values are only valid for the 68000 microprocessor. See the condensed tables in Chapter 8 for calculating times for the other microprocessors in the M68000 family.

Source	Destination											
	Dn	An	(An)	(An)+	−(An)	d(An)	d(An,Rx)	$xxxx	$xxxxxxxx	d(PC)	d(PC,Rx)	#
Dn												
An												
(An)												
(An)+												
−(An)												
d(An)												
d(An,Rx)												
$xxxx												
$xxxxxxxx												
d(PC)												
d(PC,Rx)												
#	16 3/0		28 5/2	28 5/2	30 5/2	32 6/2	34 6/2	32 6/2	36 7/2			

Number of Bytes per Instruction for Different Addressing Modes:
(Operations on Bytes and Words)

Source	Destination											
	Dn	An	(An)	(An)+	−(An)	d(An)	d(An,Rx)	$xxxx	$xxxxxxxx	d(PC)	d(PC,Rx)	#
Dn												
An												
(An)												
(An)+												
−(An)												
d(An)												
d(An,Rx)												
$xxxx												
$xxxxxxxx												
d(PC)												
d(PC,Rx)												
#	4		4	4	4	6	6	6	8			

Number of Bytes per Instruction for Different Addressing Modes:
(Operations on Long Words)

Source	Destination											
	Dn	An	(An)	(An)+	−(An)	d(An)	d(An,Rx)	$xxxx	$xxxxxxxx	d(PC)	d(PC,Rx)	#
Dn												
An												
(An)												
(An)+												
−(An)												
d(An)												
d(An,Rx)												
$xxxx												
$xxxxxxxx												
d(PC)												
d(PC,Rx)												
#	6		6	6	6	8	8	8	10			

Example:

Before the operation:	Contents of D3: (X = don't care)	$XXXXFF00
	ANDI # A0A0,D3	
Results after the operation	Contents of D3:	$XXXXA000

Applications:

A typical application for this AND instruction would consist of examining the control register for a peripheral port with a mask to see whether a bit has been set (Yes/No as result). In reverse, you could set particular bits in the control register of a peripheral port with this instruction and a mask.

ANDI to CCR   Logical AND Immediate to Condition-Code Register

Assembler Syntax:

ANDI # Constant,CCR

Operation:

#Constant ^ <CCR> → <CCR>

Flag Changes:

X   Set equal to 0 if bit 4 of constant = 0, otherwise no change.
N   Set equal to 0 if bit 3 of constant = 0, otherwise no change.
Z   Set equal to 0 if bit 2 of constant = 0, otherwise no change.
V   Set equal to 0 if bit 1 of constant = 0, otherwise no change.
C   Set equal to 0 if bit 0 of constant = 0, otherwise no change.

Operand Sizes:

This instruction operates on bytes. The CCR has a length of 8 bits, but only the lowest 5 bits can be operated upon with the ANDI-to-CCR instruction. The upper 3 bits can not be changed (see chapter 2.4).

Description of Instruction:

The ANDI-to-CCR instruction performs a logical AND operation upon a constant used as a mask and the contents of the CCR (Condition-Code Register that contains the flags). You can change individual flags in the CCR and leave the other flags unchanged with this instruction.

Format of Opcode:

15	14	13	12	11	10	9	8	7	6	5	4	3	2	1	0
0	0	0	0	0	0	1	0	0	0	1	1	1	1	0	0
0	0	0	0	0	0	0	0	\multicolumn{8}{c} 8-bit Constant

(The first word = $023C)

Bits 15–12. These bits indicate that this instruction belongs to the set of instructions {bit commands,MOVEP,immediate}. Other bits in the opcode select this particular instruction from this set.

Bits 11–0. These bits select this particular instruction as the ANDI-to-CCR instruction.

The lowest 8 bits of the following word contain the byte that is constant (the mask) in the logical AND operation.

Addressing Modes that are Allowed: The source address is specified by the byte-data immediate-addressing mode and the destination address is specified by the CCR direct-addressing mode.

Execution Times (cycles): (Operations on Bytes)

20	clock cycles
3	read cycles
0	write cycles

(These values are only valid for the 68000 microprocessor. See the condensed tables in Chapter 8 for calculating times for the other microprocessors in the M68000 family.)

Number of Bytes per Instruction for Different Addressing Modes:
(Operations on Bytes and Words)

The ANDI-to-CCR instruction always uses 4 bytes.

Example:

Before the operation:	Contents of CCR:	X	N	Z	V	C	
		1	0	1	0	0	
	ANDI #$1B,CCR	This instruction clears the Z-flag.					
After the operation:	Contents of CCR:	X	N	Z	V	C	
		1	0	0	0	0	

Applications:

You should clear the X-flag before using the ABCD instruction in order to avoid obtaining a false result. You should also clear the X-flag before using the ROXL (Rotate Left with Extend) and ROXR (Rotate Right with Extend) instructions. In these cases, you can use the ANDI-to-CCR instruction to reset the X-flag.

This is a Privileged Instruction

ANDI to SR   Logical AND Immediate to Status Register

Assembler Syntax:

ANDI #Constant,SR

Operation:

$$\# \text{Constant} \,\hat{} \, <SR> \, \rightarrow \, <SR>$$

Flag Changes:

X   Set equal to 0 if bit 4 of constant = 0, otherwise no change.
N   Set equal to 0 if bit 3 of constant = 0, otherwise no change.
Z   Set equal to 0 if bit 2 of constant = 0, otherwise no change.
V   Set equal to 0 if bit 1 of constant = 0, otherwise no change.
C   Set equal to 0 if bit 0 of constant = 0, otherwise no change.

Operand Sizes:

This instruction operates exclusively with words since the status register of an M68000 microprocessor has a length of 16 bits. Some of the bits in the status register can not be changed and therefore this instruction has no effect upon them (see Chapter 2.4).

Description of Instruction:

The ANDI-to-SR instruction performs a logical AND operation upon a constant used as a mask and the contents of the SR (Status Register). You can change individual flags in the SR and leave the other flags unchanged with this instruction. Examples include the interrupt mask, supervisor bit and the trace bit of an M68000 microprocessor. Since the ANDI-to-SR instruction changes supervisor data, it is a privileged instruction that you can only use in the supervisor mode. If you use it in the user mode, it initiates exceptional handling.

Format of Opcode:

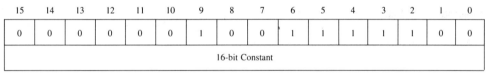

15	14	13	12	11	10	9	8	7	6	5	4	3	2	1	0
0	0	0	0	0	0	1	0	0	1	1	1	1	1	0	0
16-bit Constant																

(The first word = $027C)

Bits 15–12. These bits indicate that this instruction belongs to the set of instructions {bit commands, MOVEP, immediate}. Other bits in the opcode select this particular instruction from this set.
Bits 11–0. These bits select this particular instruction as the ANDI-to-SR instruction.
The 16 bits of the following word contain the constant (the mask) for the logical AND operation.

Addressing Modes that are Allowed:

The source address is specified by the word-data immediate-addressing mode and the destination address is specified by the status-register direct-addressing mode.

Execution Times (Cycles): (Operations on Bytes)

20   clock cycles
3   read cycles
0   write cycles

(These values are only valid for the 68000 microprocessor. See the condensed tables in Chapter 8 for calculating times for the other microprocessors in the M68000 family.)

Number of Bytes per Instruction for Different Addressing Modes:
(Operations on Words)

The ANDI-to-SR instruction always uses 4 bytes.

Example:

Before the operation:	Contents of SR:	15 14 13 12 11 10　9　　8　7 6 5 4 3 2 1 0	
		T　S　　　12　11　10　　　　　X N Z V C	
		0　1　　　0　1　1　　　　　0 0 0 0 0	
	ANDI # $A1l F,SR		
After the operation:	Contents of SR:	15 14 13 12 11 10　9　　8　7 6 5 4 3 2 1 0	
		T　S　　　12　11　10　　　　　X N Z V C	
		0　1　　　0　1　1　　　　　0 0 0 0 0	

Applications:

As illustrated in the example above, you can use the ANDI-to-SR instruction to selectively change individual bits in the status register. Examples include the trace bit, the supervisor bit (to switch an M68000 microprocessor into the user mode) and the flags. In general, this instruction performs system-control functions.

ASL, ASR　　Arithmetic Shift Left/Right

Assembler Syntax:

```
ASd.w Ds,Dd (the first d is the direction , R or L)
ASd.w # Constant,Dd
ASd < ea >
```

Operation:

Case 1: The destination address is a data register.

< Dd > is shifted by # Constant	→ < Dd > or
< Dd > is shifted by < Ds >	→ < Dy >

Case 2: The destination address is in the memory.

< Destination > is shifted by one position → < Destination >

Flag Changes:

X   Set equal to the last bit out of the operand that is shifted. If the shift counter for operations with Dd is equal to 0, then the flag is not changed.
N   Set equal to 1 if the first bit of the result is equal to 1, otherwise reset equal to 0.
Z   Set equal to 1 if result equals 0, otherwise reset equal to 0.
V   Is always reset equal to 0.
C   Set equal to the last bit out of the operand that is shifted. If the shift counter for operations with Dd is equal to 0, then it is reset equal to 0.

Operand Sizes:

Case 1: The destination address is a data register.
The operands can have the size of byte, word or long word. Therefore, the .X in the syntax refers to .B, .W or .L respectively.
Case 2: The destination address is in the memory.
The operands can only have the size of a word.

Description of Instructions:

The ASL and ASR instructions shift the bits of the operand arithmetically in the specified direction, to the left or to the right. The last bit that is shifted out of the destination register goes automatically into the C-flag and the X-flag. There are two separate cases, depending upon where the destination address points:
Case 1: The destination address is a data register.
The operands can have the size of byte, word or long word. You can specify the number of bit positions that the operand will be shifted as a value at the source address, either immediately in the instruction or directly from a data register. If this value is specified immediatly, then the number of bit positions for the rotation can range from 1 to 8. If this value is contained in a data register, then the number of bit positions for the rotation can range from 0 to 64 (modulus 64 if the data in the register is larger than 64).
Case 2: The destination address is in the memory.
The operands can only have the size of a word. You can only shift the operand by one bit position in the specified direction with each use of this instruction.
Differences between these two instructions are:
ASL: The operand is shifted the selected number of bit positions to the left. For each shift by one bit, the most-significant bit leaves the operand and enters both the C-flag and the X-flag. At the same time, a null enters the operand as the least-significant bit for each shift by one bit.

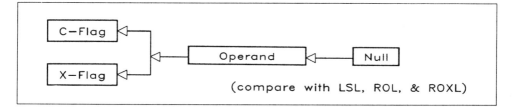

ASR: The operand is shifted the selected number of bit positions to the right. For each shift by one bit, the least-significant bit leaves the operand and enters both the C-flag and the X-flag. At the same time, the most-significant bit (sign bit) is duplicated and reentered as the most-significant bit at the left.

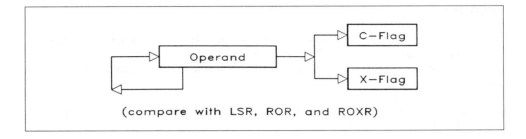

(compare with LSR, ROR, and ROXR)

Format of Opcode:

Case 1: The destination address is a data register.

15	14	13	12	11 10 9	8	7 6	5	4	3	2 1 0
1	1	1	0	Counter/Register	->Dir<-	Size	Imm/Reg	0	0	Register

Bits 15–12. These bits indicate that this instruction belongs to the set of instructions {shift,rotate}. Other bits in the opcode select this particular instruction from this set.

Counter/Register, Bits 11–9. Depending upon the contents of the Imm/Reg field, bit 5, this field contains either the number of bit positions for the shift or the number of the data register that contains the number of bit positions. In the first case, codes from 001 to 111 specify a shift of 1 to 7 bit positions respectively and a code of 000 specifies a shift of 8 bit positions.

Dir, Bit 8. This field specifies the direction of the shift. A value of 0 specifies shifting to the right and a value of 1 specifies shifting to the left.

Size Field, Bits 7–6. The size of the operand is stored in this field, defined as follows:

```
00  –   8-bit byte as operand
01  –   16-bit word as operand
10  –   32-bit long word as operand
```

Imm/Reg, Bit 5. This field determines whether the number of bit positions for the shift is contained:
0–immediate in bits 11–9 of the opcode or
1–in a data register whose number is specified in bits 11–9 of the opcode.

Bits 4–3. These two bits, 00, indicate that the operand is in a data register.

Register, Bits 2–0. These 3 bits specify the number of the data register that contains the operand.

Case 2: The destination address is in the memory.

15	14	13	12	11	10	9	8	7	6	5 4 3	2 1 0
										Effective Address <ea>	
1	1	1	0	0	0	0	->Dir<-	1	1	Mode	Register

Bits 15–12. These bits indicate that this instruction belongs to the set of instructions {shift,rotate}. Other bits in the opcode select this particular instruction from this set.

Bits 11–9. These bits select this particular instruction as an arithmetic shift operation.

Dir, Bit 8. This field specifies the direction of the shift. A value of 0 specifies shifting to the right and a value of 1 specifies shifting to the left.

Bits 7–6. These two bits indicate that the destination address is in memory and that the length of the operand is a word.

Effective Address, Bits 5–0. The effective address is stored in this pair of fields, one for the mode and the other for the register. The interpretation for this pair of fields is given in the table below:

Effective Address <ea>		Mnemonic for Addressing Mode
Mode	Register	
*	*	Dn
*	*	An
010	Register Number n	(An)
011	Register Number n	(An)+
100	Register Number n	–(An)
101	Register Number n	d(An)
110	Register Number n	d(An,Rx)
111	000	$xxxx
111	001	$xxxxxxxx
*	*	d(PC)
*	*	d(PC,Rx)
*	*	#

* means that this addressing mode is not allowed

Execution Times (Cycles):

The first number is the number of clock cycles required to: get the operands, execute the instruction, store the results and get the next opcode. The next pair of numbers is for the number of read cycles and the number of write cycles respectively. These values are only valid for the 68000 microprocessor. See the condensed tables in Chapter 8 for calculating times for the other microprocessors in the M68000 family.

Case 1: The destination address is a data register. (Operations on bytes and words.)

Source	Destination											
	Dn	An	(An)	(An)+	–(An)	d(An)	d(An,Rx)	$xxxx	$xxxxxxxx	d(PC)	d(PC,Rx)	#
Dn	6+2n I/0											
An												
(An)												
(An)+												
–(An)												
d(An)												
d(An,Rx)												
$xxxx												
$xxxxxxxx												
d(PC)												
d(PC,Rx)												
#	6+2n I/0											

Execution Times: (Case 1) (Operations on Long Words)

Source	Destination										
	Dn	An	(An)	(An)+	−(An)	d(An)	d(An,Rx)	$xxxx	$xxxxxxxx	d(PC)	d(PC,Rx)	#
Dn	8+2n I/0										
An											
(An)											
(An)+											
−(An)											
d(An)											
d(An,Rx)											
$xxxx											
$xxxxxxxx											
d(PC)											
d(PC,Rx)											
#	8+2n I/0										

Execution Times (Cycles): (Case 2) The destination address is in the memory (Operations on Words)

Source	Destination										
	Dn	An	(An)	(An)+	−(An)	d(An)	d(An,Rx)	$xxxx	$xxxxxxxx	d(PC)	d(PC,Rx)	#
			12 2/1	12 2/1	14 2/1	16 3/1	18 3/1	16 3/1	20 4/1			

Number of Bytes per Instruction for Different Addressing Modes: Operations on Bytes and Words)

Case 1: The destination address is a data register.

Source	Destination										
	Dn	An	(An)	(An)+	−(An)	d(An)	d(An,Rx)	$xxxx	$xxxxxxxx	d(PC)	d(PC,Rx)	#
Dn	2										
An											
(An)											
(An)+											
−(An)											
d(An)											
d(An,Rx)											
$xxxx											
$xxxxxxxx											
d(PC)											
d(PC,Rx)											
#	2										

Case 2: The destination address is in the memory.

	Destination										
	Dn	An	(An)	(An)+	−(An)	d(An)	d(An,Rx)	$xxxx	$xxxxxxxx	d(PC)	d(PC,Rx)	#
			2	2	2	4	4	4	6			

Examples:

There are two different possibilities for shifting an operand that is in memory by several bit positions:
Possibility 1: Repeating the operation several times in memory.

ASL (A0)	12 clock cycles
ASL (A0)	12 clock cycles
ASL (A0)	12 clock cycles
.	.
.	.
.	.
ASL (A0)	12 clock cycles

The number of cycles required to shift the operand by n bit positions is n x 12.

Possibility 2: Loading the operand into a data register, shifting the operand by several bit positions with one operation in the data register and writing the result from the data register into memory.

MOVE (A0),D1	8 clock cycles
ASL #n,D1	6+2n clock cycles
MOVE D1,(A0)	8 clock cycles

The number of cycles required to shift the operand by n bit positions is $22 + 2n$.
You can determine the optimal method, depending upon the number of bit positions required for the shift, from the following algebra:

12n	$< 22 + 2n$
10n	< 22
n	< 2.2

Therefore, if you need to shift the operand by 3 or more bit positions, it will be more efficient to use possibility 2 above.

Applications:

As an example, you could use the arithmetic shift instructions to write your own routines for multiplying by 2 and dividing by 2. The routine for division will even maintain the correct signs from these instructions.

Bcc   Conditional Branch (See Chapter 3.6.3)

Assembler Syntax:

Bcc <Label>	(The conditions cc are given in a table below.)

Operation:

If the condition cc is met, then either:

–	jump to the <Label> or	
–	<PC> + d → <PC>	(PC = Program Counter)

If the condition cc is not met, then control passes to the next instruction in the linear sequence.

Flag Changes:

None. This instruction reads the flags but does not change them.

Operand Sizes:

This instruction does not operate on operands in the conventional sense. Rather, the distinction of size is only for the size of the address distance that it can use. This size can be 8 bits (+/− 127) or 16 bits (+/− 32k).

Description of Instruction:

The Bcc instruction allows you to branch to another point in a program, if a condition is met. If the condition is not met, the program continues on to the next instruction. A distance d is specified for the conditional branch and the Bcc instruction will add this distance (forwards or backwards) to the current contents of the program counter. This distance d is written in the two's-complement format. An assembler calculates the value of d for the label that you specify. The current value in the program counter is the position of the Bcc instruction plus two. If the condition is met, control will continue at PC + d, otherwise at PC + 2. If the field in the opcode for an 8-bit distance is set equal to 0's, then the second word will be used as a 16-bit distance.

The conditions cc that you can use with this instruction are listed in the following table:

Test Condition, Decrement, and Branch		
Mnemonic	Name	Logical Condition
BEQ	equal	$Z=1$
BNE	not equal	$Z=0$
BPL	plus	$N=0$
BMI	minus	$N=1$
BHI	higher	$CvZ=0$
BLS	lower or same	$NCvZ=1$
BCS	carry flag set	$C=1$
BCC	carry flag cleared	$C=0$
BGT*	greater	$Zv(\oplus V)=0$
BLT*	less	$N \oplus V=1$
BGE*	greater or equal	$N \oplus V=0$
BLE*	less or equal	$Zv(N \oplus V)=1$
BVS*	overflow flag set	$V=1$
BVC	overflow flag cleared	$V=0$
* = two's complement arithmetic, v = logical OR, $\oplus$ = exclusive OR		

Format of Opcode:

15	14	13	12	11	10	9	8	7	6	5	4	3	2	1	0
0	1	1	0	Condition				8-bit Address Distance							
16-bit Address Distance (if 8-bit Address Distance = 0)															

Bits 15–12. These bits indicate that this instruction belongs to the set of instructions {Bcc,BSR}. Other bits in the opcode select this particular instruction from this set.

Condition, Bits 11–8. This field specifies this instruction as Bcc and specifies under which condition cc is used, as defined by the following bit patterns:

Condition	Bit pattern for Bits 11–8
EQ	0111
NE	0110
PL	1010
MI	1011
HI	0010
LS	0011
CS	0101
CC	0100
GT	1110
LT	1101
GE	1100
LE	1111
VS	1001
VC	1000

8-bit Address Distance, Bits 7–0. This field contains an integer in two's complement format that specifies the relative distance of the offset from the branch command to the label. If this field contains only zeros, then a second data word contains a 16-bit address offset. In this way, it is possible to branch to short distances that can be specified in 8 bits with a 2-byte instruction and to longer distances that can be specified in 16 bits with a 2-byte instruction plus 2-byte data word. It is not possible to branch to the next instruction with an 8-bit address distance alone, since the distance would be zero and this would imply that a 16-bit address distance follows as the next word.

Execution Times (Cycles):

The first number is the number of clock cycles required to: get the operands, execute the instruction, store the results and get the next opcode.

The next pair of numbers is for the number of read cycles and the number of write cycles respectively. These values are only valid for the 68000 microprocessor. See the condensed tables in Chapter 8 for calculating times for the other microprocessors in the M68000 family.

Condition is true, branch is executed.	Condition is not true, branch is not executed.	
8-bit	10	8
Address Distance	2/0	1/0
16-bit	10	12
Address Distance	2/0	2/0

Number of Bytes per Instruction

8-bit Address Distance	2 bytes
16-bit Address Distance	4 bytes

Example:

LABEL1	MOVE D1,D5	
	.	
	.	
	.	
	CMP #3,D2	Compare instruction, to set the flags
	BEQ LABEL1	selectively. If the contents of D2 are
	ADD D5,D3	equal to 3, then branch back to LABEL1,
		otherwise continue to the ADD instruc-
		tion.

Applications:

You can use the Bcc instruction whenever you want to control execution of the program, depending upon conditions that arise.

BCHG   Test and Change one Bit

Assembler Syntax:

BCHG Ds,<ea°
BCHG #Constant,<ea>

Operations:

Store the complement of bit x in the Z-flag and complement bit x.

Flag Changes:

X   No change.
N   No change.
Z   Set = complement of bit x.
V   No change.
C   No change.

Operand Sizes:

This instruction operates on 8-bit operands when the destination address is in memory. However, it operates on 32-bit operands when the destination address is a data register.

Destination address in memory	→ an 8-bit byte operand
Destination address is a data register	→ a 32-bit operand

Description of Instruction:

The BCHG instruction allows you to examine a particular bit in an operand, store the complement of that bit in the Z-flag and change that bit to its complement in the operand.

As the first step, the contents of the bit are read. If the value is 1, then a 0 is written into the Z-flag. If the value is 0, then a 1 is written into the Z-flag. This gives you a record of the contents of the bit before this instruction – by examining the Z-flag later or using it for a conditional branch.

As the second step, the contents of the bit are complemented. If the value was 0, then it is changed to 1. If the value was 1, then it is changed to 0.

If the destination address is a data register, then the position of the bit is specified with a modulus of 32. The most-significant bit has the number 31, and the least-significant bit has the number 0. If the destination address is in memory, then the position of the bit is specified with a modulus of 8. The most-significant bit has the number 7, and the least-significant bit has the number 0.

The number of the bit can be specified in two different ways in the opcode:

Case 1: The bit is specified directly in the word following the opcode.

Case 2: The bit is specified indirectly through a data register that is specified in the opcode.

Format of Opcode:

Case 1: The bit is specified directly in the word following the opcode.

15	14	13	12	11	10	9	8	7	6	5	4	3	2	1	0
0	0	0	0	1	0	0	0	0	1	Effective Address <ea>					
										Mode			Register		
0	0	0	0	0	0	0	0			Bit Number					

Bits 15–12. These bits indicate that this instruction belongs to the set of instructions {bit-manipulation, MOVEP,immediate}. Other bits in the opcode select this particular instruction from this set.

Bits 11–6. These bits select this particular instruction as the BCHG instruction.

Effective Address, Bits 5–0. The effective address is stored in this pair of fields, one for the mode and the other for the register. The interpretation for this pair of fields is given in the table below:

Effective Address <ea>		Mnemonic for Addressing Mode
Mode	Register	
000	Register Number n	Dn
*	*	An
010	Register Number n	(An)
011	Register Number n	(An)+
100	Register Number n	–(An)
101	Register Number n	d(An)
110	Register Number n	d(An,Rx)
111	000	$xxxx
111	001	$xxxxxxxx
*	*	d(PC)
*	*	d(PC,Rx)
*	*	#

∗ means that this addressing mode is not allowed

Case 2: The bit is specified indirectly through a data register that is specified in the opcode.

15	14	13	12	11	10	9	8	7	6	5	4	3	2	1	0
0	0	0	0		Register		1	0	1		Mode			Register	

Bits 15–12. These bits indicate that this instruction belongs to the set of instructions {bit-manipulation, MOVEP, immediate}. Other bits in the opcode select this particular instruction from this set.

Register, Bits 11–9. This field specifies the number of the data register that contains the number of the bit.
Bits 8–6. These bits select this particular instruction as the BCHG instruction.
Effective Address, Bits 5–0. The effective address is stored in this pair of fields, one for the mode and the other for the register. The interpretation for this pair of fields is given in the table below:

Effective Address <ea>		Mnemonic for Addressing Mode
Mode	Register	
000	Register Number n	Dn
*	*	An
010	Register Number n	(An)
011	Register Number n	(An)+
100	Register Number n	–(An)
101	Register Number n	d(An)
110	Register Number n	d(An,Rx)
111	000	$xxxx
111	001	$xxxxxxxx
*	*	d(PC)
*	*	d(PC,Rx)
*	*	#

∗ means that this addressing mode is not allowed

Addressing Modes that are Allowed: (for both Case 1 and Case 2)

Source	Destination											
	Dn	An	(An)	(An)+	–(An)	d(An)	d(An,Rx)	$xxxx	$xxxxxxxx	d(PC)	d(PC,Rx)	#
Dn	X		X	X	X	X	X	X	X			
An												
(An)												
(An)+												
–(An)												
d(An)												
d(An,Rx)												
$xxxx												
$xxxxxxxx												
d(PC)												
d(PC,Rx)												
#	X		X	X	X	X	X	X	X			

Execution Times (Cycles): (Operations on Bytes and Words)

The first number is the number of clock cycles required to: get the operands, execute the instruction, store the results and get the next opcode. The next pair of numbers is for the number of read cycles and the number of write cycles respectively.

These values are only valid for the 68000 microprocessor. See the condensed tables in Chapter 8 for calculating times for the other microprocessors in the M68000 family.

Case A: The destination address is in memory.

Case 1: The bit is specified directly in the word following the opcode.

	Destination											
	Dn	An	(An)	(An)+	–(An)	d(An)	d(An,Rx)	$xxxx	$xxxxxxxx	d(PC)	d(PC,Rx)	#
			16 3/1	16 3/1	18 3/1	20 4/1	22 4/1	20 4/1	24 5/1			

Case 2: The bit is specified indirectly through a data register that is specified in the opcode.

	Destination											
	Dn	An	(An)	(An)+	–(An)	d(An)	d(An,Rx)	$xxxx	$xxxxxxxx	d(PC)	d(PC,Rx)	#
			12 2/1	12 2/1	14 2/1	16 3/1	18 3/1	16 3/1	20 4/1			

Case B: The destination address is in a data register.

Case 1: The bit is specified directly in the word following the opcode.

	Destination											
	Dn	An	(An)	(An)+	–(An)	d(An)	d(An,Rx)	$xxxx	$xxxxxxxx	d(PC)	d(PC,Rx)	#
	<12 2/0											

Case 2: The bit is specified indirectly through a data register that is specified in the opcode.

	Destination											
	Dn	An	(An)	(An)+	–(An)	d(An)	d(An,Rx)	$xxxx	$xxxxxxxx	d(PC)	d(PC,Rx)	#
	<8 1/0											

Number of Bytes per Instruction for Different Addressing Modes:
(Operations on Bytes and Short Words)

Case A: The destination address is in memory.
Case 1: The bit is specified directly in the word following the opcode.

							Destination					
	Dn	An	(An)	(An)+	–(An)	d(An)	d(An,Rx)	$xxxx	$xxxxxxxx	d(PC)	d(PC,Rx)	#
			4	4	4	6	6	6	8			

Case 2: The bit is specified indirectly through a data register that is specified in the opcode.

							Destination					
	Dn	An	(An)	(An)+	–(An)	d(An)	d(An,Rx)	$xxxx	$xxxxxxxx	d(PC)	d(PC,Rx)	#
			2	2	2	4	4	4	6			

Case B: The destination address is a data register.
Case 1: The bit is specified directly in the word following the opcode.

							Destination					
	Dn	An	(An)	(An)+	–(An)	d(An)	d(An,Rx)	$xxxx	$xxxxxxxx	d(PC)	d(PC,Rx)	#
	4											

Case 2: The bit is specified indirectly through a data register that is specified in the opcode.

							Destination					
	Dn	An	(An)	(An)+	–(An)	d(An)	d(An,Rx)	$xxxx	$xxxxxxxx	d(PC)	d(PC,Rx)	#
	2											

Example:

```
Before the operation:
Contents of <$100> = 10101010     Flags:        X  N  Z  V  C
                                                 0  0  1  1  1

BCHG #3,$100

After the operation:
Contents of <$100> = 10100010     Flags:        X  N  Z  V  C
                                                 0  0  0  1  1
```

Applications:

As an example, you could use the BCHG instruction to switch the state of a LED or relay that is attached to your system over a PIA (Peripheral Interface Adapter). In this case, the former state will be stored in the Z-flag.

BCLR   Test and Clear a Bit

Assembler Syntax:

BCLR Ds, <ea>
BCLR #Constant, <ea>

Operation:

The complement of the queried bit is stored in the Z-flag.
The queried bit is cleared (reset equal to 0).

Flag Changes:

X   No change.
N   No change.
Z   Set equal to the complement of bit x.
V   No change.
C   No change.

Operand Sizes:

This instruction operates on 8-bit operands when the destination address is in memory. However, it operates on 32-bit operands when the destination address is a data register.

| Destination address in memory | → an 8-bit byte operand. |
| Destination address is a data register | → a 32-bit operand. |

Description of Instruction:

The BCLR instruction allows you to examine a particular bit in an operand, store the complement of that bit in the Z-flag and clear that bit (reset it equal to 0).

As the first step, the contents of the bit are read. This value is complemented and stored in the Z-flag. This gives you a record of the contents of the bit before this instruction–by examining the Z-flag later or using it for a conditional branch.

As the second step, the bit is cleared by resetting it equal to 0.

If the destination address is in a data register, then the position of the bit is specified with a modulus of 32. The most-significant bit has the number 31, and the least-significant bit has the number 0. If the destination address is in memory, then the position of the bit is specified with a modulus of 8. The most-significant bit has the number 7, and the least-significant bit has the number 0.

The number of the bit can be specified in two different ways in the opcode:

Case 1: The bit is specified directly in the word following the opcode.

Case 2: The bit is specified indirectly through a data register that is specified in the opcode.

Format of Opcode:

Case 1: The bit is specified directly in the word following the opcode.

15	14	13	12	11	10	9	8	7	6	5	4	3	2	1	0
										Effective Address <ea>					
0	0	0	0	1	0	0	0	1	0	Mode			Register		
0	0	0	0	0	0	0	0	Bit Number							

Bits 15–12. These bits indicate that this instruction belongs to the set of instructions {bit-manipulation, MOVEP,immediate}. Other bits in the opcode select this particular instruction from this set.

Bits 11–6. These bits select this particular instruction as the BCLR instruction.

Effective Address, Bits 5 –0. The effective address is stored in this pair of fields, one for the mode and the other for the register. The number of the selected bit is in the following word. The interpretation for this pair of fields is given in the table below:

Effective Address <ea>		Mnemonic for Addressing Mode
Mode	**Register**	
000	Register Number n	Dn
*	*	An
010	Register Number n	(An)
011	Register Number n	(An)+
100	Register Number n	–(An)
101	Register Number n	d(An)
110	Register Number n	d(An,Rx)
111	000	$xxxx
111	001	$xxxxxxxx
*	*	d(PC)
*	*	d(PC,Rx)
*	*	#

* means that this addressing mode is not allowed

Case 2: The bit is specified indirectly through a data register that is specified in the opcode.

15	14	13	12	11	10	9	8	7	6	5	4	3	2	1	0
										Effective Address <ea>					
0	0	0	0	Register			1	1	1	Mode			Register		

Bits 15–12. These bits indicate that this instruction belongs to the set of instructions {bit-manipulation, MOVEP,immediate}. Other bits in the opcode select this particular instruction from this set.

Register, Bits 11–9. This field specifies the number of the data register that contains the number of the bit.

Bits 8–6. These bits select this particular instruction as the BCLR instruction.

Effective Address, Bits 5–0. The effective address is stored in this pair of fields, one for the mode and the other for the register. The interpretation for this pair of fields is given in the table below:

Effective Address <ea>		Mnemonic for Addressing Mode
Mode	**Register**	
000	Register Number n	Dn
*	*	An
010	Register Number n	(An)
011	Register Number n	(An)+
100	Register Number n	–(An)
101	Register Number n	d(An)
110	Register Number n	d(An,Rx)
111	000	$xxxx
111	001	$xxxxxxxx
*	*	d(PC)
*	*	d(PC,Rx)
*	*	#

* means that this addressing mode is not allowed

Execution Times (Cycles):

The first number is the number of clock cycles required to: get the operands, execute the instruction, store the results and get the next opcode. The next pair of numbers is for the number of read cycles and the number of write cycles respectively.

These values are only valid for the 68000 microprocessor. See the condensed tables in Chapter 8 for calculating times for the other microprocessors in the M68000 family.

Case A: The destination address is in memory.

Case 1: The bit is specified directly in the word following the opcode.

		Destination									
Dn	An	(An)	(An)+	–(An)	d(An)	d(An,Rx)	$xxxx	$xxxxxxxx	d(PC)	d(PC,Rx)	#
		16 3/1	16 3/1	18 3/1	20 4/1	22 4/1	20 4/1	24 5/1			

Case 2: The bit is specified indirectly through a data register that is specified in the opcode.

		Destination									
Dn	An	(An)	(An)+	–(An)	d(An)	d(An,Rx)	$xxxx	$xxxxxxxx	d(PC)	d(PC,Rx)	#
		12 2/1	12 2/1	14 2/1	16 3/1	18 3/1	16 3/1	20 4/1			

Case B: The destination address is a data register.

Case 1: The bit is specified directly in the word following the opcode.

		Destination									
Dn	An	(An)	(An)+	–(An)	d(An)	d(An,Rx)	$xxxx	$xxxxxxxx	d(PC)	d(PC,Rx)	#
<14 2/0											

Case 2: The bit is specified indirectly through a data register that is specified in the opcode.

	Destination										
	Dn	An	(An)	(An)+	–(An)	d(An)	d(An,Rx)	$xxxx	$xxxxxxxx	d(PC)	d(PC,Rx)	#
	<12 1/0										

Number of Bytes per Instruction for Different Addressing Modes:

Case A: The destination address is in memory.
Case 1: The bit is specified directly in the word following the opcode.

	Destination										
	Dn	An	(An)	(An)+	–(An)	d(An)	d(An,Rx)	$xxxx	$xxxxxxxx	d(PC)	d(PC,Rx)	#
			4	4	4	6	6	6	8		

Case 2: The bit is specified indirectly through a data register that is specified in the opcode.

	Destination										
	Dn	An	(An)	(An)+	–(An)	d(An)	d(An,Rx)	$xxxx	$xxxxxxxx	d(PC)	d(PC,Rx)	#
			2	2	2	4	4	4	6		

Case B: The destination address is in a data register.
Case 1: The bit is specified directly in the word following the opcode.

	Destination										
	Dn	An	(An)	(An)+	–(An)	d(An)	d(An,Rx)	$xxxx	$xxxxxxxx	d(PC)	d(PC,Rx)	#
	4										

Case 2: The bit is specified indirectly through a data register that is specified in the opcode.

	Destination										
	Dn	An	(An)	(An)+	–(An)	d(An)	d(An,Rx)	$xxxx	$xxxxxxxx	d(PC)	d(PC,Rx)	#
	2										

Example:

Before the operation:
Contents of <$100> = 10101010   Flags: X N Z V C
                                                     0 0 1 1 1

BCLR #3,$100

After the operation:
Contents of <$100> = 10100010   Flags: X N Z V C
                                                     0 0 0 1 1

Applications:

To give an example, you could use the BCLR instruction to turn an LED or relay off that is attached to your system over a PIA (Peripheral Interface Adapter). In this case, the former state will be stored in the Z-flag.

BRA   Unconditional Branch (Branch Always)

Assembler Syntax:

> BRA Label

Operation:

> $<PC> + d \rightarrow <PC>$

Flag Changes:

> None.

Operand Sizes:

This instruction does not operate on operands in the conventional sense. Rather, the distinction of size is only for the size of the address distance that it can use. This size can be 8 bits (+/− 127) or 16 bits (+/− 32k).

Description of Instruction:

The BRA instruction allows you to branch to another point in a program, independent of any conditions. The execution of the program will continue at the point $<PC> + d$. A distance d is specified in two's complement code. An assembler calculates the value of d for the label that you specify. The current value in the program counter is the position of the BRA instruction plus 2. This instruction adds d to $<PC>$ (forwards or backwards). The size of d can be specified with either 8 bits or 16 bits. The 8-bit field is included in the opcode. If the 8-bit field contains zeros, then the following word contains the 16-bit field.

Format of Opcode:

15	14	13	12	11	10	9	8	7	6	5	4	3	2	1	0
0	1	1	0	0	0	0	0	8-bit Address Distance							
16-bit Address Distance (if 8-bit Address Distance = 0)															

Bits 15–12. These bits indicate that this instruction belongs to the set of instructions {Bcc,BSR}. Other bits in the opcode select this particular instruction from this set.

Bits 11–8. These bits define this instruction to be the BRA instruction.

8-bit Address Distance, Bits 7–0. This field contains an integer in two's complement format that specifies the relative distance of the offset from the branch command to the label. If this field contains only zeros, then a second data word contains a 16-bit address offset. In this way, it is possible to branch to short distances that can be specified in 8 bits with a 2-byte instruction and to longer distances that can be specified in 16 bits with a 2-byte instruction plus 2-byte data word. It is not possible to branch to the next instruction with an 8-bit address distance alone, since the distance would be zero and this would imply that a 16-bit address distance follows as the next word.

Addressing Modes that are Allowed:

The address distance can be specified directly.

Execution Times (Cycles):

The first number is the number of clock cyles required to: get the operands, execute the instruction, store the results and get the next opcode. The next pair of numbers is for the number of read cycles and the number of write cycles respectively.

These values are only valid for the 68000 microprocessor. See the condensed tables in Chapter 8 for calculating times for the other microprocessors in the M68000 family.

Branch is executed.	8-bit	10	
Address Distance 2/0	16-bit	10	
Address Distance 2/0			

Number of Bytes per Instruction

8-bit Address Distance	2 bytes
16-bit Address Distance	4 bytes

Example:

The structure of a DO-WHILE loop is illustrated below:

DO	MOVE D1,D4
	.
	.
	.
	CMP # 3,D2 BEQ EXIT
	BRA DO ADD D5,D3
EXIT	MOVE D3,D6l

Applications:

You can use the BRA instruction to make unconditional jumps in a program, such as for creating infinite loops with exits through other conditional jumps (such as Bcc). One such example is the construction of a DO-WHILE loop as implemented directly in some languages, such as PASCAL and FORTRAN, and can be constructed indirectly with other commands in other languages, such as BASIC.

BSET   Test and Set a Bit

Assembler Syntax:

```
BSET Ds, <ea>
BSET #Constant, <ea>
```

Operation:

The complement of the queried bit is stored in the Z-flag.
The queried bit is set equal to 1.

Flag Changes:

X	No change.
N	No change.
Z	Set equal to the complement of bit x.
V	No change.
C	No change.

Operand Sizes:

This instruction operates on 8-bit operands when the destination address in in memory. However, it operates on 32-bit operands when the destination address is a data register.

Destination address in memory	→ an 8-bit byte operand.
Destination address is a data register	→ a 32-bit operand.

Description of Instruction:

The BSET instruction allows you to examine a particular bit in an operand, store the complement of that bit in the Z-flag and set that bit equal to 1.

As the first step, the contents of the bit are read. This value is complemented and stored in the Z-flag. This gives you a record of the contents of the bit before this instruction–by examining the Z-flag later or using it for a conditional branch.

As the second step, the bit is set equal to 1.

If the destination address is a data register, then the position of the bit is specified with a modulus of 32. The most-significant bit has the number 31, and the least-significant bit has the number 0. If the destination address is in memory, then the position of the bit is specified with a modulus of 8. The most-significant bit has the number 7, and the least-significant bit has the number 0.

The number of the bit can be specified in two different ways in the opcode:

Case 1: The bit is specified directly in the word following the opcode.

Case 2: The bit is specified indirectly through a data register that is specified in the opcode.

Format of Opcode:

Case 1: The bit is specified directly in the word following the opcode.

15	14	13	12	11	10	9	8	7	6	5	4	3	2	1	0
0	0	0	0	1	0	0	0	1	1	Effective Address <ea>					
										Mode			Register		
0	0	0	0	0	0	0	0	Bit Number							

Bits 15–12. These bits indicate that this instruction belongs to the set of instructions {bit-manipulation, MOVEP,immediate}. Other bits in the opcode select this particular instruction from this set.

Bits 11–6. These bits select this particular instruction as the BSET instruction.

Effective Address, Bits 5–0. The effective address is stored in this pair of fields, one for the mode and the other for the register. The interpretation for this pair of fields is given in the table below:

Effective Address \<ea\>		Mnemonic for Addressing Mode
Mode	Register	
000	Register Number n	Dn
*	*	An
010	Register Number n	(An)
011	Register Number n	(An)+
100	Register Number n	−(An)
101	Register Number n	d(An)
110	Register Number n	d(An,Rx)
111	000	$xxxx
111	001	$xxxxxxxx
*	*	d(PC)
*	*	d(PC,Rx)
*	*	#

* means that this addressing mode is not allowed

Case 2: The bit is specified indirectly through a data register that is specified in the opcode.

15	14	13	12	11	10	9	8	7	6	5	4	3	2	1	0
0	0	0	0		Register		1	1	1			Effective Address \<ea\>			
										Mode			Register		

Bits 15–12. These bits indicate that this instruction belongs to the set of instructions {bit-manipulation, MOVEP,immediate}. Other bits in the opcode select this particular instruction from this set.

Register, Bits 11–9. This field specifies the number of the data register that contains the number of the bit.

Bits 8–6. These bits select this particular instruction as the BSET instruction.

Effective Address, Bits 5–0. The effective address is stored in this pair of fields, one for the mode and the other for the register. The interpretation for this pair of fields is given in the table below:

Effective Address \<ea\>		Mnemonic for Addressing Mode
Mode	Register	
000	Register Number n	Dn
*	*	An
010	Register Number n	(An)
011	Register Number n	(An)+
100	Register Number n	−(An)
101	Register Number n	d(An)
110	Register Number n	d(An,Rx)
111	000	$xxxx
111	001	$xxxxxxxx
*	*	d(PC)
*	*	d(PC,Rx)
*	*	#

* means that this addressing mode is not allowed

Execution Times (Cycles):

The first number is the number of clock cycles required to: get both operands, execute the instruction, store the results and get the next opcode. The next pair of numbers is for the number of read cycles and the number of write cycles respectively.

These values are only valid for the 68000 microprocessor. See the condensed tables in Chapter 8 for calculating times for the other microprocessors in the M68000 family.

Case A: The destination address is in memory.

Case 1: The bit is specified directly in the word following the opcode.

						Destination						
	Dn	An	(An)	(An)+	−(An)	d(An)	d(An,Rx)	$xxxx	$xxxxxxxx	d(PC)	d(PC,Rx)	#
			16 3/1	16 3/1	18 3/1	20 4/1	22 4/1	20 4/1	24 5/1			

Case 2: The bit is specified indirectly through a data register that is specified in the opcode.

						Destination						
	Dn	An	(An)	(An)+	−(An)	d(An)	d(An,Rx)	$xxxx	$xxxxxxxx	d(PC)	d(PC,Rx)	#
			12 2/1	12 2/1	14 2/1	16 3/1	18 3/1	16 3/1	20 4/1			

Case B: The destination address is a data register.

Case 1: The bit is specified directly in the word following the opcode.

						Destination						
	Dn	An	(An)	(An)+	−(An)	d(An)	d(An,Rx)	$xxxx	$xxxxxxxx	d(PC)	d(PC,Rx)	#
	<12 2/0											

Case 2: The bit is specified indirectly through a data register that is specified in the opcode.

						Destination						
	Dn	An	(An)	(An)+	−(An)	d(An)	d(An,Rx)	$xxxx	$xxxxxxxx	d(PC)	d(PC,Rx)	#
	<8 1/0											

Number of Bytes per Instruction for Different Addressing Modes:

Case A: The destination address is in memory.

Case 1: The bit is specified directly in the word following the opcode.

						Destination						
	Dn	An	(An)	(An)+	−(An)	d(An)	d(An,Rx)	$xxxx	$xxxxxxxx	d(PC)	d(PC,Rx)	#
			4	4	4	6	6	6	8			

Case 2: The bit is specified indirectly through a data register that is specified in the opcode.

						Destination						
	Dn	An	(An)	(An)+	−(An)	d(An)	d(An,Rx)	$xxxx	$xxxxxxxx	d(PC)	d(PC,Rx)	#
			2	2	2	4	4	4	6			

Case B: The destination address is a data register.

Case 1: The bit is specified directly in the word following the opcode.

						Destination						
	Dn	An	(An)	(An)+	−(An)	d(An)	d(An,Rx)	$xxxx	$xxxxxxxx	d(PC)	d(PC,Rx)	#
	4											

Case 2: The bit is specified indirectly through a data register that is specified in the opcode.

						Destination						
	Dn	An	(An)	(An)+	−(An)	d(An)	d(An,Rx)	$xxxx	$xxxxxxxx	d(PC)	d(PC,Rx)	#
	2											

Example:

Before the operation: Contents of <$1000> = 01010000	Flags:　X　N　Z　V　C 　　　　　1　0　0　0　0 　　　　　BSET #3,$1000
After the operation Contents of <$1000> = 01011000	Flags:　X　N　Z　V　C 　　　　　1　0　1　0　0

Applications:

To give an example, you could use the BCHG instruction to turn an LED or relay on that is attached to your system over a PIA (Peripheral Interface Adapter). In this case, the former state will be stored in the Z-flag.

BSR　　　　Branch to a Subroutine

Assembler Syntax:

BSR Label

Operation:

<PC>　　　　　　　　　　　　　→ –(A7)
<PC> + d　　　　　　　　　　　→ <PC>

Flag Changes:

None.

Operand Sizes:

This instruction does not operate on operands in the conventional sense. Rather, the distinction of size is only for the size of the address distance that it can use. This size can be 8 bits (+/– 127) or 16 bits (+/– 32k).

Description of Instruction:

The BRA instruction allows you to branch to a specific subroutine in a program, after first storing the <PC> (Program Counter) as the return address on the stack.

As the first step, this instruction stores the address the next instruction after the BSR instruction as a long word on the stack.

As the next step, this instruction transfers control to the first instruction in the subroutine, by incrementing the <PC> by an address distance d. (<PC> + d → <PC>). The distance d is specified in two's complement format. An assembler calculates the value of d for the label that you specify. The current value in the program counter is the position of the BRA instruction plus 2. This instruction adds d to <PC> (forwards or backwards). The size of d can be specified with either 8 bits or 16 bits. The 8-bit field is included in the opcode. If the 8-bit field contains zeros, then the following word contains the 16-bit field.

Format of Opcode:

15	14	13	12	11	10	9	8	7	6	5	4	3	2	1	0
0	1	1	0	0	0	0	1	8-bit Address Distance							
16-bit Address Distance (if 8-bit Address Distance = 0)															

Bits 15–12. These bits indicate that this instruction belongs to the set of instructions {Bcc,BSR}. Other bits in the opcode select this particular instruction from this set.

Bits 11–8. These bits define this instruction to be the BSR instruction.

8-bit Address Distance, Bits 7–0. This field contains an integer in two's complement format that specifies the relative distance of the offset from the branch command to the label. If this field contains only zeros, then a second data word contains a 16-bit address offset. In this way, it is possible to branch to short distances that can be specified in 8 bits with a 2-byte instruction and to longer distances that can be specified in 16 bits with a 2-byte instruction plus 2-byte data word. It is not possible to branch to the next instruction with an 8-bit address distance alone since the distance would be zero and this would imply that a 16-bit address distance follows as the next word.

Addressing Modes that are Allowed:

The address distance can be specified directly.

Execution Times (cycles):

The first number is the number of clock cycles required to: get the operands, execute the instruction, store the results and get the next opcode. The next pair of numbers is for the number of read cycles and the number of write cycles respectively.

These values are only valid for the 68000 microprocessor. See the condensed tables in Chapter 8 for calculating times for the other microprocessors in the M68000 family.

Branch is executed.	
8-bit	18
Address Distance	2/2
16-bit	18
Address Distance	2/2

Number of Bytes per Instruction

8-bit Address Distance	2 bytes
16-bit Address Distance	4 bytes

Example:

Branching to the subroutine TEST is illustrated below:

	.	
	.	
	.	
	MOVE D1,D5	
	BSR TEST	Save the < PC > on the stack. Jump to the beginning of the subroutine TEST.
	MOVE D4,$100	The next instruction that will be executed after the return from TEST.
TEST	MOVE D5,$1000	Beginning of the subroutine TEST
	.	
	.	
	.	
	RTS	Return from subroutine. Load < PC > from the stack.

Applications:

If you need to use a special routine several times in a program (such as for floating-point addition), you can create this routine as a subroutine. Then, you can call this subroutine from different points in your program. After the subroutine has executed, it will return control to the next command in the program after the command that called it. The use of subroutines shortens programs since you don't have to duplicate the same code at different places in the program, and it reduces the chances for errors since you don't have to test similar code at different places in the program. In addition, modular programs are easier to read, understand and maintain.

BTST   Test one Bit

Assembler Syntax:

```
BTST Ds, <ea>
BTST #Constant, <ea>
```

Operation:

The complement of the queried bit is stored in the Z-flag.
The bit is not changed in the operand.

Flag Changes:

X   No change.
N   No change.
Z   Set equal to the complement of bit x.
V   No change.
C   No change.

Operand Sizes:

This instruction operates on 8-bit operands when the destination address is in memory. However, it operates on 32-bit operands when the destination address is in a data register.

Destination address in memory	→ an 8-bit byte operand.
Destination address is a data register	→ a 32-bit operand.

Description of Instruction:

The BTST instruction allows you to examine a particular bit in an operand, store the complement of that bit in the Z-flag and leave that bit unchanged in the operand. You can later use this result in the Z-flag, such as for conditional branching with Bcc.

If the destination address is a data register, then the position of the bit is specified with a modulus of 32. The most-significant bit has the number 31, and the least-significant bit has the number 0. If the destination address is in memory, then the position of the bit is specified with a modulus of 8. The most-significant bit has the number 7, and the least-significant bit has the number 0.

The number of the bit can be specified in two different ways in the opcode:

Case 1: The bit is specified directly in the word following the opcode.

Case 2: The bit is specified indirectly through a data register that is specified in the opcode.

Format of Opcode:

Case 1: The bit is specified directly in the word following the opcode.

15	14	13	12	11	10	9	8	7	6	5	4	3	2	1	0
										Effective Address <ea>					
0	0	0	0	1	0	0	0	0	0	Mode			Register		
0	0	0	0	0	0	0	0	Bit Number							

Effective Address table:

15	14	13	12	11	10	9	8	7	6	5	4	3	2	1	0
										Effective Address <ea>					
0	0	0	0	1	0	0	0	0	0	Mode			Register		
0	0	0	0	0	0	0	0	Bit Number							

Bits 15–12. These bits indicate that this instruction belongs to the set of instructions {bit-manipulation, MOVEP,immediate}. Other bits in the opcode select this particular instruction from this set.

Bits 11–6. These bits select this particular instruction as the BTST instruction.

Effective Address, Bits 5–0. The effective address is stored in this pair of fields, one for the mode and the other for the register. The interpretation for this pair of fields is given in the table below:

Effective Address <ea>		Mnemonic for Addressing Mode
Mode	**Register**	
000	Register Number n	Dn
*	*	An
010	Register Number n	(An)
011	Register Number n	(An)+
100	Register Number n	–(An)
101	Register Number n	d(An)
110	Register Number n	d(An,Rx)
111	000	$xxxx
111	001	$xxxxxxxx
111	010	d(PC)
111	011	d(PC,Rx)
*	*	#

∗ means that this addressing mode is not allowed

Case 2: The bit is specified indirectly through a data register that is specified in the opcode.

15	14	13	12	11	10	9	8	7	6	5	4	3	2	1	0
0	0	0	0	Register			1	0	0	Effective Address \<ea\>					

| 0 | 0 | 0 | 0 | Register | | | 1 | 0 | 0 | Mode | | | Register | | |

Bits 15–12. These bits indicate that this instruction belongs to the set of instructions {bit-manipulation, MOVEP,immediate}. Other bits in the opcode select this particular instruction from this set.

Register, Bits 11–9. This field specifies the number of the data register that contains the number of the bit.

Bits 8–6. These bits select this particular instruction as the BTST instruction.

Effective Address, Bits 5–0. The effective address is stored in this pair of fields, one for the mode and the other for the register. The interpretation for this pair of fields is given in the table below:

Effective Address \<ea\>		Mnemonic for Addressing Mode
Mode	**Register**	
000	Register Number n	Dn
*	*	An
010	Register Number n	(An)
011	Register Number n	(An)+
100	Register Number n	–(An)
101	Register Number n	d(An)
110	Register Number n	d(An,Rx)
111	000	$xxxx
111	001	$xxxxxxxx
111	010	d(PC)
111	011	d(PC,Rx)
*	*	#

* means that this addressing mode is not allowed

Execution Times (Cycles):

The first number is the number of clock cycles required to: get the operands, execute the instruction, store the results and get the next opcode. The next pair of numbers is for the number of read cycles and the number of write cycles respectively.

These values are only valid for the 68000 microprocessor. See the condensed tables in Chapter 8 for calculating times for the other microprocessors in the M68000 family.

Case A: The destination address is in memory.

Case 1: The bit is specified directly in the word following the opcode.

	Destination										
	Dn	An	(An)	(An)+	–(An)	d(An)	d(An,Rx)	$xxxx	$xxxxxxxx	d(PC)	d(PC,Rx)	#
			12 3/0	12 3/0	14 3/0	16 4/0	18 4/0	16 4/0	20 5/0	16 4/0	18 4/0	

Case 2: The bit is specified indirectly through a data register that is specified in the opcode.

	Destination										
	Dn	An	(An)	(An)+	–(An)	d(An)	d(An,Rx)	$xxxx	$xxxxxxxx	d(PC)	d(PC,Rx)	#
			8 2/0	8 2/0	10 2/0	12 3/0	14 3/0	12 3/0	16 4/0	12 3/0	14 3/0	

Case B: The destination address is a data register.
Case 1: The bit is specified directly in the word following the opcode.

	Destination											
	Dn	An	(An)	(An)+	–(An)	d(An)	d(An,Rx)	$xxxx	$xxxxxxxx	d(PC)	d(PC,Rx)	#
	10 2/0											

Case 2: The bit is specified indirectly through a data register that is specified in the opcode.

	Destination											
	Dn	An	(An)	(An)+	–(An)	d(An)	d(An,Rx)	$xxxx	$xxxxxxxx	d(PC)	d(PC,Rx)	#
	6 1/0											

Number of Bytes per Instruction for Different Addressing Modes:

Case A: The destination address is in memory.
Case 1: The bit is specified directly in the word following the opcode.

	Destination											
	Dn	An	(An)	(An)+	–(An)	d(An)	d(An,Rx)	$xxxx	$xxxxxxxx	d(PC)	d(PC,Rx)	#
			4	4	4	6	6	6	8	6	6	

Case 2: The bit is specified indirectly through a data register that is specified in the opcode.

	Destination											
	Dn	An	(An)	(An)+	–(An)	d(An)	d(An,Rx)	$xxxx	$xxxxxxxx	d(PC)	d(PC,Rx)	#
			2	2	2	4	4	4	6	4	4	

Case B: The destination address is a data register.
Case 1: The bit is specified directly in the word following the opcode.

	Destination											
	Dn	An	(An)	(An)+	–(An)	d(An)	d(An,Rx)	$xxxx	$xxxxxxxx	d(PC)	d(PC,Rx)	#
	4											

Case 2: The bit is specified indirectly through a data register that is specified in the opcode.

	Destination											
	Dn	An	(An)	(An)+	–(An)	d(An)	d(An,Rx)	$xxxx	$xxxxxxxx	d(PC)	d(PC,Rx)	#
	2											

Example:

The value of bit 3 in the memory cell at $1000 is examined. Then, a conditional branch follows that depends upon this value.

```
          BTST #3,$1000     Examine bit 3 at location $1000.
          BEQ Label         Branch to Label if bit 3 = 0.
          ADD D3,D7         Continue here if bit 3 = 1.
          .
          .
          .
Label     MOVE D3,D
```

Applications:

To give an example, you could use the BTST instruction to examine the state of a LED, relay or a bit in a control register. You could use it to examine an interrupt flag in a PIA (Peripheral Interface Adapter) or the DSR-bit in an ACIA (Asynchronous Communications Interface Adapter).

CHK   Check Whether Data Register is out of Range

Assembler Syntax:

CHK <ea>,Dd

Operation:

If Dd < 0 or Dd > <ea> then →
start exception handling, with the N-flag indicating why.

Flag Changes:

X   No change.
N   Set equal to 1 if Dd < 0, reset equal to 0 if Dd > contents of <ea>, otherwise undefined.
Z   Undefined.
V   Undefined.
C   Undefined.

Operand Sizes:

This instruction operates on the lower half of the specified data register (bits 15–0). Therefore, it operates only on words.

Description of Instruction:

The CHK instruction compares the contents in the lower half of the specified data register with
–   0 as the lower bound and
–   the word starting at <ea> as the upper bound.
If the contents of the data register are out of this bounded range, then the CHK instruction
–   sets or resets the N-flag to indicate whether the lower bound (N-flag = 1) or the upper bound (N-flag = 0) was exceeded and
–   starts exception handling.
The M68000 microprocessors have a special exception vector, with the number 6, for this particular exception.
If the contents of the data register are within this bounded range, then control passes to the next instruction, without starting exception handling.
The word starting at <ea> that this instruction uses as the upper bound is in the two's complement format. The logic of the CHK instruction is illustrated in the flow diagram below:

CHK instruction   0 < Dd < <ea>   –→ next instruction yes

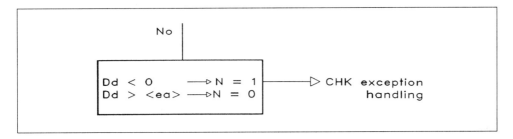

Format of Opcode:

15	14	13	12	11	10	9	8	7	6	5	4	3	2	1	0

0	1	0	0	Register	1	1	0	Effective Address <ea>	
								Mode	Register

Bits 15–12. These bits indicate that this instruction belongs to the set of instructions {PEA,SWAP, NBCD,CHK}. Other bits in the opcode select this particular instruction from this set.

Register, Bits 11–9. This field contains the number of the data register for this instruction.

Bits 8–6. These bits select this particular instruction as the CHK instruction.

Effective Address, Bits 5–0. The effective address is stored in this pair of fields, one for the mode and the other for the register. The interpretation for this pair of fields is given in the table below:

Effective Address <ea>		Mnemonic for Addressing Mode
Mode	**Register**	
000	Register Number n	Dn
*	*	An
010	Register Number n	(An)
011	Register Number n	(An)+
100	Register Number n	–(An)
101	Register Number n	d(An)
110	Register Number n	d(An,Rx)
111	000	$xxxx
111	001	$xxxxxxxx
111	010	d(PC)
111	011	d(PC,Rx)
111	100	#

* means that this addressing mode is not allowed

Execution Times (Cycles):

Case 1: Contents of Dd are within the boundary range.

The first number is the number of clock cycles required to: get the operands, execute the instruction, store the results and get the next opcode. The next pair of numbers is for the number of read cycles and the number of write cycles respectively.

These values are only valid for the 68000 microprocessor. See the condensed tables in Chapter 8 for calculating times for the other microprocessors in the M68000 family.

Source	Destination											
	Dn	An	(An)	(An)+	–(An)	d(An)	d(An,Rx)	$xxxx	$xxxxxxxx	d(PC)	d(PC,Rx)	#
Dn	10 1/0											
An												
(An)	14 2/0											
(An)+	14 2/0											
–(An)	16 2/0											
d(An)	18 3/0											
d(An,Rx)	20 3/0											
$xxxx	18 3/0											
$xxxxxxxx	22 4/0											
d(PC)	18 3/0											
d(PC,Rx)	20 3/0											
#	14 2/0											

Execution Times (Cycles):

Case 2: Contents of Dd are out of the boundary range → exception handling.

The first number is the number of clock cycles required to: get the operands, execute the instruction, store the results and get the next opcode. The next pair of numbers is for the number of read cycles and the number of write cycles respectively.

These values are only valid for the 68000 microprocessor. See the condensed tables in Chapter 8 for calculating times for the other microprocessors in the M68000 family.

Source	Destination											
	Dn	An	(An)	(An)+	–(An)	d(An)	d(An,Rx)	$xxxx	$xxxxxxxx	d(PC)	d(PC,Rx)	#
Dn	44 5/4											
An												
(An)	48 6/4											
(An)+	48 6/4											
–(An)	50 6/4											
d(An)	52 7/4											
d(An,Rx)	54 7/4											
$xxxx	52 7/4											
$xxxxxxxx	56 8/4											
d(PC)	52 7/4											
d(PC,Rx)	54 7/4											
#	48 6/4											

Number of Bytes per Instruction for Different Addressing Modes:

Source	Destination											
	Dn	An	(An)	(An)+	–(An)	d(An)	d(An,Rx)	$xxxx	$xxxxxxxx	d(PC)	d(PC,Rx)	#
Dn	2											
An												
(An)	2											
(An)+	2											
–(An)	2											
d(An)	4											
d(An,Rx)	4											
$xxxx	4											
$xxxxxxxx	6											
d(PC)	4											
d(PC,Rx)	4											
#	4											

Example:

Working with a table that contains the length of the table as the first entry is a typical example. You can use the CHK instruction to test whether the pointer for this table still points to addresses within the table.
A0 contains the address in memory for the length of the table.
A1 contains the address in memory where the values start.
D0 is the pointer to the table.

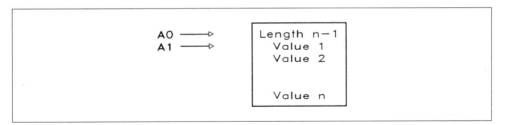

Following is the program segment:

	CLR.L D0	
LOOP	MOVE.W 0(A1,D0),(A5)+	Addressing values in table.
	.	
	.	
	.	
	ADDQ.W #2,D0	Incrementing the pointer by 2 for the next value in the table (working with words).
	.	
	CHK (A0),D0	Testing whether the pointer D0 points to a value within the table.
	.	
	,	
	.	
	BEQ LOOP	

Applications:

You can use the CHK instruction to check whether a running index for a table still points to a valid address for a value within the table. You can also use this instruction to check whether the addresses for vectors and matrices are within the dimensions of the vector or matrix. This instruction is used in high-level languages such as PASCAL and FORTRAN for handling vectors and matrices.

CLR   Clear an Operand

Assembler Syntax:

CLR.w <ea>

Operation:

$0 \rightarrow$ <ea>

Flag Changes:

X	Not changed.
N	Reset equal to 0.
Z	Set equal to 1.
V	Reset equal to 0.
C	Reset equal to 0.

Operand Sizes:

This instruction operates on bytes, words and long words. You can reset the lowest 8 bits in a data register equal to 0 or reset all 32 bits equal to zero. You can apply it to bytes, words and long words in memory. The .w in the syntax refers to .B, .W or .L respectively.

Description of Instruction:

The .CLR instruction clears the contents of a data register or a location in memory. It resets all of the specified bits in the operand equal to 0. You can not clear an address register with the CLR instruction. However, you can use the MOVEA instruction for clearing address registers. An M68000 microprocessor reads an operand from memory before clearing it, with a normal bus access, but does not use this information in any way. The CLR instruction is a unitary operation that operates on a single operand.

Format of Opcode:

15	14	13	12	11	10	9	8	7	6	5	4	3	2	1	0
0	1	0	0	0	0	1	0	Size		Effective Address <ea>					
										Mode			Register		

Bits 15–12. These bits indicate that this instruction belongs to the set of instructions {PEA,SWAP, NBCD,CHK,CLR,etc.}. Other bits in the opcode select this particular instruction from this set.
Bits 11–8. These bits select this particular instruction as the CLR instruction.

Size Field, Bits 7–6. The size of the operand that will be cleared is stored in this field, defined as follows:

00	–	8-bit byte as operand
01	–	16-bit word as operand
10	–	32-bit long word as operand

Effective Address, Bits 5–0. The effective address is stored in this pair of fields, one for the mode and the other for the register. The interpretation for this pair of fields is given in the table below:

Effective Address <ea>		Mnemonic for Addressing Mode
Mode	Register	
000	Register Number n	Dn
*	*	An
010	Register Number n	(An)
011	Register Number n	(An)+
100	Register Number n	–(An)
101	Register Number n	d(An)
110	Register Number n	d(An,Rx)
111	000	$xxxx
111	001	$xxxxxxxx
*	*	d(PC)
*	*	d(PC,Rx)
*	*	#

* means that this addressing mode is not allowed

Execution Times (Cycles):

The first number is the number of clock cycles required to: get the operand, execute the instruction, store the results and get the next opcode. The next pair of numbers is for the number of read cycles and the number of write cycles respectively.

These values are only valid for the 68000 microprocessor. See the condensed tables in Chapter 8 for calculating times for the other microprocessors in the M68000 family.

(Operations on Bytes and Words)

	Destination										
	Dn	An	(An)	(An)+	–(An)	d(An)	d(An,Rx)	$xxxx	$xxxxxxxx	d(PC)	d(PC,Rx)	#
	4 1/0		12 2/1	12 2/1	14 2/1	16 3/1	18 3/1	16 3/1	20 4/1			

(Operations on Long Words)

	Destination										
	Dn	An	(An)	(An)+	–(An)	d(An)	d(An,Rx)	$xxxx	$xxxxxxxx	d(PC)	d(PC,Rx)	#
	6 1/0		20 3/2	20 3/2	22 3/2	24 4/2	26 4/2	24 4/2	28 5/2			

Number of Bytes per Instruction for Different Addressing Modes:
(Operations on Bytes and Words)

	Destination										
	Dn	An	(An)	(An)+	–(An)	d(An)	d(An,Rx)	$xxxx	$xxxxxxxx	d(PC)	d(PC,Rx)	#
	2		2	2	2	4	4	4	6			

(Operation on Long Words)

	Destination										
	Dn	An	(An)	(An)+	–(An)	d(An)	d(An,Rx)	$xxxx	$xxxxxxxx	d(PC)	d(PC,Rx)	#
	2		2	2	2	4	4	4	6			

Example:

Clearing the contents of a data register:

Before the operation:	Contents of D1	= $12345678
		CLR.W D1
After the operation:	Contents of D1	= $12340000
		CLR.L D1
After the operation:	Contents of D1	= $00000000

Applications:

To give an example, you can use the CLR instruction to clear the index register that you use for addressing a table with the address-register indirect-addressing mode, d(An,Di) in order to start at the first value in the table. In this case, the starting address for the table must be stored in An. As another example, you can use the CLR instruction to clear a complete 32-bit data register before loading the divident for a DIVS or DIVU instruction–in order to avoid an overflow.

CMP   Compare Two Operands

Assembler Syntax:

CMP.w <ea>,Dd

Operation:

<Destination> – <Source> → Setting flags accordingly.

Flag Changes:

X   Not changed.
N   Set equal to 1 if result is negative, otherwise reset to 0.
Z   Set equal to 1 if result equals 0, otherwise reset to 0.
V   Set equal to 1 if an overflow occurs, otherwise reset to 0.
C   Set equal to 1 if a "borrow" is used, otherwise reset to 0.

Operand Sizes:

This instruction compares a pair of bytes, words or long words and sets or resets several flags depending upon the result. The .w in the syntax refers to .B, .W or .L respectively.

Description of Instruction:

The CMP instruction compares the values of two operands. It subtracts the first operand from the second operand without changing the second operand. It reads the first and second oeprands from the source and destination addresses and it writes the result back into the destination address. It sets or resets several flags, depending upon the results of this operation.

Format of Opcode:

15	14	13	12	11	10	9	8	7	6	5	4	3	2	1	0
										Effective Address <ea>					
1	0	1	1		Register		0	Size		Mode			Register		

Bits 15–12. These bits indicate that this instruction belongs to the set of instructions {CMP,EOR}. Other bits in the opcode select this particular instruction from this set.

Register, Bits 11–9. This field contains the number of the data register for this instruction.

Size, Bits 7–6. Bit 8 is always equal to 0 for the CMP instruction (equal to 1 for the CMPA and EOR instructions).

Bits 7 and 6 define the size of the operands as follows:

00	–	8-bit bytes as operands
01	–	16-bit words as operands
10	–	32-bit long words as operands

Effective Address, Bits 5–0. The effective address is stored in this pair of fields, one for the mode and the other for the register. The interpretation for this pair of fields is given in the table below:

Effective Address <ea>		Mnemonic for Addressing Mode
Mode	**Register**	
000	Register Number n	Dn
001	Register Number n	An
010	Register Number n	(An)
011	Register Number n	(An)+
100	Register Number n	–(An)
101	Register Number n	d(An)
110	Register Number n	d(An,Rx)
111	000	$xxxx
111	001	$xxxxxxxx
111	010	d(PC)
111	011	d(PC,Rx)
111	100	#

If the source address is an address register, then only the sizes of word and long word are allowed for both operands.

For the special case where the destination address is an address register, there is a separate mnemonic, CMPA (see the description for CMPA that follows as the next instruction after CMP). If the source address is an immediate number, then the appropriate mnemonic is CMPI # Number,Dd. If you want to compare two numbers in memory, the appropriate compare instruction is CMPM. However, most assemblers will also accept just CMP as the mnemonic, together with the appropriate syntax for all of these different cases.

Execution Times (Cycles): (Operations on Bytes and Words)

The first number is the number of clock cycles required to: get the operands, execute the instruction, store the results and get the next opcode. The next pair of numbers is for the number of read cycles and the number of write cycles respectively.

These values are only valid for the 68000 microprocessor. See the condensed tables in Chapter 8 for calculating times for the other microprocessors in the M68000 family.

Source	Destination											
	Dn	An	(An)	(An)+	–(An)	d(An)	d(An,Rx)	$xxxx	$xxxxxxxx	d(PC)	d(PC,Rx)	#
Dn	4 1/0											
An	4 1/0											
(An)	8 2/0											
(An)+	8 2/0											
–(An)	10 2/0											
d(An)	12 3/0											
d(An,Rx)	14 3/0											
$xxxx	12 3/0											
$xxxxxxxx	16 4/0											
d(PC)	12 3/0											
d(PC,Rx)	14 3/0											
#	8 2/0											

Execution Times (Cycles): (Operations on Long Words)

The first number is the number of clock cycles required to: get the operands, execute the instruction, store the results and get the next opcode. The next pair of numbers is for the number of read cycles and the number of write cycles respectively.

These values are only valid for the 68000 microprocessor. See the condensed tables in Chapter 8 for calculating times for the other microprocessors in the M68000 family.

Source	Destination											
	Dn	An	(An)	(An)+	–(An)	d(An)	d(An,Rx)	$xxxx	$xxxxxxxx	d(PC)	d(PC,Rx)	#
Dn	6 1/0											
An	6 1/0											
(An)	14 3/0											
(An)+	14 3/0											
–(An)	16 3/0											
d(An)	18 4/0											
d(An,Rx)	20 4/0											
$xxxx	18 4/0											
$xxxxxxxx	22 5/0											
d(PC)	18 4/0											
d(PC,Rx)	20 4/0											
#	14 3/0											

Number of Bytes per Instruction for Different Addressing Modes:
(Operations on Bytes and Words)

Source	Destination											
	Dn	An	(An)	(An)+	−(An)	d(An)	d(An,Rx)	$xxxx	$xxxxxxxx	d(PC)	d(PC,Rx)	#
Dn	2											
An	2											
(An)	2											
(An)+	2											
−(An)	2											
d(An)	4											
d(An,Rx)	4											
$xxxx	4											
$xxxxxxxx	6											
d(PC)	4											
d(PC,Rx)	4											
#	4											

Number of Bytes per Instruction for Different Addressing Modes:
(Operations on Long Words)

Source	Destination											
	Dn	An	(An)	(An)+	−(An)	d(An)	d(An,Rx)	$xxxx	$xxxxxxxx	d(PC)	d(PC,Rx)	#
Dn	2											
An	2											
(An)	2											
(An)+	2											
−(An)	2											
d(An)	4											
d(An,Rx)	4											
$xxxx	4											
$xxxxxxxx	6											
d(PC)	4											
d(PC,Rx)	4											
#	6											

Example:

Compare the results of a data register with a constant:

Before the operation:	Contents of the data register:	D0 = $0005
	Contents of the flags:	X N Z V C
		0 0 0 0 0
		CMP.W #5,D0
After the operation:	Contents of the data register:	D0 = $0005
	Contents of the flags:	X N Z V C
		0 0 1 0 0

After the CMP instruction executed in this example, the BEQ instruction would have its condition met and cause a branch to occur.

Applications:

You can use the CMP instruction whenever you need to compare two operands. After the comparison, you can use the Bcc instruction for conditional branching, depending upon the results of this comparison. For example, you can determine whether a counter has reached its limit. You can also use the CMP instruction when you sort the values in a table according to their values.

CMPA   Compare an Operand with the Contents of an Address Register

Assembler Syntax:

CMPA.w <ea>,Ad

Operation:

<Destination>–<Source> → Setting flags accordingly.
The CMPA instruction is the only instruction that uses an address register as destination address and changes the flags.

Flag Changes:

X   Not changed.
N   Set equal to 1 if result is negative, otherwise reset to 0.
Z   Set equal to 1 if result equals 0, otherwise reset to 0.
V   Set equal to 1 if an overflow occurs, otherwise reset to 0.
C   Set equal to 1 if a "borrow" is used, otherwise reset to 0.

Operand Sizes:

Since this instruction uses an address register for the destination address, it can only work with words and long words. The .w in the syntax refers to .W or .L respectively.

Description of Instruction:

The CMPA instruction compares an operand from a source address with the contents of an address register as the destination address. It subtracts the first operand (at the source address) from the second operand (at the destination address = address register) without changing the second operand. It sets or resets several flags, depending upon the results of this operation, it sets or resets several flags.

The CMPA instruction is the only instruction that uses an address register as the destination address and changes the flags.

If the size of the operands is specified as word, then the 16-bit first operand will be expanded, with the correct sign, into a 32-bit operand before it is subtracted from all 32 bits of the second operand in the address register.

Format of Opcode:

15	14	13	12	11	10	9	8	7	6	5	4	3	2	1	0
										Effective Address <ea>					
1	0	1	1	Register			Opmode			Mode			Register		

Bits 15–12. These bits indicate that this instruction belongs to the set of instructions {CMP,EOR}. Other bits in the opcode select this particular instruction from this set.

Register, Bits 11–9. This field contains the number of the address register for this instruction.

Opmode, Bits 8–6. This field defines this instruction to be the CMPA instruction and defines the size of the operands as follows:

> 011 – 16-bit word as first operand (it will be expanded to 32-bits and will then be subtracted from all 32 bits of the address register.)
>
> 110 – 32-bit words as operands

Effective Address, Bits 5–0. effective address is stored in this pair of fields, one for the mode and the other for the register. The interpretation for this pair of fields is given in the table below:

Effective Address <ea>		Mnemonic for Addressing Mode
Mode	**Register**	
000	Register Number n	Dn
001	Register Number n	An
010	Register Number n	(An)
011	Register Number n	(An)+
100	Register Number n	–(An)
101	Register Number n	d(An)
110	Register Number n	d(An,Rx)
111	000	$xxxx
111	001	$xxxxxxxx
111	010	d(PC)
111	011	d(PC,Rx)
111	100	#

If the source address is an address register, then only the sizes of word and long word are allowed for both operands.

Execution Times (Cycles): (Operations on Words)

The first number is the number of clock cycles required to: get the operands, execute the instruction, store the results and get the next opcode. The next pair of numbers is for the number of read cycles and the number of write cycles respectively.

These values are only valid for the 68000 microprocessor. See the condensed tables in Chapter 8 for calculating times for the other microprocessors in the M68000 family.

Source	Destination											
	Dn	An	(An)	(An)+	−(An)	d(An)	d(An,Rx)	$xxxx	$xxxxxxxx	d(PC)	d(PC,Rx)	#
Dn		6 1/0										
An		6 1/0										
(An)		10 2/0										
(An)+		10 2/0										
−(An)		12 2/0										
d(An)		14 3/0										
d(An,Rx)		16 3/0										
$xxxx		14 3/0										
$xxxxxxxx		18 3/0										
d(PC)		14 3/0										
d(PC,Rx)		16 3/0										
#		8 2/0										

Execution Times (Cycles): (Operations on Long Words)

The first number is the number of clock cycles required to: get the operands, execute the instruction, store the results and get the next opcode. The next pair of numbers is for the number of read cycles and the number of write cycles respectively.

These values are only valid for the 68000 microprocessor. See the condensed tables in Chapter 8 for calculating times for the other microprocessors in the M68000 family.

Source	Destination											
	Dn	An	(An)	(An)+	−(An)	d(An)	d(An,Rx)	$xxxx	$xxxxxxxx	d(PC)	d(PC,Rx)	#
Dn		6 1/0										
An		6 1/0										
(An)		14 3/0										
(An)+		14 3/0										
−(An)		16 3/0										
d(An)		18 4/0										
d(An,Rx)		20 4/0										
$xxxx		18 4/0										
$xxxxxxxx		22 5/0										
d(PC)		18 4/0										
d(PC,Rx)		20 4/0										
#		18 3/0										

Number of Bytes per Instruction for Different Addressing Modes: (Operations on Words)

Source	Destination											
	Dn	An	(An)	(An)+	−(An)	d(An)	d(An,Rx)	$xxxx	$xxxxxxxx	d(PC)	d(PC,Rx)	#
Dn		2										
An		2										
(An)		2										
(An)+		2										
−(An)		2										
d(An)		4										
d(An,Rx)		4										
$xxxx		4										
$xxxxxxxx		6										
d(PC)		4										
d(PC,Rx)		4										
#		4										

Number of Bytes per Instruction for Different Addressing Modes:
(Operations on Long Words)

Source	Destination											
	Dn	An	(An)	(An)+	–(An)	d(An)	d(An,Rx)	$xxxx	$xxxxxxxx	d(PC)	d(PC,Rx)	#
Dn	2											
An	2											
(An)	2											
(An)+	2											
–(An)	2											
d(An)	4											
d(An,Rx)	4											
$xxxx	4											
$xxxxxxxx	6											
d(PC)	4											
d(PC,Rx)	4											
#	6											

Example:

Compare the results of an address register with a constant:

Before the operation:	Contents of the address register:	A0 = $0005
	Contents of the flags:	X N Z V C
		0 0 0 0 0
		CMPA.W #5,A0
After the operation:	Contents of the address register:	A0 = $0005
	Contents of the flags:	X N Z V C
		0 0 1 0 0

After the CMP instruction executed in this example, the BEQ instruction would have its condition met and cause a branch to occur.

Applications:

You can use the CMP instruction whenever you need to compare two operands. After the comparison, you can use the Bcc instruction for conditional branching, depending upon the results of this comparison. For example, you can determine whether a counter has reached its limit. You can also use the CMP instruction when you sort the entries in a table according to their values.

CMPI   Compare an Operand with a Constant

Assembler Syntax:

CMPI.w #Constant, <ea>

Operation:

<ea> – #Constant → Setting flags accordingly.

Flag Changes:

X   Not changed.
N   Set equal to 1 if result is negative, otherwise reset to 0.
Z   Set equal to 1 if result equals 0, otherwise reset to 0.
V   Set equal to 1 if an overflow occurs, otherwise reset to 0.
C   Set equal to 1 if a "borrow" is used, otherwise reset to 0.

Operand Sizes:

This instruction compares a pair of bytes, words or long words and sets or resets several flags depending upon the result. The .w in the syntax refers to .B, .W or .L respectively.

Description of Instruction:

The CMPI instruction compares the value of a constant with an operand at the destination address. It subtracts the constant from the operand without changing the operand. It sets or resets several flags, depending upon the results of this operation, it sets or resets several flags.

Format of Opcode:

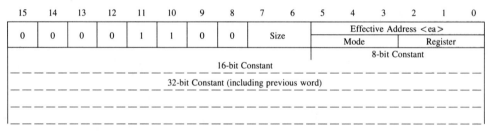

Bits 15–12. These bits indicate that this instruction belongs to the set of instructions {Bit-manipulation, MOVEP,immediate}. Other bits in the opcode select this particular instruction from this set.
Bits 11–8. These bits select this instruction as the CMPI instruction.
Size, Bits 7–6. The size of the operands is stored in this field as follows:

00   –   8-bit bytes as operands
01   –   16-bit words as operands
10   –   32-bit long words as operands

Effective Address, Bits 5–0. The effective address is stored in this pair of fields, one for the mode and the other for the register. The interpretation for this pair of fields is given in the table below:

Effective Address <ea>		Mnemonic for Addressing Mode
Mode	**Register**	
000	Register Number n	Dn
*	*	An
010	Register Number n	(An)
011	Register Number n	(An)+
100	Register Number n	−(An)
101	Register Number n	d(An)
110	Register Number n	d(An,Rx)
111	000	$xxxx
111	001	$xxxxxxxx
*	*	d(PC)
*	*	d(PC,Rx)
*	*	#

* means that this addressing mode is not allowed

The constants follow immediately after the opcode as follows:

Size field = 00   –   the byte as constant is in the least significant half of the next word.
Size field = 01   –   the word as constant is the next word after the opcode.
Size field = 10   –   the long word as constant is the next two words after the opcode.

Execution Times (Cycles): (Operations on Bytes and Words)

The first number is the number of clock cycles required to: get the operands, execute the instruction, store the results and get the next opcode. The next pair of numbers is for the number of read cycles and the number of write cycles respectively.

These values are only valid for the 68000 microprocessor. See the condensed tables in Chapter 8 for calculating times for the other microprocessors in the M68000 family.

Source	Destination											
	Dn	An	(An)	(An)+	−(An)	d(An)	d(An,Rx)	$xxxx	$xxxxxxxx	d(PC)	d(PC,Rx)	#
Dn												
An												
(An)												
(An)+												
−(An)												
d(An)												
d(An,Rx)												
$xxxx												
$xxxxxxxx												
d(PC)												
d(PC,Rx)												
#	8 2/0		12 3/0	12 3/0	14 3/0	16 4/0	18 4/0	16 4/0	20 5/0			

Execution Times (Cycles): (Operations on Long Words)

The first number is the number of clock cycles required to: get the operands, execute the instruction, store the results and get the next opcode. The next pair of numbers is for the number of read cycles and the number of write cycles respectively.

These values are only valid for the 68000 microprocessor. See the condensed tables in Chapter 8 for calculating times for the other microprocessors in the M68000 family.

Source	Destination											
	Dn	An	(An)	(An)+	−(An)	d(An)	d(An,Rx)	$xxxx	$xxxxxxxx	d(PC)	d(PC,Rx)	#
Dn												
An												
(An)												
(An)+												
−(An)												
d(An)												
d(An,Rx)												
$xxxx												
$xxxxxxxx												
d(PC)												
d(PC,Rx)												
#	14 3/0		20 5/0	20 5/0	22 5/0	24 6/0	26 6/0	24 6/0	28 7/0			

Number of Bytes per Instruction for Different Addressing Modes:
(Operations on Bytes and Words)

Source	Destination											
	Dn	An	(An)	(An)+	−(An)	d(An)	d(An,Rx)	$xxxx	$xxxxxxxx	d(PC)	d(PC,Rx)	#
Dn												
An												
(An)												
(An)+												
−(An)												
d(An)												
d(An,Rx)												
$xxxx												
$xxxxxxxx												
d(PC)												
d(PC,Rx)												
#	4		4	4	4	6	6	6	8			

Number of Bytes per Instruction for Different Addressing Modes:
(Operations on Long Words)

Source	Destination											
	Dn	An	(An)	(An)+	−(An)	d(An)	d(An,Rx)	$xxxx	$xxxxxxxx	d(PC)	d(PC,Rx)	#
Dn												
An												
(An)												
(An)+												
−(An)												
d(An)												
d(An,Rx)												
$xxxx												
$xxxxxxxx												
d(PC)												
d(PC,Rx)												
#	6		6	6	6	8	8	8	10			

Example:

Compare the contents of a memory location with a constant:

Before the operation:	Contents of the memory location $<\$100> = 7$
Contents of the flags	X N Z V C
	0 1 0 1 0
	CMPI.W #5,$100
After the operation:	Contents of the memory location $<\$100> = 7$
Contents of the flags	X N Z V C
	0 0 0 0 0

Applications:

You can use the CMP instruction whenever you know the value that you want to compare with an operand. You can then see the value of this constant in the assembler listing.

CMPM   Compare Contents of Two Memory Locations

Assembler Syntax:

CMPM.w (As)+,(Ad)+

Operation:

$<$Destination$> - <$Source$> \rightarrow$ Setting flags accordingly.

Flag Changes:

X	Not changed.
N	Set equal to 1 if result is negative, otherwise reset to 0.
Z	Set equal to 1 if result equals 0, otherwise reset to 0.
V	Set equal to 1 if an overflow occurs, otherwise reset to 0.
C	Set equal to 1 if a "borrow" is used, otherwise reset to 0.

Operand Sizes:

This instruction compares a pair of bytes, words or long words and sets or resets several flags depending upon the result. The .w in the syntax refers to .B, .W or .L respectively.

Description of Instruction:

The CMP instruction compares the values of two operands in memory. It subtracts the first operand (at the source address) from the second operand (at the destination address) without changing the second operand. It sets or resets several flags, depending upon the results of this operation.

Format of Opcode:

15	14	13	12	11	10	9	8	7	6	5	4	3	2	1	0
1	0	1	1	Register Ad			1	Size		0	0	1	Register As		

Bits 15–12. These bits indicate that this instruction belongs to the set of instructions {CMP,EOR}. Other bits in the opcode select this particular instruction from this set.

Register Ad, Bits 11–9. This field contains the number of the address register with the destination address that is addressed with the address-register indirect-addressing mode with post increment.

Size, Bits 7–6. This field defines the size of the operands as follows:

00	–	8-bit bytes as operands
01	–	16-bit words as operands
10	–	32-bit long words as operands

Register As, Bits 2–0. The field contains the number of the address register with the source address that is addressed with the address-register indirect-addressing mode with post increment.

Execution Times (Cycles): (Operations on Bytes and Words)

The first number is the number of clock cycles required to: get the operands, execute the instruction, store the results and get the next opcode. The next pair of numbers is for the number of read cycles and the number of write cycles respectively.

These values are only valid for the 68000 microprocessor. See the condensed tables in Chapter 8 for calculating times for the other microprocessors in the M68000 family.

Source	Destination											
	Dn	An	(An)	(An)+	–(An)	d(An)	d(An,Rx)	$xxxx	$xxxxxxxx	d(PC)	d(PC,Rx)	#
Dn												
An												
(An)												
(An)+				12 3/0								
–(An)												
d(An)												
d(An,Rx)												
$xxxx												
$xxxxxxxx												
d(PC)												
d(PC,Rx)												
#												

Execution Times (Cycles): (Operations on Long Words)

The first number is the number of clock cycles required to: get the operands, execute the instruction, store the results and get the next opcode. The next pair of numbers is for the number of read cycles and the number of write cycles respectively.

These values are only valid for the 68000 microprocessor. See the condensed tables in Chapter 8 for calculating times for the other microprocessors in the M68000 family.

Source	Destination											
	Dn	An	(An)	(An)+	–(An)	d(An)	d(An,Rx)	$xxxx	$xxxxxxxx	d(PC)	d(PC,Rx)	#
Dn												
An												
(An)												
(An)+				20 5/0								
–(An)												
d(An)												
d(An,Rx)												
$xxxx												
$xxxxxxxx												
d(PC)												
d(PC,Rx)												
#												

Number of Bytes per Instruction for Different Addressing Modes:
(Operations on Bytes, Words and Long Words)

Source	Destination											
	Dn	An	(An)	(An)+	–(An)	d(An)	d(An,Rx)	$xxxx	$xxxxxxxx	d(PC)	d(PC,Rx)	#
Dn												
An												
(An)												
(An)+				2								
–(An)												
d(An)												
d(An,Rx)												
$xxxx												
$xxxxxxxx												
d(PC)												
d(PC,Rx)												
#												

Example:

Compare the values stored in two memory locations:

Before the operation:	Contents at $1000 in memory:	$1234
	Contents at $2000 in memory:	$2345
	Contents in address register A1:	$1000
	Contents in address register A2:	$2000
	Contents of the flags:	X N Z V C
		0 1 0 1 0
		CMPM.W (A1)+,(A2)+
After the operation:	Contents at $1000 in memory:	$1234
	Contents at $2000 in memory:	$2345
	Contents in address register A1:	$1000
	Contents in address register A2:	$2000
	Contents of the flags:	X N Z V C
		0 0 0 0 0

After the CMP instruction executed in this example, the BEQ instruction would have its condition met and cause a branch to occur.

Applications:

You can use the CMPM instruction whenever you need to compare two operands that are stored in memory. This instruction has the advantage that you do not need to first load these operands into data registers before comparing them. This simplifies the programming and saves the data registers for other variables.

For example, it is easy to compare the values in two tables with this CMPM instruction.

DBcc Test Condition, Decrement, and Branch

Assembler Syntax:

DBcc Ds,Label

Operation:

If condition is satisfied then $<PC> + 2 \rightarrow <PC>$ (continue with next instruction) else Dn–1 → Dn if Dn = –1 then $<PC> + 2 \rightarrow <PC>$ (continue next instruction) else $<PC> + d \rightarrow <PC>$ (branch to label)

Flag Changes:

None.
This instruction reads the flags but does not change them.

Operand Sizes:

This instruction operates only with words as operands. This means that the loop counter in Ds occupies only the least-significant half of the data register and the address distance d can only be up to 16 bits long. Therefore, branches of –32 k to + 32 k from the current value in the program counter $<PC>$ are possible. The current value in the program counter $<PC>$ at the time when this instruction is executed is the address of the DBcc instruction plus 2.

Description of Instruction:

The DBcc instruction enables you to construct a counter for a loop in assembler language. This instruction leads to the execution of 3 actions by an M68000 microprocessor:

1	Test the flags for the condition cc.
2	Decrement the data register containing the loop counter, if appropriate.
3	Branch, if appropriate.

The condition cc in this instruction is completely independent of the value in the data register Dn containing the loop counter. The condition cc merely checks the status of the flags before executing the rest of the instruction. You can use this characteristic to set conditions for jumping out of a loop (see the example below).

When an M68000 microprocessor encounters this instruction, it first tests the flags with the given condition. If the condition is met, then the microprocessor continues to the next instruction, ie. branches out of the loop without testing or changing the contents of the data register containing the loop counter. The loop counter is only relevant when the condition for the flags is not met. In this case, an M68000 microprocessor subtracts 1 from the least-significant half of the data register and tests whether the result is equal to –1. If the result equals –1, this implies that the loop is completed and therefore, the microprocessor continues with the next instruction. However, if the result is not yet equal to –1, the loop is not finished and the microprocessor branches to the label (usually a return to the beginning of the loop), by adding the value of d to the contents of the program counter <PC>.

This complete process is illustrated in the following flow chart:

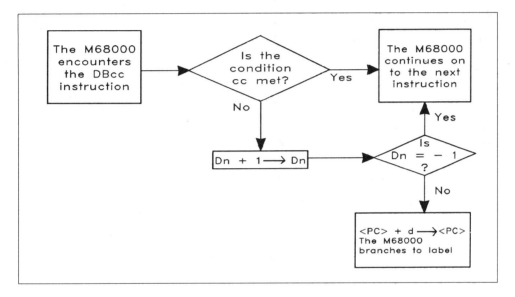

The conditions for the DBcc instruction are presented in the following table. You should note that the DBcc instruction branches only when the condition is not met, in contrast to the simpler Bcc instruction that branches when the condition is met.

Test Condition, Decrement, and Branch						
Mnemonic	Name	Logical Condition	Bit Pattern			
			11	10	9	8
DBT	true	1	0	0	0	0
DBF**	false	0	0	0	0	1
DBEQ	equal	Z=1	0	1	1	1
DBNE	not equal	Z=0	0	1	1	0
DBPL	plus	N=0	1	0	1	0
DBMI	minus	N=1	1	0	1	1
DBHI	higher	CvZ=0	0	0	1	1
DBLS	lower or same	CvZ=1	0	0	1	0
DBCS	carry flag set	C=1	0	1	0	1
DBCC	carry flag cleared	C=0	0	1	0	0
DBGT*	greater	$Zv (\oplus V)=0$	1	1	1	0
DBLT	less	$N \oplus V=1$	1	1	0	1
DBGE	greater or equal	$N \oplus V=0$	1	1	0	0
DBLE	less or equal	$Zv (N \oplus V)=1$	1	1	1	1
DBVS*	overflow flag set	V=1	1	0	0	1
DBVC*	overflow flag cleared	V=0	1	0	0	0

* = two's complement arithmetic, ** = some assemblers use the syntax RA = always branch, v = logical OR, $\oplus$ = exclusive OR

Format of Opcode:

15	14	13	12	11	10	9	8	7	6	5	4	3	2	1	0
0	1	0	1		Condition			1	1	0	0	1		Register	
16-bit Address Distance															

Bits 15–12. These bits indicate that this instruction belongs to the set of instructions {ADDQ,SUBQ, Scc,DBcc}. Other bits in the opcode select this particular instruction from this set.

Condition, Bits 11–8. This field specifies the condition cc for the DBcc instruction, as defined by the bit patterns in the table above.

Bits 7–3. These bits define this instruction to be the DBcc instruction.

Register, Bits 2–0. This field specifies the number of the data register that contains the loop counter.

Execution Times (Cycles):

The first number is the number of clock cycles required to: get the operands, execute the instruction, store the results and get the next opcode. The next pair of numbers is for the number of read cycles and the number of write cycles respectively.

These values are only valid for the 68000 microprocessor. See the condensed tables in Chapter 8 for calculating times for the other microprocessors in the M68000 family.

The processor branches	The processor does not branch	
Condition cc is met:	– (Ds > –1)	12 (Ds =–1 or Ds > –1) 2/0
Condition cc is not met:	10 (Ds > –1)	14 (Ds = –1) 3/0

Number of Bytes per Instruction

Always 4 bytes.

Example:

Construction of a loop with exit conditions:

CLR.L D0	Clear the contents of D0 for use as the loop counter.
MOVE.W #(Loop counter–1),D0	Set the loop counter at its normal value –1, since the query is for –1 by DBcc.

LOOP	MOVE	
	CMP EPS,D3	Exit from the loop when a boundary value is reached.
	DBEQ D0,LOOP	Exit from the loop if EPS = D3, otherwise, continue until the loop counter reaches –1.
	MOVE...	

Applications:

You can use the Bcc instruction to construct a number of loops with different exit conditions. Together with the DBLE and CMP instructions, you can construct a loop that corresponds to the following type of loop in a high-level programming language:

REPEAT . . .		
UNTIL (X > EPS	AND Z > 0)	
Exit Condition	Loop Counter	

For constructing a normal loop without conditions in an assembler language (corresponding to a FOR–NEXT loop in some high-level languages), you can use the DBF instruction (condition always false) or DBRA instruction (decrement and branch always) as appropriate.

There are two ways to enter a loop consisting of a segment of code between a label at the beginning of the loop and the DBcc instruction at the end of the loop:

Case 1: Start at the first instruction, proceed through the body of the loop, and execute the DBcc instruction at the end of the loop to determine whether to repeat the loop.

Case 2: Branch first to the DBcc instruction at the end of the loop to determine whether to go back to the label and execute the body of the loop.

In case 1, the body of the loop will automatically be executed at least once and in case 2, the body of the loop may never be executed (if the conditions are not met). These two cases are illustrated below:

Case 1: Start at the beginning of the loop.

LOOP	MOVE ...	
	.	
	.	Body of the loop
	.	
	DBcc Dn,LOOP	

In this case, you should set the value in the loop counter, Dn, 1 smaller than the number of times that the loop should execute when no exit occurs. This is due to the comparison with –1 and the fact that the body of the loop is executed before the test in the DBcc instruction at the end. This case is particularly useful when you are using address-register indirect-addressing mode, with index and offset, or bit instructions with dynamic bit numbers.

Case 2: Start at the end of the loop.

	.	
	BRA LOOPEND	
LOOPBEG	MOVE ...	
	.	
	.	Body of the loop
	.	
LOOPEND	DBcc Dn,LOOPBEG	

In this case, you should set the value in the loop counter, Dn, exactly equal to the number of times that the loop should execute when no exit occurs. The comparison with –1 and the fact that the test is performed before the body of the loop is executed for the first time cancel each other.

DIVS   Signed Division

Assembler Syntax:

DIVS <ea>,Dd

Operation:

<Destination> / <Source> → <Destination>

Flag Changes:

X Not changed.
N Set equal to 1 if quotient is negative, otherwise set to 0. Undefined if an overflow occurs.
Z Set equal to 1 if quotient equals 0, otherwise set to 0. Undefined if an overflow occurs.
V Set equal to 1 if an overflow occurs, otherwise set to 0.
C Always reset to 0.

Operand Sizes:

This instruction operates on a 32-bit signed dividend that is in a data register and a 16-bit signed divisor from memory. The result is a 32-bit signed quotient in the same data register. Since the sizes are predefined, there is no .w in the syntax. However, some assemblers allow .W.

Description of Instruction:

The DIVS instruction divides signed numbers, using two's complement arithmetic. The resulting quotient automatically has the correct sign. The 32-bit signed dividend is in a data register that serves as the destination address. The 16-bit signed divisor is in memory at the source address. The 32-bit signed quotient as the result is left in the same data register as the dividend. This quotient is in two parts:

quotient $=$ in the lower half of the register, bits 15 to 0
remainder $=$ in the upper half of the register, bits 31 to 16

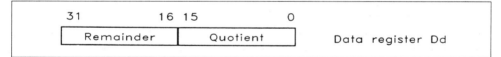

The quotient is in two's complement format and has the correct sign. The remainder has the same sign as the dividend whenever the remainder is not equal to zero.
Two error conditions can arise during this division operation:

Error 1: Division by zero

The microprocessor switches automatically to exception handling whenever it encounters division by zero.

Error 2: Overflow

If the quotient is larger than allowed for a 16-bit signed number, then the flags are set but neither the divisor nor the dividend is changed.

Format of Opcode:

15	14	13	12	11	10	9	8	7	6	5	4	3	2	1	0
1	0	0	0		Register		1	1	1	Effective Address \<ea\>					
										Mode			Register		

Bits 15-12. These bits indicate that this instruction belongs to the set of instructions {OR,DIV,SBCD}. Other bits in the opcode select this particular instruction from this set.

Register, Bits 11-9. This field contains the number of the data register that serves as the destination address (dividend before the operation and result after the operation.

Bits 8-6. These bits select this particular instruction as the DIVS instruction.

Effective Address, Bits 5-0. The effective address is stored in this pair of fields, one for the mode and the other for the register. The interpretation for this pair of fields is given in the table below:

Effective Address <ea>		Mnemonic for Addressing Mode
Mode	Register	
000	Register Number n	Dn
*	*	An
010	Register Number n	(An)
011	Register Number n	(An)+
100	Register Number n	−(An)
101	Register Number n	d(An)
110	Register Number n	d(An,Rx)
111	000	$xxxx
111	001	$xxxxxxxx
111	010	d(PC)
111	011	d(PC,Rx)
111	100	#

* means that this addressing mode is not allowed

Execution Times (Cycles):

The first number is the number of clock cycles required to: get the operands, execute the instruction, store the results and get the next opcode. The next pair of numbers is for the number of read cycles and the number of write cycles respectively.

These values are only valid for the 68000 microprocessor. See the condensed tables in Chapter 8 for calculating times for the other microprocessors in the M68000 family.

Source	Destination											
	Dn	An	(An)	(An)+	−(An)	d(An)	d(An,Rx)	$xxxx	$xxxxxxxx	d(PC)	d(PC,Rx)	#
Dn	158 1/0											
An												
(An)	162 2/0											
(An)+	162 2/0											
−(An)	164 2/0											
d(An)	166 3/0											
d(An,Rx)	168 3/0											
$xxxx	166 3/0											
$xxxxxxxx	170 4/0											
d(PC)	166 3/0											
d(PC,Rx)	168 3/0											
#	162 2/0											

Number of Bytes per Instruction for Different Addressing Modes:

Source	Destination											
	Dn	An	(An)	(An)+	–(An)	d(An)	d(An,Rx)	$xxxx	$xxxxxxxx	d(PC)	d(PC,Rx)	#
D	2											
An												
(An)	2											
(An)+	2											
–(An)	2											
d(An)	4											
d(An,Rx)	4											
$xxxx	4											
$xxxxxxxx	6											
d(PC)	4											
d(PC,Rx)	4											
#	4											

Examples:

1. With Overflow:

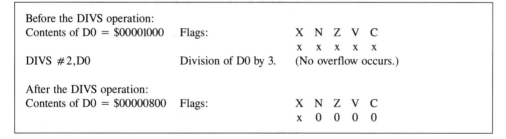

```
Before the DIVS operation:
Contents of D0 = $0FFF1234    Flags:                    X  N  Z  V  C
                                                        x  x  x  x  x
DIVS #3,D0                    Division of D0 by 3.   (An overflow occurs.)

After the DIVS operation:
Contents of D0 = $0FFF1234    Flags:                    X  N  Z  V  C
                                                        x  x  x  1  0
```

2. Without Overflow:

```
Before the DIVS operation:
Contents of D0 = $00001000    Flags:                    X  N  Z  V  C
                                                        x  x  x  x  x
DIVS #2,D0                    Division of D0 by 3.   (No overflow occurs.)

After the DIVS operation:
Contents of D0 = $00000800    Flags:                    X  N  Z  V  C
                                                        x  0  0  0  0
```

Applications:

You can use the DIVS instruction to divide signed numbers of up to 32 bits in length. However, you must remember that an overflow can occur that you will have to trap in the program. The dividend divided by the divisor must give a result in the range from –32768 to +32767 for the DIVS instruction–otherwise an overflow error will occur (that will not automatically initiate exception handling). If you want to divide signed numbers that are longer than 32 bits, you will have to use the DIVU instruction.

DIVU   Unsigned Division

Assembler Syntax:

DIVU <ea>,Dd

Operation:

<Destination> / <Source> → <Destination>

Flag Changes:

X   Not changed.
N   Set equal to 1 if quotient is negative, otherwise set to 0. Undefined if an overflow occurs.
Z   Set equal to 1 if quotient equals 0, otherwise set to 0. Undefined if an overflow occurs.
V   Set equal to 1 if an overflow occurs, otherwise set to 0.
C   Always reset to 0.

Operand Sizes:

This instruction operates on a 32-bit dividend that is in a data register and a 16-bit divisor from memory. The result is a 32-bit quotient in the same data register. Since the sizes are predefined, there is no .w in the syntax. However, some assemblers allow .W.

Description of Instruction:

The DIVU instruction divides two numbers. using two's complement arithmetic. The 32-bit dividend is in a data register that serves as the destination address. The 16-bit divisor is in memory, at the source address. The 32-bit quotient as the result is left in the same data register as the dividend. This quotient is in two parts:

quotient   =   in the lower half of the register, bits 15 to 0
remainder =   in the upper half of the register, bits 31 to 16

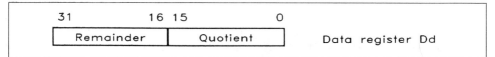

The quotient is in two's complement format and has the correct sign. The remainder has the same sign as the dividend whenever the remainder is not equal to zero.
Two error conditions can arise during this division operation:

Error 1: Division by zero

The microprocessor switches automatically to exception handling whenever it encounters division by zero.

Error 2: Overflow

If the quotient is larger than allowed for a 16-bit signed number, then the flags are set, but neither the divisor nor the dividend is changed.

Format of Opcode:

15	14	13	12	11	10	9	8	7	6	5	4	3	2	1	0
1	0	0	0	Register			0	1	1	\<ea\> Mode			Register		

Effective Address \<ea\>: Mode / Register

Bits 15–12. These bits indicate that this instruction belongs to the set of instructions {OR,DIV, SBCD}. Other bits in the opcode select this particular instruction from this set.

Register, Bits 11–9. This field contains the number of the data register that serves as the destination address (dividend before the operation and result after the operation).

Bits 8–6. These bits select this particular instruction as the DIVU instruction.

Effective Address, Bits 5–0. The effective address is stored in this pair of fields, one for the mode and the other for the register. The interpretation for this pair of fields is given in the table below:

Effective Address \<ea\>		Mnemonic for Addressing Mode
Mode	**Register**	
000	Register Number n	Dn
*	*	An
010	Register Number n	(An)
011	Register Number n	(An)+
100	Register Number n	−(An)
101	Register Number n	d(An)
110	Register Number n	d(An,Rx)
111	000	$xxxx
111	001	$xxxxxxxx
111	010	d(PC)
111	011	d(PC,Rx)
111	100	#

∗ means that this addressing mode is not allowed

Execution Times (Cycles):

The first number is the number of clock cycles required to: get the operands, execute the instruction, store the results and get the next opcode. The next pair of numbers is for the number of read cycles and the number of write cycles respectively.

These values are only valid for the 68000 microprocessor. See the condensed tables in Chapter 8 for calculating times for the other microprocessors in the M68000 family.

Source	Destination											
	Dn	An	(An)	(An)+	−(An)	d(An)	d(An,Rx)	$xxxx	$xxxxxxxx	d(PC)	d(PC,Rx)	#
Dn	140 1/0											
An												
(An)	144 2/0											
(An)+	144 2/0											
−(An)	146 2/0											
d(An)	148 3/0											
d(An,Rx)	150 3/0											
$xxxx	148 3/0											
$xxxxxxxx	152 4/0											
d(PC)	148 3/0											
d(PC,Rx)	150 3/0											
#	144 2/0											

Number of Bytes per Instruction for Different Addressing Modes:

Source	Destination											
	Dn	An	(An)	(An)+	−(An)	d(An)	d(An,Rx)	$xxxx	$xxxxxxxx	d(PC)	d(PC,Rx)	#
D	2											
An												
(An)	2											
(An)+	2											
−(An)	2											
d(An)	4											
d(An,Rx)	4											
$xxxx	4											
$xxxxxxxx	6											
d(PC)	4											
d(PC,Rx)	4											
#	4											

Example:

Program to calculate the average of 3 numbers.

CLR.L D0	Clear the data register with the dividend, to avoid the possibility of an overflow.
MOVE.W $1100,D0	Load the first number into D0.
ADD.W $1102,D0	Add the second number to the contents of D0.
ADD.W $1104,D0	Add the third number to the contents of D0.
DIVU #3,D0	The average is left in D0.

Applications:

You can use the DIVS instruction to divide numbers that are not signed. However, you must remember that an overflow can occur that you will have to trap in the program. The dividend divided by the divisor must have a result in the range from 0 to +65536 for the DIVU instruction–otherwise an overflow error will occur. In contrast, for the DIVS instruction, the dividend divided by the divisor must have a result in the range from −32768 to +32767 to avoid an overflow error.

EOR   Exclusive OR

Assembler Syntax:

EOR.w Ds,<ea>

Operation:

<Source> +o <Destination> → <Destination>

Flag Changes:

X   Not changed.
N   Set equal to 1 if first bit of result = 1, otherwise reset to 0.
Z   Set equal to 1 if result 0, otherwise reset to 0.
V   Always reset to 0.
C   Always reset to 0.

Operand Sizes:

This instruction operates on bytes, words and long words. The .w in the syntax refers to .B, .W or .L respectively.

Description of Instruction:

The EOR instruction uses the logical operation of exclusive OR upon two operands and writes the results back into the destination address. The source address is always a data register. The destination address is defined by an effective address.

Format of Opcode:

15	14	13	12	11	10	9	8	7	6	5	4	3	2	1	0
1	0	1	1	Register			1	Size		Effective Address <ea>					
										Mode			Register		

Bits 15–12. These bits indicate that this instruction belongs to the set of instructions {CMP, EOR}. Other bits in the opcode select this particular instruction from this set.

Register, Bits 11–9. This field specifies the number of the data register that serves as the source address and contains the first operand.

Bit8. This field defines this instruction to be the EOR instruction.

Size, Bits 7–6. This field defines the size of the both operands as follows:

00 –   8-bit bytes as operands
01 –   16-bit words as operands
10 –   32-bit long words as operands

Effective Address, Bits 5–0. The effective address is stored in this pair of fields, one for the mode and the other for the register. The interpretation for this pair of fields is given in the table below:

Effective Address <ea>		Mnemonic for Addressing Mode
Mode	**Register**	
000	Register Number n	Dn
*	*	An
010	Register Number n	(An)
011	Register Number n	(An)+
100	Register Number n	−(An)
101	Register Number n	d(An)
110	Register Number n	d(An,Rx)
111	000	$xxxx
111	001	$xxxxxxxx
*	*	d(PC)
*	*	d(PC,Rx)
*	*	#

* means that this addressing mode is not allowed

Execution Times (Cycles): (Operations on Bytes and Words)

The first number is the number of clock cycles required to: get the operands, execute the instruction, store the results and get the next opcode. The next pair of numbers is for the number of read cycles and the number of write cycles respectively.

These values are only valid for the 68000 microprocessor. See the condensed tables in Chapter 8 for calculating times for the other microprocessors in the M68000 family.

Source	Destination											
	Dn	An	(An)	(An)+	−(An)	d(An)	d(An,Rx)	$xxxx	$xxxxxxxx	d(PC)	d(PC,Rx)	#
Dn	4 1/0		12 2/1	12 2/1	14 2/1	16 3/1	18 3/1	16 3/1	20 4/1			
An												
(An)												
(An)+												
−(An)												
d(An)												
d(An,Rx)												
$xxxx												
$xxxxxxxx												
d(PC)												
d(PC,Rx)												
#												

Execution Times (Cycles): (Operations on Long Words)

The first number is the number of clock cycles required to: get the operands, execute the instruction, store the results and get the next opcode. The next pair of numbers is for the number of read cycles and the number of write cycles respectively.

These values are only valid for the 68000 microprocessor. See the condensed tables in Chapter 8 for calculating times for the other microprocessors in the M68000 family.

Source	Destination											
	Dn	An	(An)	(An)+	-(An)	d(An)	d(An,Rx)	$xxxx	$xxxxxxxx	d(PC)	d(PC,Rx)	#
Dn	8 1/0		20 3/2	20 3/2	22 3/2	24 4/2	26 4/2	24 4/2	28 5/2			
An												
(An)												
(An)+												
-(An)												
d(An)												
d(An,Rx)												
$xxxx												
$xxxxxxxx												
d(PC)												
d(PC,Rx)												
#												

Number of Bytes per Instruction for Different Addressing Modes:
(Operations on Bytes and Words)

Source	Destination											
	Dn	An	(An)	(An)+	-(An)	d(An)	d(An,Rx)	$xxxx	$xxxxxxxx	d(PC)	d(PC,Rx)	#
Dn	2		2	2	2	4	4	4	6			
An												
(An)												
(An)+												
-(An)												
d(An)												
d(An,Rx)												
$xxxx												
$xxxxxxxx												
d(PC)												
d(PC,Rx)												
#												

Number of Bytes per Instruction for Different Addressing Modes:
(Operations on Long Words)

Source	Destination											
	Dn	An	(An)	(An)+	-(An)	d(An)	d(An,Rx)	$xxxx	$xxxxxxxx	d(PC)	d(PC,Rx)	#
Dn	2		2	2	2	4	4	4	6			
An												
(An)												
(An)+												
-(An)												
d(An)												
d(An,Rx)												
$xxxx												
$xxxxxxxx												
d(PC)												
d(PC,Rx)												
#												

Example:

Applying the exclusive OR operation to the contents of a data register and a memory location:

Before the exclusive OR operation:
Contents of D0   = $A0A00001
Contents of $100   = $A0001101
Contents of flags :   X   N   Z   V   C
                         1   1   0   1   0

                         EOR.L D0,$100

After the exclusive OR operation:
Contents of D0   = $A0A00001
Contents of $100   = $00A01100
Contents of flags :   X   N   Z   V   C
                         1   0   0   0   0

Applications:

You can use the EOR instruction to test the status of registers for peripheral devices or for setting and resetting bits in these registers. In addition, you can combine any two operands with this logical operation.

EORI   Exclusive OR Immediate

Assembler Syntax:

EORI.w #Constant,<ea>

Operation:

#Constant +o <Destination> → <Destination>

Flag Changes:

X   Not changed.
N   Set equal to 1 if first bit of result = 1, otherwise reset to 0.
Z   Set equal to 1 if result 0, otherwise reset to 0.
V   Always reset to 0.
C   Always reset to 0.

Operand Sizes:

This instruction operates on bytes, words and long words. The .w in the syntax refers to .B, .W or .L respectively.

Description of Instruction:

The EOR instruction uses the logical operation of exclusive OR upon two operands. It writes the results back into the destination address of the second operand. The source address is always with an immediate constant. The destination address is defined by an effective address.

Format of Opcode:

15	14	13	12	11	10	9	8	7	6	5	4	3	2	1	0

0	0	0	0	1	0	1	0	Size		Effective Address <ea>					
										Mode			Register		
										8-bit Constant					

16-bit Constant

32-bit Constant (including previous word)

Bits 15–12. These bits indicate that this instruction belongs to the set of instructions {bit-manipulation, MOVEP, immediate}. Other bits in the opcode select this particular instruction from this set.

Bits 11–8. This field defines this instruction to be the EORI instruction.

Size, Bits 7–6. This field defines the size of the operands for this instruction as follows:

00	–	8-bit bytes as operands
01	–	16-bit words as operands
10	–	32-bit long words as operands

Effective Address, Bits 5–0. The effective address is stored in this pair of fields, one for the mode and the other for the register. The interpretation for this pair of fields is given in the table below:

Effective Address <ea>		Mnemonic for Addressing Mode
Mode	**Register**	
000	Register Number n	Dn
*	*	An
010	Register Number n	(An)
011	Register Number n	(An)+
100	Register Number n	–(An)
101	Register Number n	d(An)
110	Register Number n	d(An,Rx)
111	000	$xxxx
111	001	$xxxxxxxx
*	*	d(PC)
*	*	d(PC,Rx)
*	*	#

* means that this addressing mode is not allowed

Execution Times (Cycles): (Operations on Bytes and Words)

The first number is the number of clock cycles required to: get the operands, execute the instruction, store the results and get the next opcode. The next pair of numbers is for the number of read cycles and the number of write cycles respectively.

These values are only valid for the 68000 microprocessor. See the condensed tables in Chapter 8 for calculating times for the other microprocessors in the M68000 family.

Source	Destination											
	Dn	An	(An)	(An)+	–(An)	d(An)	d(An,Rx)	$xxxx	$xxxxxxxx	d(PC)	d(PC,Rx)	#
Dn												
An												
(An)												
(An)+												
–(An)												
d(An)												
d(An,Rx)												
$xxxx												
$xxxxxxxx												
d(PC)												
d(PC,Rx)												
#	8 2/0		16 3/1	16 3/1	18 3/1	20 4/1	22 4/1	20 4/1	24 5/1			

Execution Times (Cycles): (Operations on Long Words)

The first number is the number of clock cycles required to: get the operands, execute the instruction, store the results and get the next opcode. The next pair of numbers is for the number of read cycles and the number of write cycles respectively.

These values are only valid for the 68000 microprocessor. See the condensed tables in Chapter 8 for calculating times for the other microprocessors in the M68000 family.

Source	Destination											
	Dn	An	(An)	(An)+	–(An)	d(An)	d(An,Rx)	$xxxx	$xxxxxxxx	d(PC)	d(PC,Rx)	#
Dn												
An												
(An)												
(An)+												
–(An)												
d(An)												
d(An,Rx)												
$xxxx												
$xxxxxxxx												
d(PC)												
d(PC,Rx)												
#	16 3/0		28 5/2	28 5/2	30 5/2	32 6/2	34 6/2	32 6/2	36 7/2			

Number of Bytes per Instruction for Different Addressing Modes:
(Operations on Bytes and Words)

Source	Destination											
	Dn	An	(An)	(An)+	–(An)	d(An)	d(An,Rx)	$xxxx	$xxxxxxxx	d(PC)	d(PC,Rx)	#
Dn												
An												
(An)												
(An)+												
–(An)												
d(An)												
d(An,Rx)												
$xxxx												
$xxxxxxxx												
d(PC)												
d(PC,Rx)												
#	4		4	4	4	6	6	6	8			

Number of Bytes per Instruction for Different Addressing Modes:
(Operations on Long Words)

Source	Destination											
	Dn	An	(An)	(An)+	–(An)	d(An)	d(An,Rx)	$xxxx	$xxxxxxxx	d(PC)	d(PC,Rx)	#
Dn												
An												
(An)												
(An)+												
–(An)												
d(An)												
d(An,Rx)												
$xxxx												
$xxxxxxxx												
d(PC)												
d(PC,Rx)												
#	6		6	6	6	8	8	8	10			

Example:

Applying the exclusive OR operation to a constant and the contents of a memory location:

```
Before the exclusive OR operation:
Contents of $100          =    $A0001101
Contents of flags         :    X  N  Z  V  C
                               1  1  0  1  0

EOR.L  # $A0A00001,$100

After the exclusive OR operation:
Contents of $100          =    $00A01100
Contents of flags         :    X  N  Z  V  C
                               1  0  0  0  0
```

Applications:

You can use the EORI instruction to test the status of registers for peripheral devices or for setting and resetting bits in these registers. In addition, you can combine any operand with an immediate constant using this logical operation.

EORI to CCR   Exclusive OR to Condition-Code Register

Assembler Syntax:

```
EORI  # Constant,CCR
```

Operation:

$$\#\text{Constant} \oplus <\text{CCR}> \rightarrow <\text{CCR}>$$

Flag Changes:

X	Inverted if bit 4 of the constant = 1, otherwise unchanged.
N	Inverted if bit 3 of the constant = 1, otherwise unchanged.
Z	Inverted if bit 2 of the constant = 1, otherwise unchanged.
V	Inverted if bit 1 of the constant = 1, otherwise unchanged.
C	Inverted if bit 0 of the constant = 1, otherwise unchanged.

Operand Sizes:

This instruction operates only on bytes since the Condition-Code Register is only 1 byte long in the least-significant half of the 16-bit Status Register.

Description of Instruction:

The EORI-to-CCR instruction selectively changes particular flags in the Condition-Code Register, using the exclusive OR operation upon an immediate constant and the current contents of this register.

Format of Opcode:

15	14	13	12	11	10	9	8	7	6	5	4	3	2	1	0
0	0	0	0	1	0	1	0	0	0	1	1	1	1	0	0
0	0	0	0	0	0	0	0				8-bit data				

(1st word = $0A3C)

Bits 15–12. These bits indicate that this instruction belongs to the set of instructions {bit-manipulation, MOVEP,immediate}. Other bits in the opcode select this particular instruction from this set.
Bits 11–0. These bits select this particular instruction as the EORI-to-CCR instruction.
The least-significant half of the following word contains the constant used as first operand.

Addressing Modes that are Allowed:

The first operand is always an immediate constant.
The second operand is always the Condition-Code Register.

Execution Times (cycles):

20 clock cycles	(to get the operands, execute the instruction, store the results and get the next opcode.)
3 read cycles	
0 write cycles	

(These values are only valid for the 68000 microprocessor. See the condensed tables in Chapter 8 for calculating times for the other microprocessors in the M68000 family.)

Number of Bytes per Instruction for Different Addressing Modes:

Always 4 bytes.

Example:

Before executing the instruction:
Contents of the CCR: X N Z V C
                                  1 0 1 0 0
EORI #$1A,CCR   This will invert the X, N and V-flags.

After executing the instruction:
Contents of the CCR: X N Z V C
                                  0 1 1 1 0

Applications:

You know the contents of the flags; you can selectively invert some of them with the EORI-to-CCR instruction.

This is a Privileged Instruction!

EORI to SR   Exclusive OR to Status Register

Assembler Syntax:

EORI #Constant,SR

Operation:

Case 1: An M68000 microprocessor is in the Supervisor Mod

#Constant $\oplus$ <SR> → <SR>

Case 2: An M68000 microprocessor is in the User Mode:

→ exception handling (see Chapter 2.11)

Flag Changes:

X   Inverted if bit 4 of the constant = 1, otherwise unchanged.
N   Inverted if bit 3 of the constant = 1, otherwise unchanged.
Z   Inverted if bit 2 of the constant = 1, otherwise unchanged.
V   Inverted if bit 1 of the constant = 1, otherwise unchanged.
C   Inverted if bit 0 of the constant = 1, otherwise unchanged.

Operand Sizes:

This instruction operates only on words since the Status Register is 1 word long.

Description of Instruction:

The EORI-to-SR instruction selectively changes particular flags, the interrupt mask, the supervisor bit and the trace bit in the Status Register, using the exclusive OR operation upon an immediate constant and the current contents of this register.

Format of Opcode:

15	14	13	12	11	10	9	8	7	6	5	4	3	2	1	0
0	0	0	0	1	0	1	0	0	1	1	1	1	1	0	0
16-bit constant															

(1st word = $0A7C)

Bits 15–12. These bits indicate that this instruction belongs to the set of instructions {bit-manipulation, MOVEP,immediate}. Other bits in the opcode select this particular instruction from this set.
Bits 11–0. These bits select this particular instruction as the EORI-to-CCR instruction.
The following word contains the constant used as the source address.

Addressing Modes that are Allowed:

The first operand is always a constant.
The second operand is always the Status Register.

Execution Times (Cycles):

20 clock cycles	(to get the operands, execute the instruction, store the results and get the next opcode.)
3 read cycles	
0 write cycles	

(These values are only valid for the 68000 microprocessor. See the condensed tables in Chapter 8 for calculating times for the other microprocessors in the M68000 family.)

Number of Bytes per Instruction for Different Addressing Modes:

Always 4 bytes.

Example:

Before executing the instruction:

	15 14 13 12 11 10 9	8 7 6 5 4 3 2 1 0
Contents of SR:	T S 12 11 10	X N Z V C
	0 1 0 1 1	0 0 0 0 0

EORI #$2000,SR   This will invert from Supervisor to User Mode.

After executing the instruction:

	15 14 13 12 11 10 9	8 7 6 5 4 3 2 1 0
Contents of SR:	T S 12 11 10	X N Z V C
	0 0 0 1 1	0 0 0 0 0

Applications:

You can use the EORI-to-SR instruction to selectively change the supervisor bit, as in the example above. It can also change the interrupt masks, the trace bit or the flags. It is used for controlling the system.

EXG   Exchange Register Contents

Assembler Syntax:

EXG Rs,Rd

Operation:

$<Rs> \leftrightarrow <Rd>$

Flag Changes:

None

Operand Sizes:

This instruction operates only on registers and therefore only on long words. Therefore, there is no .w in the syntax. However, some assemblers allow the use of .L.

Description of Instruction:

The EXG instruction exchanges the complete contents of two registers. Three cases are possible:

Case 1:	Exchange between two data registers.
Case 2:	Exchange between two address registers.
Case 3:	Exchange between a data register and an address register.

Format of Opcode:

15	14	13	12	11	10	9	8	7	6	5	4	3	2	1	0
1	1	0	0	Register Rd		1			Opmode				Register Rs		

Bits 15–12. These bits indicate that this instruction belongs to the set of instructions {ADD,MUL, ABCD,EXG}. Other bits in the opcode select this particular instruction from this set.

Register Field Rd, Bits 11–9. This field contains the number of either a data register or an address register, depending upon the opmode. If the transfer is between a data register and an address register, then this register must be the data register.

Opmode, Bits 7–3. This field specifies the type of exchange as follows:

01000	between two data registers
01001	between two address registers
10001	between a data register and an address register

Register Field Rs, Bits 2–0. This field contains the number of either a data register or an address register, depending upon the Opmode. If the transfer is between a data register and an address register, then this register must be the address register.

Execution Times (Cycles):

The first number is the number of clock cycles required to: get the operands, execute the instruction, store the results and get the next opcode. The next pair of numbers is for the number of read cycles and the number of write cycles respectively.

These values are only valid for the 68000 microprocessor. See the condensed tables in Chapter 8 for calculating times for the other microprocessors in the M68000 family.

Source	Destination											
	Dn	An	(An)	(An)+	–(An)	d(An)	d(An,Rx)	$xxxx	$xxxxxxxx	d(PC)	d(PC,Rx)	#
Dn	6 1/0	6 1/0										
An	6 1/0	6 1/0										
(An)												
(An)+												
–(An)												
d(An)												
d(An,Rx)												
$xxxx												
$xxxxxxxx												
d(PC)												
d(PC,Rx)												
#												

Number of Bytes per Instruction for Different Addressing Modes:

Source	Destination											
	Dn	An	(An)	(An)+	–(An)	d(An)	d(An,Rx)	$xxxx	$xxxxxxxx	d(PC)	d(PC,Rx)	#
Dn	2	2										
An	2	2										
(An)												
(An)+												
–(An)												
d(An)												
d(An,Rx)												
$xxxx												
$xxxxxxxx												
d(PC)												
d(PC,Rx)												
#												

Example:

Exchange between two data registers.

Before the operation:	Contents of D0	=	$FF001234
	Contents of D1	=	$12345678
		EXG D0,D1	
After the operation:	Contents of D0	=	$12345678
	Contents of D1	=	$FF001234

Applications:

A typical example would occur when you are working with bytes with a value in an address register and no data register is free. Another example would be when you have calculated an address in a data register and want to transfer it to an address register.

EXT   Extend Register with Sign

Assembler Syntax:

EXT.w Dd

Operation:

< Destination > expanded with proper sign → < Destination >

Flag Changes:

X   Not changed.
N   Set equal to 1 if result is negative, otherwise reset to 0.
Z   Set equal to 1 if result equals 0, otherwise reset to 0.
V   Always reset to 0.
C   Always reset to 0.

Operand Sizes:

This instruction converts a byte into a word or a word into a long word. The .w in the syntax refers to .W (byte into word) or .L (word into long word) respectively.

Description of Instruction:

The EXT instruction converts the contents of a data register from a byte into a word, or from a word into a long word, while retaining the proper sign.

In the case of converting a byte into a word, the bit 7 of the byte (with the sign) is copied into bits 15 to 8:

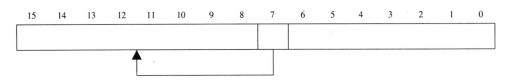

In the case of converting a word into a long word, the bit 15 of the word (with the sign) is copied into bits 31–16:

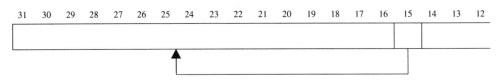

Format of Opcode:

15	14	13	12	11	10	9	8	7	6	5	4	3	2	1	0
0	1	0	0	1	0	0		Opmode		0	0	0		Register	

Bits 15–12. These bits indicate that this instruction belongs to the set of instructions {NEG, SWAP, EXT}. Other bits in the opcode select this particular instruction from this set.

Opmode, Bits 8–6. This field specifies which type of conversion is requested, as follows:

010	a byte is converted into a word
011	a word is converted into a long word

Register, Bits 2–0. This field contains the number of the data register in which the extension takes place.

Addressing Modes that are Allowed:

The EXT instruction is for a unitary operation upon the contents of a single data register that is the destination address. Therefore, only the data-register direct-addressing mode is allowed.

Execution Times (Cycles):

4 clock cycles	(to get the operand, execute the instruction, store the results and get the next opcode.)
1 read cycle	
0 write cycles	

(These values are only valid for the 68000 microprocessor. See the condensed tables in Chapter 8 for calculating times for the other microprocessors in the M68000 family.)

Number of Bytes per Instruction for Different Addressing Modes:
(Operations on Bytes and Words)

Always 2 bytes.

Examples:

1. Extending from a byte to a word in a data register.

Before the operation:	Contents of D0 = $FFFFFF73
	EXT.W D0
After the operation:	Contents of D0 = $FFFF0073

2. Extending from a word to a long word in a data register.

Before the operation:	Contents of D0 = $0010F000
	EXT.L D0
After the operation:	Contents of D0 = $FFFFF000

Applications:

If you want to work with operands of mixed lengths, then you must convert them to the same length before you can compare them. If you want to compare a byte with a long word, then you must use the EXT instruction twice, first to extend the byte into a word and second to extend the word into a long word. Another application is when you want to use a data register as an index register and you only have a byte address in the data register.

ILLEGAL   Illegal Opcode

Assembler Syntax:

None.

Operation:

\<PC\>	→ -(SSP)
\<SR\>	→ -(SSP)
	→ exception handling for an illegal opcode

Flag Changes:

None.

Operand Sizes:

None, since there are no operands.

Description of Instruction:

The EXT opcode is the only opcode of the M68000 microprocessors that is not decoded and is not forseen for a future expansion of the instruction set. Should the M68000 encounter this opcode, it will automatically go into exception handling, using the exception vector for an illegal opcode, with the vector number 4. (See Chapter 2.5.)

Assemblers for M68000 microprocessors will never create this opcode. It could only occur when an M68000 microprocessor tries to read a data area as program code or when a program is encoded by hand.

There are also other opcodes that are not decoded. They also lead to exception handling, with the same exception vector for an illegal opcode. However, they are reserved for future expansions of the instruction set.

Format of Opcode:

15	14	13	12	11	10	9	8	7	6	5	4	3	2	1	0
0	1	0	0	1	0	1	0	1	1	1	1	1	1	0	0

(= $4 PrFC)

Execution Times (Cycles):

34 clock cycles	(to get the operand, execute the instruction, store the results and get the next opcode.)
4 read cycles	
3 write cycles	

(These values are only valid for the 68000 microprocessor. See the condensed tables in Chapter 8 for calculating times for the other microprocessors in the M68000 family.)

Number of Bytes per Instruction:

Always 2 bytes.

Remark: The opcode has its own exception vector. Therefore, if an M68000 microprocessor encounters this opcode as an error, the microprocessor will still not be left in an undefined state.

Applications:

You can use the ILLEGAL opcode to insert breakpoints into a program. For example, a monitor for an M68000 microprocessor can insert this opcode into a program at the points where a breakpoint is desired. When the microprocessor encounters this opcode, it switches to exception handling and can be stopped.

JMP   Jump

Assembler Syntax:

JMP <ea>

Operation:

<ea> → <PC>

Flag Changes:

None.

Operand Sizes:

None, since this instruction does not use operands.

Description of Instruction:

The JMP instruction transfers control of the program to the specified address. This instruction loads the extended address <ea> into the program counter <PC>. This jump can be to any address in the 16-megabyte range. By contrast, the BRA instruction can only branch −32k to + 32k from the current value in the program counter. However, the jump from the BRA instruction is relocatable whereas the jump from the JMP instruction is absolute and not relocatable, unless you use one of the program-counter relative addressing modes.

Format of Opcode:

15	14	13	12	11	10	9	8	7	6	5	4	3	2	1	0
										Effective Address <ea>					
0	1	0	0	1	1	1	0	1	1	Mode			Register		

Bits 15–12. These bits indicate that this instruction belongs to the set of instructions {LINK,NEG, NOT,JMP,etc.}. Other bits in the opcode select this particular instruction from this set.
Bits 11–6. These bits select this particular instruction as the JMP instruction.
Effective Address, Bits 5–0. The effective address is stored in this pair of fields, one for the mode and the other for the register. The resulting address is stored in the program counter and the next instruction is read from this address. The interpretation for this pair of fields is given in the table below:

Effective Address <ea>		Mnemonic for Addressing Mode
Mode	**Register**	
*	*	Dn
*	*	An
010	Register Number n	(An)
*	*	(An)+
*	*	−(An)
101	Register Number n	d(An)
110	Register Number n	d(An,Rx)
111	000	$xxxx
111	001	$xxxxxxxx
111	010	d(PC)
111	011	d(PC,Rx)
*	*	#

* means that this addressing mode is not allowed

Execution Times (Cycles):

The first number is the number of clock cycles required to: get the operands, execute the instruction, store the results and get the next opcode. The next pair of numbers is for the number of read cycles and the number of write cycles respectively.
These values are only valid for the 68000 microprocessor. See the condensed tables in Chapter 8 for calculating times for the other microprocessors in the M68000 family.

						Destination					
Dn	An	(An)	(An)+	−(An)	d(An)	d(An,Rx)	$xxxx	$xxxxxxxx	d(PC)	d(PC,Rx)	#
			8 2/0		10 2/0	14 2/0	10 2/0	12 3/0	10 2/0	14 3/0	

Number of Bytes per Instruction for Different Addressing Modes:

						Destination					
Dn	An	(An)	(An)+	−(An)	d(An)	d(An,Rx)	$xxxx	$xxxxxxxx	d(PC)	d(PC,Rx)	#
		2			4	4	4	6	4	4	

Example:

Absolute jump in a program.

Address of Instruction	Instruction
$1000	MOVE.W D0,D1
$1002	JMP $2000
.	.
.	.
.	.
.	.
$2000	MOVE.W D3,D5
.	.
.	.
.	.

Applications:

You can use the JMP instruction when you want to jump absolutely to another address in memory, such as to jump over an area of memory that contains data. You could also use the BRA instruction for the same purpose. However, the BRA instruction can only jump −32k to + 32k from the current value in the program counter. The BRA instruction has an advantage in that it is relocatable whereas the JMP instruction usually is not relocatable. The JMP instruction has the advantage that you can jump to any address in the 16-megabyte address space.

JSR   Jump to a Subroutine

Assembler Syntax:

JSR <ea>

Operation:

$$<PC> \rightarrow -(SP)$$
$$<ea> \rightarrow <PC>$$

Flag Changes:

None.

Operand Sizes:

None, since this instruction does not use operands.

Description of Instruction:

The JSR instruction transfers control of the program to the address specified, which is the beginning address of a subroutine. This instruction first saves the current value in the program counter <PC> in the stack (SP) and then loads the extended address <ea> into the program counter <PC>. This jump can be to any address in the 16-megabyte range. By contrast, the BSR instruction can only branch −32k to + 32k from the current value in the program counter. However, the jump from the BSR instruction is relocatable whereas the jump from the JMP instruction is absolute and not relocatable, unless you use one of the program-counter relative-addressing modes.

Format of Opcode:

15	14	13	12	11	10	9	8	7	6	5	4	3	2	1	0
0	1	0	0	1	1	1	0	1	0	\multicolumn{6}{c} Effective Address <ea>						
										Mode			Register			

Bits 15–12. These bits indicate that this instruction belongs to the set of instructions {LINK,NEG, NOT,JMP,etc.}. Other bits in the opcode select this particular instruction from this set.

Bits 11–6. These bits select this particular instruction as the JSR instruction.

Effective Address, Bits 5–0. The effective address is stored in this pair of fields, one for the mode and the other for the register. The resulting address is stored in the program counter and the next instruction is read from this address. The interpretation for this pair of fields is given in the table below:

Effective Address <ea>		Mnemonic for Addressing Mode
Mode	Register	
*	*	Dn
*	*	An
010	Register Number n	(An)
*	*	(An)+
*	*	−(An)
101	Register Number n	d(An)
110	Register Number n	d(An,Rx)
111	000	$xxxx
111	001	$xxxxxxxx
111	010	d(PC)
111	011	d(PC,Rx)
*	*	#

* means that this addressing mode is not allowed

Execution Times (Cycles):

The first number is the number of clock cycles required to: get the operands, execute the instruction, store the results and get the next opcode. The next pair of numbers is for the number of read cycles and the number of write cycles respectively.

These values are only valid for the 68000 microprocessor. See the condensed tables in Chapter 8 for calculating times for the other microprocessors in the M68000 family.

						Destination					
Dn	An	(An)	(An)+	–(An)	d(An)	d(An,Rx)	$xxxx	$xxxxxxxx	d(PC)	d(PC,Rx)	#
		16 2/2			18 2/2	22 2/2	18 2/2	20 3/2	18 2/2	22 3/2	

Number of Bytes per Instruction for Different Addressing Modes:

						Destination					
Dn	An	(An)	(An)+	–(An)	d(An)	d(An,Rx)	$xxxx	$xxxxxxxx	d(PC)	d(PC,Rx)	#
		2			4	4	4	6	4	4	

Example:

Jump to a subroutine.

Address of Instruction	Instruction	
$1000	MOVE.W D0,D1	
$1002	JSR $2000	<PC> contains $1006 at the beginning of the instruction. <PC> is saved on the stack.
$1006	MOVE.W D3,$1888	
.	.	
.	.	
.	.	
$2000	MOVE.W D3,D5	Beginning of subroutine.
.	.	
.	.	
.	.	
$2200	RTS	End of subroutine. Load $1006 from the stack into the <PC>.

Applications:

You can use the JSR instruction when you want to jump absolutely to the beginning of a subroutine at a given address in memory. You could also use the BSR instruction for the same purpose. However, the BSR instruction can only jump –32k to + 32k from the current value in the program counter. The BSR instruction has an advantage in that it is relocatable whereas the JSR instruction usually is not relocatable. The JSR instruction has the advantage that you can jump to any address in the 16-megabyte address space which is useful when the subroutine is located more than 32 k away from the point from which it is called.

LEA   Load Effective Address in Address Register

Assembler Syntax:

LEA <ea>,Ad

Operation:

<ea> → <Ad>

Flag Changes:

None.

Operand Sizes:

This instruction operates only with long words since the address is loaded into an address register and address registers always contain long words. Therefore, there is no .w in the syntax.

Description of Instruction:

The LEA instruction loads an effective address into an address register. As the first step, it calculates the effective address. As an example, the address could be defined as 5(A0,D5.L). This instruction will load this result into the 32-bit address register, whereby all 32 bits from the source address go into this register. The difference between the LEA instruction and the MOVE instruction is that the LEA instruction moves the effective address into the address register, whereas the MOVE instruction moves the contents from the effective address into the address register.

Format of Opcode:

15	14	13	12	11	10	9	8	7	6	5	4	3	2	1	0
										Effective Address \<ea\>					
0	1	9	0	Register			1	1	1	Mode			Register		

Bits 15–12. These bits indicate that this instruction belongs to the set of instructions {LEA,CLR, NEGX,NEG,EXT,etc.}. Other bits in the opcode select this particular instruction from this set.
Register, Bits 11–9. This field specifies the number of the address register used as the destination address.
Bits 8–6. These bits select this particular instruction as the LEA instruction.
Effective Address, Bits 5–0. The effective address is stored in this pair of fields, one for the mode and the other for the register. The effective address that will be stored in the address register is calculated from the contents of these fields. The interpretation for this pair of fields is given in the table below:

Effective Address \<ea\>		Mnemonic for Addressing Mode
Mode	Register	
*	*	Dn
*	*	An
010	Register Number n	(An)
*	*	(An)+
*	*	–(An)
101	Register Number n	d(An)
110	Register Number n	d(An,Rx)
111	000	$xxxx
111	001	$xxxxxxxx
111	010	d(PC)
111	011	d(PC,Rx)
*	*	#

* means that this addressing mode is not allowed

Execution Times (Cycles):

The first number is the number of clock cycles required to: get the operands, execute the instruction, store the results and get the next opcode. The next pair of numbers is for the number of read cycles and the number of write cycles respectively.

These values are only valid for the 68000 microprocessor. See the condensed tables in Chapter 8 for calculating times for the other microprocessors in the M68000 family.

Source	Destination											
	Dn	An	(An)	(An)+	–(An)	d(An)	d(An,Rx)	$xxxx	$xxxxxxxx	d(PC)	d(PC,Rx)	#
Dn												
An												
(An)		4 1/0										
(An)+												
–(An)												
d(An)		8 2/0										
d(An,Rx)		12 2/0										
$xxxx		8 2/0										
$xxxxxxxx		12 3/0										
d(PC)		8 2/0										
d(PC,Rx)		12 2/0										
#												

Number of Bytes per Instruction for Different Addressing Modes:

Source	Destination											
	Dn	An	(An)	(An)+	–(An)	d(An)	d(An,Rx)	$xxxx	$xxxxxxxx	d(PC)	d(PC,Rx)	#
Dn												
An												
(An)		2										
(An)+												
–(An)												
d(An)		4										
d(An,Rx)		4										
$xxxx		4										
$xxxxxxxx		6										
d(PC)		4										
d(PC,Rx)		4										
#												

Examples:

Example 1:

Before the operation:	A0	=	$00044A00
	D0	=	$00008000
	A3	=	$xxxxxxxx
LEA 5(A0,D0),A3			$00044A00
			$FFFF8000
			+ $00000005
			$100003CA05
After the operation:	A0	=	$00044A00
	D0	=	$00008000
	A3	=	$0003CA05

Example 2:

Before the operation:	A0	=	$12345678
	D0	=	$00000000
	A3	=	$xxxxxxxx
LEA (A0),A3			
After the operation:	A0	=	$12345678
	D0	=	$00000000
	A3	=	$12345678

Example 3: Calculating and storing an effective address in an address register before executing a long loop:

	LEA $25(A0,D3),A5	Calculate the effective address
LOOP	MOVE.W (A5),D5	
	............,(A5)	Addressing memory cells with the
	........(A5),....	address-register indirect-address-
	........(A5),....	mode. The address $25(A0,D3)
		could be given each time, but
		would execute slower.
	DBRA D5,LOOP	

Applications:

The LEA instruction is particularly useful when you want to calculate an address and keep this address stored. An example is shown above. This saves time during execution since the address does not have to be recalculated each time, and the result is easier to read.

LINK   Link Stack Area for Subroutine

Assembler Syntax:

LINK As, # Address Distance

Operation:

$$
\begin{aligned}
<As> &\quad \rightarrow -(A7) \\
<A7> &\quad \rightarrow <As> \\
<A7> + \#\text{Address Distance} &\quad \rightarrow <A7>
\end{aligned}
$$

Flag Changes:

None.

Operand Sizes:

The address register is 32 bits wide and contains a long word. The LINK instruction uses the full 32-bit contents of the specified address register As. The address distance is specified as a 16-bit word that must be negative and is expressed in the two's complement format. However, this instruction expands the address distance, with the correct sign, into a long word before combining it with the contents of the address register.

Description of Instruction:

The LINK instruction enables you to open a separate stack area, such as for a subroutine. It performs the following steps:

1   It writes the contents of the address register, that is specified in the instruction, onto the top of the stack.
2   It loads the stack pointer itself into the same address register, from which the contents were saved in step 1.
3   It adds the address distance, that is specified in the instruction, to the stack pointer.

The result is a new stack area that you can use for another purpose, such as for a subroutine. You can use the LINK instruction in this way to open separate stack areas for each subroutine. Normally, the LINK instruction will be the first instruction in a subroutine, and it will be followed by a MOVEM instruction. Since the original stack pointer for the main program is now in an address register, you can still access the data of the main program from the subroutine in the case where this data is on the stack.
These operations are illustrated in the diagram below:

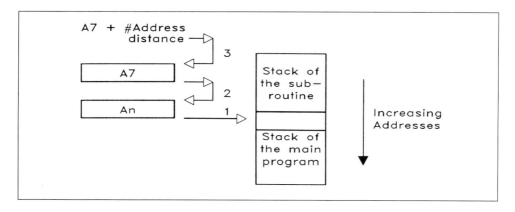

You could replace the LINK instruction by the following sequences of instructions:

Instruction Sequence 1	Instruction Sequence 2
PEA (A2) MOVEA.L A7,A2 ADDA.L # Address Distance,A7	MOVEA.L A2,-(A7) LEA (A7),A2 LEA # Address Distance (A7),A7
Equivalent Single Instruction	
LINK A2, # Address Distance	

Format of Opcode:

15	14	13	12	11	10	9	8	7	6	5	4	3	2	1	0
0	1	0	0	1	1	1	0	0	1 ·	0	1	0	Register		
16-bit Address Distance															

Bits 15–12. These bits indicate that this instruction belongs to the set of instructions {LEA,CLR, NEG,EXT,LINK,etc.}. Other bits in the opcode select this particular instruction from this set.

Bits 11–3. These bits select this particular instruction as the LINK instruction.

Register, Bits 2–0. This field contains the number of the address register into which the stack pointer is saved.

The 16-bit address distance, in two's complement format with sign, follows immediately after the opcode. It is necessary to use a negative number for this distance, since the stack for an M68000 microprocessor grows in the negative direction, and the new stack for the subroutine should not overwrite the stack of the main program.

Execution Times (Cycles):

18 clock cycles	(to get the operand, execute the instruction, store the results and get the next opcode.)
2 read cycles	
2 write cycles	

(These values are only valid for the 68000 microprocessor. See the condensed tables in Chapter 8 for calculating times for the other microprocessors in the M68000 family.)

Number of Bytes per Instruction for

Always 4 bytes

Example:

Subroutine with its own stack.

Address of Instruction	Instruction	
$1000	MOVE.L D2,D5	
$1002	JSR $2000	
$1006	MOVE.W D4,$2560	
.	.	
.	.	
.	.	
$2000	LINK A2,−$30	Construct separate stack.
$2004	MOVEM.L D0−D7/A0/A1/A3-A6,−(A7)	
.	.	
.	.	
.	.	
$2100	MOVEM.L (A7)+,D0-D7/A0/A1/A3−A6	
$2104	UNLK A2	Release the separate stack.
$2106	RTS	

Applications:

The LINK instruction is used primarily for creating separate stacks for subroutines. You can use the UNLK instruction at the end of a subroutine to release the separate stack area at the end of the subroutine. The LINK instruction is used often by compilers of high-level languages for this purpose.

This instruction is an example of how M68000 microprocessors are ideally suited for use with high-level languages.

LSL, LSR   Logical Shift (Left or Right)

Assembler Syntax:

LSd.w Ds,Dd	d can be either L (=Left) or R (Right).
LSd.w #Constant,Dd	
LSd <ea>	

Operation:

Case 1: The destination address is a data register.

<Dy> is shifted by either a #Constant or <Ds> and the results → <Dd>.

Case 2: The destination address is in the memory.

> <Destination> is shifted by one position → <Destination>

Flag Changes:

> X   Set equal to the last bit out of the operand that is shifted. If the shift counter Ds contains 0, then this flag is not changed.
> N   Set equal to 1 if the first bit of the result is equal to 1, otherwise reset equal to 0.
> Z   Set equal to 1 if the result equals 0, otherwise reset equal to 0.
> V   Is always set equal to 1.
> C   Set equal to the last bit out of the operand that is shifted. If the shift counter Ds contains 0, then this flag is reset equal to 0.

Operand Sizes:

Case 1: The destination address is a data register.

> The operands can have the size of byte, word or long word. Therefore, the .X in the syntax refers to .B, .W or .L respectively.

Case 2: The destination address is in the memory.

> The operands can only have the size of a word.

Description of Instructions:

The LSL and LSR instructions shift the bits of the operand logically in the specified direction, to the left or to the right. The last bit that is shifted out of the operand goes automatically into the C-flag and the X-flag. There are two separate cases, depending upon where the destination address is located:

Case 1: The destination address is a data register.

The operand can have the size of byte, word or long word. You can specify the number of bit positions that the operand will be shifted as a value at the source address, either immediately in the instruction or directly from a data register. If this value is specified immediately, then the number of bit positions for the rotation can range from 1 to 8. If this value is contained in a data register, then the number of bit positions for the rotation can range from 0 to 64 (modulus 64 if the data in the register is larger than 64).

Case 2: The destination address is in the memory.

The operand can only have the size of a word. You can only shift the operand by one bit position in the specified direction with each use of this instruction.

Differences between these two instructions are:

LSL: The operand is shifted the selected number of bit positions to the left. For each shift by one bit, the most-significant bit leaves the operand and enters both the C-flag and the X-flag. At the same time, a null enters the operand as the least-significant bit for each shift by one bit.

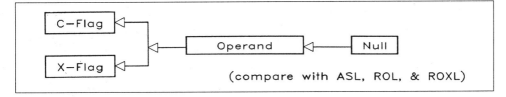

LSR: The operand is shifted by the selected number of bit positions to the right. For each shift by one bit, the least-significant bit leaves the operand and enters both the C-flag and the X-flag. At the same time, a null enters the operand as the most-significant bit at the left.

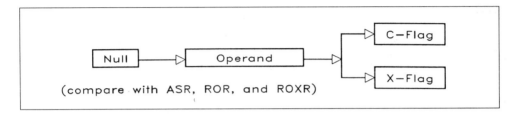

(compare with ASR, ROR, and ROXR)

Format of Opcode:

Case 1: The destination address is a data register.

15	14	13	12	11	10	9	8	7	6	5	4	3	2	1	0
1	1	1	0	Counter/Register			->Dir<-	Size		Imm/Reg	0	1	Register		

Bits 15–12. These bits indicate that this instruction belongs to the set of instructions {shift,rotate}. Other bits in the opcode select this particular instruction from this set.

Counter/Register, Bits 11–9. Depending upon the contents of the Imm/Reg field, bit 5, this field contains either the number of bit positions for the shift or the number of the data register that contains the number of bit positions. In the first case, codes from 001 to 111 specify a shift of 1 to 7 bit positions respectively and a code of 000 specifies a shift of 8 bit positions.

Dir, Bit 8. This field specifies the direction of the shift. A value of 0 specifies shifting to the right and a value of 1 specifies shifting to the left.

Size, Bits 7–6. The size of the operand is stored in this field, defined as follows:

00	–	8-bit byte as operand
01	–	16-bit word as operand
10	–	32-bit long word as operand

Imm/Reg, Bit 5. This field determines whether the number of bit positions for the shift is contained:

0	–	immediate in bits 11-9 of the opcode or
1	–	in a data register whose number is specified in bits 11-9 of the opcode.

Bits 4–3. These two bits, 01, indicate that the operand is in a data register.

Register, Bits 2–0. These three bits specify the number of the data register that contains the operand that is to be shifted.

Case 2: The destination address is in the memory.

15	14	13	12	11	10	9	8	7	6	5	4	3	2	1	0
										Effective Address <ea>					
1	1	1	0	0	0	1	->Dir<-	1	1	Mode			Register		

Bits 15–12. These bits indicate that this instruction belongs to the set of instructions {shift,rotate}. Other bits in the opcode select this particular instruction from this set.

Bits 11–9. These bits select this particular instruction as a logical shift operation.

Dir, Bit 8. This field specifies the direction of the shift. A value of 0 specifies shifting to the right, and a value of 1 specifies shifting to the left.

Bits 7–6. These two bits indicate that the destination address is in memory and that the length of the operand is a word.

Effective Address, Bits 5–0. The effective address is stored in this pair of fields, one for the mode and the other for the register. The interpretation for this pair of fields is given in the table below:

Effective Address <ea>		Mnemonic for Addressing Mode
Mode	Register	
*	*	Dn
*	*	An
010	Register Number n	(An)
011	Register Number n	(An)+
100	Register Number n	–(An)
101	Register Number n	d(An)
110	Register Number n	d(An,Rx)
111	000	$xxxx
111	001	$xxxxxxxx
*	*	d(PC)
*	*	d(PC,Rx)
*	*	#

* means that this addressing mode is not allowed

Execution Times (Cycles):

The first number is the number of clock cycles required to: get the operands, execute the instruction, store the results and get the next opcode. The next pair of numbers is for the number of read cycles and the number of write cycles respectively.

These values are only valid for the 68000 microprocessor. See the condensed tables in Chapter 8 for calculating times for the other microprocessors in the M68000 family.

Case 1: The destination address is a data register.

(Operations on bytes and words.)

Source	Destination											
	Dn	An	(An)	(An)+	–(An)	d(An)	d(An,Rx)	$xxxx	$xxxxxxxx	d(PC)	d(PC,Rx)	#
Dn	X											
An												
(An)												
(An)+												
–(An)												
d(An)												
d(An,Rx)												
$xxxx												
$xxxxxxxx												
d(PC)												
d(PC,Rx)												
#	X											

Execution Times (Cycles):
(Case 1) (Operations on Long Words)

Source	Destination											
	Dn	An	(An)	(An)+	−(An)	d(An)	d(An,Rx)	$xxxx	$xxxxxxxx	d(PC)	d(PC,Rx)	#
Dn	8+2n 1/0											
An												
(An)												
(An)+												
−(An)												
d(An)												
d(An,Rx)												
$xxxx												
$xxxxxxxx												
d(PC)												
d(PC,Rx)												
#	8+2n 1/0											

Execution Times (Cycles):
(Case 2: The Destination Address is in the Memory.)
(Operations on Words)

	Destination											
	Dn	An	(An)	(An)+	−(An)	d(An)	d(An,Rx)	$xxxx	$xxxxxxxx	d(PC)	d(PC,Rx)	#
			12 2/1	12 2/1	14 2/1	16 3/1	18 3/1	16 3/1	20 4/1			

Number of Bytes per Instruction for Different Addressing Modes:
(Operations on Bytes, Words and Words)

Case 1: The destination address is a data register.

Source	Destination											
	Dn	An	(An)	(An)+	−(An)	d(An)	d(An,Rx)	$xxxx	$xxxxxxxx	d(PC)	d(PC,Rx)	#
Dn	2											
An												
(An)												
(An)+												
−(An)												
d(An)												
d(An,Rx)												
$xxxx												
$xxxxxxxx												
d(PC)												
d(PC,Rx)												
#	2											

Case 2: The destination address is in the memory.

	Destination											
	Dn	An	(An)	(An)+	−(An)	d(An)	d(An,Rx)	$xxxx	$xxxxxxxx	d(PC)	d(PC,Rx)	#
			2	2	2	4	4	4	6			

Example:

There are two different possibilities for shifting an operand that is in memory by several bit positions:
Possibility 1: Repeating the operation several times in memory.

LSL (A0)	12 clock cycles
LSL (A0)	12 clock cycles
LSL (A0)	12 clock cycles
.	.
.	.
.	.
LSL (A0)	12 clock cycles

The number of cycles required to shift the operand by n bit positions is n x 12.

Possibility 2: Loading the operand into a data register, shifting the operand by several bit positions with one operation in the data register and writing the result from the data register into memory.

MOVE (A0),D1	8 clock cycles
LSL #n,D1	6+2n clock cycles
MOVE D1,(A0)	8 clock cycles

You can determine the optimal method, depending upon the number of bit positions required for the shift, from the following algebra:

12n	< 22 + 2n
10n	< 22
n	< 2.2

Therefore, if you need to shift the operand by 3 or more bit positions, it will be more efficient to use possibility 2 above.

Applications:

To give an example, you could use the logical shift instructions to write your own routines for multiplying by 2 and dividing by 2.

MOVE   Move Data from Source to Destination

Assembler Syntax:

MOVE.w <ea>,<ea>

Operation:

<Source> → <Destination>

Flag Changes:

X	Not changed.
N	Set equal to 1 if transfered data is negative, otherwise reset to 0.
Z	Set equal to 1 if transfered data is equal to 0, otherwise reset to 0.
V	Always reset to 0.
C	Always reset to 0.

Operand Sizes:

This instruction can transfer bytes, words and long words from the source address to the destination address. The .w in the syntax refers to .B, .W or .L respectively.

Description of Instruction:

The MOVE instruction transfers data from a source address to a destination address. It is a universal instruction, and it is certainly the most frequently used instruction of the M68000 microprocessors. There are no instructions such as LDA or STA for loading to and storing from registers in the instruction set of the M68000 microprocessors. The MOVE instruction also performs these tasks. The universal MOVE instruction can transfer data from anywhere to anywhere. It can transfer bytes, words and long words. It sets flags, depending upon the value of the data that it transfers.

Format of Opcode:

15	14	13	12	11	10	9	8	7	6	5	4	3	2	1	0
0	0	Size		Destination Address						Source Address					
				Register			Mode			Mode			Register		

Bits 15–12. These four bits specify the MOVE instruction and the last two of these four bits specify the sizes of the operands as follows:

01	–	8-bit bytes as operands
11	–	16-bit words as operands
10	–	32-bit long words as operands

Destination Address, Bits 11–6. The destination address is stored in this pair of fields, one for the mode and the other for the register. The interpretation for this pair of fields is given in the table below:

Effective Address <ea>		Mnemonic for Addressing Mode
Mode	Register	
000	Register Number n	Dn
*	*	An
010	Register Number n	(An)
011	Register Number n	(An)+
100	Register Number n	-(An)
101	Register Number n	d(An)
110	Register Number n	d(An,Rx)
111	000	$xxxx
111	001	$xxxxxxxx
*	*	d(PC)
*	*	d(PC,Rx)
*	*	#

* means that this addressing mode is not allowed

Source Address, Bits 5–0. The source address is stored in this pair of fields, one for the mode and the other for the register. The interpretation for this pair of fields is given in the table below:

Effective Address <ea>		Mnemonic for Addressing Mode
Mode	Register	
000	Register Number n	Dn
001	Register Number n	An
010	Register Number n	(An)
011	Register Number n	(An)+
100	Register Number n	-(An)
101	Register Number n	d(An)
110	Register Number n	d(An,Rx)
111	000	$xxxx
111	001	$xxxxxxxx
111	010	d(PC)
111	011	d(PC,Rx)
111	100	#

* means that this addressing mode is not allowed

Remark: The address-register direct-addressing mode, An, is not allowed for the destination address for transfers of bytes. You can use the MOVEA mnemonic when you want to transfer an operand into an address register. However, most assemblers will automatically use the opcode for the MOVEA instruction when you use the syntax MOVE <ea>,Ad.

Execution Times (Cycles): (Operations on Bytes and Words)

The first number is the number of clock cycles required to: get the operand, execute the instruction, store the results and get the next opcode. The next pair of numbers is for the number of read cycles and the number of write cycles respectively.

These values are only valid for the 68000 microprocessor. See the condensed tables in Chapter 8 for calculating times for the other microprocessors in the M68000 family.

Source	Destination											
	Dn	An	(An)	(An)+	−(An)	d(An)	d(An,Rx)	$xxxx	$xxxxxxxx	d(PC)	d(PC,Rx)	#
Dn	4 1/0		8 1/1	8 1/1	8 1/1	12 2/1	14 2/1	12 2/1	16 3/1			
An	4 1/0		8 1/1	8 1/1	8 1/1	12 2/1	14 2/1	12 2/1	16 3/1			
(An)	8 2/0		12 2/1	12 2/1	12 2/1	16 3/1	18 3/1	16 3/1	20 4/1			
(An)+	8 2/0		12 2/1	12 2/1	12 2/1	16 3/1	18 3/1	16 3/1	20 4/1			
−(An)	10 2/0		14 2/1	14 2/1	14 2/1	18 3/1	20 3/1	18 3/1	22 4/1			
d(An)	12 3/0		16 3/1	16 3/1	16 3/1	20 4/1	22 4/1	20 4/1	24 5/1			
d(An,Rx)	14 3/0		18 3/1	18 3/1	18 3/1	22 4/1	24 4/1	22 4/1	26 5/1			
$xxxx	12 3/0		16 3/1	16 3/1	16 3/1	20 4/1	22 4/1	20 4/1	24 5/1			
$xxxxxxxx	16 4/0		20 4/1	20 4/1	20 4/1	24 5/1	26 5/1	24 5/1	28 6/1			
d(PC)	12 3/0		16 3/1	16 3/1	16 3/1	20 4/1	22 4/1	20 4/1	24 5/1			
d(PC,Rx)	14 3/0		18 3/1	18 3/1	18 3/1	22 4/1	24 4/1	22 4/1	26 5/1			
#	8 2/0		12 2/1	12 2/1	12 2/1	16 3/1	18 3/1	16 3/1	20 4/1			

Execution Times (Cycles): (Operations on Long Words)

The first number is the number of clock cycles required to: get the operands, execute the instruction, store the results and get the next opcode. The next pair of numbers is for the number of read cycles and the number of write cycles respectively.

These values are only valid for the 68000 microprocessor. See the condensed tables in Chapter 8 for calculating times for the other microprocessors in the M68000 family.

Source	Destination											
	Dn	An	(An)	(An)+	−(An)	d(An)	d(An,Rx)	$xxxx	$xxxxxxxx	d(PC)	d(PC,Rx)	#
Dn	4 1/0		12 1/2	12 1/2	14 1/2	16 2/2	18 2/2	16 2/2	20 3/2			
An	4 1/0		12 1/2	12 1/2	14 1/2	16 2/2	18 2/2	16 2/2	20 3/2			
(An)	12 3/0		20 3/2	20 3/2	20 3/2	24 4/2	26 4/2	24 4/2	28 5/2			
(An)+	12 3/0		20 3/2	20 3/2	20 3/2	24 4/2	26 4/2	24 4/2	28 5/2			
−(An)	14 3/0		22 3/2	22 3/2	22 3/2	26 4/2	28 4/2	26 4/2	30 5/2			
d(An)	16 4/0		24 4/2	24 4/2	24 4/2	28 5/2	30 5/2	28 5/2	32 6/2			
d(An,Rx)	18 4/0		26 4/2	26 4/2	26 4/2	30 5/2	32 5/2	30 5/2	34 6/2			
$xxxx	16 4/0		24 4/2	24 4/2	24 4/2	28 5/2	30 5/2	28 5/2	32 6/2			
$xxxxxxxx	20 5/0		28 5/2	28 5/2	28 5/2	32 6/2	34 6/2	32 6/2	36 7/2			
d(PC)	16 4/0		24 4/2	24 4/2	24 4/2	28 5/2	30 5/2	28 5/2	32 6/2			
d(PC,Rx)	18 4/0		26 4/2	26 4/2	26 4/2	30 5/2	32 5/2	30 5/2	34 6/2			
#	12 3/0		20 3/2	20 3/2	20 3/2	24 4/2	26 4/2	24 4/2	28 5/2			

Number of Bytes per Instruction for Different Addressing Modes:
(Operations on Bytes and Words)

Source	Destination											
	Dn	An	(An)	(An)+	−(An)	d(An)	d(An,Rx)	$xxxx	$xxxxxxxx	d(PC)	d(PC,Rx)	#
Dn	2		2	2	2	4	4	4	6			
An	2		2	2	2	4	4	4	6			
(An)	2		2	2	2	4	4	4	6			
(An)+	2		2	2	2	4	4	4	6			
−(An)	2		2	2	2	4	4	4	6			
d(An)	4		4	4	4	6	6	6	8			
d(An,Rx)	4		4	4	4	6	6	6	8			
$xxxx	4		4	4	4	6	6	6	8			
$xxxxxxxx	6		6	6	6	8	8	8	10			
d(PC)	4		4	4	4	6	6	6	8			
d(PC,Rx)	4		4	4	4	6	6	6	8			
#	4		4	4	4	6	6	6	8			

Number of Bytes per Instruction for Different Addressing Modes:
(Operations on Long Words)

Source	Destination											
	Dn	An	(An)	(An)+	−(An)	d(An)	d(An,Rx)	$xxxx	$xxxxxxxx	d(PC)	d(PC,Rx)	#
Dn	2		2	2	2	4	4	4	6			
An	2		2	2	2	4	4	4	6			
(An)	2		2	2	2	4	4	4	6			
(An)+	2		2	2	2	4	4	4	6			
−(An)	2		2	2	2	4	4	4	6			
d(An)	4		4	4	4	6	6	6	8			
d(An,Rx)	4		4	4	4	6	6	6	8			
$xxxx	4		4	4	4	6	6	6	8			
$xxxxxxxx	6		6	6	6	8	8	8	10			
d(PC)	4		4	4	4	6	6	6	8			
d(PC,Rx)	4		4	4	4	6	6	6	8			
#	6		6	6	6	8	8	8	10			

Example:

The following example copies one block of data from one location in memory to another location in memory. Data register D1 contains the number of words that are to be copied. Address register A1 contains the address from which the data comes and address register A2 contains the address to which the data goes. This example shows how the block-move instruction of some other processors can be replaced by the following 3 instructions that execute faster than a single block-move instruction.

```
Label   MOVE.W (A1)+(A2)+
        DBRA D1,Label
        END
```

Applications:

The MOVE instruction is used universally whenever you need to transfer data from one location to another. As examples, you can use it to load a register or location in memory with given data, such as for setting up the counter for a loop.

MOVE to CCR   Move Data to Condition-Code Register

Assembler Syntax:

```
MOVE <ea>,CCR
```

Operation:

```
<ea> → <CCR>
```

Flag Changes:

X	Set equal to bit 4 of the source operand.
N	Set equal to bit 3 of the source operand.
Z	Set equal to bit 2 of the source operand.
V	Set equal to bit 1 of the source operand.
C	Set equal to bit 0 of the source operand.

Operand Sizes:

This instruction operates only on words as operands. The condition-code register has the length of one byte, but only the least-significant half of the word from the source address is actually transfered into the condition-code register. The most-significant half of the operand does not influence the most-significant half of the status register (that contains the condition-code register as its lower half). Only the lower 5 bits of the condition-code register can be changed, and the upper 3 bits remain unchanged (see Chapter 2.4).

Description of Instruction:

The MOVE-to-CCR instruction sets all of the flags in the condition-code register CCR to a desired value. You can set each of these flags to either 0 or 1.

Format of Opcode:

15	14	13	12	11	10	9	8	7	6	5	4	3	2	1	0
0	1	0	0	0	1	0	0	1	1	Effective Address <ea>					

| 0 | 1 | 0 | 0 | 0 | 1 | 0 | 0 | 1 | 1 | Effective Address <ea> Mode | | | Register | | |

Bits 15–12. These bits indicate that this instruction belongs to the set of instructions {CLR,NEG,NOT, NBCD,MOVE-to-CCR,etc.}. Other bits in the opcode select this particular instruction from this set.
Bits 11–6. These bits select this particular instruction as the MOVE-to-CCR instruction.
Effective Address, Bits 5–0. The effective address for the source address is stored in this pair of fields, one for the mode and the other for the register. The interpretation for this pair of fields is given in the table below:

Effective Address <ea>		Mnemonic for Addressing Mode
Mode	**Register**	
00	Register Number n	Dn
*	*	An
010	Register Number n	(An)
011	Register Number n	(An)+
100	Register Number n	−(An)
101	Register Number n	d(An)
110	Register Number n	d(An,Rx)
111	000	$xxxx
111	001	$xxxxxxxx
111	010	d(PC)
111	100	d(PC,Rx)
111	100	#

* means that this addressing mode is not allowed

Execution Times (Cycles):

The first number is the number of clock cycles required to: get the operand, execute the instruction, store the results and get the next opcode. The next pair of numbers is for the number of read cycles and the number of write cycles respectively.

These values are only valid for the 68000 microprocessor. See the condensed tables in Chapter 8 for calculating times for the other microprocessors in the M68000 family.

Source	Destination CCR
Dn	12 2/0
An	
(An)	16 3/0
(An)+	16 3/0
–(An)	18 3/0
d(An)	20 4/0
d(An,Rx)	22 4/0
$xxxx	20 4/0
$xxxxxxxx	24 5/0
d(PC)	20 4/0
d(PC,Rx)	22 4/0
#	16 3/0

Number of Bytes per Instruction for Different Addressing Modes:

Source	Destination CCR
Dn	2
An	
(An)	2
(An)+	2
–(An)	2
d(An)	4
d(An,Rx)	4
$xxxx	4
$xxxxxxxx	6
d(PC)	4
d(PC,Rx)	4
#	4

Example:

Setting the Z-flag and clearing all of the other flags.

Before the operation:	X	N	Z	V	C
	1	0	0	1	1
MOVE #4,CCR					
After the operation:	X	N	Z	V	C
	0	0	1	0	0

Applications:

To give an example, you can use the MOVE-to-CCR instruction to set the Z-flag before using the ABCD instruction. This gives you the opportunity to query later whether the result of the operation was zero or not (see ABCD instruction).

You can use the MOVE-to-CCR instruction whenever you need to set the flags to specific values.

Only Available for the 68010, 68012, 68020 and 68030
It is a Privileged Instruction!

MOVE from CCRMove Data from Condition-Code Register

Assembler Syntax:

MOVE CCR, <ea>

Operation:

<CCR> → <ea>

Flag Changes:

None.

This instruction reads the flags but does not change them.

Operand Sizes:

This instruction operates on words, even though the CCR only contains one byte. This instruction reads the missing most-significant 8 bits as nulls.

Description of Instruction:

The MOVE-from-CCR instruction of an 68010/12/20/30 microprocessor reads the flags in the condition-code register while the processor is in the user mode. This instruction was not necessary for the 68000/08 microprocessors since the MOVE-from-SR instruction allowed you to read the complete status register, including the flags in the condition-code register as its lower half. However, the MOVE-from-SR instruction is a privileged instruction of the M68010, and you can therefore not use it while in the user mode. Therefore, the new MOVE-from-CCR instruction of the 68010/12/20/30 microprocessors allows you to read the flags in the user mode of the these microprocessors. This instruction reads the CCR into the least-significant half of the destination address and writes nulls into the most-significant half.

> Note: ANDI-to-CCR, ORI-to-CCR and EORI-to-CCR are all byte operations. However, MOVE-from-CCR is a word operation.

Format of Opcode:

15	14	13	12	11	10	9	8	7	6	5	4	3	2	1	0
0	1	0	0	0	0	1	0	1	1	Effective Address <ea>					
										Mode			Register		

Bits 15–12. These bits indicate that this instruction belongs to the set of instructions {CLR,NEG,NOT, LINK,etc.}. Other bits in the opcode select this particular instruction from this set.

Bits 11–6. These bits select this particular instruction as the MOVE-from-CCR instruction.

Effective Address, Bits 5–0. The effective address is stored in this pair of fields, one for the mode and the other for the register. The interpretation for this pair of fields is given in the table below:

Effective Address <ea>		Mnemonic for Addressing Mode
Mode	**Register**	
000	Register Number n	Dn
*	*	An
010	Register Number n	(An)
011	Register Number n	(An)+
100	Register Number n	–(An)
101	Register Number n	d(An)
110	Register Number n	d(An,Rx)
111	000	$xxxx
111	001	$xxxxxxxx
*	*	d(PC)
*	*	d(PC,Rx)
*	*	#

* means that this addressing mode is not allowed

Execution Times (Cycles):

The first number is the number of clock cycles required to: get the operand, execute the instruction, store the results and get the next opcode. The next pair of numbers is for the number of read cycles and the number of write cycles respectively.

These values are only valid for the 68000 microprocessor. See the condensed tables in Chapter 8 for calculating times for the other microprocessors in the M68000 family.

Source	Destination											
	Dn	An	(An)	(An)+	–(An)	d(An)	d(An,Rx)	$xxxx	$xxxxxxxx	d(PC)	d(PC,Rx)	#
CCR	8 1/1		10 1/1	12 1/1	12 1/1	12 2/1	16 2/1	12 2/1	16 3/1			

Number of Bytes per Instruction for Different Addressing Modes:

Source	Destination											
	Dn	An	(An)	(An)+	–(An)	d(An)	d(An,Rx)	$xxxx	$xxxxxxxx	d(PC)	d(PC,Rx)	#
CCR	2		2	2	2	4	4	4	6			

Example:

Copy the CCR into memory location $1000.

Before the operation:	Contents of $1000	=	$xxxx
	Contents of CCR	=	X N Z V C
			1 1 1 0 0
MOVE CCR,$1000			
After the operation:	Contents of $1000	=	$0018
	Contents of CCR	=	X N Z V C
			1 1 0 0 0

Applications:

The MOVE-from-CCR instruction enables you to check which flags are changed in a given operation. If you do not want to test the flags with a branch instruction in a program, then the MOVE-from-CCR instruction is the instruction that you need.

This is a Privileged Instruction!

MOVE to SR   Move Data to Status Register

Assembler Syntax:

```
MOVE <ea>,SR
```

Operation:

```
If the microprocessor is in the Supervisor Mode,
then <ea> → <SR>
else → exception handling (violation of privilege)
```

Flag Changes:

```
X   Set equal to bit 4 of the source operand.
N   Set equal to bit 3 of the source operand.
Z   Set equal to bit 2 of the source operand.
V   Set equal to bit 1 of the source operand.
C   Set equal to bit 0 of the source operand.
```

Operand Sizes:

This instruction operates only on words as operands. The status register also has the length of one word.

Description of Instruction:

The MOVE-to-SR instruction sets the interrupt mask, the supervisor bit, the trace bit and all of the flags in the condition-code register CCR (lower half of the SR) to a desired value. You can set each of these bits to either 0 or 1.

The MOVE-to-SR instruction is a privileged instruction. It can only be executed from the supervisor mode of an M68000 microprocessors.

Format of Opcode:

15	14	13	12	11	10	9	8	7	6	5	4	3	2	1	0
										Effective Address <ea>					
0	1	0	0	0	1	1	0	1	1	Mode			Register		

Bits 15–12. These bits indicate that this instruction belongs to the set of instructions {CLR,NEG,NOT, NBCD,MOVE-to-CCR,etc.}. Other bits in the opcode select this particular instruction from this set.
Bits 11–6. These bits select this particular instruction as the MOVE-to-SR instruction.
Effective Address, Bits 5–0. The effective address for the destination address is stored in this pair of fields, one for the mode and the other for the register. The interpretation for this pair of fields is given in the table below:

Effective Address <ea>		Mnemonic for Addressing Mode
Mode	Register	
000	Register Number n	Dn
*	*	An
010	Register Number n	(An)
011	Register Number n	(An)+
100	Register Number n	–(An)
101	Register Number n	d(An)
110	Register Number n	d(An,Rx)
111	000	$xxxx
111	001	$xxxxxxxx
111	010	d(PC)
111	011	d(PC,Rx)
111	100	#

* means that this addressing mode is not allowed

Execution Times (Cycles):

The first number is the number of clock cycles required to: get the operand, execute the instruction, store the results and get the next opcode. The next pair of numbers is for the number of read cycles and the number of write cycles respectively.

These values are only valid for the 68000 microprocessor. See the condensed tables in Chapter 8 for calculating times for the other microprocessors in the M68000 family.

Source	Destination
	SR
Dn	12 2/0
An	
(An)	16 3/0
(An)+	16 3/0
–(An)	18 3/0
d(An)	20 4/0
d(An,Rx)	22 4/0
$xxxx	20 4/0
$xxxxxxxx	24 5/0
d(PC)	20 4/0
d(PC,Rx)	22 4/0
#	16 3/0

Number of Bytes per Instruction for Different Addressing Modes:

Source	Destination
	CCR
Dn	2
An	
(An)	2
(An)+	2
–(An)	2
d(An)	4
d(An,Rx)	4
$xxxx	4
$xxxxxxxx	6
d(PC)	4
d(PC,Rx)	4
#	4

Example:

Clearing all of the flags and switching an M68000 microprocessor from the supervisor mode into the user mode (by changing the supervisor bit).

Before the operation:	15	14	13	12	11	10	9		8	7	6	5	4	3	2	1	0				
Status register:	T		S			I2	I1	I0				X	N	Z	V	C					
	0		1			1	1	1				1	0	0	1	1					

MOVE #0700,SR

After the operation:	15	14	13	12	11	10	9		8	7	6	5	4	3	2	1	0				
Status register:	T		S			I2	I1	I0				X	N	Z	V	C					
	0		0			1	1	1				0	0	0	0	0					

Applications:

A typical application for the MOVE-to-SR instruction would be to switch an M68000 microprocessor from the supervisor mode to the user mode. You can also use it to change the interrupt mask and the trace bit. If you only want to change the flags, the MOVE-to-CCR instruction may be better. You can use the MOVE-to-SR instruction whenever you need to set the contents of the status register to specific values.

This is a Privileged Instruction for the 68010/12/20/30 But Not for the 68000/08 Microprocessors

MOVE from SR Move Data from Status Register

Assembler Syntax:

MOVE SR, <ea>

Operation:

<SR> → <Destination>

Flag Changes:

None.

This instruction reads the flags but does not change them.

Operand Sizes:

This instruction operates on words since the SR itself is one word long.

Description of Instruction:

The MOVE-from-SR instruction copies the contents of the status register into a destination address that can be a data register or an address in memory. After this operation, you can examine the contents of the status register, such as the supervisor bit, trace bit, interrupt mask and the flags. Since this is not a privileged instruction for the 68000/08 microprocessors, you can use it in user programs for this purpose. However, for the 68010/12/20/30 microprocessors, it is a privileged instruction, but you can then use the MOVE-from-CCR instruction (only for the M68010) to read the flags in the condition-code register in the lower half of the status register.

Format of Opcode:

15	14	13	12	11	10	9	8	7	6	5	4	3	2	1	0
0	1	0	0	0	0	0	0	1	1	Effective Address <ea>					

| Effective Address <ea> | | | | | | | | | | | Mode | | Register | | |

Bits 15–12. These bits indicate that this instruction belongs to the set of instructions {CLR,NEG,NOT, NBCD,MOVE-from-SR,etc.}. Other bits in the opcode select this particular instruction from this set.
Bits 11–6. These bits select this particular instruction as the MOVE-from-SR instruction.
Effective Address, Bits 5–0. The effective address for the source address is stored in this pair of fields, one for the mode and the other for the register. The interpretation for this pair of fields is given in the table below:

Effective Address <ea>		Mnemonic for Addressing Mode
Mode	**Register**	
000	Register Number n	Dn
*	*	An
010	Register Number n	(An)
011	Register Number n	(An)+
100	Register Number n	−(An)
101	Register Number n	d(An)
110	Register Number n	d(An,Rx)
111	000	$xxxx
111	001	$xxxxxxxx
*	*	d(PC)
*	*	d(PC,Rx)
*	*	#

∗ means that this addressing mode is not allowed

Execution Times (Cycles):

The first number is the number of clock cycles required to: get the operand, execute the instruction, store the results and get the next opcode. The next pair of numbers is for the number of read cycles and the number of write cycles respectively.

These values are only valid for the 68000 microprocessor. See the condensed tables in Chapter 8 for calculating times for the other microprocessors in the M68000 family.

Source	Destination											
	Dn	An	(An)	(An)+	–(An)	d(An)	d(An,Rx)	$xxxx	$xxxxxxxx	d(PC)	d(PC,Rx)	#
CCR	6 1/0		12 2/1	12 2/1	14 2/1	16 3/1	18 3/1	16 3/1	20 4/1			

Number of Bytes per Instruction for Different Addressing Modes:

Source	Destination											
	Dn	An	(An)	(An)+	–(An)	d(An)	d(An,Rx)	$xxxx	$xxxxxxxx	d(PC)	d(PC,Rx)	#
CCR	2		2	2	2	4	4	4	6			

Example:

Copy the SR into memory location $1000.

Before the operation:	Contents of D0	=	$FFFFFFFF
			15 14 13 12 11 10 9 8 7 6 5 4 3 2 1 0
	Status Register:		T S 12 11 10 X N Z V C
			0 1 1 1 1 1 0 0 1 1
MOVE SR,D0			
After the operation:	Contents of D0	=	$FFF2713
			15 14 13 12 11 10 9 8 7 6 5 4 3 2 1 0
			T S 12 11 10 X N Z V C
			0 1 1 1 1 1 0 0 1 1

Applications:

The MOVE-from-SR instruction enables you to check the contents of the status register. Since you can not change the bits, other than the flags, from a user program, you will usually only be interested in reading the flags. However, you could also want to know the current value of the interrupt mask.

This is a Privileged Instruction!

MOVE USP   Move User Stack Pointer

Assembler Syntax:

```
MOVE USP,Ad
MOVE As,USP
```

Operation:

If an M68000 microprocessor is in the supervisor mode,

then either:	
USP	→ Ad or
As	→ USP
else (microprocessor is in the user mode)	
exception handling (violation of privilege)	

Flag Changes:

None.

Operand Sizes:

Since the user stack pointer is in a 32-bit address register, this instruction uses only long words.

Description of Instruction:

The MOVE USP instruction copies either:
- the user stack pointer into a specified address register or
- the contents of a specified address register into the user stack pointer.

The MOVE USP instruction is only allowed in the supervisor mode.

Format of Opcode:

15	14	13	12	11	10	9	8	7	6	5	4	3	2	1	0
0	1	0	0	1	1	1	0	0	1	1	0	Dir		Register	

Bits 15–12. These bits indicate that this instruction belongs to the set of instructions {CLR,NEG, NOT,NBCD,MOVE USP,etc.}. Other bits in the opcode select this particular instruction from this set.
Bits 11–4. These bits define this instruction to be the MOVE USP instruction.
Dir, Bit 4. This bit defines the direction in which the user stack pointer will be moved as follows:

0	=	the contents of the address register are copied to the user stack pointer
1	=	the user stack pointer is copied into the address register

Register, Bits 2–0. This field contains the number of the address register that this instruction can use in either direction, depending upon the Dir bit.

Execution Times (Cycles):

These values are only valid for the 68000 microprocessor. See the condensed tables in Chapter 8 for calculating times for the other microprocessors in the M68000 family.

MOVE USP,An	4 clock cycles 1/0	(to get the operand, execute the instruction, store the results and get the next opcode.)
MOVE An,USP	4 clock cycles 1/0	(to get the operand, execute the instruction, store the results and get the next opcode.)

Number of Bytes per Instruction:

MOVE USP,An	2 bytes
MOVE An,USP	2 bytes

Example:

Copying the user stack pointer into the address register.

Before the operation:	A5	=	$FFFFFFFF
	USP	=	$12345677
			MOVE USP,A5
After the operation:	A5	=	$12345677
	USP	=	$12345677

Applications:

You can use this MOVE USP instruction in an operating system to obtain access to the user stack pointer. This is not possible in the user mode, alone due to the mnemonics, since the user stack pointer in the user mode has the name A7 and the supervisor stack pointer in the supervisor mode also has the name A7. For this reason, the user stack pointer has its own name, USP, in the supervisor mode.

MOVEA   Move into Address Register

Assembler Syntax:

MOVEA.w <ea>,Ad

Operation:

<ea> → <Ad>

Flag Changes:

None.

Operand Sizes:

This instruction operates on words or long words as source operands since it copies from a source address into an address register. The .w in the syntax refers to .W or .L respectively.

Description of Instruction:

The MOVEA instruction copies the operand stored at the effective address into an address register, at the destination address. If the operand from the source address contains a word, it will automatically be converted into a long word, with the correct sign.

Format of Opcode:

15	14	13	12	11	10	9	8	7	6	5	4	3	2	1	0
0	0	Size		Destination Register			0	0	1	Effective Address <ea>					
										Mode			Register		

Bits 15–12. These bits indicate that this instruction belongs to the set of instructions {MOVE, Immediate, Bit Manipulation}. Other bits in the opcode select this particular instruction from this set.

Size, Bits 13–12. This field defines whether the operand is a word (16 bits) or a long word (32 bits) as follows:

11	=	16 bits long (will be converted into 32-bit length with the correct sign)
10	=	32-bit long word

Destination Register, Bits 11–9. The contents of this field define the address register into which the operand will be copied.

Bits 8–6. These bits select this particular instruction as the MOVEA instruction.

Effective Address, Bits 5–0. The effective address for the source address is stored in this pair of fields, one for the mode and the other for the register. The interpretation for this pair of fields is given in the table below:

Effective Address <ea>		Mnemonic for Addressing Mode
Mode	**Register**	
000	Register Number n	Dn
001	Register Number n	An
010	Register Number n	(An)
011	Register Number n	(An)+
100	Register Number n	−(An)
101	Register Number n	d(An)
110	Register Number n	d(An,Rx)
111	000	$xxxx
111	001	$xxxxxxxx
111	010	d(PC)
111	011	d(PC,Rx)
111	100	#

* means that this addressing mode is not allowed

Execution Times (Cycles): (Operations on Words)

The first number is the number of clock cycles required to: get the operand, execute the instruction, store the results and get the next opcode. The next pair of numbers is for the number of read cycles and the number of write cycles respectively.

These values are only valid for the 68000 microprocessor. See the condensed tables in Chapter 8 for calculating times for the other microprocessors in the M68000 family.

Source	Destination											
	Dn	An	(An)	(An)+	−(An)	d(An)	d(An,Rx)	$xxxx	$xxxxxxxx	d(PC)	d(PC,Rx)	#
Dn		4 1/0										
An		4 1/0										
(An)		8 2/0										
(An)+		8 2/0										
−(An)		10 2/0										
d(An)		12 3/0										
d(An,Rx)		14 3/0										
$xxxx		12 3/0										
$xxxxxxxx		15 4/0										
d(PC)		12 3/0										
d(PC,Rx)		14 3/0										
#		8 2/0										

Execution Times (Cycles): (Operations on Long Words)

The first number is the number of clock cycles required to: get the operand, execute the instruction, store the results and get the next opcode. The next pair of numbers is for the number of read cycles and the number of write cycles respectively.

These values are only valid for the 68000 microprocessor. See the condensed tables in Chapter 8 for calculating times for the other microprocessors in the M68000 family.

Source	Destination											
	Dn	An	(An)	(An)+	−(An)	d(An)	d(An,Rx)	$xxxx	$xxxxxxxx	d(PC)	d(PC,Rx)	#
Dn		4 1/0										
An		4 1/0										
(An)		12 3/0										
(An)+		12 3/0										
−(An)		14 3/0										
d(An)		16 4/0										
d(An,Rx)		18 4/0										
$xxxx		16 4/0										
$xxxxxxxx		20 5/0										
d(PC)		16 4/0										
d(PC,Rx)		18 4/0										
#		12 3/0										

Number of Bytes per Instruction for Different Addressing Modes:
(Operations on Words)

Source	Destination											
	Dn	An	(An)	(An)+	−(An)	d(An)	d(An,Rx)	$xxxx	$xxxxxxxx	d(PC)	d(PC,Rx)	#
Dn		2										
An		2										
(An)		2										
(An)+		2										
−(An)		2										
d(An)		4										
d(An,Rx)		4										
$xxxx		4										
$xxxxxxxx		6										
d(PC)		4										
d(PC,Rx)		4										
#		4										

Number of Bytes per Instruction for Different Addressing Modes:
(Operations on Long Words)

Source	Destination											
	Dn	An	(An)	(An)+	–(An)	d(An)	d(An,Rx)	$xxxx	$xxxxxxxx	d(PC)	d(PC,Rx)	#
Dn	2											
An	2											
(An)	2											
(An)+	2											
–(An)	2											
d(An)	4											
d(An,Rx)	4											
$xxxx	4											
$xxxxxxxx	6											
d(PC)	4											
d(PC,Rx)	4											
#	6											

Example:

Writing the value of 0 into the address register A3.

```
Before the operation:  A3      = $12345678          X  N  Z  V  C
                                                     1  0  0  0  0
MOVEA.L  #0,A3
In this case, MOVEA.W  #0,A3 would be the equivalent.

After the operation:   A3      = $00000000          X  N  Z  V  C
                                                     1  0  0  0  0
```

Applications:

You can use the MOVEA instruction for loading the starting addresses into address registers. A typical example is the case where you use an address register as the index register for a table. You could use the MOVEA instruction to preset the address register with the address of the first value in the table.

You can also use the LEA instruction for loading the starting address into an address register. For an example, LEA LABEL,A3 is practically the same as MOVEA.L #Label,A3, whereby the LEA instruction requires only 12 clock cycles and the MOVEA instruction requires 20 clock cycles.

This Instruction is Only Available for the 68010/12/20/30
It is a Privileged Instruction!

MOVEC   Move into and out of Control Register

Assembler Syntax:

MOVEC Control Register,Rd
MOVEC Rs,Control Register

The Control Register can be:
SFC	=	Source Function-Code Register
DFC	=	Destination Function-Code Register
USP	=	User Stack Pointer
VBR	=	Vector-Base Register

Operation:

< Source > → < Destination >

Flag Changes:

None.

Operand Sizes:

This instruction operates only on long words. If a register contains less than 32 bits, the missing bits will be read as nulls.

Description of Instruction:

The MOVEC instruction copies data into a control register or reads the contents out of a control register. This instruction always copies 32 bits from a control register, even if the control register contains less than 32 bits (the missing bits are copied as nulls).

Format of Opcode:

15	14	13	12	11	10	9	8	7	6	5	4	3	2	1	0
0	1	0	0	1	1	1	0	0	1	1	1	1	0	1	Dir

A/D	Register			Control Register											

Bits 15–12. These bits indicate that this instruction belongs to the set of instructions {SWAP,TST, LINK,etc.}. Other bits in the opcode select this particular instruction from this set.
Bits 11–1. These bits select this particular instruction as the MOVEC instruction.
Dir, Bit 0. This bit defines the direction of the move as follows:

0	=	from a control register into a data register or an address register
1	=	from a data register or an address register into a control register

A/D, Bit 15. This bit defines the type for the general register as follows:

```
0   =   data register
1   =   address register
```

Register, Bits 14–12. This field contains the number of the general register whose type is defined by the A/D bit.

Control Register, Bits 11–0. This field defines the control register that is used, as follows:

Binary	Hex	Control Register
0000 0000 0000	000	Source Function Code (SFC) Register
0000 0000 0001	001	Destination Function Code (DFC) Register
1000 0000 0000	800	User Stack Pointer (USP)
1000 0000 0001	801	Vector Base Register (VBR)

All other bit combinations initiate exception handling (for an illegal instruction).

Execution Times (Cycles):

The first number is the number of clock cycles required to: get the operand, execute the instruction, store the results and get the next opcode. The next pair of numbers is for the number of read cycles and the number of write cycles respectively.

These values are only valid for the 68010/012 microprocessor. See the condensed tables in Chapter 8 for calculating times for the other microprocessors in the M68000 family.

Source	Destination					
	Dn	An	SFC	DFG	USP	VBR
Dn			10 2/0	10 2/0	10 2/0	10 2/0
An			10 2/0	10 2/0	10 2/0	10 2/0
SFC	12 2/0	12 2/0				
DFC	12 2/0	12 2/0				
USP	12 2/0	12 2/0				
VBR	12 2/0	12 2/0				

Number of Bytes per Instruction for Different Addressing Modes:

It always has 4 bytes.

Example:

The vector-base table is loaded with $F00000. Therefore, the vector table of the processor will begin at $F00000 instead of the usual address at $000000.

```
MOVE.L  #$F00000,D0
MOVEC D0,VBR
```

Applications:

You can use this MOVEC instruction for shifting the vector table and for loading the function-code registers as well as the user stack pointer. In this way, you can prepare for using the MOVES instruction by first defining the source and destination areas for this instruction (user or supervisor).

MOVEM   Move Multiple Registers

Assembler Syntax:

Case 1:	MOVEM.w Register List, <ea>
Case 2:	MOVEM.w <ea>,Register List

Operation:

Case 1:	<Registers in the list> → <ea>
Case 2:	<ea> → <Registers in the list>

Flag Changes:

None.

Operand Sizes:

This instruction operates on words and long words. When an operand at a source address has a width of only one word and it is copied into a register (always 32 bits wide), the word is first expanded to a 32-bit long word, with the correct sign. When a register is copied into a destination address with a width of only one word, then only the least-significant half of the register is copied. The .w in the syntax refers to .W or .L respectively for the operands that are copied.

Description of Instruction:

The MOVEM instruction can copy the contents of up to 16 registers (8 data registers, from D0 to D7, and 8 address registers, from A0 to A7) in one of two directions:

Case 1:	from the list of registers to an area in memory
Case 2:	from an area in memory to a list of registers

You can select an arbitrary subset of these 16 registers for this operation by defining a mask as the first word that follows the opcode. A "1" in the mask means that copying will take place for the register and a "0" in the mask means that no copying will take place for the register. Two different sequences are used for processing the registers, depending upon the addressing mode that is used, and the mask must match this sequence:

Mask 1:	A7 A6 A5 A4 A3 A2 A1 A0 D7 D6 D5 D4 D3 D2 D1 D0
Mask 2:	D0 D1 D2 D3 D4 D5 D6 D7 A0 A1 A2 A3 A4 A5 A6 A7
	(Mask 2 has the reverse sequence as that in mask 1.)

The MOVEM instruction operates differently, depending upon the addressing modes used. These differences can be summarized as follows:

– Address-register indirect-addressing mode with predecrementing

With this mode, only case 1 is allowed, with copying from registers into memory. Therefore, you can only address the destination and never the source in this situation. The sequence for the copy operations and the mask for selecting a subset is defined by mask 1. The address in the address register selected in the opcode for this instruction is decremented by 2 as each register is copied into memory. At the end of the operation, the address register selected in the opcode points to the last word that this instruction copied into memory.

– Address-register indirect-addressing mode with postincrementing

With the mode, only case 2 is allowed, with copying from memory into registers. Therefore, you can only address the source and never the destination in this situation. The sequence for the copy operations and the mask for selecting a subset is defined by mask 2. The address in the address register selected in the opcode for this instruction is incremented by 2 as addresses are read from memory into each register. At the end of the operation, the address register selected in the opcode points to the last word plus 2 that this instruction copied from memory.

Other Addressing Modes that are Allowed

With these modes, both case 1 and case 2 are allowed for copying from and to registers. The sequence for the copy operations and the mask for selecting a subset is defined by mask 2. The address in the address register selected in the opcode for this instruction is incremented by 2 by each copy operation, independent of whether it is from registers to memory or from memory to registers. Because of the order in which the registers are stored in memory, you must recall the contents back into the register using the address-register indirect-addressing mode, with predecrementing.

You can separate individual selected registers by a slash in the register list. You can also define sequences of registers with a hyphen between the first and last register in the sequence. To give some examples, the following are valid register lists for use with the MOVEM instruction:

```
D0/D5/A1/A7
D0-D5/A3-A6 = D0/D1/D2/D3/D4/D5/A3/A4/A5/A6
```

The actual order in which registers are processed depends entirely upon the order specified in the mask for the addressing mode. It is independent of the order in the register list with which you specify the names of the registers in the syntax of the instruction (see the examples).

Format of Opcode:

15	14	13	12	11	10	9	8	7	6	5	4	3	2	1	0
0	1	0	0	1	Dir	0	0	1	Size	Effective Address <ea>					
										Mode			Register		
Mask for Register List															

Bits 15–12. These bits indicate that this instruction belongs to the set of instructions {NEG,NOT,PEA, CLR,MOVEM,etc.}. Other bits in the opcode select this particular instruction from this set.
Bits 11 and 9–7. These bits select this particular instruction as the MOVEM instruction.
Dir, Bit 10. This bit determines the direction of the copy operation as follows:

0	=	from registers to memory
1	=	from memory to registers

Size, Bit 6. This bit determines the size of the operands that are copied as follows:

0	=	words (that are converted to long words with the correct signs before they are copied from memory to registers)
1	=	long words

Effective Address, Bits 5–0. The effective address is stored in this pair of fields, one for the mode and the other for the register. This address is the address in memory to which or from which data is copied from or to the registers. The interpretation for this pair of fields is given in the two tables below:

Case 1: Copying from a list of registers to an area of memory

Effective Address <ea>		Mnemonic for Addressing Mode
Mode	**Register**	
*	*	Dn
*	*	An
010	Register Number n	(An)
*	*	(An)+
100	Register Number n	−(An)
101	Register Number n	d(An)
110	Register Number n	d(An,Rx)
111	000	$xxxx
111	001	$xxxxxxxx
*	*	d(PC)
*	*	d(PC,Rx)
*	*	#

∗ means that this addressing mode is not allowed

Case 2: Copying from an area of memory to a list of registers

Effective Address <ea>		Mnemonic for Addressing Mode
Mode	**Register**	
*	*	Dn
*	*	An
010	Register Number n	(An)
011	Register Number n	(An)+
*	*	−(An)
101	Register Number n	d(An)
110	Register Number n	d(An,Rx)
111	000	$xxxx
111	001	$xxxxxxxx
111	010	d(PC)
111	011	d(PC,Rx)
*	*	#

∗ means that this addressing mode is not allowed

Execution Times (Cycles): (Operations on Words)

The first number is the number of clock cycles required to: get the operands, execute the instruction, store the results and get the next opcode. The next pair of numbers is for the number of read cycles and the number of write cycles respectively.

These values are only valid for the 68000 microprocessor. See the condensed tables in Chapter 8 for calculating times for the other microprocessors in the M68000 family.

Case 1: Copying from a list of registers to an area of memory

Source	Destination											
	Dn	An	(An)	(An)+	-(An)	d(An)	d(An,Rx)	$xxxx	$xxxxxxxx	d(PC)	d(PC,Rx)	#
Dn/An			8+4n 2/n		8+4n 2/n	12+4n 3/n	14+4n 3/n	12+4n 3/n	16+4n 4/n			

Case 2: Copying from an area of memory to a list of registers

Source	Destination											
	Dn	An	(An)	(An)+	-(An)	d(An)	d(An,Rx)	$xxxx	$xxxxxxxx	d(PC)	d(PC,Rx)	#
Dn/An			12+4n 3+n/0	12+4n 3+n/0		16+4n 4+n/0	18+4n 4+n/0	16+4n 4+n/0	20+4n 5+n/0	16+4n 4+n/0	18+4n 4+n/0	

(Operations on Long Words)

Case 1: Copying from a list of registers to an area of memory

Source	Destination											
	Dn	An	(An)	(An)+	-(An)	d(An)	d(An,Rx)	$xxxx	$xxxxxxxx	d(PC)	d(PC,Rx)	#
Dn/An			8+8n 2/2n		8+8n 2/2n	12+8n 3/2n	14+8n 3/2n	12+8n 3/2n	16+8n 4/2n			

Case 2: Copying from an area of memory to a list of registers

Source	Destination											
	Dn	An	(An)	(An)+	-(An)	d(An)	d(An,Rx)	$xxxx	$xxxxxxxx	d(PC)	d(PC,Rx)	#
Dn/An			12+8n 3+2n/0	12+8n 3+2n/0		16+8n 4+2n/0	18+8n 4+2n/0	16+8n 4+2n/0	20+8n 5+2n/0	16+8n 4+2n/0	18+8n 4+2n/0	

Number of Bytes per Instruction for Different Addressing Modes: (Operations on Words and Long Words)

Case 1: Copying from a list of registers to an area of memory

Source	Destination											
	Dn	An	(An)	(An)+	-(An)	d(An)	d(An,Rx)	$xxxx	$xxxxxxxx	d(PC)	d(PC,Rx)	#
Dn/An			4	4		6	6	6	8			

Case 2: Copying from an area of memory to a list of registers

Source	Destination											
	Dn	An	(An)	(An)+	-(An)	d(An)	d(An,Rx)	$xxxx	$xxxxxxxx	d(PC)	d(PC,Rx)	#
Dn/An			4	4		6	6	6	8	6	6	

Examples:

a) Copying contents of several registers onto the stack. Direction of copy operation →

Mask 1: A7 A6 A5 A4 A3 A2 A1 A0 D7 D6 D5 D4 D3 D2 D1 D0

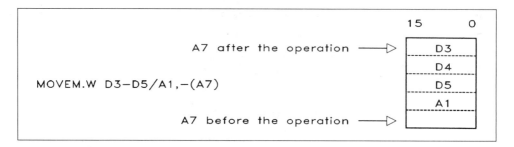

b) Copying the stack into several registers. Direction of copy operation →

Mask 2: D0 D1 D2 D3 D4 D5 D6 D7 A0 A1 A2 A3 A4 A5 A6 A7

```
                                                    15          0
                                                  ┌──────────────┐
                    A7 after the operation  ────▷ │     D3       │
                                                  ├──────────────┤
                                                  │     D4       │
    MOVEM.W  (A7)+,D3-D5/A1                        ├──────────────┤
                                                  │     D5       │
                                                  ├──────────────┤
                                                  │     A1       │
                    A7 before the operation ────▷ ├──────────────┤
                                                  │              │
                                                  └──────────────┘
```

c) Copying contents of registers into memory with the addressing mode of direct.
Direction of copy operation →

Mask 2: D0 D1 D2 D3 D4 D5 D6 D7 A0 A1 A2 A3 A4 A5 A6 A7

```
                                                    15          0
                                                  ┌──────────────┐
                                        $1000     │     D3       │
                                                  ├──────────────┤
                                        $1002     │     D4       │
    MOVEM.W  D3-D5/A1,$1000                        ├──────────────┤
                                        $1004     │     D5       │
                                                  ├──────────────┤
                                        $1006     │     A1       │
                                                  ├──────────────┤
                                                  │              │
                                                  └──────────────┘
```

d) Copying from memory into registers with the addressing mode of direct.
Direction of copy operation →

Mask 2: D0 D1 D2 D3 D4 D5 D6 D7 A0 A1 A2 A3 A4 A5 A6 A7

Applications:

You can use the MOVEM instruction to save the contents of the registers on a stack when an interrupt occurs and to retrieve the contents from the stack after the interrupt has been processed. When an M68000 microprocessor recognizes an interrupt, it automatically saves only the program counter and status register on a stack. This has the advantage that it can begin faster with handling the interrupt. This gives you the flexibility to decide which of the other registers you want to save on a stack for such interrupts since most interrupts do not need to use all of the registers.

If you place the MOVEM instruction at the beginning of a subroutine, you can make the subroutine reentrant.

You could, of course, also use individual MOVE instructions to replace one single MOVEM instruction.

MOVEP   Move Data for Peripherals

Assembler Syntax:

MOVEP.w Ds,d(Ad)
MOVEP.w d(As),Dd

Operation:

| Contents of register Ds | → address d(Ad) |
| Contents at address d(As) | → register <Dd> |

Flag Changes:

None.

Operand Sizes:

This instruction copies words and long words. The .w in the syntax refers to .W or .L respectively.

Description of Instruction:

The MOVEP instruction copies data between a data register and every second address in memory or a peripheral register. This operation begins at the given address and then increments the address by two. However, the contents of the address register that is specified in the instruction are not changed.

The MOVEP instruction copies data one byte at a time. The most-significant byte in the data registers is copied first and the least-significant byte is copied last.

A peripheral device is always addressed in the address-register indirect-addressing mode, with address offset. If the resulting address is an even number, then the byte is transfered on the upper half of the data bus. If the resulting address is an odd number, then the byte is transfered on the lower half of the data bus. Either two bytes or four bytes are transfered, depending upon the length of the operand.

Copying a Long Word into or out of an Even Address with MOVEP:

The organization of the bytes of data in the data register appears as follows:

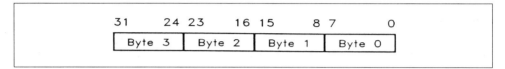

The bytes are transfered on the data bus in the following order:

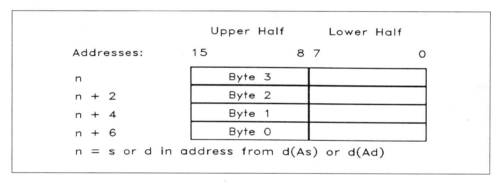

Copying a Word into or out of an Odd Address with MOVEP:

The organization of the bytes of data in the data register appears as follows:

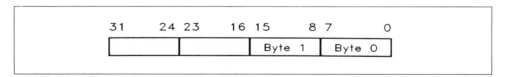

The bytes are transfered on the data bus in the following order:

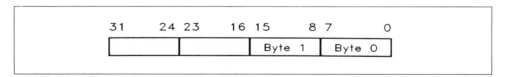

The MOVEP instruction is the only instruction of the M68000 microprocessors with which you can directly read or write to an uneven address in memory.

Format of Opcode:

15	14	13	12	11	10	9	8	7	6	5	4	3	2	1	0
0	0	0	0	Data Register			Opmode			0	0	1	Address Register		
Address Offset															

Bits 15–12. These bits indicate that this instruction belongs to the set of instructions {bit manipulation, immediate, MOVEP}. Other bits in the opcode select this particular instruction from this set.

Data Register, Bits 11–9. The MOVEP instruction always copies data from or into a data register. This field specifies that register.

Opmode, Bits 8–6. This field specifies both the direction of the copying operation and the size of the operands as follows:

100	a word from memory or a peripheral to a data register
101	a long word from memory or a peripheral to a data register
110	a word from a data register to memory or a peripheral
111	a long word from a data register to memory or a peripheral

Bits 5–3. These bits select this particular instruction as the MOVEP instruction.
Address Register, Bits 2–0. The MOVEP instruction always uses the address-register indirect-addressing mode, with address offset. This field specifies this address register.
The 16-bit address offset follows immediately after the opcode.

Execution Times (Cycles): (Operations on Words)

The first number is the number of clock cycles required to: get the operand, execute the instruction, store the results and get the next opcode. The next pair of numbers is for the number of read cycles and the number of write cycles respectively.

These values are only valid for the 68000 microprocessor. See the condensed tables in Chapter 8 for calculating times for the other microprocessors in the M68000 family.

Source	Destination											
	Dn	An	(An)	(An)+	–(An)	d(An)	d(An,Rx)	$xxxx	$xxxxxxxx	d(PC)	d(PC,Rx)	#
Dn	16 2/2											
An												
(An)												
(An)+												
–(An)												
d(An)	16 4/0											
d(An,Rx)												
$xxxx												
$xxxxxxxx												
d(PC)												
d(PC,Rx)												
#												

Execution Times (Cycles): (Operations on Long Words)

The first number is the number of clock cycles required to: get the operand, execute the instruction, store the results, and get the next opcode. The next pair of numbers is for the number of read cycles and the number of write cycles respectively.

These values are only valid for the 68000 microprocessor. See the condensed tables in Chapter 8 for calculating times for the other microprocessors in the M68000 family.

Source	Destination											
	Dn	An	(An)	(An)+	–(An)	d(An)	d(An,Rx)	$xxxx	$xxxxxxxx	d(PC)	d(PC,Rx)	#
Dn						24 2/4						
An												
(An)												
(An)+												
–(An)												
d(An)	24 6/0											
d(An,Rx)												
$xxxx												
$xxxxxxxx												
d(PC)												
d(PC,Rx)												
#												

Number of Bytes per Instruction for Different Addressing Modes:
(Operations on Words and Long Words)

Source	Destination											
	Dn	An	(An)	(An)+	–(An)	d(An)	d(An,Rx)	$xxxx	$xxxxxxxx	d(PC)	d(PC,Rx)	#
Dn						4						
An												
(An)												
(An)+												
–(An)												
d(An)	4											
d(An,Rx)												
$xxxx												
$xxxxxxxx												
d(PC)												
d(PC,Rx)												
#												

Example:

See the description of instruction.

Applications:

The MOVEP instruction simplifies communications between an M68000 microprocessor and 8-bit peripheral devices. All of the registers of the peripheral device that the M68000 addresses in a single MOVEP instruction must be even or odd.

MOVEQ   Move Constant Quickly into Data Register

Assembler Syntax:

MOVEQ #Constant,Dd

Operation:

#Constant → <Dd>

Flag Changes:

X   Not changed.
N   Set equal to 1 if constant is negative, otherwise set to 0.
Z   Set equal to 1 if constant equals 0, otherwise set to 0.
V   Always reset to 0.
C   Always reset to 0.

Operand Sizes:

The constant can have up to 8 bits since 8 bits are free for it in the 16-bit opcode. This constant should be in the two's complement form and must have a value within the range from –128 to +127 due to the limitation of having only 8 bits available. However, this instruction will expand this constant into the 32-bit format, with the correct sign, before writing it into the data register. No .w is added to the mnemonic for the size of operands.

Description of Instruction:

The MOVEQ instruction serves to load a data register with a constant. This constant must have a value in the range from –128 to +127. You specify this constant in decimal form; the assembler converts it into an 8-bit constant in two's complement format and puts it into the least-significant half of the opcode, and an M68000 microprocessor expands it into a 32-bit constant in two's complement format (with the correct sign) when writing the number into a data register.

Format of Opcode:

15	14	13	12	11	10	9	8	7	6	5	4	3	2	1	0
0	1	1	1		Register		0				8-bit Constant				

Bits 15–12. These bits indicate that this instruction is the MOVEQ instruction.
Register, Bits 11–9. This field specifies the data register into which the MOVEQ instruction writes the constant.
8-bit Constant, Bits 7–0. This field specifies the 8-bit constant in the two's complement format. The MOVEQ instruction will expand it into the 32-bit two's complement format when it writes the constant into the specified data register.

4 clock cycles	(to execute the instruction, store the results and get the next opcode.)
1 read cycle	
0 write cycles	

(These values are only valid for the 68000 microprocessor. See the condensed tables in Chapter 8 for calculating times for the other microprocessors in the M68000 family.)

Number of Bytes per Instruction for Different Addressing Modes:

Always 2 bytes.

Example:

a) Loading a positive number into the data register D0, such as for a loop counter:

Before the operation:	Contents of D0 = $12345678
	MOVEQ #$55,D0
After the operation:	Contents of D0 = $00000055

b) Loading a negative number into the data register D0.

Before the operation:	Contents of D0 = $12345678
	MOVEQ #$88,D0
After the operation:	Contents of D0 = $FFFFFF88

Applications:

You can use the MOVEQ instruction for loading a starting value into a data register, such as when you use the register as the counter for a loop. You can also use it for loading shift and rotation counters into a data register before an operation of shifting or rotating.

This Instruction is Only Available for the 68010/12/20/30
It is a Privileged Instruction!

MOVES   Move Data Between Supervisor and User Memory Areas

Assembler Syntax:

```
MOVES.w Rs,<ea>
MOVES.w <ea>,Rd
```

Operation:

< Source > → < Destination >
(depending upon the contents of the Function-Code Register)

Flag Changes:

None.

Operand Sizes:

This instruction can operate on bytes, words or long words. The .w in the syntax refers to .B, .W or .L respectively.

Description of Instruction:

The MOVES instruction serves for transfering data between the supervisor address area and the user address area. Depending upon the contents of a function-code register, a byte, word, or long word will be copied to or from an address register or a data register from or to memory in the supervisor address area or the user address area. Depending upon the direction of this transfer, the destination function-code register (DFC) is used for a transfer from a register to memory and the source function-code register (SFC) is used for a transfer from memory to a register. To do this, the function-code outputs of the processor are set according the contents of the destination function-code register (DFC) or source function-code register (SFC), as appropriate.

If the destination is a data register, then the least-significant part of the register will be filled by a byte or word whereas the whole register will be filled by a long word. If the destination is an address register, the operand will be extended into the 32-bit two's complement format, with the correct sign, and be written into the whole register. If the source or destination of the operation is an address register, then only 16-bit words and 32-bit long words are allowed as operands.

Format of Opcode:

15	14	13	12	11	10	9	8	7	6	5	4	3	2	1	0
										Effective Address < ea >					
0	0	0	0	1	1	1	0	Size		Mode			Register		
Add/Dat	Register			->Dir<-	0	0	0	0	0	0	0	0	0	0	0

Bits 15–12. These bits indicate that this instruction belongs to the set of instructions {bit manipulation, immediate, MOVEP, MOVES}. Other bits in the opcode select this particular instruction from this set.

Bits 11–8. These bits select this particular instruction as the MOVES instruction.

Size Field, Bits 7–6. The size of the operands is stored in this field, defined as follows:

00	–	8-bit bytes as operands
01	–	16-bit words as operands
10	–	32-bit long words as operands

Effective Address, Bits 5–0. The effective address is stored in this pair of fields, one for the mode and the other for the register. The interpretation for this pair of fields is given in the table below:

Effective Address <ea>		Mnemonic for Addressing Mode
Mode	**Register**	
*	*	Dn
*	*	An
010	Register Number n	(An)
011	Register Number n	(An)+
100	Register Number n	−(An)
101	Register Number n	d(An)
110	Register Number n	d(An,Rx)
111	000	$xxxx
111	001	$xxxxxxxx
*	*	d(PC)
*	*	d(PC,Rx)
*	*	#

* means that this addressing mode is not allowed

Add/Dir Bit. This bit specifies the type of source or destination register as follows:

0   –   data register
1   –   address register

Register. This field specifies the source or destination register.
Dir Bit. This bit specifies the direction of the transfer as follows:

0   –   effective address to register
1   –   register to effective address

Execution Times (Cycles): (Operations on Bytes and Words)

The first number is the number of clock cycles required to: get the operand, execute the instruction, store the results and get the next opcode. The next pair of numbers is for the number of read cycles and the number of write cycles respectively.

These values are only valid for the 68010/012 microprocessor. See the condensed tables in Chapter 8 for calculating times for the other microprocessors in the M68000 family.

Source	Destination											
	Dn	An	(An)	(An)+	−(An)	d(An)	d(An,Rx)	$xxxx	$xxxxxxxx	d(PC)	d(PC,Rx)	#
Dn			8 1/1	8 1/1	8 1/1	12 2/1	14 2/1	12 2/1	16 3/1			
An			8 1/1	8 1/1	8 1/1	12 2/1	14 2/1	12 2/1	16 3/1			
(An)	8 2/0	8 2/0										
(An)+	8 2/0	8 2/0										
−(An)	10 2/0	10 2/0										
d(An)	12 3/0	12 3/0										
d(An,Rx)	14 3/0	14 3/0										
$xxxx	12 3/0	12 3/0										
$xxxxxxxx	16 4/0	16 4/0										
d(PC)												
d(PC,Rx)												
#												

Execution Times (Cycles): (Operations on Long Words)

The first number is the number of clock cycles required to: get the operand, execute the instruction, store the results and get the next opcode. The next pair of numbers is for the number of read cycles and the number of write cycles respectively.

These values are only valid for the 68010/012 microprocessor. See the condensed tables in Chapter 8 for calculating times for the other microprocessors in the M68000 family.

Source	Destination											
	Dn	An	(An)	(An)+	−(An)	d(An)	d(An,Rx)	$xxxx	$xxxxxxxx	d(PC)	d(PC,Rx)	#
Dn			12 1/2	12 1/2	14 1/2	16 2/2	18 2/2	16 2/2	20 3/2			
An			12 1/2	12 1/2	14 1/2	16 2/2	18 2/2	16 2/2	20 3/2			
(An)	12 3/0	12 3/0										
(An)+	12 3/0	12 3/0										
−(An)	14 3/0	14 3/0										
d(An)	16 4/0	16 4/0										
d(An,Rx)	18 4/0	18 4/0										
$xxxx	16 4/0	16 4/0										
$xxxxxxxx	20 5/0	20 5/0										
d(PC)												
d(PC,Rx)												
#												

Number of Bytes per Instruction for Different Addressing Modes:
(Operations on Bytes, Words and Long Words)

Source	Destination											
	Dn	An	(An)	(An)+	−(An)	d(An)	d(An,Rx)	$xxxx	$xxxxxxxx	d(PC)	d(PC,Rx)	#
Dn			4	4	4	6	6	6	8			
An			4	4	4	6	6	6	8			
(An)	4	4										
(An)+	4	4										
−(An)	4	4										
d(An)	6	6										
d(An,Rx)	6	6										
$xxxx	6	6										
$xxxxxxxx	8	8										
d(PC)	4											
d(PC,Rx)												
#												

Examples:

Contents of both function-code registers:

```
DFC = 001
SFC = 101
```

MOVES.L D0,$1000
Four bytes will be written from D0 into the user address area, starting with the address $1000 (due to the contents of DFC).
MOVES.L $1000,D0

Four bytes will be written from the supervisor address area, starting with the address $1000, into D0 (due to the contents of SFC).

Applications:

This instruction is used primarily in operating systems. It allows the processor to read data out of the user address area and write data into this area when the processor is in the supervisor mode. In this way, the operating system has access to the data in the user address area at all times – which is not directly possible for the processor itself if the function-code pins are used for address decoding.

MULS   Multiply with Signs

Assembler Syntax:

MULS <ea>,Dd

Operation:

< Source >	x < Destination >	→ < Destination >
(16 bits)	(16 bits)	(32 bits)

Flag Changes:

X Not changed.
N Set equal to 1 if result is negative, otherwise reset to 0.
Z Set equal to 1 if result equals 0, otherwise reset to 0.
V Always reset to 0.
C Always reset to 0.

Operand Sizes:

This instruction operates on a 16-bit first operand from a source address and a 16-bit second operand in a destination data register. The result is a 32-bit operand in the same destination data register. All operands have signs. The sizes of the operands are fixed for this instruction.

Description of Instruction:

The MULS instruction multiplies two signed 16-bit numbers using two's complement arithmetic, and the result is a signed 32-bit number. The destination address for obtaining the second operand and for storing the results is a data register. Before the operation, only the least-significant half is used, but after the operation, the whole register is used. Therefore, any data that may have been in the most-significant half of this register before the operation will be overwritten by the operation.

Format of Opcode:

15	14	13	12	11	10	9	8	7	6	5	4	3	2	1	0
1	1	0	0		Register		1	1	1	Effective Address <ea>					
										Mode			Register		

Bits 15–12. These bits indicate that this instruction belongs to the set of instructions {AND,ABCD, EXG,MUL}. Other bits in the opcode select this particular instruction from this set.

Register, Bits 11–9. This field specifies the destination data register that contains the second operand before the operation and the product after the operation.

Bits 8–6. These bits select this particular instruction as the MULS instruction.

Effective Address, Bits 5–0. This address for the source address is stored in this pair of fields, one for the mode and the other for the register. The interpretation for this pair of fields is given in the table below:

Effective Address <ea>		Mnemonic for Addressing Mode
Mode	Register	
000	Register Number n	Dn
*	*	An
010	Register Number n	(An)
011	Register Number n	(An)+
100	Register Number n	–(An)
101	Register Number n	d(An)
110	Register Number n	d(An,Rx)
111	000	$xxxx
111	001	$xxxxxxxx
111	010	d(PC)
111	011	d(PC,Rx)
111	100	#

* means that this addressing mode is not allowed

Execution Times (Cycles):

The first number is the number of clock cycles required to: get the operands, execute the instruction, store the results and get the next opcode. The next pair of numbers is for the number of read cycles and the number of write cycles respectively.

These values are only valid for the 68000 microprocessor. See the condensed tables in Chapter 8 for calculating times for the other microprocessors in the M68000 family.

Source	Destination											
	Dn	An	(An)	(An)+	–(An)	d(An)	d(An,Rx)	$xxxx	$xxxxxxxx	d(PC)	d(PC,Rx)	#
Dn	70 1/0											
An												
(An)	74 2/0											
(An)+	74 2/0											
–(An)	76 2/0											
d(An)	78 3/0											
d(An,Rx)	80 3/0											
$xxxx	78 3/0											
$xxxxxxxx	82 4/0											
d(PC)	78 3/0											
d(PC,Rx)	80 3/0											
#	74 2/0											

Number of Bytes per Instruction for Different Addressing Modes:

Source	Destination											
	Dn	An	(An)	(An)+	−(An)	d(An)	d(An,Rx)	$xxxx	$xxxxxxxx	d(PC)	d(PC,Rx)	#
Dn	2											
An												
(An)	2											
(An)+	2											
−(An)	2											
d(An)	4											
d(An,Rx)	4											
$xxxx	4											
$xxxxxxxx	6											
d(PC)	4											
d(PC,Rx)	4											
#	4											

Example:

Multiplication of a negative number by a positive number (the same example as for the MULU instruction).

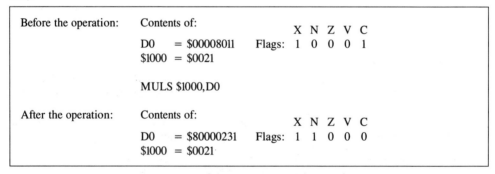

```
Before the operation:    Contents of:              X  N  Z  V  C
                         D0   = $00008011  Flags:  1  0  0  0  1
                         $1000 = $0021

                         MULS $1000,D0

After the operation:     Contents of:              X  N  Z  V  C
                         D0   = $80000231  Flags:  1  1  0  0  0
                         $1000 = $0021
```

Applications:

You can use the MULS instruction to multiply two signed 16-bit numbers and obtain the signed 32-bit product. If you need to multiply larger numbers, you will need to write an algorithm that uses the MULU instruction for the less-significant words. An example of such an algorithm is given in Chapter 6.

MULU   Multiply without Signs

Assembler Syntax:

```
MULU <ea>,Dd
```

Operation:

<Source>	x <Destination>	→ <Destination>
(16 bits)	(16 bits)	(32 bits)

Flag Changes:

X   Not changed.
N   Set equal to 1 if result is negative, otherwise reset to 0.
Z   Set equal to 1 if result equals 0, otherwise reset to 0.
V   Always reset to 0.
C   Always reset to 0.

Operand Sizes:

This instruction operates on a 16-bit first operand from a source address and a 16-bit second operand in a destination data register. The result is a 32-bit operand that is written back into the same data register. The sizes of the operands are fixed for this instruction.

Description of Instruction:

The MULU instruction multiplies two unsigned 16-bit numbers and the result is an unsigned 32-bit number. The destination address is a data register. Before the operation, only the least-significant half is used, but after the operation, the whole register is used. Therefore, any data that may have been in the most-significant half of this register before the operation will be written over by the operation.

Format of Opcode:

15	14	13	12	11	10	9	8	7	6	5	4	3	2	1	0
1	1	0	0		Register		0	1	1	Effective Address <ea>					
										Mode			Register		

Bits 15–12. These bits indicate that this instruction belongs to the set of instructions {AND,ABCD, EXG,MUL}. Other bits in the opcode select this particular instruction from this set.
Register. This field specifies the destination data Bits 11–9 register that contains the second operand before the operation and the product after the operation.
Bits 8–6. These bits select this particular instruction as the MULU instruction.
Effective Address, Bits 5–0. The effective address for the source address is stored in this pair of fields, one for the mode and the other for the register. The interpretation for this pair of fields is given in the table below:

Effective Address <ea>		Mnemonic for Addressing Mode
Mode	Register	
000	Register Number n	Dn
*	*	An
010	Register Number n	(An)
011	Register Number n	(An)+
100	Register Number n	–(An)
101	Register Number n	d(An)
110	Register Number n	d(An,Rx)
111	000	$xxxx
111	001	$xxxxxxxx
111	010	d(PC)
111	011	d(PC,Rx)
111	100	#

* means that this addressing mode is not allowed

Execution Times (Cycles):

The first number is the number of clock cycles required to: get the operands, execute the instruction, store the results and get the next opcode. The next pair of numbers is for the number of read cycles and the number of write cycles respectively.

These values are only valid for the 68000 microprocessor. See the condensed tables in Chapter 8 for calculating times for the other microprocessors in the M68000 family.

Source	Destination											
	Dn	An	(An)	(An)+	−(An)	d(An)	d(An,Rx)	$xxxx	$xxxxxxxx	d(PC)	d(PC,Rx)	#
Dn	70 1/0											
An												
(An)	74 2/0											
(An)+	74 2/0											
−(An)	76 2/0											
d(An)	78 3/0											
d(An,Rx)	80 3/0											
$xxxx	78 3/0											
$xxxxxxxx	82 4/0											
d(PC)	78 3/0											
d(PC,Rx)	80 3/0											
#	74 2/0											

Number of Bytes per Instruction for Different Addressing Modes:

Source	Destination											
	Dn	An	(An)	(An)+	−(An)	d(An)	d(An,Rx)	$xxxx	$xxxxxxxx	d(PC)	d(PC,Rx)	#
Dn	2											
An												
(An)	2											
(An)+	2											
−(An)	2											
d(An)	4											
d(An,Rx)	4											
$xxxx	4											
$xxxxxxxx	6											
d(PC)	4											
d(PC,Rx)	4											
#	4											

Example:

Multiplication of two numbers (the same example as for the MULS instruction).

Before the operation:	Contents of:		X N Z V C	
	D0	= $00008011	Flags: 1 0 0 0 1	
	$1000	= $0021		
	MULU $1000,D0			

After the operation:	Contents of:		X N Z V C
	D0	= $00108231	Flags: 1 1 0 0 0
	$1000	= $0021	

Applications:

You can use the MULU instruction to multiply two unsigned 16-bit numbers and obtain the unsigned 32-bit product. For signed numbers of 16 bits or less, you can use the MULS instruction. If you need to multiply larger signed numbers, you will need to write an algorithm (see the example in Chapter 6).

NBCD   Negate BCD Number with Extend

Assembler Syntax:

NBCD <ea>

Operation:

0–(<Destination> + <X-flag>) → <Destination>

Flag Changes:

X   Set the same as the C-bit.
N   Undefined after the operation.
Z   Set equal to 0 if result not equal 0, otherwise undefined.
V   Undefined after the operation.
C   Set equal to 1 if a "borrow" was required, otherwise reset equal to 0.

Operand Sizes:

This instruction operates only on bytes.

Description of Instruction:

The NBCD instruction serves to create the 9's complement of a number if the X-flag was set or the 10's complement of a number if the X-flag was not set. This instruction subtracts both the original number and the value of the X-flag from 0. This operation implements a unary operation upon a byte, whereby the byte contains two digits of a BCD-encoded number.

Format of Opcode:

15	14	13	12	11	10	9	8	7	6	5	4	3	2	1	0
0	1	0	0	1	0	0	0	0	0	Effective Address <ea>					
										Mode			Register		

Bits 15–12. These bits indicate that this instruction belongs to the set of instructions {CLR,CHK, NBCD,etc.}. Other bits in the opcode select this particular instruction from this set.

Bits 11–6. These bits select this particular instruction as the NBCD instruction.

Effective Address, Bits 5–0. The effective address is stored in this pair of fields, one for the mode and the other for the register. The interpretation for this pair of fields is given in the table below:

Effective Address <ea>		Mnemonic for Addressing Mode
Mode	Register	
000	Register Number n	Dn
*	*	An
010	Register Number n	(An)
011	Register Number n	(An)+
100	Register Number n	–(An)
101	Register Number n	d(An)
110	Register Number n	d(An,Rx)
111	000	$xxxx
111	001	$xxxxxxxx
*	*	d(PC)
*	*	d(PC,Rx)
*	*	#

∗ means that this addressing mode is not allowed

Execution Times (Cycles):

The first number is the number of clock cycles required to: get the operand, execute the instruction, store the results and get the next opcode. The next pair of numbers is for the number of read cycles and the number of write cycles respectively.

These values are only valid for the 68000 microprocessor. See the condensed tables in Chapter 8 for calculating times for the other microprocessors in the M68000 family.

	Destination										
	Dn	An	(An)	(An)+	–(An)	d(An)	d(An,Rx)	$xxxx	$xxxxxxxx	d(PC)	d(PC,Rx)	#
	6 1/0		12 2/1	12 2/1	14 2/1	16 3/1	18 3/1	16 3/1	20 4/1			

Number of Bytes per Instruction for Different Addressing Modes:

	Destination										
	Dn	An	(An)	(An)+	–(An)	d(An)	d(An,Rx)	$xxxx	$xxxxxxxx	d(PC)	d(PC,Rx)	#
	2		2	2	2	4	4	4	6			

Example:

Before the operation:	Contents of		X N Z V C
	D0	= $xxxxxx34	Flags: 1 0 0 0 0
	NBCD D0		
After the operation:	Contents of		X N Z V C
	D0	= $xxxxxx65	Flags: 1 0 0 1 1

Applications:

You can use the NBCD instruction to create negative numbers in the BCD format.

NEG   Negate Binary Number

Assembler Syntax:

NEG.w <ea>

Operation:

0–<ea> → <ea>

Flag Changes:

X   Set the same as the C-bit.
N   Set equal to 1 if result is negative (<ea> larger than 0 before the operation), otherwise reset to 0.
Z   Set equal to 1 if result equals 0 (<ea> = 0 before the operation), otherwise reset to 0.
V   Set equal to 1 if there is an overflow, otherwise set to 0.
C   Set equal to 1 if result is not equal to 0, otherwise reset equal to 0.

Operand Sizes:

This instruction operates on bytes, words and long words. The .w in the syntax refers to .B, .W. or .L respectively.

Description of Instruction:

The NEG instruction serves to create the two's complement of a number. It subtracts the operand at the destination address, <ea>, from 0 and writes the results into the destination address. It can convert a byte, a word or a long word into two's complement format.

Format of Opcode:

15	14	13	12	11	10	9	8	7	6	5	4	3	2	1	0
0	1	0	0	0	1	0	0	Size		Effective Address <ea>					

| 0 | 1 | 0 | 0 | 0 | 1 | 0 | 0 | Size | | Mode | | | Register | | |

Bits 15–12. These bits indicate that this instruction belongs to the set of instructions {NOT,NBCD, SWAP,EXT,NEG,etc}. Other bits in the opcode select this particular instruction from this set.
Bits 11–8. These bits select this particular instruction as the NEG instruction.
Size, Bits 7–6. The size of the operand is stored in this field as follows:

00 –   8-bit byte as operand
01 –   16-bit word as operand
10 –   32-bit long word as operand

Effective Address, Bits 5–0. The effective address is stored in this pair of fields, one for the mode and the other for the register. The interpretation for this pair of fields is given in the table below:

Effective Address <ea>		Mnemonic for Addressing Mode
Mode	**Register**	
000	Register Number n	Dn
*	*	An
010	Register Number n	(An)
011	Register Number n	(An)+
100	Register Number n	–(An)
101	Register Number n	d(An)
110	Register Number n	d(An,Rx)
111	000	$xxxx
111	001	$xxxxxxxx
*	*	d(PC)
*	*	d(PC,Rx)
*	*	#

* means that this addressing mode is not allowed

Execution Times (Cycles):

The first number is the number of clock cycles required to: get the operand, execute the instruction, store the results and get the next opcode. The next pair of numbers is for the number of read cycles and the number of write cycles respectively.

These values are only valid for the 68000 microprocessor. See the condensed tables in Chapter 8 for calculating times for the other microprocessors in the M68000 family.

(Unary operations on bytes and words)

						Destination					
	Dn	An	(An)	(An)+	–(An)	d(An)	d(An,Rx)	$xxxx	$xxxxxxxx	d(PC)	d(PC,Rx)	#
	4 1/0		12 2/1	12 2/1	14 2/1	16 3/1	18 3/1	16 3/1	20 4/1			

(Unary operations on long words)

						Destination					
	Dn	An	(An)	(An)+	–(An)	d(An)	d(An,Rx)	$xxxx	$xxxxxxxx	d(PC)	d(PC,Rx)	#
	6 1/0		20 3/2	20 3/2	22 3/2	24 4/2	26 4/2	24 4/2	28 5/2			

Number of Bytes per Instruction for Different Addressing Modes:
(Unary Operations on Bytes and Words)

						Destination					
	Dn	An	(An)	(An)+	–(An)	d(An)	d(An,Rx)	$xxxx	$xxxxxxxx	d(PC)	d(PC,Rx)	#
	2		2	2	2	4	4	4	6			

(Unary operations on long words)

						Destination					
	Dn	An	(An)	(An)+	–(An)	d(An)	d(An,Rx)	$xxxx	$xxxxxxxx	d(PC)	d(PC,Rx)	#
	2		2	2	2	4	4	4	6			

Examples:

a) Negating a positive number

Before the operation:	Contents at		X N Z V C
	$1000 = #$5073	Flags:	1 0 0 0 1
	NEG.W $1000		
After the operation:	Contents at		X N Z V C
	$1000 = #$AF8D	Flags:	1 1 0 0 1

b) Negating a negative number

Before the operation:	Contents at		X N Z V C
	$1000 = #$8073	Flags:	1 0 0 0 1
	NEG.W $1000		
After the operation:	Contents at		X N Z V C
	$1000 = #$7F8D	Flags	1 0 0 0 1

Applications:

You can use the NEG instruction to convert a positive number into a negative number in the two's complement format. If you need to convert a number with more than 32 bits, then you must also use the NEGX instruction.

NEGX   Negate Binary Number with Extend

Assembler Syntax:

NEGX.w <ea>

Operation:

0–(<ea> + <X-flag>) → <ea>

Flag Changes:

X   Set the same as the C-bit.
N   Set equal to 1 if result is negative (<ea> larger than 0 before the operation), otherwise reset to 0.
Z   Set equal to 1 if result equals 0 (<ea> = 0 before the operation), otherwise reset to 0.
V   Set equal to 1 if there is an overflow, otherwise set to 0.
C   Set equal to 1 if result is not equal to 0, otherwise reset equal to 0.

Operand Sizes:

This instruction operates on bytes, words and long words. The .w in the syntax refers to .B, .W. or .L respectively.

Description of Instruction:

The NEGX instruction serves to create the two's complement of a number. It subtracts both the operand, at <ea>, and the X-flag from 0 and writes the results into the same location. It can convert a byte, a word or a long word into two's complement format.

Format of Opcode:

15	14	13	12	11	10	9	8	7	6	5	4	3	2	1	0
0	1	0	0	0	0	0	0	\multicolumn{2}{c}{Size}	\multicolumn{6}{c}{Effective Address <ea>}

| | | | | | | | | | | Mode | | | Register | | |

Bits 15–12. These bits indicate that this instruction belongs to the set of instructions {NOT,NBCD, SWAP,EXT,NEG,etc}. Other bits in the opcode select this particular instruction from this set.

Bits 11–8. These bits select this particular instruction as the NEGX instruction.

Size, Bits 7–6. The size of the operand is stored in this field as follows:

00	–	8-bit byte as operand
01	–	16-bit word as operand
10	–	32-bit long word as operand

Effective Address, Bits 5–0. The effective address is stored in this pair of fields, one for the mode and the other for the register. The interpretation for this pair of fields is given in the table below:

Effective Address <ea>		Mnemonic for Addressing Mode
Mode	**Register**	
000	Register Number n	Dn
*	*	An
010	Register Number n	(An)
011	Register Number n	(An)+
100	Register Number n	–(An)
101	Register Number n	d(An)
110	Register Number n	d(An,Rx)
111	000	$xxxx
111	001	$xxxxxxxx
*	*	d(PC)
*	*	d(PC,Rx)
*	*	#

* means that this addressing mode is not allowed

Execution Times (Cycles):

The first number is the number of clock cycles required to: get the operand, execute the instruction, store the results and get the next opcode. The next pair of numbers is for the number of read cycles and the number of write cycles respectively.

These values are only valid for the 68000 microprocessor. See the condensed tables in Chapter 8 for calculating times for the other microprocessors in the M68000 family.

(Unary operations on bytes and words)

						Destination						
Dn	An	(An)	(An)+	–(An)	d(An)	d(An,Rx)	$xxxx	$xxxxxxxx	d(PC)	d(PC,Rx)	#	
4 1/0		12 2/1	12 2/1	14 2/1	16 3/1	18 3/1	16 3/1	20 4/1				

(Unary operations on long words)

						Destination						
Dn	An	(An)	(An)+	–(An)	d(An)	d(An,Rx)	$xxxx	$xxxxxxxx	d(PC)	d(PC,Rx)	#	
6 1/0		20 3/2	20 3/2	22 3/2	24 4/2	26 4/2	24 4/2	28 5/2				

Number of Bytes per Instruction for Different Addressing Modes:
(Unary Operations on Bytes and Words)

						Destination						
Dn	An	(An)	(An)+	–(An)	d(An)	d(An,Rx)	$xxxx	$xxxxxxxx	d(PC)	d(PC,Rx)	#	
2		2	2	2	4	4	4	6				

(Unary operations on long words)

						Destination						
Dn	An	(An)	(An)+	–(An)	d(An)	d(An,Rx)	$xxxx	$xxxxxxxx	d(PC)	d(PC,Rx)	#	
2		2	2	2	4	4	4	6				

Examples:

Negating positive number when the X-flag is equal to 1.

Before the operation:	Contens at	X N Z V C	
	$1000 = #$0123	Flags: 1 0 0 0 0	
NEGX.W $1000			
After the operation:	Contens at	X N Z V C	
	$1000 = #$FEDC	Flags: 1 1 0 0 1	

Applications:

You can use the NEGX instruction to convert a positive number with more than 32 bits into a negative number in the two's complement format.

NOP   No Operation

Assembler Syntax:

NOP

Operation:

No operation, but $<PC> + 2 \rightarrow <PC>$

Flag Changes:

None.

Operand Sizes:

No operands are used.

Description of Instruction:

The NOP instruction does not execute any operation. The only change or effect from this instruction is that the program counter advances by 2 in order to fetch the next instruction. An M68000 microprocessor will then continue with the next instruction.

Format of Opcode:

15	14	13	12	11	10	9	8	7	6	5	4	3	2	1	0
0	1	0	0	1	1	1	0	0	1	1	1	0	0	0	1

= $4E71

Bits 15–12. These bits indicate that this instruction belongs to the set of instructions {NOT,NEG, SWAP,EXT,NOP,etc.}. Other bits in the opcode select this particular instruction from this set.
Bits 11–0. These bits select this particular instruction as the NOP instruction.

Addressing Modes that are Allowed:

None, since this instruction does not use any operands.

Execution Times (Cycles):

4 clock cycles
(This value is only valid for the 68000 microprocessor. See the condensed tables in Chapter 8 for calculating times for the other microprocessors in the M68000 family.)

Number of Bytes per Instruction:

2 bytes

Applications:

You can use the NOP instruction to temporarily replace other instructions, such as when testing a program, ie. the NOP instruction serves as a 2-byte space filler in the code. You could also use the DBT instruction as a 4-byte space filler, since it also does nothing more than to advance the program counter. You could also use the NOP instruction as a time delay in a loop or to reserve space in a program for code that has not yet been written.

NOT   Logical Complement

Assembler Syntax:

NOT.w <ea>

Operation:

<Destination> → <Destination>   (contents are complemented)

Flag Changes:

X   Not changed.
N   Set equal to 1 if result is negative, otherwise reset to 0.
Z   Set equal to 1 if result equals 0, otherwise reset to 0.
V   Always reset to 0.
C   Always reset to 0.

Operand Sizes:

This instruction operates on bytes, words and long words. The .w in the syntax refers to .B, .W or .L respectively.

Description of Instruction:

The NOT instruction creates the one's complement of the operand from the destination address and rewrites it back into the same location. This means that every 1 is changed into a 0 and every 0 is changed into a 1. If you add 1 to the result, the result will then be the same as from the NEG instruction.

Format of Opcode:

15	14	13	12	11	10	9	8	7	6	5	4	3	2	1	0
0	1	0	0	0	1	1	0	Size		Effective Address <ea>					
										Mode			Register		

Bits 15–12. These bits indicate that this instruction belongs to the set of instructions {NEG,SWAP, EXT,NOT,etc.}. Other bits in the opcode select this particular instruction from this set.
Size Field, Bits 7–6. The size of the operand is stored in this field, defined as follows:

00	–	8-bit byte as operand
01	–	16-bit word as operand
10	–	32-bit long word as operand

Effective Address, Bits 5–0. The effective address is stored in this pair of fields, one for the mode and the other for the register. The interpretation for this pair of fields is given in the table below:

Effective Address <ea>		Mnemonic for Addressing Mode
Mode	**Register**	
000	Register Number n	Dn
*	*	An
010	Register Number n	(An)
011	Register Number n	(An)+
100	Register Number n	–(An)
101	Register Number n	d(An)
110	Register Number n	d(An,Rx)
111	000	$xxxx
111	001	$xxxxxxxx
*	*	d(PC)
*	*	d(PC,Rx)
*	*	#

∗ means that this addressing mode is not allowed

Execution Times (Cycles):

The first number is the number of clock cycles required to: get the operand, execute the instruction, store the results and get the next opcode. The next pair of numbers is for the number of read cycles and the number of write cycles respectively.

These values are only valid for the 68000 microprocessor. See the condensed tables in Chapter 8 for calculating times for the other microprocessors in the M68000 family.

(Unary operations on bytes and words)

	Destination										
	Dn	An	(An)	(An)+	–(An)	d(An)	d(An,Rx)	$xxxx	$xxxxxxxx	d(PC)	d(PC,Rx)	#
	4 1/0		12 2/1	12 2/1	14 2/1	16 3/1	18 3/1	16 3/1	20 4/1			

(Unary operations on long words)

	Destination										
	Dn	An	(An)	(An)+	–(An)	d(An)	d(An,Rx)	$xxxx	$xxxxxxxx	d(PC)	d(PC,Rx)	#
	6 1/0		20 3/2	20 3/2	22 3/2	24 4/2	26 4/2	24 4/2	28 5/2			

Number of Bytes per Instruction for Different Addressing Modes:

(Unary operations on Bytes and Words)

	Destination										
	Dn	An	(An)	(An)+	–(An)	d(An)	d(An,Rx)	$xxxx	$xxxxxxxx	d(PC)	d(PC,Rx)	#
	2		2	2	2	4	4	4	6			

(Unary operations on long words)

	Destination										
	Dn	An	(An)	(An)+	–(An)	d(An)	d(An,Rx)	$xxxx	$xxxxxxxx	d(PC)	d(PC,Rx)	#
	2		2	2	2	4	4	4	6			

Example:

Before the operation:	Contents of		X N Z V C	
	D0	= $xxxx3333	Flags: 1 0 0 0 0	
	NOT.W D0			
After the operation:	Contents of		X N Z V C	
	D0	= $xxxxCCCC	Flags: 1 1 0 0 0	

Applications:

You can use the NOT instruction to complement or invert the contents of a memory location. It is similar to the BCHG instruction, except that the BCHG instruction operates upon only 1 bit.

OR   Logical Inclusive OR

Assembler Syntax:

```
OR.w <ea>,Dd
OR.w Ds,<ea>
```

Operation:

<Source> V <Destination> → <Destination>

Flag Changes:

X   Not changed.
N   Set equal to 1 if most-significant bit of result equals 1, otherwise reset to 0.
Z   Set equal to 1 if result equals 0, otherwise reset to 0.
V   Always reset to 0.
C   Always reset to 0.

Operand Sizes:

This instruction operates on bytes, words and long words. The .w in the syntax refers to .B, .W or .L respectively.

Description of Instruction:

The OR instruction performs the logical operation of inclusive OR on a pair of bytes, words, or long words. Each bit in the result will be 1 if either one or both of the corresponding bits in the two operands are equal to 1. Each bit in the result will be a 0 if both of the corresponding bits in the two operands are the same.

Format of Opcode:

15	14	13	12	11	10	9	8	7	6	5	4	3	2	1	0
1	0	0	0	Register			Opmode			Effective Address <ea>					
										Mode			Register		

Bits 15–12. These bits indicate that this instruction belongs to the set of instructions {OR, DIV, SBCD}. Other bits in the opcode select this particular instruction from this set.

*Register, Bits11–9.*This field specifies the data register that serves either the source address or the destination address.

Opmode, Bits 8–6. This field specifies the direction of the operation and the size of the operands. The first bit specifies the directions as follows:

0	–	destination is a data register
1	–	source is a data register

The last two bits specify the size as follows:

00	–	8-bit bytes as operands
01	–	16-bit words as operands
10	–	32-bit long words as operands

Effective Address, Bits 5–0. The effective address is stored in this pair of fields, one for the mode and the other for the register. The interpretation for this pair of fields is given in the tables below that also show the differences between the two cases of:

Case 1: The source address is defined by an effective address and the destination address is a data register.
Case 2: The source address is a data register and the destination address is defined by an effective address.
Case 1: Source address is defined by an effective address; destination address is a data register.

Effective Address <ea>		Mnemonic for Addressing Mode
Mode	Register	
000	Register Number n	Dn
*	*	An
010	Register Number n	(An)
011	Register Number n	(An)+
100	Register Number n	–(An)
101	Register Number n	d(An)
110	Register Number n	d(An,Rx)
111	000	$xxxx
111	001	$xxxxxxxx
111	010	d(PC)
111	011	d(PC,Rx)
111	100	#

* means that this addressing mode is not allowed

Case 2: Source address is a data register; destination address is defined by an effective address.

Effective Address <ea>		Mnemonic for Addressing Mode
Mode	**Register**	
000	Register Number n	Dn
*	*	An
010	Register Number n	(An)
011	Register Number n	(An)+
100	Register Number n	–(An)
101	Register Number n	d(An)
110	Register Number n	d(An,Rx)
111	000	$xxxx
111	001	$xxxxxxxx
*	*	d(PC)
*	*	d(PC,Rx)
*	*	#

* means that this addressing mode is not allowed

Execution Times (Cycles): (Operations on Bytes and Words)

The first number is the number of clock cycles required to: get the operands, execute the instruction, store the results and get the next opcode. The next pair of numbers is for the number of read cycles and the number of write cycles respectively.

These values are only valid for the 68000 microprocessor. See the condensed tables in Chapter 8 for calculating times for the other microprocessors in the M68000 family.

Source	Destination											
	Dn	An	(An)	(An)+	–(An)	d(An)	d(An,Rx)	$xxxx	$xxxxxxxx	d(PC)	d(PC,Rx)	#
Dn	4 1/0		12 2/1	12 2/1	14 2/1	16 3/1	18 3/1	16 3/1	20 4/1			
An												
(An)	8 2/0											
(An)+	8 2/0											
–(An)	10 2/0											
d(An)	12 3/0											
d(An,Rx)	14 3/0											
$xxxx	12 3/0											
$xxxxxxxx	16 4/0											
d(PC)	12 3/0											
d(PC,Rx)	14 3/0											
#	8 2/0											

Execution Times (cycles): (Operations on Long Words)

The first number is the number of clock cycles required to: get the operands, execute the instruction, store the results and get the next opcode. The next pair of numbers is for the number of read cycles and the number of write cycles respectively.

These values are only valid for the 68000 microprocessor. See the condensed tables in Chapter 8 for calculating times for the other microprocessors in the M68000 family.

Source	Destination											
	Dn	An	(An)	(An)+	−(An)	d(An)	d(An,Rx)	$xxxx	$xxxxxxxx	d(PC)	d(PC,Rx)	#
Dn	6 1/0		16 3/1	16 3/1	18 3/1	20 4/1	22 4/1	20 4/1	24 5/1			
An												
(An)	14 3/0											
(An)+	14 3/0											
−(An)	16 3/0											
d(An)	18 4/0											
d(An,Rx)	20 4/0											
$xxxx	18 4/0											
$xxxxxxxx	22 5/0											
d(PC)	18 4/0											
d(PC,Rx)	20 4/0											
#	14 3/0											

Number of Bytes per Instruction for Different Addressing Modes:
(Operations on Bytes and Words)

Source	Destination											
	Dn	An	(An)	(An)+	−(An)	d(An)	d(An,Rx)	$xxxx	$xxxxxxxx	d(PC)	d(PC,Rx)	#
Dn	2		2	2	2	4	4	4	6			
An												
(An)	2											
(An)+	2											
−(An)	2											
d(An)	4											
d(An,Rx)	4											
$xxxx	4											
$xxxxxxxx	6											
d(PC)	4											
d(PC,Rx)	4											
#	4											

Number of Bytes per Instruction for Different Addressing Modes:
(Operations on Long Words)

Source	Destination											
	Dn	An	(An)	(An)+	−(An)	d(An)	d(An,Rx)	$xxxx	$xxxxxxxx	d(PC)	d(PC,Rx)	#
Dn	2		2	2	2	4	4	4	6			
An												
(An)	2											
(An)+	2											
−(An)	2											
d(An)	4											
d(An,Rx)	4											
$xxxx	4											
$xxxxxxxx	6											
d(PC)	4											
d(PC,Rx)	4											
#	6											

Example:

Before the operation:	Contents of:		X	N	Z	V	C
	D0 = $xxxxAAAA	Flags:	1	0	0	0	1
	$1000 = $5555						

OR.W $1000,D0

After the operation:	Contents of:		X	N	Z	V	C
	D0 = $xxxxFFFF	Flags:	1	1	0	0	0
	$1000 = $5555						

Applications:

You can use the OR instruction to perform the logical inclusive OR operation on two operands. For example, you could use this instruction to set individual bits or read individual bits in a control register. You could also do the same in memory.

ORI   Logical Inclusive OR with a Constant (Immediate)

Assembler Syntax:

ORI.w #Constant,<ea>

Operation:

#Constant V <Destination> → <Destination>

Flag Changes:

X   Not changed.
N   Set equal to 1 if the most-significant bit of the result is 1, otherwise reset to 0.
Z   Set equal to 1 if result equals 0, otherwise reset to 0.
V   Always reset to 0.
C   Always reset to 0.

Operand Sizes:

This instruction operates on bytes, words and long words. The .w in the syntax refers to .B, .W or .L respectively.

Description of Instruction:

The ORI instruction performs a logical inclusive OR operation upon a constant together with an operand from a destination address and stores the result back into the destination address.

Format of Opcode:

| 15 | 14 | 13 | 12 | 11 | 10 | 9 | 8 | 7 | 6 | 5 | 4 | 3 | 2 | 1 | 0 |

0	0	0	0	0	0	0	0	Size		Effective Address <ea>					
										Mode			Register		
										8-bit Constant					

16-bit Constant

32-bit Constant (including previous word)

Bits 15–12. These bits indicate that this instruction belongs to the set of instructions {Immediate, MOVEP,Bit Manipulation}. Other bits in the opcode select this particular instruction from this set.

Bits 11–8. These bits select this particular instruction as the ORI instruction

Size Field, Bits 7–6. The size of the operands is stored in this field, defined as follows:

00	–	8-bit bytes as operands
01	–	16-bit words as operands
10	–	32-bit long words as operands

Effective Address, Bits 5–0. The effective address for the destination address is stored in this pair of fields, one for the mode and the other for the register. The interpretation for this pair of fields is given in the table below:

Effective Address <ea>		Mnemonic for Addressing Mode
Mode	Register	
000	Register Number n	Dn
*	*	An
010	Register Number n	(An)
011	Register Number n	(An)+
100	Register Number n	–(An)
101	Register Number n	d(An)
110	Register Number n	d(An,Rx)
111	000	$xxxx
111	001	$xxxxxxxx
*	*	d(PC)
*	*	d(PC,Rx)
*	*	#

* means that this addressing mode is not allowed

The constant follows immediately after the opcode. Depending upon the size of the constant specified in bits 7 and 6, a byte as the constant is in the least-significant half of the next word, a word uses a full word and a long word uses two words.

Execution Times (Cycles): (Operations on Bytes and Words)

The first number is the number of clock cycles required to: get the operands, execute the instruction, store the results and get the next opcode. The next pair of numbers is for the number of read cycles and the number of write cycles respectively.

These values are only valid for the 68000 microprocessor. See the condensed tables in Chapter 8 for calculating times for the other microprocessors in the M68000 family.

Source	Destination											
	Dn	An	(An)	(An)+	-(An)	d(An)	d(An,Rx)	$xxxx	$xxxxxxxx	d(PC)	d(PC,Rx)	#
Dn												
An												
(An)												
(An)+												
-(An)												
d(An)												
d(An,Rx)												
$xxxx												
$xxxxxxxx												
d(PC)												
d(PC,Rx)												
#	8 2/0		16 3/1	16 3/1	18 3/1	20 4/1	22 4/1	20 4/1	24 5/1			

Execution Times (Cycles): (Operations on Long Words)

The first number is the number of clock cycles required to: get the operands, execute the instruction, store the results and get the next opcode. The next pair of numbers is for the number of read cycles and the number of write cycles respectively.

These values are only valid for the 68000 microprocessor. See the condensed tables in Chapter 8 for calculating times for the other microprocessors in the M68000 family.

Source	Destination											
	Dn	An	(An)	(An)+	-(An)	d(An)	d(An,Rx)	$xxxx	$xxxxxxxx	d(PC)	d(PC,Rx)	#
Dn												
An												
(An)												
(An)+												
-(An)												
d(An)												
d(An,Rx)												
$xxxx												
$xxxxxxxx												
d(PC)												
d(PC,Rx)												
#	16 3/0		28 5/2	28 5/2	30 5/2	32 6/2	34 6/2	32 6/2	36 7/2			

Number of Bytes per Instruction for Different Addressing Modes:
(Operations on Bytes and Words)

Source	Destination											
	Dn	An	(An)	(An)+	-(An)	d(An)	d(An,Rx)	$xxxx	$xxxxxxxx	d(PC)	d(PC,Rx)	#
Dn												
An												
(An)												
(An)+												
-(An)												
d(An)												
d(An,Rx)												
$xxxx												
$xxxxxxxx												
d(PC)												
d(PC,Rx)												
#	4		4	4	4	6	6	6	8			

Number of Bytes per Instruction for Different Addressing Modes:
(Operations on Long Words)

Source	Destination											
	Dn	An	(An)	(An)+	–(An)	d(An)	d(An,Rx)	$xxxx	$xxxxxxxx	d(PC)	d(PC,Rx)	#
Dn												
An												
(An)												
(An)+												
–(An)												
d(An)												
d(An,Rx)												
$xxxx												
$xxxxxxxx												
d(PC)												
d(PC,Rx)												
#	6		6	6	6	8	8	8	10			

Example:

Before the operation:	Contents of			X	N	Z	V	C	
	D0	= $xxxxAAAA	Flags:	1	0	0	0	1	
ORI.W #$55555,D0									
After the operation:	Contents of			X	N	Z	V	C	
	D0	= $xxxxFFFF	Flags:	1	1	0	0	0	

Applications:

You can use the ORI instruction to set or read individual bits in a control register. You could also do the same in memory.

ORI to CCR　Inclusive OR with Constant to Condition-Code Register

Assembler Syntax:

ORI #Constant,CCR

Operation:

#Constant V <CCR> → <CCR>

Flag Changes:

X	Set equal to 1 if bit 4 of the constant = 1, otherwise unchanged.
N	Set equal to 1 if bit 3 of the constant = 1, otherwise unchanged.
Z	Set equal to 1 if bit 2 of the constant = 1, otherwise unchanged.
V	Set equal to 1 if bit 1 of the constant = 1, otherwise unchanged.
C	Set equal to 1 if bit 0 of the constant = 1, otherwise unchanged.

Operand Sizes:

This instruction operates only on bytes since the condition-code register (CCR) has a length of 8 bits.

Description of Instruction:

The ORI-to-CCR instruction is useful for changing individual flags in the condition-code register (CCR). You can set any particular flags equal to 1 and leave the other flags unchanged.

Format of Opcode:

15	14	13	12	11	10	9	8	7	6	5	4	3	2	1	0
0	0	0	0	0	0	0	0	0	0	1	1	1	1	0	0
0	0	0	0	0	0	0	0	Constant							

(The first word = $003C)

Bits 15–12. These bits indicate that this instruction belongs to the set of instructions {Bit Instructions, MOVEP, Immediate}. Other bits in the opcode select this particular instruction from this set. *Bits 11–0.* These bits select this particular instruction as the ORI-to-CCR instruction.

The immediate constant is contained in the least-significant half of the following word. The rest of the word contains nulls.

Addressing Modes that are Allowed:

Source address   = #
Destination address   = CCR immediate

Execution Times (cycles):

20	clock cycles
3	read cycles
0	write cycles

(These values are only valid for the 68000 microprocessor. See the condensed tables in Chapter 8 for calculating times for the other microprocessors in the M68000 family.)

Number of Bytes per Instruction for Different Addressing Modes:

Always 4 bytes.

Example:

Before the operation:	X N Z V C Flags: 0 0 0 0 0
ORI #FF,CCR	
After the operation:	X N Z V C Flags: 1 1 1 1 1

Applications:

It is desirable to set some flags equal to 1 before executing some instructions, such as ROXL and ROXR. You can use the ORI-to-CCR instruction for this purpose.

Privileged Instruction!

ORI to SR Inclusive OR with Constant to Status Register

Assembler Syntax:

ORI #Constant,SR

Operation:

Case 1: An M68000 microprocessor is in the supervisor mode
    #Constant V <SR> → <SR>
Case 2: An M68000 microprocessor is in the user mode
        privilege violation → exception handling (see Chapter 2.5)

Flag Changes:

X Set equal to 1 if bit 4 of the constant = 1, otherwise unchanged.
N Set equal to 1 if bit 3 of the constant = 1, otherwise unchanged.
Z Set equal to 1 if bit 2 of the constant = 1, otherwise unchanged.
V Set equal to 1 if bit 1 of the constant = 1, otherwise unchanged.
C Set equal to 1 if bit 0 of the constant = 1, otherwise unchanged.

Operand Sizes:

This instruction operates only on words since the status register (SR) has a length of 16 bits.

Description of Instruction:

The ORI-to-SR instruction is useful for changing individual flags, the interrupt mask and the trace bit in the status register (SR). You can set any particular bits equal to 1 and leave the other bits unchanged. However, the ORI-to-SR instruction can not change the supervisor bit since it must be equal to 1 for the instruction to be allowed and the instruction can only change each bit to 1.

Since this instruction changes supervisor information (the trace bit and the interrupt mask), it is a privileged instruction that is only allowed when an M68000 microprocessor is in the supervisor mode. Otherwise, when the microprocessor is in the user mode, this instruction will lead to exception-handling.

Format of Opcode:

15	14	13	12	11	10	9	8	7	6	5	4	3	2	1	0
0	0	0	0	0	0	0	0	0	1	1	1	1	1	0	0
Word Constant															

(The first word = $007C)

Bits 15–12. These bits indicate that this instruction belongs to the set of instructions {Bit Instructions, MOVEP, Immediate}. Other bits in the opcode select this particular instruction from this set.
Bits 11–0. These bits select this particular instruction as the ORI-to-SR instruction.

The immediate constant is contained in the following word.

Addressing Modes that are Allowed:

Source address   = #
Destination address   = SR immediate

Execution Times (Cycles):

20	clock cycles
3	read cycles
0	write cycles

(These values are only valid for the 68000 microprocessor. See the condensed tables in Chapter 8 for calculating times for the other microprocessors in the M68000 family.)

Number of Bytes per Instruction for Different Addressing Modes:

Always 4 bytes.

Example:

Setting the interrupt mask at level 7.

Before the operation:

		15	14	13	12	11	10	9	8	7	6	5	4	3	2	1	0
Status Register:		T		S			12	11	10				X	N	Z	V	C
		0		1			0	0	0				1	0	0	0	0

ORI #0700,SR

After the operation:

		15	14	13	12	11	10	9	8	7	6	5	4	3	2	1	0
Status Register:		T		S			12	11	10				X	N	Z	V	C
		0		1			1	1	1				1	0	0	0	0

Applications:

As shown in the example above, you can use the ORI-to-SR instruction to selectively set bits in the status register equal to 1, such as for changing the trace bit or the interrupt mask. By setting the trace bit equal to 1, you can implement single stepping for testing a program (see Chapter 2.4). You can also change the flags with this instruction, but it may be easier to use the ORI-to-CCR instruction (not privileged) for the flags.

PEA   Push Effective Address onto Stack

Assembler Syntax:

```
PEA  <ea>
```

Operation:

Effective Address → -(A7)

Flag Changes:

None.

Operand Sizes:

This instruction operates only with a 32-bit long word as operand since the operand is an address for the stack. Therefore, there is no .w in the syntax.

Description of Instruction:

The PEA instruction pushes an address onto the stack that is currently used. If an M68000 microprocessor is in the user mode, it will use the user stack. If the microprocessor is in the supervisor mode, it will use the supervisor stack.

As a first step, this instruction will calculate the effective address. Then, it will write this address onto the appropriate stack. It is similar to the LEA instruction, except that the LEA instruction stores the effective address in an address register rather than on a stack.

Format of Opcode:

15	14	13	12	11	10	9	8	7	6	5	4	3	2	1	0
0	1	0	0	1	0	0	0	0	1	\multicolumn{6}{c}{Effective Address <ea>}

Effective Address <ea>: Mode (bits 5–3), Register (bits 2–0)

Bits 15–12. These bits indicate that this instruction belongs to the set of instructions {LEA,CLR,NEG, PEA,etc.}. Other bits in the opcode select this particular instruction from this set.

Bits 11–6. These bits select this particular instruction as the PEA instruction.

Effective Address, Bits 5–0. The effective address is stored in this pair of fields, one for the mode and the other for the register. The interpretation for this pair of fields is given in the table below:

Effective Address <ea>		Mnemonic for Addressing Mode
Mode	**Register**	
*	*	Dn
*	*	An
010	Register Number n	(An)
*	*	(An)+
*	*	–(An)
101	Register Number n	d(An)
110	Register Number n	d(An,Rx)
111	000	$xxxx
111	001	$xxxxxxxx
111	010	d(PC)
111	011	d(PC,Rx)
*	*	#

* means that this addressing mode is not allowed

Execution Times (Cycles):

The first number is the number of clock cycles required to: get the operand, execute the instruction, store the results and get the next opcode. The next pair of numbers is for the number of read cycles and the number of write cycles respectively.

These values are only valid for the 68000 microprocessor. See the condensed tables in Chapter 8 for calculating times for the other microprocessors in the M68000 family.

						Destination						
	Dn	An	(An)	(An)+	–(An)	d(An)	d(An,Rx)	$xxxx	$xxxxxxxx	d(PC)	d(PC,Rx)	#
			12 1/2			16 2/2	20 2/2	16 2/2	20 2/2	16 2/2	20 2/2	

Number of Bytes per Instruction for Different Addressing Modes:

						Destination						
	Dn	An	(An)	(An)+	–(An)	d(An)	d(An,Rx)	$xxxx	$xxxxxxxx	d(PC)	d(PC,Rx)	#
			2			4	4	4	6	4	4	

Example:

Saving an address before jumping to a subroutine that changes the contents of the address register, so that the address can be retrieved after the return from the subroutine.

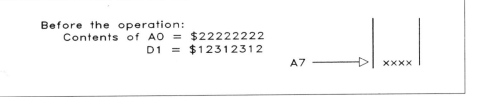

```
        Before the operation:
          Contents of A0 = $22222222
                     D1 = $12312312
                                      A7 ——————▷| xxxx |
```

```
PEA 5(A0,D5.L)
RTS
```

```
          After the operation:
            Contents of A0 = $22222222
                       D5 = $12312312
                                         A7  ─────────▷  3453
                                                         4539
                                                         ××××
```

Applications:

You can use the PEA instruction to store addresses on the current stack, such as when the number of address registers is not sufficient and when you will need the calculated address later. You can then get the address and put it back into an address register later with the instruction MOVE.L (A7)+,An.

Privileged Instruction!

RESET   Reset External Peripherals

Assembler Syntax:

RESET

Operation:

Case 1:   An M68000 microprocessor is in the supervisor mode. The microprocessor will hold its RESET line low for 124 cycles.

Case 2:   Ab M68000 microprocessor is in the user mode. This is a violation of the privilege status that leads to exception handling (see Chapter 2.5).

Flag Changes:

None.

Operand Sizes:

This instruction does not use operands.

Description of Instruction:

If an M68000 microprocessor is in the supervisor status, then the RESET instruction will cause it to hold its RESET line low for 124 clock cycles. This resets all peripheral devices that are attached to the RESET line. However, it does not reset the microprocessor itself. Rather the microprocessor continues on to the next instruction after waiting 124 clock cycles.

If an M68000 microprocessor is in the user status, then the RESET instruction will start exception handling, since the RESET instruction is not allowed in this mode (see Chapter 2.5).

Format of Opcode:

15	14	13	12	11	10	9	8	7	6	5	4	3	2	1	0
0	1	0	0	1	1	1	0	0	1	1	1	0	0	0	0

(= $4E70)

Bits 15–12. These bits indicate that this instruction belongs to the set of instructions {LEA,CLR,NEG, PEA,RESET,etc.}. Other bits in the opcode select this particular instruction from this set.

Bits 11–0. These bits select this particular instruction as the RESET instruction.

Addressing Modes that are Allowed:

There are none, since this instruction does not use operands.

Execution Times (Cycles):

132	clock cycles
1	read cycle
0	write cycles

(These values are only valid for the 68000 microprocessor. See the condensed tables in Chapter 8 for calculating times for the other microprocessors in the M68000 family.)

Number of Bytes per Instruction for Different Addressing Modes:

Always 2 bytes.

Applications:

You can use the RESET instruction in an operating system, particularly for taking care of catastrophic errors in the peripheral devices. (See also Chapter 2.10: Resetting an IPC device with the 68120.)

ROL,ROR   Rotate Left or Right (Without Extend)

Assembler Syntax:

ROd.w Ds,Dd	
ROd.w #Constant,Dd	(the first d is the direction, R or L)
ROd <ea>	

Operation:

Case 1:	The destination address is a data register.	
	The operand at the destination address is rotated the number of bit positions specified by the operand at the source address → <Destination>	
Case 2:	The destination address is in memory.	
	The operand at the destination address is rotated by one bit position and rewritten at the destination address.	

Flag Changes:

X   Not changed.
N   Set equal to 1 if the most-significant bit of the result is 1, otherwise reset to 0.
Z   Set equal to 1 if result equals 0, otherwise reset to 0.
V   Always reset to 0.
C   Set equal to the same value as the last bit shifted out of the operand. If the operand is shifted by 0 bit positions (source address is a data register containing 0), then this bit will be reset to 0.

Operand Sizes:

Case 1:   The destination address is a data register.
          This instruction can operate on a byte, word or long words. The .w in the syntax refers to .B, .W or .L respectively.
Case 2:   The destination address is in memory.
          This instruction can only operate on words.

Description of Instruction:

The ROL and ROR instructions rotate the operand at the destination address. Each bit that leaves the operand in the given direction goes back into the operand from the other direction and goes into the C-flag. There are two cases, depending upon where the destination address is located:

Case 1: The destination address is a data register.

The size of the operand can be a byte, word or long word. You can specify the number of bit positions for the rotation as a value at the source address, either immediately in the instruction or directly from a data register. If this value is specified immediately, then the number of bit positions for the rotation can range from 1 to 8. If this value is contained in a data register, then the number of bit positions for the rotation can range from 0 to 64 (modulus 64 if the data in the register is larger than 64).

Case 2: The destination address is in memory.

The size of the operand can only be a word. This word will be rotated 1 bit position in the specified direction.

There are also two cases, depending upon the direction of the rotation:

ROL: The operand will be rotated by the given number of bit positions to the left. The bits that leave the operand at the left (most-significant bits) are fed back into the operand from the right (as least-significant bits). The last bit to leave the operand is also stored in the C-flag.

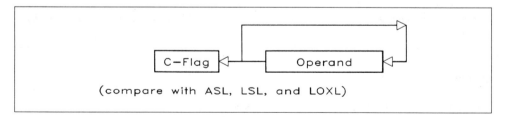

(compare with ASL, LSL, and LOXL)

ROR: The operand will be rotated by the given number of bit positions to the right. The bits that leave the operand at the right (least-significant bits) are fed back into the operand at the left (as most-significant bits). The last bit to leave the operand is also stored in the C-flag.

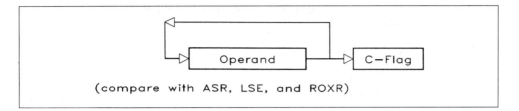

(compare with ASR, LSE, and ROXR)

Format of Opcode:

Case 1: The destination address is a data register.

15	14	13	12	11	10	9	8	7	6	5	4	3	2	1	0
1	1	1	0	Counter/Register			->Dir<-	Size		Imm/Reg	1	1	Register		

Bits 15–12. These bits indicate that this instruction belongs to the set of instructions {Shift, Rotate}. Other bits in the opcode select this particular instruction from this set.

Counter/Register, Bits 11–9. Depending upon the value of bit 5, this field contains either the counter (immediate constant) that defines the number of bit positions for the rotation ($001 = 1$, $010 = 2$, ... $111 = 7$, and $000 = 8$) or the number of the data register that contains the number of bit positions (modulus 64).

Direction, Bit 8. This bit specifies the direction of the rotation as follows:

0	–	to the right
1	–	to the left

Size Field, Bits 7–6. The size of the operand is stored in this field, defined as follows:

00	–	8-bit byte as operand
01	–	16-bit word as operand
10	–	32-bit long word as operand

Imm/Reg, Bit 5. This bit specifies whether bits 11–9 contain a counter (immediate value) for the shift or the number of a data register as follows:

0	–	counter (value from 1 to 8)
1	–	data register (the number of bit positions for the rotation will be read from this register with a modulus of 64)

Register, Bits 2–0. This field specifies the number of the data register that serves as the destination address.

Case 2: The destination address is in memory.

15	14	13	12	11	10	9	8	7	6	5	4	3	2	1	0
										Effective Address <ea>					
1	1	1	0	0	1	1	->Dir<-	1	1	Mode			Register		

Bits 15–12. These bits indicate that this instruction belongs to the set of instructions {shift, rotate}. Other bits in the opcode select this particular instruction from this set.

Bits 11–9. These bits select this particular instruction as a rotation instruction.

Direction, Bit 8. This bit specifies the direction of the rotation as follows:

0	–	to the right
1	–	to the left

Bits 7–6. These bits specify that the destination address is in memory and that the size of the operand is word.

Effective Address, Bits 5–0. The effective address for the destination address is stored in this pair of fields, one for the mode and the other for the register. The interpretation for this pair of fields is given in the table below:

Effective Address <ea>		Mnemonic for Addressing Mode
Mode	Register	
*	*	Dn
*	*	An
010	Register Number n	(An)
011	Register Number n	(An)+
100	Register Number n	–(An)
101	Register Number n	d(An)
110	Register Number n	d(An,Rx)
111	000	$xxxx
111	001	$xxxxxxxx
*	*	d(PC)
*	*	d(PC,Rx)
*	*	#

∗ means that this addressing mode is not allowed

Execution Times (Cycles):

The first number is the number of clock cycles required to: get the operand, execute the instruction, store the results and get the next opcode. The next pair of numbers is for the number of read cycles and the number of write cycles respectively.

These values are only valid for the 68000 microprocessor. See the condensed tables in Chapter 8 for calculating times for the other microprocessors in the M68000 family.

Case 1: The destination address is a data register. (Operations on Bytes and Words)

Source	Destination											
	Dn	An	(An)	(An)+	–(An)	d(An)	d(An,Rx)	$xxxx	$xxxxxxxx	d(PC)	d(PC,Rx)	#
Dn	6+2n 1/0											
An												
(An)												
(An)+												
–(An)												
d(An)												
d(An,Rx)												
$xxxx												
$xxxxxxxx												
d(PC)												
d(PC,Rx)												
#	6+2n 1/0											

Execution Times (Cycles):

(Case 1)
(Operations on Long Words)

Source	Destination										
	Dn	An	(An)	(An)+	−(An)	d(An)	d(An,Rx)	'$xxxx	$xxxxxxxx	d(PC)	d(PC,Rx)	#
Dn	8+2n 1/0										
An											
(An)											
(An)+											
−(An)											
d(An)											
d(An,Rx)											
$xxxx											
$xxxxxxxx											
d(PC)											
d(PC,Rx)											
#	8+2n 1/0										

Execution Times (Cycles):

(Case 2: The destination address is in memory.) (Operations on Words)

	Destination										
	Dn	An	(An)	(An)+	−(An)	d(An)	d(An,Rx)	$xxxx	$xxxxxxxx	d(PC)	d(PC,Rx)	#
			12 2/1	12 2/1	14 2/1	16 3/1	18 3/1	16 3/1	20 4/1			

Number of Bytes per Instruction for Different Addressing Modes:

Case 1: The destination address is a data register. Always 2 bytes, independent of the operand size.
Case 2: The destination address is in memory.

	Destination										
	Dn	An	(An)	(An)+	−(An)	d(An)	d(An,Rx)	$xxxx	$xxxxxxxx	d(PC)	d(PC,Rx)	#
			2	2	2	4	4	4	6			

Example:

Case 1: The destination address is a data register.

Before the operation:	Contents of		X N Z V C
	D0	= $xxxxxx88	Flags: 1 0 0 0 1
	ROR.B #2,D0		
After the operation:	Contents of		X N Z V C
	D0	= $xxxxxx22	Flags: 1 0 0 0 0

Case 2: The destination address is in memory. There are two different methods for rotating an operand by more than one bit position when the operand is in memory:

Method a: Using one rotation instruction per bit position.

ROL (A0)	12 clock cycles
ROL (A0)	12 clock cycles
.	
.	
.	
ROL (A0)	12 clock cycles
n times	12n clock cycles

Method b: Loading the operand into a data register, rotating the operand in the data register and writing the results back into memory.

MOVE.W (A0),D1	8 clock cycles
ROL.W #n,D1	6+2n clock cycles
MOVE.W D1,(A0)	8 clock cycles
	22 + 2n clock cycles

Comparing these two alternative methods, we find that the breakeven point is for n = 2.2. This means that method b is more efficient if the number of bit positions for the shift is greater than 2. The calculations are shown below:

12n	< 22 + 2n
10n	< 22
n	< 2.2

Applications:

You can use the ROd instructions in order to process the 3 most-significant bytes in a data register, using byte processing. The instruction ROL #8,Dn will bring the most-significant byte into the former position of the least-significant byte. With three such operations, you can bring any one of the 3 higher bytes into the bottom of the data register for byte processing.

ROXL,ROXR   Rotate Left or Right (with Extend)

Assembler Syntax:

ROXd.w Ds,Dd	
ROXd.w #Constant,Dd	(the first d is the direction, R or L)
ROXd <ea>	

Operation:

Case 1:	The destination address is a data register.
	The operand is rotated the number of bit positions specified at the source
	address → <Destination>
Case 2:	The destination address is in memory.
	The operand is rotated by one bit position and rewritten at the destination
	address.

Flag Changes:

X   Set equal to the same value as the last bit shifted out of the operand. If the operand is shifted by 0 bit positions (source address is a data register containing 0), then this flag will not be changed.

N   Set equal to 1 if the most-significant bit of the result is 1, otherwise reset to 0.

Z   Set equal to 1 if result equals 0, otherwise reset to 0.

V   Always reset to 0.

C   Set equal to the same value as the last bit shifted out of the operand. If the operand is shifted by 0 bit positions (source address is a data register containing 0), then this bit will be reset to 0.

Operand Sizes:

Case 1:   The destination address is a data register.
This instruction can operate on a byte, word or long words. The .X in the syntax refers to .B, .W or .L respectively.

Case 2:   The destination address is in memory.
This instruction can only operate on words.

Description of Instruction:

The ROXL and ROXR instructions rotate the operand. Each bit that leaves the operand in the given direction goes first into the X-flag, and the value that was in the X-flag goes back into the operand from the other direction. Each bit also goes into the C-flag so that the last bit will be left in both the X-flag and the C-flag. The difference between this pair of ROXL and ROXR instructions versus the pair of ROL and ROR instructions is that the X-flag serves as an intermediate buffer for 1 bit in the cyclical shifting. Depending upon where the destination address is located, there are two cases:

Case 1: The destination address is a data register. The size of the operand can be a byte, word, or long word. You can specify the number of bit positions for the rotation as a value at the source address, either immediately in the instruction or directly from a data register. If this value is specified immediately, then the number of bit positions for the rotation can range from 1 to 8. If this value is contained in a data register, then the number of bit positions for the rotation can range from 0 to 64 (modulus 64 if the data in the register is larger than 64).

Case 2: The destination address is in memory. The size of the operand can only be a word. This word word will be rotated 1 bit position in the specified direction.

There are also two cases, depending upon the direction of the rotation:

ROXL: The operand will be rotated by the given number of bit positions to the left. The bits that leave the operand at the left (most-significant bits) are fed into the C-flag and X-flag. The bits that were in the X-flag are fed back into the other end of the operand from the right (as least-significant bits).

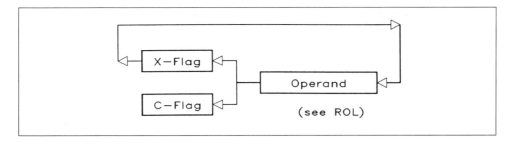

ROXR: The operand will be rotated by the given number of bit positions to the right. The bits that leave the operand at the right (least-significant bits) are fed into the C-flag and X-flag. The bits that were in the X-flag are fed back into the operand at the left (as most-significant bits). The last bit to leave the operand is also stored in the C-flag.

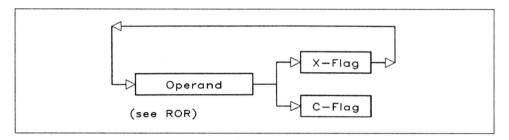

Format of Opcode:

Case 1: The destination is a data register.

15	14	13	12	11	10	9	8	7	6	5	4	3	2	1	0
1	1	1	0	Counter/Register			->Dir<-	Size		Imm/Reg	1	0	Register		

Bits 15–12. These bits indicate that this instruction belongs to the set of instructions {Shift, Rotate}. Other bits in the opcode select this particular instruction from this set.

Counter/Register, Bits 11–9. Depending upon the value of bit 5, this field contains either the counter (immediate constant) that defines the number of bit positions for the rotation (001 = 1, 010 = 2, ... 111 = 7, and 000 = 8) or the number of the data register that contains the number of bit positions (modulus 64).

Direction Bit 8. This bit specifies the direction of the rotation as follows:

0	–	to the right
1	–	to the left

Size Field, Bits 7–6. The size of the operand is stored in this field, defined as follows:

00	–	8-bit byte as operand
01	–	16-bit word as operand
10	–	32-bit long word as operand

Imm/Reg, Bit 5. This bit specifies whether bits 11–9 contain a counter (immediate value) for the shift or the number of a data register as follows:

0	–	counter (value from 1 to 8)
1	–	data register (the number of bit positions for the rotation will be read from this register with a modulus of 64)

Register, Bits 2–0. This field specifies the number of the data register that serves as the destination address.
Case 2: The destination address is in memory.

15	14	13	12	11	10	9	8	7	6	5	4	3	2	1	0
1	1	1	0	0	1	0	->Dir<-	1	1	Effective Address <ea>					
										Mode			Register		

Bits 15–12. These bits indicate that this instruction belongs to the set of instructions {shift, rotate}. Other bits in the opcode select this particular instruction from this set.

Bits 11–9. These bits select this particular instruction as a rotation instruction.

Direction, Bit 8. This bit specifies the direction of the rotation as follows:

```
0   –   to the right
1   –   to the left
```

Bits 7–6. These bits specify that the operand is in memory and that the size of the operand is word.

Effective Address, Bits 5–0. The effective address for the destination address is stored in this pair of fields, one for the mode and the other for the register. The interpretation for this pair of fields is given in the table below:

Effective Address <ea>		Mnemonic for Addressing Mode
Mode	**Register**	
*	*	Dn
*	*	An
010	Register Number n	(An)
011	Register Number n	(An)+
100	Register Number n	–(An)
101	Register Number n	d(An)
110	Register Number n	d(An,Rx)
111	000	$xxxx
111	001	$xxxxxxxx
*	*	d(PC)
*	*	d(PC,Rx)
*	*	#

* means that this addressing mode is not allowed

Execution Times (Cycles):

The first number is the number of clock cycles required to: get the operand, execute the instruction, store the results and get the next opcode. The next pair of numbers is for the number of read cycles and the number of write cycles respectively.

These values are only valid for the 68000 microprocessor. See the condensed tables in Chapter 8 for calculating times for the other microprocessors in the M68000 family.

Case 1: The destination address is a data register. (Operations on Bytes and Words)

Source	Destination											
	Dn	An	(An)	(An)+	–(An)	d(An)	d(An,Rx)	$xxxx	$xxxxxxxx	d(PC)	d(PC,Rx)	#
Dn	6+2n 1/0											
An												
(An)												
(An)+												
–(An)												
d(An)												
d(An,Rx)												
$xxxx												
$xxxxxxxx												
d(PC)												
d(PC,Rx)												
#	6+2n 1/0											

Execution Times (Cycles):

(Case 1) (Operations on Long Words)

Source	Destination											
	Dn	An	(An)	(An)+	–(An)	d(An)	d(An,Rx)	$xxxx	$xxxxxxxx	d(PC)	d(PC,Rx)	#
Dn	8+2n 1/0											
An												
(An)												
(An)+												
–(An)												
d(An)												
d(An,Rx)												
$xxxx												
$xxxxxxxx												
d(PC)												
d(PC,Rx)												
#	8+2n 1/0											

Execution Times (Cycles):

(Case 2: The destination address is in memory.) (Operations on Long Words)

	Destination											
	Dn	An	(An)	(An)+	–(An)	d(An)	d(An,Rx)	$xxxx	$xxxxxxxx	d(PC)	d(PC,Rx)	#
			12 2/1	12 2/1	14 2/1	16 3/1	18 3/1	16 3/1	20 4/1			

Number of Bytes per Instruction for Different Addressing Modes:

Case 1:	The destination address is a data register.
	Always 2 bytes, independent of the operand size.
Case 2:	The destination address is in memory.

	Destination											
	Dn	An	(An)	(An)+	–(An)	d(An)	d(An,Rx)	$xxxx	$xxxxxxxx	d(PC)	d(PC,Rx)	#
			2	2	2	4	4	4	6			

Example:

Case 1: The destination address is a data register.

Before the operation:	Contents of		X N Z V C
	D0 = $xxxxxx88	Flags:	1 0 0 0 1
	ROXR.B #2,D0		
After the operation:	Contents of		X N Z V C
	D0 = $xxxxxx62	Flags:	0 0 0 0 0

Case 2: The destination address is in memory. There are two different methods for rotating an operand by more than one bit position when the operand is in memory:

Method a: Using one rotation instruction per bit position.

ROXL (A0)	12 clock cycles
ROXL (A0)	12 clock cycles
.	
.	
.	
ROXL (A0)	12 clock cycles
n times	12n clock cycles

Method b: Loading the operand into a data register, rotating the operand in the data register, and writing the results back to memory.

MOVE.W (A0),D1	8 clock cycles
ROXL.W #n,D1	6+2n clock cycles
MOVE.W D1,(A0)	8 clock cycles
	22 + 2n clock cycles

Comparing these two alternative methods, we find that the breakeven point is for n = 2.2. This means that method b is more efficient if the number of bit positions for the shift is greater than 2. The calculations are shown below:

12n	< 22 + 2n
10n	< 22
n	< 2.2

Applications:

You can use the ROXd instructions in order to rotate numbers that have more than 32 bits.

This Instruction is Only Available for the 68010/12/20/30 Microprocessors

RTD   Return and Delete Temporary Parameters

Assembler Syntax:

RTD #Address Distance

Operation:

(SP)+   → <PC>
(SP)+ #Address Distance   → (SP)

Flag Changes:

None.

Operand Sizes:

This instruction operates on an address distance as an operand, and this operand can have a maximum of 16 bits.

Description of Instruction:

The RTD instruction returns control from a subroutine. It loads the program counter from the stack. Then, it expands the address distance to 32 bits, with the correct sign, and adds the result to the stack pointer. This creates a new stack pointer.

This instruction is only available for the 68010/12/20/30 microprocessors, but its functions can be duplicated with the following combinations of instructions of the 68000/08 microprocessors:

```
        MC68010                    M68000

        RTD # 12                   MOVE.L (A7)+,An
                                   LEA  12(A7),A7
                                   JMP (An)
```

Format of Opcode:

15	14	13	12	11	10	9	8	7	6	5	4	3	2	1	0
0	1	0	0	1	1	1	0	0	1	1	1	0	1	0	0

16-bit Address Distance

(The first word = $4E74)

Bits 15–12. These bits indicate that this instruction belongs to the set of instructions {RTS,SWAP, NOT,NEG,RTE,RTD}. Other bits in the opcode select this particular instruction from this set.
Bits 11–0. These bits select this particular instruction as the RTD instruction.

Addressing Modes that are Allowed:

Only the immediate mode is allowed.

Execution Times (cycles):

> 16 clock cycles
> 4 read cycles
> 0 write cycles

These values are only valid for the 68000 microprocessor. See the condensed tables in Chapter 8 for calculating times for the other microprocessors in the M68000 family.

Number of Bytes per Instruction for Different Addressing Modes:

> Always 4 bytes.

Applications:

If a subroutine stores temporary variables on the stack, then you must clear these temporary variables from the stack when the control returns from the subroutine. You must also reset the stack pointer to the value that it had just before calling the subroutine. By adding the appropriate address distance to the stack pointer, you can return the stack pointer to its original value and no longer have to worry about the temporary variables.

This Instruction is Modified for the 68010/12/20/30 Microprocessors
It is a Privileged Instruction!

RTE   Return from Exception Handling

Assembler Syntax:

> RTE

Operation:

> Case 1:   An M68000 microprocessor is in the supervisor mode.
>   It gets the SR and PC from the stack to continue where an interrupt occurred.
>   (A7)+   → <SR>
>   (A7)+   → <PC>
>   (A7)+   → Processor (only for 68010/12/20/30 microprocessors)
> Case 2:   An M68000 microprocessor is in the user mode.
>   → exception handling (violation of privilege)

Flag Changes:

This instruction loads the status register, containing the flags, from the stack and does not change them.

Operand Sizes:

This instruction does not use operands.

Description of Instruction:

The RTE instruction provides a return from routines for an interrupt, a trap or other exception-handling routine. It loads the status register, SR, and the program counter, PC, from the stack. This puts the microprocessor back into the same status that it was in before it was interrupted. The contents of the status register and the program counter at the end of this routine are lost. All of the bits in the status register are loaded, including the trace bit, supervisor bit, interrupt mask and flags.

The difference in this instruction for the 68010/12/20/30 microprocessors versus the 68000/08 microprocessors is that it reads an extra word with the 68010/12/20/30 microprocessors. The BERR signal of the 68010 microprocessor saves all of the internal information on the stack. All of the other exceptions of the 68010/12/20/30 microprocessors save only one extra word on the stack. This word contains information regarding whether more data is on the stack that must also be read.

The RTE instruction reads first the status register and then the program counter from the stack with both the 68010/12/20/30 microprocessors and the 68000/08 microprocessors. However, with the 68010/12/20/30 microprocessors, it continues and reads the next word from the stack for all situations except with a BERR signal. In the case of a BERR signal, it reads the next 25 words from the stack. The first word from the stack, after reading the status register and program counter, contains information on any other data that needs to be read. This word has the following format:

15	14	13	12	11	10	9	8	7	6	5	4	3	2	1	0
		Format		0	0					Vector Offset					

Format, Bits 15–12. Only two entries are allowed in this field as follows:

0000	– Short Format
	The instruction only needs to get 4 words from the stack (SR, PC and this extra word).
1000	– Long Format
	The instruction needs to get 29 words from the stack (SR, PC, this extra word and an additional 25 extra words. (These 25 extra words are loaded into the internal microcode register of a 68010/12/20/30 microprocessor.)

Any other entries in this field will lead to a format-error exception.

Vector Offset, Bits 9–0. This field contains the vector number for the exception that triggered this exceptionhandling.

The following flow chart shows how the RTE instuction works with the 68010/12/20/30 microprocessors:

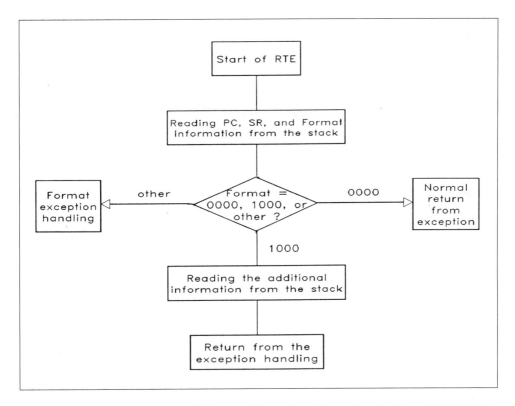

After a BERR exception, the previously-interruped bus cycle can be continued at the end of the RTE instruction. This can be a read or write access and even the beginning of a new instruction. These differences make a small difference in the times of execution for this instruction.

Format of Opcode:

15	14	13	12	11	10	9	8	7	6	5	4	3	2	1	0
0	1	0	0	1	1	1	0	0	1	1	1	0	0	1	1

(= $4E73)

Bits 15–12. These bits indicate that this instruction belongs to the set of instructions {RTS,SWAP, NOT,NEG,RTE}. Other bits in the opcode select this particular instruction from this set.
Bits 11–0. These bits select this particular instruction as the RTE instruction.

Addressing Modes that are Allowed:

None, since the RTE instruction does not use operands.

Execution Times (Cycles):

The first number is the number of clock cycles required to: get the operands, execute the instruction, store the results and get the next opcode. The next pair of numbers is for the number of read cycles and the number of write cycles respectively.

These values are only valid for the 68000 microprocessor. See the condensed tables in Chapter 8 for calculating times for the other microprocessors in the M68000 family.

68000/08	68010/12/20/30
20 5/0	
Short Format	24
	6/0
Long Format	112
(Continue interrupted read cycle)	27/0
Long Format	112
(Continue interrupted write cycle)	26/1
Long Format	110
(Without continuing interrupted cycle)	26/0

Number of Bytes per Instruction for Different Addressing Modes:

Always 2 bytes.

Example (for a 68000/08 microprocessor): Before the operation:

```
Before the operation:
    Contents of PC = $xxxxxxxx        A7 ──────▷   0405    SR
                SR = $xxxx                         0012    PC
                                                   ABCE    PC
```

RTE: After the operation:

```
After the operation:
    Contents of PC = $0012ABCE                     0405    SR
                SR = $0405                         0012    PC
                                                   ABCE    PC
                                      A7 ──────▷
```

Applications:

You can use the RTE instruction to return from all types of exception-handling with a 68000/08 microprocessor.

You can use the RTE instruction to return from all types of exception-handling, in particular from the BERR signal, with a 68010/10/20/30 microprocessor. Together with the special feature for saving the internal information of the 68010/12/20/30 microprocessors, the RTE instruction allows the 68010/12/20/30 microprocessors to work with virtual memory.

RTR   Return and Restore Flags

Assembler Syntax:

RTR

Operation:

Restore contents of PC and CCR from the stack
(A7)+ → <CCR>
(A7)+ → <PC>

Flag Changes:

This instruction loads the condition-code register, containing the flags, from the stack and does not change them.

Operand Sizes:

This instruction does not use operands.

Description of Instruction:

The RTR instruction provides a return from routines for an interrupt, a trap or other exception-handling routine, as well as from a normal subroutine. It loads the condition-code register, CCR, and the program counter, PC, from the stack. This allows you to continue a user program or user subroutine in the supervisor mode. The operating system must carefully monitor such a possibility.

In a return from a subroutine, not only the program counter, but also the flags are reset from the stack. Of course, you must have saved the condition-code register on the stack before starting the subroutine. With the RTE instruction, you can save the MOVE instruction at the end of the subroutine that would have been necessary to restore the condition-code register.

The contents of the condition-code register and the program counter at the end of this routine are lost.

Format of Opcode:

15	14	13	12	11	10	9	8	7	6	5	4	3	2	1	0
0	1	0	0	1	1	1	0	0	1	1	1	0	1	1	1

= $4E77

Bits 15–12. These bits indicate that this instruction belongs to the set of instructions {RTS,SWAP, NOT,NEG,RTR}. Other bits in the opcode select this particular instruction from this set.
Bits 11–0. These bits select this particular instruction as the RTR instruction.

Addressing Modes that are Allowed:

None, since the RTR instruction does not use operands.

Execution Times (Cycles):

20 clock cycles (for executing the operations)
5 read cycles
0 write cycles

(These values are only valid for the 68000 microprocessor. See the condensed tables in Chapter 8 for calculating times for the other microprocessors in the M68000 family.)

Number of Bytes per Instruction:

Always 2 bytes.

Example (for a 68000/08 microprocessor): Before the operation:

```
Before the operation:
    Contents of PC = $xxxxxxxx     A7 ──────▷│  xx05  │  CCR
                CCR = X N Z V C              │  0012  │  PC
             (Flags) = x x x x x             │  ABCE  │  PC
```

RTR: After the operation:

```
After the operation:
    Contents of PC = $0012ABCE              │  xx05  │  CCR
                CCR = X N Z V C              │  0012  │  PC
             (Flags) = 0 0 1 0 1            │  ABCE  │  PC
                                 A7 ──────▷│
```

Applications:

You can use the RTR instruction to return from all types of exception handling with a 68000/08 microprocessor, except for returning to the user mode.

A major use for the RTR is to return from subroutines since it saves programming effort.

RTS   Return from Subroutine

Assembler Syntax:

RTS

Operation:

Restore contents of PC from the stack
$(A7)+ \rightarrow <PC>$

Flag Changes:

None.

Operand Sizes:

This instruction does not use operands.

Description of Instruction:

The RTS instruction provides a return from a routine. It loads the program counter, PC, from the stack. The contents of the program counter at the end of the subroutine are overwritten and lost. This allows the program to continue from the next instruction after the instruction that called the subroutine–if the address for the next instruction is on the top of the stack. The BSR and JSR instructions automatically store the address of the next instruction on the stack before branching or jumping to the beginning of a subroutine.

Format of Opcode:

15	14	13	12	11	10	9	8	7	6	5	4	3	2	1	0
0	1	0	0	1	1	1	0	0	1	1	1	0	1	0	1

= $4E75

Bits 15–12. These bits indicate that this instruction belongs to the set of instructions {RTS,SWAP, NOT,NEG,RTS}. Other bits in the opcode select this particular instruction from this set.
Bits 11–0. These bits select this particular instruction as the RTS instruction.

Addressing Modes that are Allowed:

None, since the RTS instruction does not use operands.

Execution Times (Cycles):

16 clock cycles (for executing the operations)
4 read cycles
0 write cycles

(These values are only valid for the 68000 microprocessor. See the condensed tables in Chapter 8 for calculating times for the other microprocessors in the M68000 family.)

Number of Bytes per Instruction:

Always 2 bytes.

Example (for a 68000/08 microprocessor): Before the operation:

```
Before the operation:
    Contents of PC = $xxxxxxxx      A7 ──▷   0012      PC
                                             ABCE      PC
```

RTS: After the operation:

```
After the operation:
    Contents of PC = $0012ABCE               0012      PCR
                                             ABCE      PC
                                    A7 ──▷
```

Applications:

You can use the RTS instruction to return from a subroutine. It does not give you the convenience of the RTR instruction since you must reset the flags yourself with the RTS instruction.

SBCD   Subtraction of BCD Numbers

Assembler Syntax:

SBCD Ds,Dd
SBCD –(As),–(Ad)

Operation:

$< Destination > – (< Source > + \text{X-flag}) \rightarrow < Destination >$

Flag Changes:

X   Set the same as the C-flag.
N   Undefined after the operation.
Z   Set equal to 0 if result not equal 0, otherwise unchanged.
V   Undefined after the operation.
C   Set equal to 1 if a decimal "borrow" occurs, otherwise set to 0.

It is advisable to set the Z-flag equal to 1 before this instruction so that you can later check for a result of 0.

Operand Sizes:

This instruction operates on bytes. Therefore, there is no .w in the syntax.

Description of Instruction:

The SBCD instruction subtracts a first operand (at the source address) from a second operand (at the destination address). It writes the result back into the destination address. It uses the X-flag to take any previous "borrow" into account. Therefore, you can use this instruction to subtract numbers with more than two digits.

This instruction operates upon bytes and therefore upon pairs of BCD digits since each byte contains two BCD digits. You can use the subroutine in the example below to subtract numbers with more than two digits.

Format of Opcode:

15	14	13	12	11	10	9	8	7	6	5	4	3	2	1	0
1	0	0	0	Register Rx			1	0	0	0	0	R/M	Register Ry		

Bits 15–12. These bits indicate that this instruction belongs to the set of instructions {OR,DIV, SBCD}. Other bits in the opcode select this particular instruction from this set.

Register Field Rd, Bits 11–9. Depending upon the contents of the R/M field, this field contains the number of either the destination data register that contains the second operand (R/M = 0) or the address register for the address-register indirect-addressing mode, with predecrement (R/M = 1).

Bits 8–4. These bits select this particular instruction as the SBCD instruction.

R/M Field, Bit 3. This field determines whether the registers Rs and Rd are data registers for the data-register direct-addressing mode (R/M = 0) or address registers for the address-register indirect-addressing mode, with predecrement (R/M = 1).

Register Field Rs, Bits 2–0. Depending upon the contents of the R/M field, this field contains the number of either the source data register that contains the first operand (R/M = 0) or the address register for the address-register indirect-addressing mode, with predecrement (R/M = 1).

Execution Times (Cycles):

The first number is the number of clock cycles required to: get the operands, execute the instruction, store the results and get the next opcode. The next pair of numbers is for the number of read cycles and the number of write cycles respectively.

These values are only valid for the 68000 microprocessor. See the condensed tables in Chapter 8 for calculating times for the other microprocessors in the M68000 family.

Source	Destination											
	Dn	An	(An)	(An)+	–(An)	d(An)	d(An,Rx)	$xxxx	$xxxxxxxx	d(PC)	d(PC,Rx)	#
Dn	6 1/0											
An												
(An)												
(An)+												
–(An)					18 3/1							
d(An)												
d(An,Rx)												
$xxxx												
$xxxxxxxx												
d(PC)												
d(PC,Rx)												
#												

Number of Bytes per Instruction for Different Addressing Modes:

Source	Destination											
	Dn	An	(An)	(An)+	–(An)	d(An)	d(An,Rx)	$xxxx	$xxxxxxxx	d(PC)	d(PC,Rx)	#
Dn	2											
An												
(An)												
(An)+												
–(An)					2							
d(An)												
d(An,Rx)												
$xxxx												
$xxxxxxxx												
d(PC)												
d(PC,Rx)												
#												

Example:

Subtracting BCD numbers with more than two digits in memory.

1st number	= 504345	(from destination address)
2nd number	= 225713	(from source address)

Before the operation:		Contents of memory:	
1st number		2nd number	
Address	Contents	Address	Contents
$1007	45	$2007	13
$1006	43	$2006	57
$1005	50	$2005	22

MOVE #4,CCR	Clear the X-flag, to prevent a false borrow, and set the Z-flag, to determine whether the result is null.
MOVE #$1008,A	Load the address registers with starting
MOVE #$2008,A0	values.
SBCD –(A0),–(A1)	Subtract the least-significant two digits.
SBCD –(A0),–(A1)	Subtract the middle pair of digits.
SBCD –(A0),–(A1)	Subtract the most-significant two digits.

After the operation:		Contents of memory:	
1st number		2nd number	
Address	Contents	Address	Contents
$1007	32	$2007	13
$1006	86	$2006	57
$1005	27	$2005	22

Applications:

If the system uses BCD displays for the results, it is often convenient to perform the arithmetic with BCD numbers. The SBCD instruction performs subtraction, just as the ABCD instruction performs addition.

Scc   Set or Clear a Byte Conditionally

Assembler Syntax:

Scc <ea>

Operation:

If cc = true	then 11111111	→ <Destination>
If cc = false	then 00000000	→ <Destination>

Flag Changes:

None, since this instruction merely reads the flags.

Operand Sizes:

This instruction operates only on bytes. Therefore, there is no .w in the syntax.

Description of Instruction:

The Scc instruction will either set all bits in the specified byte equal to ones or will reset all bits equal to nulls, depending upon whether the condition is true or false.

The conditions cc that you can use with this instruction are listed in the following table:

Mnemonic	Meaning	Flags that are queried
CC	Carry flag = 0?	$C = 0$
CS	Carry flag = 1?	$C = 1$
EQ	Equal (Z-flag = 1)?	$Z = 1$
F	False, never satisfied	0
GE*	Greater than or equal to?	$N\char94 V v N\char94 V = 1$
GT*	Greater than?	$N\char94 V\char94 Z v N\char94 V\char94 Z = 1$
HI	Higher?	$C\char94 Z = 1$
LE*	Less than or equal to?	$Z v N\char94 V v N\char94 V = 1$
LS	Lower or identical?	$C v Z = 1$
LT*	Less than?	$N\char94 V v N\char94 V = 1$
MI	Negative?	$N = 1$
NE	Not equal (Z-flag = 0)?	$Z = 0$
PL	Positive?	$N = 0$
T	True, always satisfied	1
VC*	No overflow (V-flag = 0)?	$V = 0$
VS*	Overflow (V-flag = 1)?	$V = 1$

* = These conditions use two's-complement arithmetic

Format of Opcode:

15	14	13	12	11	10	9	8	7	6	5	4	3	2	1	0
											Effective Address <ea>				
0	1	0	1		Condition			1	1	Mode			Register		

Bits 15–12. These bits indicate that this instruction belongs to the set of instructions {ADDQ,SUBQ, Scc,DBcc}. Other bits in the opcode select this particular instruction from this set.

Condition, Bits 11–8. This field specifies which condition cc is used, as defined by the bit patterns shown in the figure above.

Condition	Bit pattern for Bits 11–8
CC	0100
CS	0101
EQ	0111
F	0001
GE	1100
GT	1110
HI	0010
LE	1111
LS	0011
LT	1101
MI	1011
NE	0110
PL	1010
T	0000
VC	1000
VS	1001

Effective Address, Bits 5–0. The effective address is stored in this pair of fields, one for the mode and the other for the register. The interpretation for this pair of fields is given in the table below:

Effective Address <ea>		Mnemonic for Addressing Mode
Mode	Register	
000	Register Number n	Dn
*	*	An
010	Register Number n	(An)
011	Register Number n	(An)+
100	Register Number n	−(An)
101	Register Number n	d(An)
110	Register Number n	d(An,Rx)
111	000	$xxxx
111	001	$xxxxxxxx
*	*	d(PC)
*	*	d(PC,Rx)
*	*	#

* means that this addressing mode is not allowed

Execution Times (cycles): (Operations on Bytes)

The first number is the number of clock cycles required to: get the operand, execute the instruction, store the results and get the next opcode. The next pair of numbers is for the number of read cycles and the number of write cycles respectively.

These values are only valid for the 68000 microprocessor. See the condensed tables in Chapter 8 for calculating times for the other microprocessors in the M68000 family.

	Destination											
	Dn	An	(An)	(An)+	–(An)	d(An)	d(An,Rx)	$xxxx	$xxxxxxxx	d(PC)	d(PC,Rx)	#
cc = true	6 1/0		12 2/1	12 2/1	14 2/1	16 3/1	18 3/1	16 3/1	20 4/1			
cc = false	4 1/0		12 2/1	12 2/1	14 2/1	16 3/1	18 3/1	16 3/1	20 4/1			

Number of Bytes per Instruction for Different Addressing Modes:

(Operations on Bytes)

	Destination											
	Dn	An	(An)	(An)+	–(An)	d(An)	d(An,Rx)	$xxxx	$xxxxxxxx	d(PC)	d(PC,Rx)	#
	2		2	2	2	4	4	4	6			

Example:

```
CLR.W D0
CLR.W D1
CMP.W D0,D1       Z-flag set = 1, since <D0> = <D1>.
SEQ D2            Lower byte of D2 set = $FF, since <Z-flag> = 1.
ADDQ.W #1,D0
CMP.W D0,D1       Z-flag set = 0, since <D0> = 1 and <D1> = 0.
SEQ D2            Lower byte of D2 reset = $00, since <Z-flag> = 0.
```

Applications:

You can use the Scc instruction to save the contents of flags after a given instruction for later use. Then, you can determine later whether particular flags were set earlier in the program.

If you use the NEG instruction after the Scc instruction, it will change the contents of the byte from either $00 or $FF into either 1 or 0.

This is a Privileged Instruction!

STOP   Load the Status Register and Stop

Assembler Syntax:

```
STOP #Constant
```

Operation:

Case 1:	An M68000 microprocessor is in the supervisor mode.
	#Constant → <SR>. The microprocessor stops.
Case 2:	An M68000 microprocessor is in the user mode.
	→ exception-handling (violation of privilege)

Flag Changes:

X	Set equal to bit 4 of the constant.
N	Set equal to bit 3 of the constant.
Z	Set equal to bit 2 of the constant.
V	Set equal to bit 1 of the constant.
C	Set equal to bit 0 of the constant.

Operand Sizes:

The constant must be a 16-bit word since the status register is 16 bits wide.

Description of Instruction:

Assuming that an M68000 microprocessor is in the supervisor mode, the STOP instruction will copy the constant from the instruction into the status register. This will overwrite any contents of the status register, including the trace bit, interrupt mask, supervisor bit and the flags. Then, it increments the program counter to point to the next instruction, and it stops the microprocessor.

An M68000 microprocessor will not start executing again until one of the following conditions is met:

1 If the STOP instruction is executed while the trace bit is set, then the microprocessor will proceed to trace-exception handling.

2 If an interrupt arrives that has a higher priority than the value set in the interrupt mask by the constant of the STOP instruction, then the interrupt will be serviced. If the priority is lower, then nothing will happen.

3 The user resets the microprocessor. A reset has a higher priority than anything else that can occur in the microprocessor.

Since the STOP instruction is a privileged instruction, bit 13 (for the supervisor status) must be set equal to 1 at the time when the STOP instruction is executed and the constant in the instruction must reset it equal to 1. Otherwise, a violation of the privilege status occurs and exception-handling is initiated.

Format of Opcode:

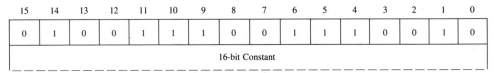

15	14	13	12	11	10	9	8	7	6	5	4	3	2	1	0
0	1	0	0	1	1	1	0	0	1	1	1	0	0	1	0

16-bit Constant

(1st word = $4E72)

Bits 15–12. These bits indicate that this instruction belongs to the set of instructions {SWAP,NOT, NEG,STOP,etc.}. Other bits in the opcode select this particular instruction from this set.

Bits 11–0. These bits select this particular instruction as the STOP instruction.

The next 16-bit word after the opcode contains the constant that will be copied into the status register.

Addressing Modes that are Allowed:

None, since it does not use operands other than the constant.

Execution Times (Cycles):

4 clock cycles

(This value is only valid for the 68000 microprocessor. See the condensed tables in Chapter 8 for calculating times for the other microprocessors in the M68000 family.)

Number of Bytes per Instruction for Different Addressing Modes:

Always 4 bytes.

Example:

Before the operation:

	15	14	13	12	11	10	9	8	7	6	5	4	3	2	1	0
Status Register =	T		S			12	11	10				X	N	Z	V	C
	0		1			0	0	0				1	0	0	0	0

STOP #$FFFF

After the operation:

	15	14	13	12	11	10	9	8	7	6	5	4	3	2	1	0
Status Register =	T		S			12	11	10				X	N	Z	V	C
	1		1			1	1	1				1	1	1	1	1

Applications:

There are many possible end points in an operating system that an M68000 microprocessor could reach with a STOP instruction. This is particularly the case when a catastrophic error occurs that the operating system can not repair. By coding a number into the constant that is used in different STOP instructions in an operating system, you can later read the status register, determine this number and thereby determine which STOP instruction stopped the microprocessor.

SUB   Binary Subtraction, Without Extend (for Borrow)

Assembler Syntax:

SUB.w <ea>,Dd
SUB.w Ds,<ea>

Operation:

<Destination> – <Source> → <Destination>

Flag Changes:

X	Set equal to 1 if a "borrow" occurs, otherwise reset to 0.
N	Set equal to 1 if result is negative, otherwise reset to 0.
Z	Set equal to 1 if result equals 0, otherwise reset to 0.
V	Set equal to 1 if an overflow occurs, otherwise reset to 0.
C	Set equal to 1 if a "borrow" occurs, otherwise reset to 0.

Operand Sizes:

This instruction can operate on bytes, words or long words. The .w in the syntax refers to .B, .W or .L respectively.

Description of Instruction:

The SUB instruction subtracts a first operand (at the source address) from a second operand (at the destination address). It writes the results back into the destination address. This instruction does not take any previous borrow into account. If you need to subtract numbers with more than 32 bits, you must use the SUBX instruction to take the borrow from a less-significant operation into account in the next more significant operation. Either the source address or the destination address must be a data register.

Format of Opcode:

15	14	13	12	11	10	9	8	7	6	5	4	3	2	1	0
1	0	0	1		Register			Opmode			Effective Address <ea>				
											Mode			Register	

Bits 15–12. These bits indicate that this instruction belongs to the set of instructions {SUB,SUBX}. Other bits in the opcode select this particular instruction from this set.

Register, Bits 11–9. This field specifies the data register that is used either as the source register or the destination register by this instruction.

Opmode, Bits 8–6. Bit 8 of this field determines whether the data register specified in bits 11–9 is used for the source address (this bit = 1) or for the destination address (this bit = 0). The other two bits define the size of the operands as follows:

00	–	8-bit bytes as operands
01	–	16-bit words as operands
11	–	32-bit long words as operands

Effective Address, Bits 5–0. The effective address is stored in this pair of fields, one for the mode and the other for the register. The interpretation for this pair of fields is different, depending upon whether it defines the source address or the destination address, as given in the two tables below:

Case 1: The effective address defines the source address:

Effective Address <ea>		Mnemonic for Addressing Mode
Mode	Register	
000	Register Number n	Dn
001	Register Number n	An
010	Register Number n	(An)
011	Register Number n	(An)+
100	Register Number n	–(An)
101	Register Number n	d(An)
110	Register Number n	d(An.Rx)
111	000	$xxxx
111	001	$xxxxxxxx
111	010	d(PC)
111	011	d(PC.Rx)
111	100	#

For the address-register direct-addressing mode, An, only words and long words are allowed since processing of bytes in address registers is not allowed.

Case 2: The effective address defines the destination address:

Effective Address <ea>		Mnemonic for Addressing Mode
Mode	Register	
*	*	Dn
*	*	An
010	Register Number n	(An)
011	Register Number n	(An)+
100	Register Number n	−(An)
101	Register Number n	d(An)
110	Register Number n	d(An,Rx)
111	000	$xxxx
111	001	$xxxxxxxx
*	*	d(PC)
*	*	d(PC,Rx)
*	*	#

* means that this addressing mode is not allowed

For the case of an address register as the destination address, there is a special mnemonic, SUBA, that is described as the next instruction below.

Execution Times (Cycles): (Operations on Bytes and Words)

The first number is the number of clock cycles required to: get the operands, execute the instruction, store the results and get the next opcode. The next pair of numbers is for the number of read cycles and the number of write cycles respectively.

These values are only valid for the 68000 microprocessor. See the condensed tables in Chapter 8 for calculating times for the other microprocessors in the M68000 family.

Source	Destination											
	Dn	An	(An)	(An)+	−(An)	d(An)	d(An,Rx)	$xxxx	$xxxxxxxx	d(PC)	d(PC,Rx)	#
Dn	4 1/0		12 2/1	12 2/1	14 2/1	16 3/1	18 3/1	16 3/1	20 4/1			
An	4 1/0											
(An)	8 2/0											
(An)+	8 2/0											
−(An)	10 2/0											
d(An)	12 3/0											
d(An,Rx)	14 3/0											
$xxxx	12 3/0											
$xxxxxxxx	16 4/0											
d(PC)	12 3/0											
d(PC,Rx)	14 3/0											
#	8 2/0											

Execution Times (cycles): (Operations on Long Words)

The first number is the number of clock cycles required to: get the operands, execute the instruction, store the results and get the next opcode. The next pair of numbers is for the number of read cycles and the number of write cycles respectively.

These values are only valid for the 68000 microprocessor. See the condensed tables in Chapter 8 for calculating times for the other microprocessors in the M68000 family.

Source	Destination										
	Dn	An	(An)	(An)+	–(An)	d(An)	d(An,Rx)	$xxxx	$xxxxxxxx d(PC)	d(PC,Rx)	#
Dn	6 1/0		20 3/2	20 3/2	22 3/2	24 4/2	26 4/2	24 4/2	28 5/2		
An	8 1/0										
(An)	14 3/0										
(An)+	14 3/0										
–(An)	16 3/0										
d(An)	18 4/0										
d(An,Rx)	20 4/0										
$xxxx	18 4/0										
$xxxxxxxx	22 5/0										
d(PC)	18 4/0										
d(PC,Rx)	20 4/0										
#	14 3/0										

Number of Bytes per Instruction for Different Addressing Modes:

(Operations on Bytes and Words)

Source	Destination										
	Dn	An	(An)	(An)+	–(An)	d(An)	d(An,Rx)	$xxxx	$xxxxxxxx d(PC)	d(PC,Rx)	#
D	2		2	2	2	4	4	4	6		
An	2										
(An)	2										
(An)+	2										
–(An)	2										
d(An)	4										
d(An,Rx)	4										
$xxxx	4										
$xxxxxxxx	6										
d(PC)	4										
d(PC,Rx)	4										
#	4										

Number of Bytes per Instruction for Different Addressing Modes:

(Operations on Long Words)

Source	Destination										
	Dn	An	(An)	(An)+	–(An)	d(An)	d(An,Rx)	$xxxx	$xxxxxxxx d(PC)	d(PC,Rx)	#
D	2		2	2	2	4	4	4	6		
An	2										
(An)	2										
(An)+	2										
–(An)	2										
d(An)	4										
d(An,Rx)	4										
$xxxx	4										
$xxxxxxxx	6										
d(PC)	4										
d(PC,Rx)	4										
#	6										

Examples:

1. Subtraction of byte operands

Before the operation:	Contents of	D1	= $xxxxxx53
		D2	= $xxxxxx23
SUB.B D3,D1		Subtraction of <D1>-<D3> → <D1>	
After the operation:	Contents of	D1	= $xxxxxx30 X N Z V C
		Flags	= 0 0 0 0 0

2. Subtraction of word operands

Before the operation:	Contents of	D1	= $xxxx1234
		$1000	= $1111
SUB.W $1000,D1		Subtraction of <D1>-<$1000> → <D1>	
After the operation:	Contents of	D1	= $xxxx0123 X N Z V C
		Flags	= 0 0 0 0 0

3. Subtraction of long-word operands

Before the operation:	Contents of	D1	= $33333333
		$1000	= $11111111
SUB.L $1000,D1		Subtraction of <D1>-<$1000> → <D1>	
After the operation:	Contents of	D1	= $22222222 X N Z V C
		Flags	= 0 0 0 0 0

Applications:

You can use the SUB instruction for subtracting binary numbers that are up to 32 bits long. For longer numbers, you will need to use the SUBX instruction that also takes the borrow from a previous operation into account.

SUBA   Binary Subtraction with Address Register as Destination

Assembler Syntax:

SUBA.w <ea>,Ad

Operation:

<Ad>-<Source> → <Ad>

Flag Changes:

None.

Operand Sizes:

This instruction can operate only on words or long words since only words and long words can be processed in address registers. The .w in the syntax refers to only .W or .L respectively.

Description of Instruction:

The SUBA instruction subtracts the first operand from the operand in a destination address register. This instruction does not take any previous borrow into account. The SUBA instruction is a mnemonic extension to the SUB instruction for the special case using an address register as the destination address. For most compilers, it does not matter whether you use SUB < ea >,Ad or SUBA < ea >,Ad in your program. Both will generate the same opcode.

Format of Opcode:

15	14	13	12	11	10	9	8	7	6	5	4	3	2	1	0
										Effective Address <ea>					
1	0	0	1	Register			Opmode			Mode			Register		

Bits 15–12. These bits indicate that this instruction belongs to the set of instructions {SUB,SUBX}. Other bits in the opcode select this particular instruction from this set.

Register, Bits 11–9. This field specifies the address register that this instruction uses as the destination address.

Opmode, Bits 8–6. This field determines the size of the first operand as follows:

011	– 16-bit word as first operand
111	– 32-bit long word as first operand

In the case of a 16-bit word as the first operand, this instruction will first expand the 16-bit operand to 32 bits, with the correct sign, and then use the full 32-bit long word as the first operand.

Effective Address, Bits 5–0. The effective address for the source address (first operand) is stored in this pair of fields, one for the mode and the other for the register. It applies only to the source operand, as explained in the table below:

Effective Address <ea>		Mnemonic for Addressing Mode
Mode	**Register**	
000	Register Number n	Dn
001	Register Number n	An
010	Register Number n	(An)
011	Register Number n	(An)+
100	Register Number n	–(An)
101	Register Number n	d(An)
110	Register Number n	d(An,Rx)
111	000	$xxxx
111	001	$xxxxxxxx
111	010	d(PC)
111	011	d(PC,Rx)
111	100	#

Execution Times (cycles): (Operations on Words)

The first number is the number of clock cycles required to: get the operands, execute the instruction, store the results and get the next opcode. The next pair of numbers is for the number of read cycles and the number of write cycles respectively.

These values are only valid for the 68000 microprocessor. See the condensed tables in Chapter 8 for calculating times for the other microprocessors in the M68000 family.

Source	Destination											
	Dn	An	(An)	(An)+	–(An)	d(An)	d(An,Rx)	$xxxx	$xxxxxxxx	d(PC)	d(PC,Rx)	#
Dn	8 1/0											
An	8 1/0											
(An)	12 2/0											
(An)+	12 2/0											
–(An)	14 2/0											
d(An)	16 3/0											
d(An,Rx)	18 3/0											
$xxxx	16 3/0											
$xxxxxxxx	20 4/0											
d(PC)	16 3/0											
d(PC,Rx)	18 3/0											
#	12 2/0											

Execution Times (Cycles): (Operations on Long Words)

The first number is the number of clock cycles required to: get the operands, execute the instruction, store the results and get the next opcode. The next pair of numbers is for the number of read cycles and the number of write cycles respectively.

These values are only valid for the 68000 microprocessor. See the condensed tables in Chapter 8 for calculating times for the other microprocessors in the M68000 family.

Source	Destination											
	Dn	An	(An)	(An)+	−(An)	d(An)	d(An,Rx)	$xxxx	$xxxxxxxx	d(PC)	d(PC,Rx)	#
Dn		8 1/0										
An		8 1/0										
(An)		14 3/0										
(An)+		14 3/0										
−(An)		16 3/0										
d(An)		18 4/0										
d(An,Rx)		20 4/0										
$xxxx		18 4/0										
$xxxxxxxx		22 5/0										
d(PC)		20 4/0										
d(PC,Rx)		20 4/0										
#		14 3/0										

Number of Bytes per Instruction for Different Addressing Modes:

(Operations on Words)

Source	Destination											
	Dn	An	(An)	(An)+	−(An)	d(An)	d(An,Rx)	$xxxx	$xxxxxxxx	d(PC)	d(PC,Rx)	#
D		2										
An		2										
(An)		2										
(An)+		2										
−(An)		2										
d(An)		4										
d(An,Rx)		4										
$xxxx		4										
$xxxxxxxx		6										
d(PC)		4										
d(PC,Rx)		4										
#		4										

Number of Bytes per Instruction for Different Addressing Modes:

(Operations on Long Words)

Source	Destination											
	Dn	An	(An)	(An)+	−(An)	d(An)	d(An,Rx)	$xxxx	$xxxxxxxx	d(PC)	d(PC,Rx)	#
D		2										
An		2										
(An)		2										
(An)+		2										
−(An)		2										
d(An)		4										
d(An,Rx)		4										
$xxxx		4										
$xxxxxxxx		6										
d(PC)		4										
d(PC,Rx)		4										
#		6										

Examples:

1. Subtraction of words as operands

Before the operation:	Contents of	A1	=	$00001234
		~ <source>	=	$ 1111
SUBA.W #$1000,A1			Subtraction of <A1>-$1111 → <A1>	
After the operation:	Contents of	A1	=	$00000123
		Flags	=	unchanged

2. Subtraction of long-word operands

Before the operation:	Contents of	A1	=	$12345678
		$1000	=	$11111111
SUBA.L #$11111111,A1			Subtraction: <A1>-$11111111 → <A1>	
After the operation:	Contents of	A1	=	$01234567
		Flags	=	unchanged

Applications:

You can use the SUB instruction for subtracting binary numbers that are up to 32 bits long, particularly for calculating addresses. After calculating the address, you can access the desired operand using the address-register indirect-addressing mode.

SUB   Binary Subtraction, Immediate (with a Constant as Source)

Assembler Syntax:

SUBI.w #Constant, <ea>

Operation:

<Destination> - #Constant → <Destination>

Flag Changes:

X   Set equal to 1 if a "borrow" occurs, otherwise reset to 0.
N   Set equal to 1 if result is negative, otherwise reset to 0.
Z   Set equal to 1 if result equals 0, otherwise reset to 0.
V   Set equal to 1 if an overflow occurs, otherwise reset to 0.
C   Set equal to 1 if a "borrow" occurs, otherwise reset to 0.

Operand Sizes:

This instruction can operate on bytes, words or long words. The .w in the syntax refers to .B, .W or .L respectively.

Description of Instruction:

The SUBI instruction subtracts an immediate constant of an operand from a destination address. This instruction does not take any previous borrow into account. If you need to subtract numbers with more than 32 bits, you must use the SUBX instruction to take the borrow from a less-significant operation into account in the next more-significant operation.

Format of Opcode:

15	14	13	12	11	10	9	8	7	6	5	4	3	2	1	0
										Effective Address <ea>					
0	0	0	0	0	1	0	0	Size		Mode			Register		
								8-bit Constant							
16-bit Constant															
32-bit Constant (including the previous 16-bit word)															

Bits 15–12. These bits indicate that this instruction belongs to the set of instructions {Bit manipulation,MOVEP,Immediate}. Other bits in the opcode select this particular instruction from this set.

Bits 11–8. These bits select this particular instruction as the SUBI instruction.

Size, Bits 7–6. This field defines the size of the operands as follows:

00	–	8-bit bytes as operands
01	–	16-bit words as operands
11	–	32-bit long words as operands

Effective Address, Bits 5–0. The effective address for the operand at the destination address is stored in this pair of fields, one for the mode and the other for the register.

Effective Address <ea>		Mnemonic for Addressing Mode
Mode	**Register**	
000	Register Number n	Dn
*	*	An
010	Register Number n	(An)
011	Register Number n	(An)+
100	Register Number n	–(An)
101	Register Number n	d(An)
110	Register Number n	d(An,Rx)
111	000	$xxxx
111	001	$xxxxxxxx
*	*	d(PC)
*	*	d(PC,Rx)
*	*	#

* means that this addressing mode is not allowed

When the operands have the size of bytes, one 16-bit word follows the opcode, containing the byte used as the constant in its least-significant half. If the size is words, then one word follows the opcode, containing the word used as the constant. If the size is long words, then two words follow the opcode, containing the two halves of the 32-bit constant.

Execution Times (Cycles): (Operations on Bytes and Words)

The first number is the number of clock cycles required to: get the operands, execute the instruction, store the results and get the next opcode. The next pair of numbers is for the number of read cycles and the number of write cycles respectively.

These values are only valid for the 68000 microprocessor. See the condensed tables in Chapter 8 for calculating times for the other microprocessors in the M68000 family.

Source	Destination											
	Dn	An	(An)	(An)+	−(An)	d(An)	d(An,Rx)	$xxxx	$xxxxxxxx	d(PC)	d(PC,Rx)	#
Dn												
An												
(An)												
(An)+												
−(An)												
d(An)												
d(An,Rx)												
$xxxx												
$xxxxxxxx												
d(PC)												
d(PC,Rx)												
#	8 2/0		16 3/1	16 3/1	18 3/1	20 4/1	22 4/1	20 4/1	24 5/1			

Execution Times (Cycles): (Operations on Long Words)

The first number is the number of clock cycles required to: get the operands, execute the instruction, store the results and get the next opcode. The next pair of numbers is for the number of read cycles and the number of write cycles respectively.

These values are only valid for the 68000 microprocessor. See the condensed tables in Chapter 8 for calculating times for the other microprocessors in the M68000 family.

Source	Destination											
	Dn	An	(An)	(An)+	−(An)	d(An)	d(An,Rx)	$xxxx	$xxxxxxxx	d(PC)	d(PC,Rx)	#
Dn												
An												
(An)												
(An)+												
−(An)												
d(An)												
d(An,Rx)												
$xxxx												
$xxxxxxxx												
d(PC)												
d(PC,Rx)												
#	16 3/0		28 5/2	28 5/2	30 5/2	32 6/2	34 6/2	32 6/2	36 7/2			

Number of Bytes per Instruction for Different Addressing Modes:

(Operations on Bytes and Words)

Source	Destination											
	Dn	An	(An)	(An)+	–(An)	d(An)	d(An,Rx)	$xxxx	$xxxxxxxx	d(PC)	d(PC,Rx)	#
Dn												
An												
(An)												
(An)+												
–(An)												
d(An)												
d(An,Rx)												
$xxxx												
$xxxxxxxx												
d(PC)												
d(PC,Rx)												
#	4		4	4	4	6	6	6	8			

Number of Bytes per Instruction for Different Addressing Modes:

(Operations on Long Words)

Source	Destination											
	Dn	An	(An)	(An)+	–(An)	d(An)	d(An,Rx)	$xxxx	$xxxxxxxx	d(PC)	d(PC,Rx)	#
Dn												
An												
(An)												
(An)+												
–(An)												
d(An)												
d(An,Rx)												
$xxxx												
$xxxxxxxx												
d(PC)												
d(PC,Rx)												
#	6		6	6	6	8	8	8	10			

Example:

Program to address values in a table.

Structure of the table:

The table starts at address $100 in memory. This starting address of $100 is stored in address register A0. The number of the entry in the table, that you want to get, is stored in data register D1. The destination address is stored in address register A5.

Table

Start Address $100

```
        CLR.L D1
        MOVE  #(Number of value-1),D0
        MOVE  #(Numer of value*2)-2,D1
        LEA START,A0
LOOP  MOVE(A0,D1),(A5)+
        SUBI #2,D1
        DBRA D0,LOOP
```

Applications:

You can use the SUB instruction for decrementing the contents of a data register in order to calculate the address for a value in a table, where this addressing takes place in a loop that uses a data register as index register. An example is given above.

SUB   Quick Binary Subtraction, Immediate (with a Small Constant)

Assembler Syntax:

SUBQ.w #Constant, <ea>

Operation:

<Destination> - #Constant → <Destination>

Flag Changes:

X   Set equal to 1 if a "borrow" occurs, otherwise reset to 0.
N   Set equal to 1 if result is negative, otherwise reset to 0.
Z   Set equal to 1 if result equals 0, otherwise reset to 0.
V   Set equal to 1 if an overflow occurs, otherwise reset to 0.
C   Set equal to 1 if a "borrow" occurs, otherwise reset to 0.

If the destination address is an address register, the flags will not be changed.

Operand Sizes:

This instruction can subtract small constants, with a value from 1 to 8, as the first operand from a byte, word or long word as the second operand (at the destination address). The .w in the syntax refers to .B, .W or .L respectively for the second operand.

Description of Instruction:

The SUBQ instruction differs from the SUBI instruction primarily in that it subtracts a smaller constant (with a value from 1 to 8) as the first operand from the second operand (at the destination address), but faster. This instruction does not take any previous borrow into account.

Format of Opcode:

15	14	13	12	11	10	9	8	7	6	5	4	3	2	1	0
0	1	0	1		Constant		1		Size		Effective Address <ea>				
											Mode			Register	

Bits 15–12. These bits indicate that this instruction belongs to the set of instructions {ADDQ,SUBQ, Scc,DBcc}. Other bits in the opcode select this particular instruction from this set.

Constant, Bits 11– 9. This field contains the value of the immediate constant, whereby 001 = 1, 010 = 2, etc. to 111 = 7 and 000 = 8.

Size, Bits 7–6. This field specifies the size of the second operand as follows:

00	–	8-bit byte as operand
01	–	16-bit word as operand
11	–	32-bit long word as operand

Effective Address,Bits 5–0. The effective address for the operand at the destination address is stored in this pair of fields, one for the mode and the other for the register.

Effective Address <ea>		Mnemonic for Addressing Mode
Mode	**Register**	
000	Register Number n	Dn
001	Register Number n	An
010	Register Number n	(An)
011	Register Number n	(An)+
100	Register Number n	–(An)
101	Register Number n	d(An)
110	Register Number n	d(An,Rx)
111	000	$xxxx
111	001	$xxxxxxxx
*	*	d(PC)
*	*	d(PC,Rx)
*	*	#

∗ means that this addressing mode is not allowed

Execution Times (Cycles): (Operations on Bytes and Words)

The first number is the number of clock cycles required to: get the operands, execute the instruction, store the results and get the next opcode. The next pair of numbers is for the number of read cycles and the number of write cycles respectively.

These values are only valid for the 68000 microprocessor. See the condensed tables in Chapter 8 for calculating times for the other microprocessors in the M68000 family.

Source	Destination											
	Dn	An	(An)	(An)+	–(An)	d(An)	d(An,Rx)	$xxxx	$xxxxxxxx	d(PC)	d(PC,Rx)	#
Dn												
An												
(An)												
(An)+												
–(An)												
d(An)												
d(An,Rx)												
$xxxx												
$xxxxxxxx												
d(PC)												
d(PC,Rx)												
#	4 1/0	8 1/0	12 2/1	12 2/1	14 2/1	16 3/1	18 3/1	16 3/1	20 4/1			

Execution Times (Cycles): (Operations on Long Words)

The first number is the number of clock cycles required to: get the operands, execute the instruction, store the results and get the next opcode. The next pair of numbers is for the number of read cycles and the number of write cycles respectively.

These values are only valid for the 68000 microprocessor. See the condensed tables in Chapter 8 for calculating times for the other microprocessors in the M68000 family.

Source	Destination											
	Dn	An	(An)	(An)+	–(An)	d(An)	d(An,Rx)	$xxxx	$xxxxxxxx	d(PC)	d(PC,Rx)	#
Dn												
An												
(An)												
(An)+												
–(An)												
d(An)												
d(An,Rx)												
$xxxx												
$xxxxxxxx												
d(PC)												
d(PC,Rx)												
#	8 1/0	8 1/0	20 3/2	20 3/2	22 3/2	24 4/2	26 4/2	24 4/2	28 5/2			

Number of Bytes per Instruction for Different Addressing Modes:

(Operations on Bytes and Words)

Source	Destination											
	Dn	An	(An)	(An)+	–(An)	d(An)	d(An,Rx)	$xxxx	$xxxxxxxx	d(PC)	d(PC,Rx)	#
Dn												
An												
(An)												
(An)+												
–(An)												
d(An)												
d(An,Rx)												
$xxxx												
$xxxxxxxx												
d(PC)												
d(PC,Rx)												
#	2	2	2	2	2	4	4	4	6			

Number of Bytes per Instruction for Different Addressing Modes:

(Operations on Long Words)

Source	Destination											
	Dn	An	(An)	(An)+	−(An)	d(An)	d(An,Rx)	$xxxx	$xxxxxxxx	d(PC)	d(PC,Rx)	#
Dn												
An												
(An)												
(An)+												
−(An)												
d(An)												
d(An,Rx)												
$xxxx												
$xxxxxxxx												
d(PC)												
d(PC,Rx)												
#	2	2	2	2	2	4	4	4	6			

Example:

Subtracting 2 from the value in data register D0.

Before the operation:	Contents of D0 = $xxxxxx78,
SUBQ.B #2,D0	
After the operation:	Contents of D0 = $xxxxxx76,

Applications:

You can use the SUBQ instruction for decrementing the contents of a data register or address register, such as for calculating the addresses for values in a table using an index register in a loop. The criteria for selecting the SUBQ instruction are:

- the short time of execution,
- saving bytes for data after the opcode and
- the limitation to values between 1 and 8.

SUBX   Binary Subtraction, with Extend (for Borrow)

Assembler Syntax:

SUB.w Ds,Dd
SUB.w −(As),−(Ad)

Operation:

$$< Destination > - (< Source > + X\text{-flag}) \rightarrow < Destination >$$

Flag Changes:

X   Set equal to 1 if a "borrow" occurs, otherwise reset to 0.
N   Set equal to 1 if result is negative, otherwise reset to 0.
Z   Set equal to 1 if result equals 0, otherwise unchanged.
V   Set equal to 1 if an overflow occurs, otherwise reset to 0.
C   Set equal to 1 if a "borrow" occurs, otherwise reset to 0.

Just as with the ABCD instruction, it is advisable to set the Z-flag equal to 1 before the operation so that the Z-flag will contain the correct result even if the result is equal to 0.

Operand Sizes:

This instruction can operate on bytes, words or long words. The .w in the syntax refers to .B, .W or .L respectively.

Description of Instruction:

The SUBX instruction subtracts the first operand (at the source address) from second operand (at the destination address). It writes the results back into the destination address. This instruction does take any previous borrow into account by also subtracting the Z-flag from the second operand. If you need to subtract numbers with more than 32 bits, you must use this SUBX instruction to take the borrow from a less-significant operation into account in the next more-significant operation.

Format of Opcode:

15	14	13	12	11	10	9	8	7	6	5	4	3	2	1	0
1	0	0	1	Register Rx			1	Size		0	0	R/M	Register Ry		

Bits 15–12. These bits indicate that this instruction belongs to the set of instructions {SUB,SUBX}. Other bits in the opcode select this particular instruction from this set.
Register Rd, Bits 11–9. Depending upon the value of the R/M field, this field defines the destination register, either as the number of the data register containing the second operand or the number of the address register that contains the address for accessing the second operand with the address-register indirect-addressing mode, with predecrement.
Size, Bits 7–6. This field specifies the sizes of both operands as follows:

00	–	8-bit bytes as operands
01	–	16-bit words as operands
11	–	32-bit long words as operands

R/M Field, Bit 3. This field specifies the addressing mode for both operands together as follows:

0	–	both operands are in data registers
1	–	both operands are in memory and are accessed with the address-register indirect-addressing mode, with predecrement

Register Ry, Bits 2–1. Depending upon the value of the R/M field, this field defines the source register, either as the number of the data register containing the first operand or the number of the address register that contains the address for accessing the first operand with the address-register indirect-addressing mode, with predecrement.

Execution Times (Cycles): (Operations on Bytes and Words)

The first number is the number of clock cycles required to: get the operands, execute the instruction, store the results and get the next opcode. The next pair of numbers is for the number of read cycles and the number of write cycles respectively.

These values are only valid for the 68000 microprocessor. See the condensed tables in Chapter 8 for calculating times for the other microprocessors in the M68000 family.

Source	Destination											
	Dn	An	(An)	(An)+	–(An)	d(An)	d(An,Rx)	$xxxx	$xxxxxxxx	d(PC)	d(PC,Rx)	#
Dn	4 1/0											
An												
(An)												
(An)+												
–(An)				18 3/1								
d(An)												
d(An,Rx)												
$xxxx												
$xxxxxxxx												
d(PC)												
d(PC,Rx)												
#												

Execution Times (Cycles): (Operations on Long Words)

The first number is the number of clock cycles required to: get the operands, execute the instruction, store the results and get the next opcode. The next pair of numbers is for the number of read cycles and the number of write cycles respectively.

These values are only valid for the 68000 microprocessor. See the condensed tables in Chapter 8 for calculating times for the other microprocessors in the M68000 family.

Source	Destination											
	Dn	An	(An)	(An)+	–(An)	d(An)	d(An,Rx)	$xxxx	$xxxxxxxx	d(PC)	d(PC,Rx)	#
Dn	8 1/0											
An												
(An)												
(An)+												
–(An)				30 5/2								
d(An)												
d(An,Rx)												
$xxxx												
$xxxxxxxx												
d(PC)												
d(PC,Rx)												
#												

Number of Bytes per Instruction for Different Addressing Modes:
(Operations on Bytes and Words)

Source	Destination											
	Dn	An	(An)	(An)+	–(An)	d(An)	d(An,Rx)	$xxxx	$xxxxxxxx	d(PC)	d(PC,Rx)	#
Dn	2											
An												
(An)												
(An)+												
–(An)					2							
d(An)												
d(An,Rx)												
$xxxx												
$xxxxxxxx												
d(PC)												
d(PC,Rx)												
#												

Number of Bytes per Instruction for Different Addressing Modes:
(Operations on Long Words)

Source	Destination											
	Dn	An	(An)	(An)+	–(An)	d(An)	d(An,Rx)	$xxxx	$xxxxxxxx	d(PC)	d(PC,Rx)	#
Dn	2											
An												
(An)												
(An)+												
–(An)					2							
d(An)												
d(An,Rx)												
$xxxx												
$xxxxxxxx												
d(PC)												
d(PC,Rx)												
#												

Examples:

Subtraction of two numbers that are longer than 32 bits each.

```
1st number = $7765432176543210
2nd number = $1234567801234567
```

```
Before the operation:          Contents of      D1 = $01234567
                                                D2 = $76543210
                                                D3 = $12345678
                                                D4 = $77654321


SUB.L D1,D2 corresponding to: $7765432176543210
ORI #$04,CCR–$1234567801234567
SUBX.L D3,D4 $6530ECA97530ECA9
```

After the operation:	Contents of	D1 = $01234567
		D2 = $7530ECA9
		D3 = $12345678
		D4 = $6530ECA9

Applications:

You can use the SUBX instruction for subtracting the more significant components of numbers with more than 32 bits. You can use the simpler and faster SUB instruction for the least-significant 32 bits of these numbers. Both the SUB and SUBX instructions will set the X-flag if they use a borrow and subsequent SUBX instructions will take this borrow into account.

If you later want to determine whether the result of a SUBX instruction is zero, you should first set the Z-flag equal to 1, such as with the ORI instruction, as in the example above.

SWAP   Swap Halves of Data Register

Assembler Syntax:

SWAP Dn

Operation:

$<$Dd (bits 31–16)$> \longleftrightarrow <$Dd (bits 15–0)$>$

Flag Changes:

X   Not changed.
N   Set equal to 1 if the most-significant bit in the 32-bit register is equal to 1 after the operation, otherwise reset to 0.
Z   Set equal to 1 if result in the whole register equals 0, otherwise reset to 0.
V   Always reset to 0.
C   Always reset to 0.

Operand Sizes:

This instruction operates on the two 16-bit halves of a 32-bit data register. Therefore, the size of the operands is that of words.

Description of Instruction:

The SWAP instruction exchanges or swaps the most-significant half of a data register with the least-significant half.

Format of Opcode:

15	14	13	12	11	10	9	8	7	6	5	4	3	2	1	0
0	1	0	0	1	0	0	0	0	1	0	0	0	Register		

Bits 15–12. These bits indicate that this instruction belongs to the set of instructions {NOT,NEG, SWAP,etc.}. Other bits in the opcode select this particular instruction from this set.

Bits 11–3. These bits select this particular instruction as the SWAP instruction.

Register, Bits 2–0. This field specifies the number of the data register in which the SWAP operation takes place.

Execution Times (Cycles):

```
4 clock cycles
1 read cycle
0 write cycles
```

(These values are only valid for the 68000 microprocessor. See the condensed tables in Chapter 8 for calculating times for the other microprocessors in the M68000 family.)

Number of Bytes per Instruction:

Always 2 bytes.

Example:

Before the operation:	Contents of D0 = $FFFFAAAA,
SWAP D0	
After the operation:	Contents of D0 = $AAAAFFFF

Applications:

You can use the SWAP instruction to obtain access to the remainder after a division operation, since this remainder is stored in the most-significant half of the data register. When using words, you can use the SWAP instruction in order to be able to fully use both halves of all data registers.

TAS   Test and Set a Bit in an Operand

Assembler Syntax:

TAS <ea>

Operation:

<Destination> queried	→ <CCR>
1	→ <Destination (bit 7)>

Flag Changes:

X   Not changed.
N   Set equal to 1 if the most-significant bit of the 8-bit operand was equal to 1 before the operation, otherwise reset to 0.
Z   Set equal to 0 if the 8-bit operand was equal to 0 before the operation, otherwise reset to 0.
V   Always reset to 0.
C   Always reset to 0.

Operand Sizes:

This instruction operates on a byte as the operand.

Description of Instruction:

The TAS instruction examines a byte as operand and writes the results in the flags. In particular, the most-significant bit that determines whether the value of the byte is postive or negative is stored in the N-flag. Then, a 1 is written as the most-significant bit, regardless of whether it was 0 or 1 before the operation. This instruction performs a read-modify-write bus cycle that is not interruptable (see Chapter 2.6).
The TAS instruction is used primarily to synchronize different processors that are working with the same memory or to synchronize peripherals, such as a printer.

Format of Opcode:

15	14	13	12	11	10	9	8	7	6	5	4	3	2	1	0
										Effective Address <ea>					
0	1	0	0	1	0	1	0	1	1	Mode			Register		

Bits 15–12. These bits indicate that this instruction belongs to the set of instructions {NOT,NEG,EXT, TAS,etc.}. Other bits in the opcode select this particular instruction from this set.
Bits 11–6. These bits select this particular instruction as the TAS instruction.
Effective Address, Bits 5–0. The effective address is stored in this pair of fields, one for the mode and the other for the register. The interpretation for this pair of fields is given in the table below:

Effective Address <ea>		Mnemonic for Addressing Mode
Mode	Register	
000	Register Number n	Dn
*	*	An
010	Register Number n	(An)
011	Register Number n	(An)+
100	Register Number n	–(An)
101	Register Number n	d(An)
110	Register Number n	d(An,Rx)
111	000	$xxxx
111	001	$xxxxxxxx
*	*	d(PC)
*	*	d(PC,Rx)
*	*	#

* means that this addressing mode is not allowed

Execution Times (Cycles): (Unary operation on bytes)

The first number is the number of clock cycles required to: get the operand, execute the instruction, store the results and get the next opcode. The next pair of numbers is for the number of read cycles and the number of write cycles respectively.

These values are only valid for the 68000 microprocessor. See the condensed tables in Chapter 8 for calculating times for the other microprocessors in the M68000 family.

						Destination					
Dn	An	(An)	(An)+	–(An)	d(An)	d(An,Rx)	$xxxx	$xxxxxxxx	d(PC)	d(PC,Rx)	#
4 1/0		14 2/1	14 2/1	16 2/1	18 3/1	20 3/1	18 3/1	22 4/1			

Number of Bytes per Instruction for Different Addressing Modes:

(Unary Operations on Bytes)

						Destination					
Dn	An	(An)	(An)+	–(An)	d(An)	d(An,Rx)	$xxxx	$xxxxxxxx	d(PC)	d(PC,Rx)	#
2		2	2	2	4	4	4	6			

Examples:

1. Bit 7 of the operand is already equal to 1.

```
Before the operation:      Contents at address   $1000  = $80
                                                     X  N  Z  V  C
                                          Flags  =   1  0  0  0  1,

TAS $1000

After the operation:       Contents at address   $1000  = $80
                                                     X  N  Z  V  C
                                          Flags  =   1  1  0  0  0
```

2. Bit 7 of the operand is initially equal to 0.

```
Before the operation:      Contents at address   $1000  = $00
                                                     X  N  Z  V  C
                                          Flags  =   1  0  0  0  1,

TAS $1000

After the operation:       Contents at address   $1000  = $80
                                                     X  N  Z  V  C
                                          Flags  =   1  0  1  0  0
```

Applications:

You can use the TAS instruction for synchronizing the accesses of different processors to a common memory in a multi-processor system. The byte of data in memory that the TAS instruction operates upon is the equivalent of a semaphore, whereas a semaphore is similar to a signal or a flag.

TRAP   Trap to Initiate Exception Handling

Assembler Syntax:

TRAP # Vector Number   0 < = Vector Number < = 15

Operation:

Four steps: 1.   Switch the microprocessor into the Supervisor Mode of operation.
2.   < PC >   → –(A7) (supervisor stack)
3.   < SR >   → –(A7) (supervisor stack)
4.   <Vector>   → < PC >

Flag Changes:

None.

Operand Sizes:

This instruction does not use operands.

Description of Instruction:

The TRAP instruction initiates exception-handling. As the first step, it switches an M68000 microprocessor into the supervisor mode of operation. Then, it copies the contents of both the program counter and the status register into the supervisor stack. It multiplies the exception-vector number by four to obtain the address of the exception vector in memory. Finally, it loads the exception vector from that address into the program counter and starts the microprocessor in the supervisor mode.

These vector numbers, from 0 to 15, correspond to the lowest 16 exception vectors in the table of 256 exception vectors of the M68000 microprocessors. Using the TRAP instruction is equivalent to a "software interrupt" for other processors (see Chapter 2.4.4 and 2.5).

Format of Opcode:

15	14	13	12	11	10	9	8	7	6	5	4	3	2	1	0
0	1	0	0	1	1	1	0	0	1	0	0	Vector Number			

Bits 15–12. These bits indicate that this instruction belongs to the set of instructions {SWAP,NOT, NEG,EXT,TRAP,etc.}. Other bits in the opcode select this particular instruction from this set.

Bits 11–4. These bits select this particular instruction as TRAP instruction.

Vector Number, Bits 3–0. This field contains the exception-vector number, from 0 to 15. It is multiplied by 4 to obtain an address in memory for a unique exception vector.

Addressing Modes that are Allowed:

None.

Execution Times (Cycles):

> 32 clock cycles
> 4 read cycles
> 4 write cycles

(These values are only valid for the 68000 microprocessor. See the condensed tables in Chapter 8 for calculating times for the other microprocessors in the M68000 family.)

Number of Bytes per Instruction:

> Always 2 bytes.

Example:

> A typical call to the operating system.
> LEA PARAMETER,A0
> MOVE.L #1,D0
> TRAP #2   The call to the operating system will be processed after
>   this instruction and the functions that are specified in the
>   parameter block will be performed.
>
> PARAMETER   DC.W xxxx
>   DC.L xxxxxxxx
>   DC.L xxxxxxxx   Block of parameters
>   DC.L xxxxxxxx
>   DC.W xxxx

Applications:

You can use the TRAP instruction to switch into the supervisor mode from a user program that is running in the user mode. What happens next depends upon the routine that is started at the exception-vector address selected by the trap. TRAP instructions are often used for system calls to the operating system, as in the example above (see also Chapter 2.4.4 and 3.6). For example, the TRAP instruction could be used to allow a user program to present an output to a terminal or a printer in a multi-user system. This instruction allows a user program to use functions of the operating system. However, the operating system must control whether the user program is authorized to use these functions.

TRAPV   Trap upon Overflow

Assembler Syntax:

> TRAPV

Operation:

> If V-flag = 1
> then → trap
> else → continue with next instruction

Flag Changes:

None. The flags are read but not changed.

Operand Sizes:

None, since this instruction does not use operands.

Description of Instruction:

The TRAPV instruction checks the overflow flag, ie. the V-flag. If this flag has a value of 1, then it initiates exception-handling. If this flag has a value of 0, then it continues on to the next instruction in the normal sequence.

An M68000 microprocessor has a separate vector for the TRAPV instruction.

Format of Opcode:

15	14	13	12	11	10	9	8	7	6	5	4	3	2	1	0
0	1	0	0	1	1	1	0	0	1	1	1	0	1	1	0

(= $4E76)

Bits 15–12. These bits indicate that this instruction belongs to the set of instructions {NOT,SWAP, NEG,EXT,TRAPV,etc.}. Other bits in the opcode select this particular instruction from this set.

Bits 11–0. These bits select this particular instruction as the TRAPV instruction.

Execution Times (Cycles):

These values are only valid for the 68000 microprocessor. See the condensed tables in Chapter 8 for calculating times for the other microprocessors in the M68000 family.

Case 1: trap is initiated

34 clock cycles
5 read cycles
3 write cycles

Case 2: trap is not initiated

4 clock cycles
1 read cycle
0 write cycles

Number of Bytes per Instruction:

Always 2 bytes.

Example:

```
DIVU #3,D5,
TRAPV              Check to determine whether an overflow occurred during
   .               division–that prevented the division from being
   .               completed.
   .
```

Applications:

You have two options when you need to be certain that an overflow did not occur in a given operation:

1　use the BVS instruction (branch on overflow set) or
2　use the TRAPV instruction

The first option is adequate for simple situations. However, as in the example above, you may trap the occurrance of an overflow and branch to a routine in the operating system. In this case, such a subroutine must exist in the supervisor code and in fact most operating systems contain such a routine.

TST　　　　Test the Contents of an Operand

Assembler Syntax:

```
TST.w <ea>
```

Operation:

```
<Destination> querried, results → <flags>
```

Flag Changes:

```
X   Not changed.
N   Set equal to 1 if operand is negative, otherwise reset to 0.
Z   Set equal to 1 if operand equals 0, otherwise reset to 0.
V   Always reset to 0.
C   Always reset to 0.
```

Operand Sizes:

This instruction can operate on a byte, word or long word at the destination address. The .w in the syntax refers to .B, .W or .L respectively.

Description of Instruction:

The TST instruction tests the operand at the destination address to determine whether the value of the operand is smaller than, equal to or larger than 0. The result of this test is stored in the flags, without changing the operand.

Format of Opcode:

15	14	13	12	11	10	9	8	7	6	5	4	3	2	1	0
0	1	0	0	1	0	1	0	Size		Effective Address <ea>					
										Mode			Register		

Bits 15–12. These bits indicate that this instruction belongs to the set of instructions {SWAP,NOT, NEG,EXT,TST,etc.}. Other bits in the opcode select this particular instruction from this set.

Bits 11–8. These bits select this particular instruction as the TST instruction.

Size Field, Bits 7–6. The size of the operand is stored in this field, defined as follows:

00	–	8-bit byte as operand
01	–	16-bit word as operand
10	–	32-bit long word as operand

Effective Address, Bits 5–0. The effective address is stored in this pair of fields, one for the mode and the other for the register. The interpretation for this pair of fields is given in the table below:

Effective Address <ea>		Mnemonic for Addressing Mode
Mode	**Register**	
000	Register Number n	Dn
*	*	An
010	Register Number n	(An)
011	Register Number n	(An)+
100	Register Number n	–(An)
101	Register Number n	d(An)
110	Register Number n	d(An,Rx)
111	000	$xxxx
111	001	$xxxxxxxx
*	*	d(PC)
*	*	d(PC,Rx)
*	*	#

* means that this addressing mode is not allowed

Execution Times (Cycles): (Operations on Bytes and Words)

The first number is the number of clock cycles required to: get the operand, execute the instruction, store the results and get the next opcode. The next pair of numbers is for the number of read cycles and the number of write cycles respectively.

These values are only valid for the 68000 microprocessor. See the condensed tables in Chapter 8 for calculating times for the other microprocessors in the M68000 family.

	Destination										
	Dn	An	(An)	(An)+	–(An)	d(An)	d(An,Rx)	$xxxx	$xxxxxxxx	d(PC)	d(PC,Rx)	#
	4 1/0		8 2/0	8 2/0	10 2/0	12 3/0	14 3/0	12 3/0	16 4/0			

Execution Times (Cycles): (Operations on Long Words)

					Destination					
Dn	An	(An)	(An)+	–(An)	d(An)	d(An,Rx)	$xxxx	$xxxxxxxx	d(PC)	d(PC,Rx)	#
4 1/0		12 3/0	12 3/0	14 3/0	16 4/0	18 4/0	16 4/0	20 5/0			

Number of Bytes per Instruction for Different Addressing Modes:

(Operations on Bytes, Words and Long Words)

					Destination					
Dn	An	(An)	(An)+	–(An)	d(An)	d(An,Rx)	$xxxx	$xxxxxxxx	d(PC)	d(PC,Rx)	#
2		2	2	2	4	4	4	6			

Example:

1. Testing a positive value in a byte.

Before the operation:	Contents at	$1000 = $27	
			X N Z V C
		Flags =	1 0 0 1 1
TST.B $1000			
After the operation:	Contents at	$1000 = $27	
			X N Z V C
		Flags =	1 0 0 0 0

2. Testing a negative value in a word.

Before the operation:	Contents at	$1000 = $8779	
			X N Z V C
		Flags =	1 0 0 0 1
TST.W $1000			
After the operation:	Contents at	$1000 = $8779	
			X N Z V C
		Flags =	1 1 0 0 0

Applications:

You can use the TST instruction to test the contents of an operand. This test determines whether the value is less than, equal to or greater than null. It is similar to the instruction CMPI #0, <ea>, except that the TST instruction is faster.

UNLK   Unlink and Retrieve the Stack Pointer

Assembler Syntax:

UNLK Ad

Operation:

```
<Ad>  →  <A7>
<A7)+  →  <Ad>
```

Flag Changes:

None.

Operand Sizes:

This instruction operates only on 32-bit long words since it operates on the contents of address registers.

Description of Instruction:

The UNLK instruction is the complement that undoes a LINK instruction (see the LINK instruction). It releases the stack area of a subroutine and returns the control to the main program.

As step 1, the UNLK instruction retrieves the stack pointer of the main program that the LINK instruction stored in an address register Ad and copies it into the stack pointer A7.

As step 2, the UNLK instruction retrieves from the stack area of the main program the previous contents of the address register that was used by the main program and copies it into the address register Ad.

As a·result, for the main program both the stack pointer A7 and the address register An are restored to their original values before the subroutine was started.

These operations are illustrated in the diagram below:

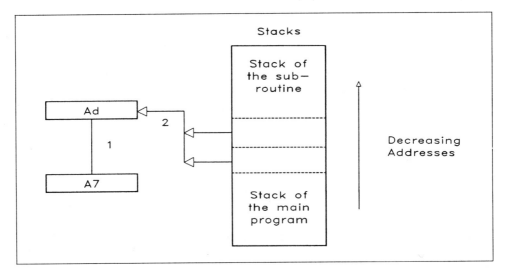

You could replace the UNLK instruction by the following sequences of instructions:

Instruction Sequence 1	Instruction Sequence 2
MOVEA.L As,A7 MOVEA.L (A7)+,AD	LEA (As),A7 MOVEA.L (A7)+,Ad

Format of Opcode:

15	14	13	12	11	10	9	8	7	6	5	4	3	2	1	0
0	1	0	0	1	1	1	0	0	1	0	1	1	Register		

Bits 15–12. These bits indicate that this instruction belongs to the set of instructions {LEA,CLR, NEG,EXT,LINK,UNLK,etc.}. Other bits in the opcode select this particular instruction from this set.
Bits 11–3. These bits select this particular instruction as the UNLK instruction.
Register, Bits 2–0. This field specifies the number of the address register for the stack pointer of the main program.

Execution Times (Cycles):

12 clock cycles
3 read cycles
0 write cycles

(These values are only valid for the 68000 microprocessor. See the condensed tables in Chapter 8 for calculating times for the other microprocessors in the M68000 family.)

Number of Bytes per Instruction:

Always 2 bytes.

Example:

A subroutine with its own stack.

Address of Instruction	Instruction	
$1000	MOVE.L D2,D5	
$1002	JSR $2000	
$1006	MOVE.W D4,$2560	
.	.	
.	.	
.	.	
$2000	LINK A2,−$30	Creating stack for subroutine
$2004	MOVEM.L D0−D7/A0/A1/A3−A6,−(A7)	
.	.	
.	.	
.	.	
$2100	MOVEM.L (A7)+,D0−D7/A0/A1/A3−A6	
$2104	UNLK A2	Deleting stack for subroutine
$2106	RTS	

Applications:

You can use the combination of the LINK and UNLK instructions to create and delete separate stack areas for subroutines. The UNLK instruction is used frequently by compilers of high-level languages. The availability of this pair of instructions demonstrates how the M68000 microprocessors are optimized for use with high-level languages.

4.3 Summary of Differences Among All M68000 Microprocessors

The differences in the instruction sets of the different microprocessors of the M68000 family can be summarized as follows:
- The 68000 and 68008 microprocessors both have the same identical set of instructions.
- The 68010 and 68012 microprocessors modify 2 instructions (MOVE from SR and RTE) and add 4 instructions (MOVEC, MOVES, MOVE from CCR and RTD) to the basic set of instructions for the 68000 and 68008 microprocessors – in order to support virtual memory.
- The 68020 microprocessor has all of the instructions of the 68010 and 68012 microprocessors, but it extends two to support the PC relative-addressing mode (CMPI and TST),
  extends 9 to support 32-bit offsets and/or operands (Bcc, BRA, BSR, CHK, DIVS, DIVU, LINK, MULS and MULU),
  extends 1 for new control registers (MOVEC),
  adds 21 new instructions (BFCHG, BFCLR, BFEXTS, BFEXTU, BFFFO, BFINS, BFSET, BFTST, BKPT, CALLM, CAS, CAS2, CHK2, CMP2, DIVL, DIVUL, EXTB, PACK, RTM, TRAPcc and UNPK), and
  adds a category of general coprocessor instructions (cp) that are processed without a TRAP, as was the case for earlier microprocessors in this family.
- The 68030 microprocessor has all of the instructions of the 68020 microprocessor, plus 4 of the 12 instructions of the 68851 PMMU (PFLUSH, PMOVE, PTEST, and PLOAD are included–PVALID, PFLUSHR, PBcc, PDBcc, PScc, PTRAPcc, PSAVE and PRESTORE are not included).

All of the instructions for the 68000, 68008, 68010 and 68012 are listed in alphabetical order in Section 4.2 above and are described in detail there. The changes and additions for the 68020 and 68030 microprocessors are described in Chapter 8 under the respective sections for these two microprocessors. The instructions of the 68851 PMMU are described in Chapter 7 in the section for this support device. Figure 4-12 below lists all of the current instructions for the M68000 family (except for the detailed instructions for the coprocessors) to show the differences from one microprocessor to another.

Mnemonic	Description	68000 68008	68010 68012	68020	68851 PMMU	68030
ABCD	Add BCD with extend	X	X	X		X
ADD	Add binary	X	X	X		X
ADDA	Add address	X	X	X		X
ADDI	Add immediate	X	X	X		X
ADDQ	Add quick	X	X	X		X
ADDX	Add binary with ext	X	X	X		X
AND	Logical AND	X	X	X		X
ANDI	AND immediate	X	X	X		X
ANDI to CCR	AND imm. to CCR	X	X	X		X
ASL	Arith. shift left	X	X	X		X
ASR	Arith. shift right	X	X	X		X
Bcc	Branch on condition	X	X	32-bit		X

Mnemonic	Description	68000 68008	68010 68012	68020	68851 PMMU	68030
BCHG	Test bit & change	X	X	X		X
BCLR	Test bit & clear	X	X	X		X
BFCHG	Test field & ch			X		X
BFCLR	Test bit field & cl			X		X
BFEXTS	BF extract signed			X		X
BFEXTU	BF extract unsigned			X		X
BFFFO	BF find first one			X		X
BFINS	BF insert			X		X
BFSET	Test BF & set			X		X
BFTST	Test bit field			X		X
BKPT	Breakpoint			X		X
BRA	Branch	X	X	32-bit		X
BSET	Test bit and set	X	X	X		X
BSR	Branch to subrout.	X	X	32-bit		X
BTST	Test bit	X	X	X		X
CALLM	Call Module			X		X
CAS	Compare & swap op's			X		X
CAS2	Compare & swap 2x o			X		X
CHK	Check reg. w. bound	X	X	32-bit		X
CHK2	Check reg. w. U&L B			X		X
CLR	Clear	X	X	X		X
CMP	Compare	X	X	X		X
CMPA	Compare address	X	X	X		X
CMPI	Compare immediate	X	X	+PC Rel		X
CMPM	Comp. mem. to mem.	X	X	X		X
CPM2	Comp. reg. w. U&L B			X		X
cp	Coprocessor instr's	trap	trap	intern.		intern.
DBcc	Decr. & branch on c	X	X	X		X
DIVS	Division signed	X	X	32/64 b		X
DIVSL	Div. signed & long			X		X
DIVU	Division unsigned	X	X	32/64 b		X
DIVUL	Div. unsign. & long			X		X
EOR	Exlusive OR	X	X	X		X
EORI	Excl. OR immediate	X	X	X		X
EORI to CCR	Excl. OR to CCR	X	X	X		X
EORI to SR	Excl. OR to SR	X	X	X		X
EXG	Exchange registers	X	X	X		X
EXT	Sign extend	X	X	X		X
EXTB	Sign extended 8 to 32			X		X
JMP	Jump	X	X	X		X
JSR	Jump to subroutine	X	X	X		X
LEA	Load eff. address	X	X	X		X
LINK	Link and allocacte	X	X	32-bit		X
LSL	Logical shift left	X	X	X		X
LSR	Logical shift right	X	X	X		X
MOVE	Move	X	X	X		X
MOVEA	Move address	X	X	X		X
MOVEC	Move control reg.		X	+ new R		X

Mnemonic	Description	68000 68008	68010 68012	68020	68851 PMMU	68030
MOVEM	Move multiple reg's	X	X	X		X
MOVEP	Move peripheral	X	X	X		X
MOVEQ	Move quick	X	X	X		X
MOVES	Move alt. add. sp.		X	X		X
MOVE to CCR	Move to CCR	X	X	X		X
MOVE from CCR	Move from CCR		X	X		X
MOVE to SR	Move to SR	X	X	X		X
MOVE from SR	Move from SR	X	X	X		X
MOVE USP	Move user stack p.	X	X	X		X
MULS	Multiply signed	X	X	32-bit		X
MULU	Multiply unsigned	X	X	32-bit		X
NBCD	Negate BCD w. ext	X	X	X		X
NEG	Negate	X	X	X		X
NEGX	Negate with extend	X	X	X		X
NOP	No operation	X	X	X		X
NOT	Logical NOT	X	X	X		X
OR	Logical incl. OR	X	X	X		X
ORI	OR immediate	X	X	X		X
ORI to CCR	ORI to CCR	X	X	X		X
ORI to SR	ORI to SR	X	X	X		X
PACK	Pack BCD			X		X
PBcc	Branch on PMMU cond				X	
PDBcc	Decr. & branch on P.				X	
PEA	Push eff. address	X	X	X		X
PFLUSH	Flush tr. cache				X	X
PFLUSHR					X	
PLOAD					X	X
PMOVE	Move to/from PMMU r				X	X
PRESTORE	Restore PMMU				X	
PSAVE	Save state of PMMU				X	
PScc	Set oper. by PMMU c				X	
PTRAPcc	Trap by PMMU condit				X	
PTEST	Determin access r.				X	X
PVALID	Test access rights				X	
RESET	Reset ext. devices	X	X	X		X
ROL	Rotate left	X	X	X		X
ROR	Rotate right	X	X	X		X
ROXL	Rotate left w. ext.	X	X	X		X
ROXR	Rotate right s. ext.	X	X	X		X
RTD	Return & deallocate		X	X		X
RTE	Return from except.	X	Mod	X		X
RTM	Return from module			X		X
RTR	Ret & restore CCR	X	X	X		X
RTS	Return from subrout	X	X	X		X
SBCD	Subtract BCD w ext.	X	X	X	X	
Scc	Set conditionally	X	X	X		X
STOP	Stop	X	X	X		X
SUB	Subtract	X	X	X		X

Mnemonic	Description	68000 68008	68010 68012	68020	68851 PMMU	68030
SUBA	Subtract address	X	X	X		X
SUBI	Subtract immediate	X	X	X		X
SUBQ	Subtract quick	X	X	X		X
SUBX	Subtract w. extend	X	X	X		X
SWAP	Swap registers	X	X	X		X
TAS	Test oper. & set	X	X	X		X
TRAP	Trap	X	X	X		X
TRAPcc	Trap conditionally			X		X
TRAPV	Trap on overflow	X	X	X		X
TST	Test operand	X	X	+PC Rel		X
UNLK	Unlink	X	X	X		X
UNPK	Unpack BCD			X		X
Total Number of Instructions		82	86	107	12	111

Figure 4-12: Comparison of the Instruction Sets for M68000 Microprocessors

It is difficult to count the number of instructions in a given instruction set since there are many options for counting, such as whether

− ALS and ASR are two separate instructions or one instruction with two variants (same for LSL & LSR, ROL & ROR and ROXL & ROXR) and
− Bcc is one instruction, or 14 different instructions where each condition is a separate instruction (same for DBcc, PBcc, PDBcc, PScc, Scc and TRAPcc).

Supporters of the RISC philosophy will tend to bend the rules of counting in order to obtain smaller numbers than given in Figure 4-12 above whereas supporters of the CISC philosophy will tend to bend the rules of counting in order to obtain larger numbers than given in Figure 4-12 above. It is important for comparisons of instruction sets that you use the same rules for counting in each set. Therefore, the comparisons at the bottom of Figure 4-12 above are valid since the numbers are counted in the same way for each microprocessor.

5
Masks of the 68000 Microprocessor

5.1 Introduction to Masks

The "masks" of an integrated circuit refer to the photographic masks that are used for manufacturing the wafers with integrated circuits upon them. Therefore, the internal reference number for a mask is the ultimate specification for one of possibly several different versions of the same product. In this chapter, we will present the masks for the first 68000 microprocessor as an example.

Each 68000 microprocessor has a printed label on it that includes the number of the mask used as well as the year and the week when the integrated circuit was manufactured. See Figure 5-1 for an illustration of where this information is printed.

It is only natural in any design process that several versions of the same product will be developed over time. Later versions usually represent small technical improvements. In the case of the 68000 microprocessor, only the first mask had significant functional differences from the later masks. The later masks differed from one another primarily as changes in the layout on the chip – in order to reduce hot spots in higher-speed versions. The 6 masks that have been used for manufacturing 68000 microprocessors are listed in Figure 5-2 below. You will find references to these mask numbers in the data sheets that give detailed technical specifications. You will note that the 68000 is by now a very stable product and that no new masks have been introduced since 1981. Only the masks CC1 and GN7 were ever used for producing large numbers of microprocessors, and all 68000 microprocessors since 1981 have been manufactured with the GN7 mask (except for CMOS versions).

Mask Number	Date When First Used	
R9M	July	1979
T6E	April	1980
BF4	May	1980
CC1	September	1980
DL6	March	1981
GN7	December	1981

Figure 5-2: Motorola's Mask Numbers for the 68000 Microprocessor

Second-source manufacturers of the 68000 microprocessors receive original copies of the masks from Motorola, but they often use different mask numbers internally.

5.2 The Prototype "XC68000" Microprocessor

The first prototype of the 68000 microprocessor was introduced in 1979 under the name "XC68000". The R9M mask was used to produce it and it was sold in small quantities. It is the only mask that differs significantly in its logical and electrical properties from the rest of the masks that were developed later. Therefore, these differences are summarized here to indicate the magnitude of such differences in a typical case. You should not attempt to design microcomputers today based upon this XC68000 microprocessor from the R9M mask, but rather, should use the current versions from the latest GN7 mask.

General Specifications:

The microprocessor was tested under the following conditions:

- 5.0 Volts =/- 3% (supply voltage)
- only at 25°C (room temperature)
- maximum clock frequency = 4 megahertz
- minimum clock frequency = 1 megahertz

Differences in the Instruction Set:

1 CHK	CHK only initiates a trap when Dn > EA.
2 MOVE USP	A MOVE from or to the USP is not privileged.
3 STOP	STOP does stop the processor. However, it does not initiate an interrupt. The only way to free the microprocessor from this status therefore is with a RESET. The user should therefore not use the STOP instruction with microprocessors fabricated with the R9M mask.
4 Logical Operations on CCR	The instructions ANDI to CCR, EORI to CCR, EOR to CCR and ORI to CCR modify the complete status register (SR), and not just the CCR half.
5 DCNT (DBcc)	The DCNT instruction corresponds roughly in its functions to the DBRA and DBF instructions. However, it has its own opcode, and it is not expandable for use with the other conditions, such as NE, EQ, etc. In contrast to DBcc, the loop is terminated when the data register contains 0. The mnemonic for the instruction is:
DCNT Dn,LABEL	The opcode has the following structure:

15	14	13	12	11	10	9	8	7	6	5	4	3	2	1	0
0	1	1	1		DN		1				Address Offset				

The address offset is also different than for DBcc, since it can only range from −1 to −256.

NOTE: The Motorola assembler has an option (Mask2) that generates the equivalent of the DBcc instruction as a macro instruction for the XC68000 microprocessor.

6 Bit Manipulation	The XC68000 microprocessor performs bit manipulations upon words of data. This turned out to be inconvenient when working with 8-bit peripheral-interface devices and therefore this was changed to performing bit manipulations on bytes of data for all microprocessors fabricated with later mask versions.

| 7 Z-Bit for ADDX, SUBX, NEGX, ABCD, SBCD, and NBCD | These instructions are the primitive components of multiple instructions, such as for adding large numbers together. The XC68000 microprocessor sets the Z-bit only according to the last instruction, such as ADDX. |

Other Differences in the Operation:

1 Double Bus Error	When an address error or a bus error occurs during a power-on reset, the XC68000 microprocessor does not go into the HALT state, but rather into the corresponding exception routine.
2 Double Exception	If the exception vector for a non-implemented instruction contains an odd address (ie. the error is purely an address error), then the saved address of the program counter on the stack is the same as the stack pointer itself.
3 Error in Executing Instructions	When a MOVE.W or MOVE.L <ea>,–(An) instruction is followed by a MOVEP instruction, the XC68000 microprocessor generates a UDS but doesn't generate a LDS strobe signal on the last write cycle of the MOVE instruction.
4 Bus-Control Error	If a bus request arrives from another bus master during a bus cycle and a bus error occurs in the same bus cycle, then the XC68000 will not initiate the bus-error exception routine but rather will initiate the next normal bus cycle with an odd address.
5 Synchronous-Bus Timing	The XC68000 does not always execute two consecutive VPA accesses.

5.3 The Main Mask Versions

Figure 5-3 illustrates the differences among the different masks for the 68000 microprocessor after the first R9M mask for the prototype version. Since the specifications are being held even for expanded temperature ranges and faster versions, no significant changes are expected for the future.

As you can see from Figure 5-3, there are only two families of masks for the 68000 microprocessor, ie. T6E and CC1, whereby only the CC1 mask and variants thereof have been used for producing significant quantities of 68000 microprocessors. All of the other masks are very nearly identical.

A typical example for a nearly identical pair of masks is CC1 and DL6. When a new version is required for a different temperature range or a higher operating frequency, or both, then warm spots may develop that require a small change in the layout on the surface of the chip–without any changes in the functional or electrical specifications.

	Masks						See
	T6E	**BF4**	**CC1**	**DL6**	**GN7**	**Future**	**Chapter**
Minimum number of clock cycles for a write bus cycle	5	same as T6E	4	same as CC1	same as CC1	same as CC1	2.6.1
Interrupt synchronization	No		Yes				2.9.6
Combination of DTACK, BERR and HALT (Case 5)	undefined		defined				2.10
FC0–FC2 lines in high-impedance state after HALT	Yes		No				2.3
R/W valid before AS, DS, An and Dn after a bus error	Yes		No				**
UDs and LDs active during a bus error	Yes		Yes			No	2.5.1
Wait for acknowledge-ment after tri-state for bus access	Yes		Yes		No	No	2.11

** Bus conflicts could occur in the external bus interface for the masks T6E and BF4 (also R9M) when a bus error occured during a write bus cycle that switched the R/W signal to read before AS, DS, the address lines, and the data lines were inactivated.

Figure 5-3: Comparision of Production Masks for 68000 Microprocessors

Bibliography

1 E. A. Snow and D. Siewiorek Impact of Implementation Design Tradeoffs on Performance: The PDP 11, A Case Study Dept. of EE and Comp. Sci., Carnegie-Mellon University (July, 1977)
2 A. Craselli The Design of Program-Modifiable Microprogrammed Control Units
3 S. Stritter, N. Tredennick Microprogrammed Implementation of A Single Chip Microprocessor, Proc. 11th Annual Microprogramming Workshop, November 1978
4 J. Zolnowsky, N. Tredennick Design and Implementation of System Features for the MC68000, Proc. Compcon Fall 1979
5 E. Stritter, T. Gunter A Microprocessor Architecture for a Changing World, Computer, Vol. 12, No. 2
6 Motorola Inc. MC68000 16-Bit Users Manual, Third Edition, Prentice Hall Inc. Englewood Cliffs, N. J.
7 J. Zolnowsky Instruction Prefetch on the MC68000, Motorola internal publication
8 Leo J. Scanlon The 68000: Principles and Programming, Howard W. Sams & Co., Inc., Indianapolis
9 Gerry Kane, Doug Hawkins, Lance Leventhal 68000 Assembly Language Programming, 1st Printing 1981, Osborne/McGraw Hill, California
10 Motorola Inc. MC6801 8-Bit Single-Chip Microcomputer Reference Manual
11 Peter Stuhlmueller 16-bit Generation Z8000–Aufbau und Anwendung, 1st Printing, 1980, tewi-Verlag, Munich
12 Mostek Corp. Microelectronic Data Book 1982/1983, May 1982
13 Motorola Inc. MC68000 Course Notes, Version January 1980
14 Motorola Inc. MC68120/MC68121 Intelligent Peripheral Controller User's Manual, 1st Edition
15 Motorola Inc. MC68000 16-bit Microprocessor Data Sheet, Edition April 1983
16 Parveen Grupta Multiprocessing Improves Robotic Accuracy and Control, Computer Design, November 1983
17 Signetics Corp. SCB68430 Direct Memory Access Interface (DMAI), Data Sheet, Edition January 1983
18 Thomas W. Cantrell A Versatile DMA Controller For High Performance System Design, Proc. Session 20, Wescon 1982, Anaheim, California
19 Werner Hilf Neue Peripheribausteine fuer den MC68000, Elektronik 19/1981
20 Rockwell International Corp. R68465 Double-Density Floppy Disk Controller, Data Sheet, Edition February 1983
21 Rockwell International Corp. R68560, R68561 Multi-Protocol Communications Controller (MPCC), Data Sheet, Edition March 1983
22 Alex Goldberger, Stephen Y. Lau Understand Datacomm Protocols by Examining Their Structures, EDN, March 3, 1983
23 Motorola Inc. Application Note AN808–Interfacing 6800 Peripherals to the MC68000 Asynchronously
24 Motorola Inc. Application Note AN854–The MC68230 Parallel/Timer Provides An Effective Printer Interface
25 Erwin Niebauer Minimalsystem MC68000, Abschlussarbeit an der Fachhochschule Munich
26 Motorola Inc. MC68451 Memory-Management Unit, Data Sheet, April 1983 (ADI-872-RI)
27 John F. Wakerly Microcomputer Architecture and Programming, John Wiley & Sons, New York, 1981
28 Motorola Inc. MEX68KDM(D2) Design Modul User's Guide, 2nd Printing, August 1979
29 Motorola Inc. M68VECPU100(D1) VMEmodules User's Guide, 1st Printing, September 1981
30 Motorola Inc. M68KMBUG(DI) MACSbug Initialization and I/O Routines
31 Motorola Inc. MC68010 16-bit Virtual-Memory Microprocessor, Advance Information, December 1982
32 Motorola Inc. Virtual-System Course Notes, October 1982
33 Knaizuk and Hartmann Memory Test Algorithmus, published in IEEE Transactions on Computers, April 1977
34 Brinch Hansen Per Operating System Principles, 1st Printing 1973, Prentice Hall Inc., London
35 E. G. Coffmann, M. J. Elphick, A. Shoshani System deadlocks, Computing Surveys 3, 2, Pages 67–78, June 1971
36 E. W. Dijkstra A short introduction to the art of programming, Technological University, Eindhoven, The Netherlands, August 1971
37 N. Wirth The programming language PASCAL, Acta Informatica, 1, Pages 35–63, 1971
38 Dave Bursky MC68000 16-bit Microprocessor to Offer Wide Address Range, Powerful Commands, Electronic Design 15; July 19, 1978

39   Ian Lemair, Robert Nobis Complex Systems are Simple to Design, Electronic Design 18, September 1, 1978

40   Heather Bryce Microprogramming Makes the MC68000 a Processor Ready for the Future, Electronic Design 22, October 25, 1979

41   Thomas W. Starnes Compact Instructions give the MC68000 Power While Simplifying its Operation, Electronic Design 20, September 27, 1979

42   John Stockton, V. Scherer Learn the Timing and Interfacing of MC68000 Peripheral Circuits, Electronic Design 23, November 8, 1979

43   Jim Farrell MC68000 Microprocessor Combines Powerful Instruction Set with 16MByte Addressing Range, Electronic Products, October 1979

44   R. Grappel, Jack Hemenway The MC68000–a 32-bit uP Masquerading as a 16-bit Device, EDN, February 20, 1980

45   Motorola Inc. EB84 Engineering Bulletin–Interrupt Synchronisation on the MC68000 (T6E)

46   Motorola Inc. EB97 Engineering Bulletin–A Discussion of Interrupts for the MC68000

47   Bernd Pol Betriebssysteme–Eine Einfuehrung-, Elektronik Heft 2, 1981

48   Peter Stuhlmueller Aufgaben eines Betriebssystems, Elektronik Heft 2, 1981

49   John F. Stockton The MC68010 Virtual-Memory Machine Brings Mainframe Features to Microcomputers, Computer Design, 11 May 1982

50   Loebel, Mueller, and Schmid Lexikon der Datenverarbeitung, 1st Printing, 1969

51   Ron L. Cates Mapping An Alterable Reset Vector For the MC68000, Electronics / July 28, 1982

52   Gary Kane 68000 Microprocessor Handbook, Osborne McGraw Hill, Berkeley, California

53   Dr. Adam Osborne Einfuehrung in die Mikrocomputertechnik, tewi-Verlag, Munich

54   P. von Bechen / Mostek Inc. Einchip-Mikrocomputer ist zur 68000-Familie kompatibel, Elektronik 13, 7.1.1983

55   Andrew Barth 32-Bit Prozessor ersetzt 8-bit CPU, Elektronik 17, 8.26.1983

56   Andrew Barth Entwicklungen mit dem Mikroprozessor MC68008, Elektronik-Report, April 1984

57   Hans-Juergen Nischik 68008 ersetzt Z80, Elektronik 14, 7.13.1984

58   Peter von Bechen 8-Bit-Prozessor bietet 32-Bit-Architektur, Elektronik 1, 1.14.1983

59   Werner Hilf MC68020–32-Bit-Prozessor fuer zukunftsichere Systeme, Elektronik 14, 7.13.1983

60   Motorola Inc. MC68440 Dual-Channel Direct Memory Access Controller, Data Sheet, Feburary 1984 (ADI-1002)

61   Motorola Inc. MC68010, Data Sheet, August 1983 (ADI-942-R1)

62   Motorola Inc. MC68008, Data Sheet, August 1983 (ADI-939-R1)

63   Motorola Inc. MC68153, Data Sheet, 1984 (ADI-1057)

64   Motorola Inc. MC68452, Data Sheet, 1983 (ADI-696-R1)

65   Motorola Inc. MC68000 Educational Computer Board–User's Manual, 2. Edition, July 1982

66   Motorola Inc. MC68020 32-Bit Virtual-Memory Microprocessor–User's Manual, 1. Edition, May 1984

67   J. A. Eibner Simple Cache Steps Up Performance Of 16-Bit Systems, Electronic Design, Dec. 22, 1983

68   Motorola Inc. Application Note AN897–MC68008 Minimum Configuration System

69   Motorola Inc. Application Note AN899–A Terminal Interface, Printer Interface, and Background Printing for a MC68000-Based System Using the MC68681 DUART

70   Robert Beims Meet the MC68020 Microprocessor, Motorola Systems News, Summer 1984

71   D. McGregor, D. S. Mothersole Virtual Memory and the MC68010, IEEE Micro, Vol. 3, No. 3, Pages 24–39, June 1983

72   H. Yonezawa, H. Maejima, K. Minorikawa CRT chip controls bit-mapped graphics and alphanumerics (HD63484), Electronic Design, June 14, 1984

73   Motorola Inc. MC6881 Design Specifications, July 1983

74   Motorola Inc. Application Note AN896–Serial I/O, Timer, and Interface Capabilities of the MC68901 Multifunction Peripheral

75   Motorola Inc. Application Note AN819–Prioritized Individually-Vectored Interrupts For Multiple Peripheral Systems with the MC68000

76   Hermann H. Goldstine The Computer from Pacal to von Neumann, Princeton University Press, Princeton, NJ, 1972

77   Amar Gupta and Hoo-Min D. Toong Microprocessors–The First Twelve Years, Proc. of the IEEE, Vol 71, No 11, pages 1236–1256, November 1983

78   Robert N. Noyce and Marcian E. Hoff, Jr. A History of Microprocessor Development at Intel, IEEE Micro, pages 8–21, February 1981

79   Hoo-min D. Toong and Amar Gupta An Architectural Comparison of Contemporary 16-Bit Microprocessors, IEEE Micro, pages 26–37, May 1981

80   James J. Farrel III The Advancing Technology of Motorola's Microprocessors and Microcomputers, IEEE Micro, pages 55–63, October 1984

81   Motorola Inc. MC68020 32-Bit Microprocessor User's Manual, 2nd Edition, Prentice-Hall, Inc., Englewood Cliffs, N.J., 1985

82   Motorola Inc. MC68020 32-Bit Microprocessor Course Notes (MTT20–Motorola Technical Training)

83   Motorola Inc. Motorola Microprocessor Software Catalog, 3rd Edition, 1984

84   Andrew L. Rood, Robert C. Cline, and Jon A. Brewster
UNIX and the MC68000: A Software Perspective on the MC6800 CPU Architecture and UNIX Compatibility, pages 179–200, BYTE, September 1986

85   Thomas L. Johnson A Comparison of MC68000 Family Processors: A Look at the Architecture and Hardware and Software Compatibility, pages 205–218, BYTE, September 1986

86   Ken Marrin Modified Harvard architecture doubles performance of 68020, Computer Design, pages 26–28, October 1, 1986

87   John Bond 32-Bit Micros Advance Art of Memory Management, Computer Design, pages 21–30, October 15, 1986

Notes

Notes

Notes

Notes

Notes

Notes

Notes

Notes

Notes

Notes

PRENTICE HALL ORDER FORM

To order additional copies of this book as well as other Prentice Hall titles on the Motorola 68000 family of microprocessors, kindly complete this form:

QUANTITY	TITLE/AUTHOR	TITLE CODE	PRICE	TOTAL
_____	M 68000 Family, Volume I Hilf/Nausch	54152–4	$40.00	_____
_____	M 68000 Family, Volume II Hilf/Nausch	54153–2	$40.00	_____
_____	M 68000 8-/16-/32-Bit Microprocessor User's Manual Motorola, Inc., 6th Ed.	60924–8	$22.95	_____
_____	MC 68020 32-Bit Microprocessor User's Manual, 3rd Ed. Motorola, Inc.	56701–6	$22.95	_____
_____	MC 68851 Paged Memory Management Unit User's Manual, 2nd Ed. Motorola, Inc.	56699–2	$22.95	_____
_____	MC 68881/882 Floating-Point Coprocessor User's Manual, 2nd Ed. Motorola, Inc.	56700–8	$22.95	_____
_____	MC 68030 32-Bit Microprocessor User's Manual Motorola, Inc.	56695–0	$22.95	_____
_____	MC 68 HC11 Reference Manual Motorola, Inc.	56671–1	$24.95	_____
_____	Single- and Multiple-Chip Microcomputer Interfacing Lipovski	81055–6	$42.00	_____

Total $ _____

SAVE! If payment accompanies order, plus your state's sales tax where applicable, Prentice Hall pays postage and handling charges. Same return privilege refund guaranteed. Please do not mail in cash.

☐ **PAYMENT ENCLOSED**—shipping and handling to be paid by publisher (please include your state's tax where applicable).

☐ **SEND BOOKS ON 15-DAY TRIAL BASIS** & bill me (with small charge for shipping and handling).

Name _____

Address _____

City _____ State _____ Zip _____

I prefer to charge my ☐ Visa ☐ MasterCard

Card Number _____ Expiration Date _____

Signature _____

All prices listed are subject to change without notice. *OFFER NOT VALID OUTSIDE U.S.*

MAIL YOUR ORDER TO: Prentice Hall, Book Distribution Center, Route 59 at
Brook Hill Drive, West Nyack, NY 10994

Attention Corporate Customers: For orders over 20 copies to be billed to a corporate address, call (201) 529–2498.

For individuals ordering fewer than 20 copies, call (201) 767–5937.

Government Customers: please call 201–767–5994

Available at better bookstores

D–TENT–BX (0)

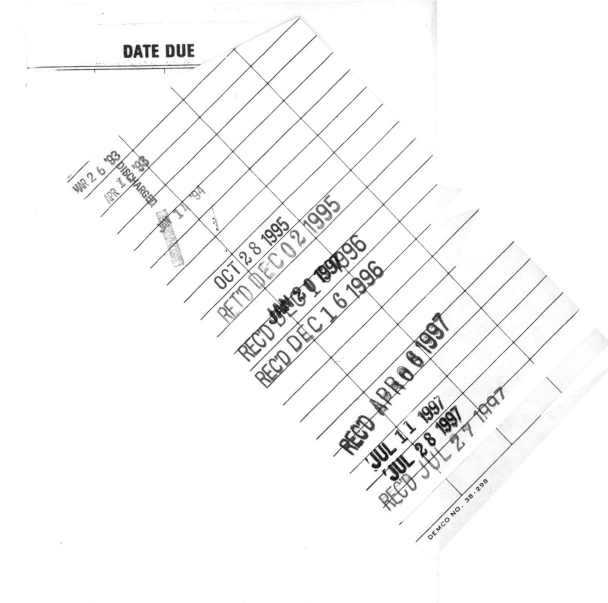